Ozark Folklore

Ozark Folklore

An Annotated Bibliography
Volume II

Vance Randolph
and
Gordon McCann

With a Foreword by
W. K. McNeil

University of Missouri Press
Columbia, 1987

Library of Congress Cataloging-in-Publication Data
Randolph, Vance, 1892–1980.

   Ozark folklore.

   Vol. 2 by Vance Randolph and Gordon McCann.
   Includes bibliographies and indexes.
   1. Folklore—Ozark Mountains Region—Bibliography.
2. Ozark Mountains Region—Social life and customs—
Bibliography.   I. McCann, Gordon, 1931–   .
II. Title.
Z5984.U620937   1987   016.398'09767'1   86–16071
[GR110.M77]
ISBN 0-8262-0627-1 (v. 1: alk. paper)
ISBN 0-8262-0486-4 (v. 2: alk. paper)

   ∞|™ This paper meets the minimum requirements of
the American National Standard for Permanence of Paper
for Printed Library Materials, Z39.48, 1984.

Contents

Foreword

Vance Randolph's Contributions to Folklore Scholarship

Too often a man's accomplishments are not properly appreciated until after he is dead. Fortunately, this was not the case with Vance Randolph, although he did not receive appropriate recognition until the last decade of his life. During that era most of his major books were reissued, a biography was undertaken, at least two official programs honoring him were held in Arkansas, he was elected to membership in the Fellows of the American Folklore Society, a special issue of *Mid-South Folklore* was dedicated to him, and one of his books became an academic bestseller, the most popular in terms of sales of his many volumes. Despite all of this acclaim, Vance remained modest, in fact too much so, for he often said that he was no scholar. Nevertheless, he made significant contributions to the study of American folklore, and as one of his many friends I am proud to have the honor of briefly discussing them here.

Probably everyone who discusses self-educated folklorists like Randolph is inclined to point out that such persons are difficult to fit into any prearranged category. Certainly that is true in Randolph's case, for he is a mass of contradictions. He was an amateur folklorist, but a professional writer. He had no doctorate, yet he was a Fellow of the American Folklore Society, one of only two people without a Ph.D. to achieve that honor. He could not transcribe music, but is rightly regarded as an authority on folk music. He held no academic position, but produced a number of works of lasting scholarly value. He had no training in fieldwork, yet his fieldwork stands as a model. He was mainly interested in a single region, but wrote books that are must reading for anyone interested in American folklore. He was no analyst, yet he produced volumes that are essential to folklore theorists. He is somewhere between the amateur gentleman collector of the nineteenth century and the systematic, theoretically minded scholar of the twentieth century. This assessment is not intended to dismiss or condemn Vance and his work, for it is often the case that an interested and knowledgeable person acting solely on his own resources makes greater scholarly contributions than all the Ph.D.'s; the history of American folklore studies contains numerous testimonies to this fact, Clifton Johnson and George Korson being just two examples.

One of the great virtues of Randolph's folklore writings is that they were produced for the best of reasons, sheer love of the subject. Certainly there is little money, even now, to be made from books on folklore, and a half-century ago when Vance began work the profit potential was even less. To be sure, as a professional writer he, like university professors, had to "publish or perish," but for him this was literally true rather than figuratively so. Nevertheless, from the very start of his career he produced a number of publications for scholarly journals for which he received no pay. This fact alone indicates Randolph's love both of the Ozark people and their oral traditions. More importantly, in these articles and later in his books Vance set a high standard, demonstrating that scholarly works could be both readable and worthwhile. Someone once said that "scholarly writing is not a style but an industrial disease." This evaluation does not apply to anything Randolph wrote, for, as a man who had to live by his words, he knew better than most academics the value of good writing. As Richard Dorson noted thirty years ago, Vance knew best how to "avoid commercial shoddiness and scholarly dullness." Thus, his status as a professional writer was a decided strength.

As a self-educated folklorist without university affiliation, Randolph never had the benefit of sabbaticals and the security of tenure. His research was mostly undertaken without financial backing. Indeed, for much of his career he lived at the poverty level and conducted his work without either monetary support or even encouragement. On at least one occasion he was publicly denounced for collecting Ozark folklore. Yet, in a sense, these disadvantages and problems were also strengths. Without formal training in folklore, Vance did not adopt many of the academic biases prevalent when he began his career. Prior to his time, American folklore studies were primarily text compilations, generally dealing with exotic groups such as the American Indian. These emphases are largely traceable to the influence of such early scholars as Franz Boas and George Lyman Kittredge, the latter a ballad scholar and the former a collector of aboriginal narratives now best remembered as the father of American anthropology. Boas could see little value in conducting research among Ozark mountaineers and, in 1915, tried to persuade Randolph to do fieldwork among the Indians of British Columbia. When Vance refused to go along with the idea his hopes of obtaining a degree under Boas ended.

Boas, unlike some other folklorists of his day, did do fieldwork, but solely as a means of amassing texts of myths and folktales, not because he had much interest in informants. Indeed, he seems to have made it a point of pride to avoid much contact with the natives from whom he recorded oral traditions. Typically he sought out a competent informant who was fluent in English and the native language, knew the old stories and customs, and was willing to dictate and translate texts by the hour. Boas rigidly directed all of his fieldwork sessions and rarely veered from the task of procuring narratives. In short, he had no intellectual interest in the informant except as a repository of oral traditions. As anyone knows who has read Randolph's numerous books, this model is one that Vance did not follow. Instead his volumes, like *The Ozarks* (1931), *Ozark Mountain Folks* (1932), and *Ozark Superstitions* (1947), are of considerable appeal because they are not just collections of texts. They are, rather, presentations of folklore in its social context, studies that give not only texts but also some consideration of what the items of lore mean to those that pass them on. As one means of achieving this goal, he published *Ozark Mountain Folks* largely in the words of his informants.

Prior to World War II most folklorists were primarily past oriented. One of the reasons Boas, Kittredge, and others were little concerned with informants was that they saw folklore mainly as a means of arriving at historical information. When

Kittredge encouraged W. Roy Mackenzie to describe and discuss the singers from whom he collected, it was not from an interest in modern ballad singing but simply to find out if contemporary tradition could shed light on ballad origins. Similarly, Boas was mainly interested in using myths and tales to reconstruct tribal histories. While he evidently had some concern for the modern welfare of the Indians he knew, he was really only interested in those aspects of lore that could shed light on the past. Randolph did not entirely escape this bias, for certainly in his earliest work he subscribed to a survivalist concept of lore, but he did at least go beyond the examples of Kittredge, Boas, and others in depicting the contemporary mountaineer, even if he thought of him as a survivor of a past era.

Being self-educated and innovative, Randolph paid attention to matters that most scholars ignored; in this way he helped expand his chosen discipline. For example, in the area of folksongs, Vance was one of the first authorities to concern himself with the influence of mass media on traditional singers. At a time when other ballad and folksong collectors were busy amassing versions and variants of the Child corpus, Randolph gathered these and much more. To him everything in a folksinger's repertoire was of some importance. Therefore, he placed items learned from hillbilly records alongside versions of "Edward," "Lord Bateman," and other old British ballads. He was also among the first scholars to include tune transcriptions with song texts, and his *Ozark Folksongs* remains one of the most extensive collections of tunes published in America. Obviously, it is foolhardy to suggest that these innovations resulted solely because Vance lacked a Ph.D. and worked on his own. Nevertheless, it seems likely that had he been a member of the academic world he would have been more bound by accepted conventions among his university folklore colleagues. He might have realized that ballad specialists were not supposed to pay attention to songs derived from singers like Jimmie Rodgers.

One positive academic influence on Randolph was the University of Missouri scholar Henry Marvin Belden (1864–1954). His *Ballads and Songs Collected by the Missouri Folklore Society* (1940) is a significant example of American folksong scholarship that departs in a number of respects from most early ballad collections. It includes variants, some tunes, identification of informants, mention of informants' sources, and, most importantly, readable annotations. Prior to 1940, regional collections generally contained notes that merely listed other texts or were copied from earlier ballad volumes. Belden set a superior example by giving seminal and interesting headnotes that are rich in detail, erudite, and valuable. This tradition was continued by Randolph in his *Ozark Folksongs*.

Vance's lack of university affiliation with its accompanying benefits was, in several other respects, fortuitous. Freed from the necessities of teaching, he had more time to devote to fieldwork. Where the professor might have a couple of weeks or months at most to spend in recording folklore, Vance had virtually unlimited amounts of time. Thus, where the academic collector could be little more than a transient gatherer of oral traditions, Randolph became not just a folklorist but also a close friend to his informants. This situation in turn meant that he was capable of recording greater amounts of material and also much more intimate data than could the university collector. Moreover, Randolph compensated for the lack of academic securities and advantages with unusual strength, vigor, and dedication.

Often the professor utilizes his students as collectors, either to save time or simply because the teacher is not a good fieldworker. Much of the material amassed by Henry Belden, Frank C. Brown, and even Franz Boas was obtained in this way. Student collecting is, of course, a valuable teaching device, but it is no adequate substitute for the folklorist recording traditions firsthand. The teacher is wholly at the mercy of the student's abilities, and under the very best conditions there is little control over the collecting method and only secondhand contact with informants. Having no students, Vance was left to his own resources and, as a result, is one of the very few American folklorists of whom it can be correctly said that he person- ally collected virtually every item of oral tradition he published. Thus, he was better able than most scholars to provide contextual information and to answer questions about what meaning the lore had to the folk who preserved it.

Merely collecting folklore in the Ozarks was a ground-breaking action in the 1920s and 1930s. As I stated earlier, many academics of the time were not con- cerned with Anglo-American lore. Those concerned with this lore focused mainly on Appalachia, where they sought out "contemporary ancestors." Randolph, more than anyone else, helped change that popular image, and he did it not by showing "quaint and colorful characters" but by presenting the traditions of Ozark mountain people with respect. This attitude was atypical at the time, for most scholars of the day regarded their informants as social and intellectual inferiors.

At the time Randolph began his work, most folklorists specialized in a single genre or genres. Kittredge's major concern was balladry, Boas was mainly interested in myths and folktales, and so on. Randolph's work was more broad ranging, dealing with most of the folklore genres found in America. In a sense all of his publications on oral tradition can be seen as a single study, an ethnography of the Ozarks. In fairness it must be pointed out that, unlike most other collectors, Randolph's work stems not just from an interest in folklore per se, but from the love and understand- ing of a region and its people. This led him, in books like *Ozark Mountain Folks*, to consider aspects of material culture, home life, and other topics that most folklorists during the first half of the century ignored. In so doing he provided a total folklife approach rather than a mere listing or an examination of a limited aspect of folk tradition.

Because many early collectors were certain that folklore was rapidly dying, they sought material only among the elderly. Randolph also inclined to the view that folklore was fading, but he was shrewd enough to understand that oral traditions are not the exclusive property of any age group. Consequently he gathered much of the material he published from younger people, even teenagers, a group rarely utilized by folklorists active during the first half of the century. It sometimes happened that younger people were his most important and willing sources for some genres. For example, Irene Carlisle, eventually a folksong collector herself, and Pauline Mc-

Cullough are two relatively young people who made significant contributions to *Ozark Folksongs*.

Anyone discussing Randolph's contributions to scholarship will likely feel bound to cite what he considers the greatest of Vance's achievements. Certainly there are many and the choice is difficult. He was an excellent writer, an early proponent of the folklife approach, one of the leading forces in changing the Appalachian bias, and an innovative fieldworker, and he possessed many other attributes that might be singled out. I think, though, that I am safe in stating that his most significant accomplishment is the compilation of the most complete collection from a single region of the United States. To some this choice may seem mundane, especially to those who hold theory more important than collecting. But, as William Wells Newell correctly said nearly a century ago, "One fact is worth a thousand theories," and Vance certainly left us with a multitude of facts with which to work. For all the talk in recent years about folk regions, only one region has been collected with any degree of thoroughness. That region is the Ozarks, and much of the important work there was done by Vance Randolph.

Because all of the commentary until now has been laudatory, it seems necessary to add that Randolph's work was not flawless. Certainly folklorists, like other people, are not perfect, and the writings of all of us could be improved. Randolph's books and articles are not ideal, but it is fair to say that what mistakes he made were also made by most of his contemporaries, and their works lacked many of the virtues of Vance's publications.

It is fitting that in this, his last book, Randolph, who was for many years the dean of Ozark scholars, should comment on and evaluate the myriad publications that have been issued concerning his beloved mountain region. It is also fitting that the work on this book was completed by Gordon McCann, who like Vance is an amateur folklorist with great energy, sound judgment, and a deep knowledge of and love for the Ozarks. Gordon sacrificed large amounts of his time and resources in gathering material for Vance to read, and then after Vance's death Gordon collected and annotated many sources on his own and invested much time in bringing the work to press. All of us who use this volume are indebted to Vance Randolph and Gordon McCann for gathering this wealth of material and sharing their knowledge of Ozark folklore.

W. K. McNeil
The Ozark Folk Center
Mountain View, Arkansas

Acknowledgments

A work such as this is heavily dependent upon the assistance of many individuals and institutions. And a sincere expression of thanks goes out to those who in any way aided us in the compilation of the bibliography, whether it was helping to locate a book on a library shelf or showing the responsibility and the courtesy to answer our innumerable inquiries. But to recognize all these people would produce pages of names and would also risk my unintentional omission of some.

Some, however, merit special recognition. When Vance died in November 1980 I found myself left with this undertaking, having made the promise and now with the obligation to see it completed and published. For five years I had worked with the assuredness that the final decisions on what was to be reviewed and written would be decided by the dean of Ozark folklorists—suddenly I alone held the reins. My greatest help came by way of the Ozark Folk Center. In 1976 Dr. W. K. "Bill" McNeil had become their folklorist and moved to Mountain View. Vance had met him a few weeks before I did. "We must get to know this McNeil," he wrote me, "He may be of some use to us." And then he added his most complimentary assessment of a person, "He knows his stuff!" And Dr. McNeil has certainly been "of use." After Vance's passing, Bill became this project's advisor, proofreader, grammarian, and typist, and my good friend. I can never thank him enough for his guidance toward its completion.

For their many words of encouragement and valued support these past years, a special thanks is due to these people: Ernie Deane, Vance and Mary's most considerate friend, who took the time to see to their needs and comforts in their last years; Vance's good friend who became my good friend, Dr. Herbert Halpert, professor emeritus of folklore at the Memorial University of Newfoundland; Dr. Norm Cohen, editor of the one-volume *Ozark Folksongs*; Dr. Charles Wolfe, a transplanted Ozarker now professor of English at Middle Tennessee State University; Clay Anderson, editor of the *Ozarks Mountaineer*, a publication that has done much to set the facts straight and to preserve a record of our Ozark heritage; Ellen Massey of Lebanon, Missouri, teacher par excellence, whose Bittersweet classes and their publication have been an inspiration to all of us; and Douglas Mahnkey of Forsyth, Missouri, and Aunt Ella Dunn of Bear Creek, each of whom is reason enough for anyone to love the Ozarks.

This publication is also indebted to the following archives for their particular help and patience: Jewell Smith and staff, Springfield–Greene County Libraries; the Duane G. Meyer Library, Southwest Missouri State University; Ellen Shipley, Special Collections–University of Arkansas at Fayetteville; Judith Armstrong, Drury College Library, Springfield; Charlotte Dugan, reference librarian, School of the Ozarks Library, Point Lookout, Missouri; and the State Historical Society of Missouri.

Finally, and most important, is my gratitude to my family, my wife Mona and her years of forbearance of my reading and typing at all hours of the day and night, and my children, Chuck and Abba, who kept the store open. Without them none of this would have been possible.

Gordon McCann
Springfield, Missouri
December 1986

Introduction

On 8 April 1977, three years before his death, Vance Randolph wrote concerning this volume:

> When *Ozark Folklore: A Bibliography* was published by Indiana University in 1972 I regarded it as a good job well done. It was a big book, 572 pages, 2,643 entries, and it seemed to me that the subject was pretty well covered. Almost immediately, however, came letters from Ozarkers and ex-Ozarkers all over the country, listing books and papers not included in my magnum opus. I began work on a bulky appendix to be printed for future editions of the *Bibliography*.
>
> In 1975 I met Gordon McCann, of Springfield, Missouri, a native Missourian and an indefatigable student of the Ozark scene. He is not a professional folklorist, but just an enthusiastic amateur like me. A dedicated regionalist, his primary interest is pioneer history, but he has a remarkable library of Ozark folk material, including many rare and obscure items hitherto unknown to me. We decided to combine our stuff and publish it as a supplement to the *Bibliography* of 1972.
>
> This book is the product of two authors, Gordon McCann and me. But in order to preserve a style and format consistent with the original *Bibliography*, and to avoid a lot of rewriting, it seems best to retain the first-person singular pronoun throughout. The annotations reflect two men's opinions, of course, but McCann and I are pretty well agreed. In case we differ about any particular item, the difference will be indicated in a footnote.

To Vance Randolph it came as a welcomed challenge that the renaissance of interest in and information about Ozark folklore presented the need for a second volume of his bibliography. He left it to me to finish the job of completing the volume, but my rationale for choosing the items and for writing the annotations is no different than his.

Randolph's definition of *folklore* as stated in the preface to the first volume of this bibliography remained the guideline used in assembling and categorizing the material for this supplement. He described it as touching all knowledge that is casually transmitted from one generation to the next by word of mouth or by example, including not only the traditional ballads, tales, and proverbs, but much of our common speech, social customs, folk arts, and crafts, besides many manifestations of folk belief and religion, these patterns depending upon folk tradition, not upon schools or printing presses. Also in that preface, he described that first volume as the compilation of "material gathered by amateurs who are interested in popular rather than scholarly publication, the annotations reflecting personal opinions and observations." Vance Randolph always considered himself one of those "amateurs." He adopted the Ozarks and for most of his eighty-eight years focused his entire being upon the study of this one region.

*   *   *   *

This supplement represents that one man's dedication and determination to continue his life's work up until the time he was neither mentally nor physically capable of doing so. Vance often mentioned that he hoped he would be able to work right up to his very last breath. He came very close, to within three weeks, when surgery at age eighty-eight proved too much for him to overcome. He died on 1 November 1980 in the Veteran's Hospital in Fayetteville, Arkansas. When I picked up his belongings at the hospital, there in his battered old black leather briefcase were a copy of a festschrift for Herbert Halpert and the latest issue of *The Ozarks Mountaineer*.

Thus ended the life of the greatest chronicler of Ozark culture we shall ever know. His work represents an eighty-year love affair between a man and a people, for if there is one absolute truth that can be said about Vance Randolph, it is that he truly loved the Ozarks. In 1919 this "flat-lander" from Kansas moved to Pineville in the southwest corner of Missouri, near where he later bought a cabin. Though he left for a brief time, he returned and married a girl from the area and published his first writings about the Ozarks.

Randolph involved himself completely in the lives of the people of southwest Missouri and northwest Arkansas. He learned the old ballads, the stories and tall tales, from young and old alike, but he concentrated his efforts on the old-timers, for he thought they were the last purveyors of this unique culture, an assumption he later had reason to refute. He knew the pillars of the community but also ran with the boys from "up the creek." He drank their moonshine with them, and he always made it a point to know who turned out the best stuff. He gambled with them, becoming wise in the ways of poker and pitch. He joined in their manly sports of hunting and trapping, and he knew the rivers. He went along with the boys that guided as they floated the city slickers and their money down the rivers in johnboats. He also was with them when they gigged, grabbed, and noodled, and when an occasional stick of blasting powder was tossed into the water. But guns were his passion. He was particularly proud of a pair of matched derringers and took great pride in his marksmanship with them. He was never too specific about the degree of his skill, but from our conversations I suspect he sent many a bottle and tin can to its maker as it floated down the James River in Stone County, Missouri.

Vance knew the fiddlers and their tunes and calls, and he square danced until either a ruckus or the rising sun stilled the fiddler's bow. After each of these adventures he would run back to his room and put everything down while it was still fresh on his mind. One of the Short family with whom he lived for a while in Galena told me that his clearest recollection of Vance was the sound of his typewriter at all hours of the day or night. Vance often mentioned that he felt an urgency, an immediate obligation, to record as much of this culture as possible, for it was poised on the brink of extinction. He felt that much of his success was due to the fact that he happened to be in the right place at the right time. By the end of the forties he thought the last of the pioneers was gone. But in the fifties, when he became acquainted with his future wife, Mary Celestia Parler, and her folklore classes at the University of Arkansas, he found to his amazement that her students, grandchildren and great-grandchildren of his informants, were still telling the stories and still singing the ballads he thought were no longer remembered. They had been listening more than he suspected.

*   *   *   *

When I met Randolph in March 1975, he was eighty-three years of age, confined to the very cramped quarters of a room in a rest home in Fayetteville, Arkansas, a room he shared with his wife Mary, who was nearly blind. He was suffering from a variety of illnesses, including hardening of the arteries and serious heart problems, and his hands and feet were severely crippled from arthritis. Among the many inconveniences that griped Vance about his old age was the fact that he could no longer use the typewriter. Arthritis had crippled his fingers to such a degree that it became terribly uncomfortable just to hold the pen, let alone write with it. But he continued his work as well as he could. After our preliminary introductory remarks, we had no trouble establishing common ground for conversation. My being an Ozark "native"—with family ties and friends in most parts of the southwest Missouri–northwest Arkansas Ozarks, the areas where Vance lived and did most of his collecting (many of the informants listed in his writings were relatives or acquaintances of mine)—prolonged what was to have been a brief meeting into a lengthy visit as I brought him up to date about people and places he hadn't seen nor heard from in years. This first visit set the theme for subsequent ones, the swapping of stories and anecdotes about all of these individuals.

At the time of this first meeting he was finishing the final proofreading of *Pissing in the Snow* (University of Illinois Press, 1976), and he had started working on a supplement to his 1972 bibliography, having compiled about a hundred reviews. He was very limited in his access to material. Many of his old friends who would have looked after his reading needs were either dead or retired or had lost contact with him. Only his good friend, former *Arkansas Gazette* feature writer and teacher Ernie Deane, and occasionally a friend of Mary's would bring him anything to read. Most of his reviewing was limited to what he might receive through the mail. He was pretty much on his own just as he had been throughout his career. He had become out of touch with happenings outside the rest home, and, as he stated in the few paragraphs he wrote for the the introduction to this supplement, he did not realize the extent of the renewed interest in folklore that had taken place.

The reasons for my becoming involved after meeting Vance were well described by him. I am the offspring of a north Arkansas mother and a south Missouri father, was raised in and have lived all of my life in the Ozarks. I've been a devoted "Ozark-watcher," witnessing (and bemoaning) the inevitable cultural shocks caused by changing life-styles and the in-migration of the mid-twentieth century but marveling at the time-honored folkways that appear to be surviving, preserved and/or revived by a younger generation who proclaim a certain reverence for the ways of their forefathers.

During our first visits Vance mentioned to me each time that he was going to give up trying to work on a supplement. He was discouraged about his health and it was too difficult for him to get material on his own. Besides, he didn't think there was going to be enough available to justify the effort. I became involved in the project when, after one of these visits, I compared the contents of the 1972 bibliography with my private library. I found that I had sixty-nine titles not shown and promptly sent him a list of them. Immediately I received this enthusiastic reply:

April 12, 1975

Dear McCann:

I'm still in the hospital, but Mary Celestia brought me your letter of the 9th. Your list of titles is astounding. Of your 69 items, I recognize only about 10 or 15. I have copied 50 of your titles into my notebook, and shall try to check those for folklore references when I get to feeling better. Some of the rare items I shall not be able to get at all—such as Groom & McConkey's *Baldknobbers*, the eight-act tragedy played by the students at Sparta in 1887, and Vandeventer's Baldknobber MS. If you are willing to trust me with any of these treasures by all means send them to me at Sunrise Manor.

I want to take full advantage of your splendid collection of Ozark books, and your willingness to share it with me, but I shall try to call on you for material that I can't get anywhere else—such as the *Bald Knobber Play* in Sparta, Mo. and Judge Vandeventer MSS. This material and the stories about it should be included in my *Supplement I* to my Bibliography.

I am still overwhelmed by the extent and value of your work in this field. There are few people around nowadays who are interested in such matters, and they usually become collectors of coins or antique pistols or butterflies or postage stamps. Since Rayburn died and Halpert went to be a professor in Canada and Ted Worley is off for Fiddler's Green I have felt pretty much alone in these here parts.

I wish to God we had met years ago! Maybe we could have collaborated on this Ozark business and come up with a really *valuable* Ozarks bibliography.

Vance Randolph

So now, besides our shared memories of people and places in the Ozarks, we found a common interest in the printed word, and thus began my involvement with the second volume of the Ozark folklore bibliography (or Supplement I, as we referred to it) and a close friendship that was to last the five and one-half years he had left to live. From that time on I was to witness that Vance was truly an example of the power of mind over body. He was a sad paradox. In spite of his deteriorating physical condition, his mind remained unbelievably alert until his very last days. He was ever aware of this, and occasionally when he felt bad he would become disheartened by the reality of the many things he could no longer do. But after a few minutes of conversation about the Ozarks he would improve remarkably. He replaced these discomforts with his eagerness to keep going.

In June 1977 I received the following:

Dear McCann:

Perhaps we should work as if we thought that other enthusiasts (fools like you and me) will add more supplements to ours: Maybe you, if you reach my age, may recruit some young collaborator just as I found you, and produce *Supplement II*, McCann and Blank, University of Missouri Press, 1995 etc. Comes then two more damn fools to sweat out *Supplement III*, and so on until the Ozark country becomes an urbanized hell full of refugees from the cities, and there is nothing more worth writing about.

The excitement and privilege of collaborating with Vance Randolph changed what had been for me years of casual accumulation of Ozarks material into a determined effort to locate and obtain as much as time and opportunity would permit.

By this time a change had occurred in the social attitudes of the public, especially among young adults, changes that became evident in the fifties and reached proportions of national significance in the sixties. A social rebellion against the "modern" way of life, with its urban blight, environmental abuse and destruction, involvement in a no-win war, and constant reminders of the possibility of nuclear disaster, formed. A desire for a better way of life, with freedom from the confusion and emotional stress of today's world, engendered a nostalgic look at our pioneer past, and an interest in things "old-timey" became a national pastime. Even the stereotype of the Ozark hillbilly, living his seemingly uncomplicated nineteenth-century pioneer life in an isolated hollow with clean water and air and an abundance of food, received its share of attention. By the 1970s large numbers of books, journals, dissertations, and magazine and newspaper articles concerning Ozark folklore and related subjects became available. Rather than the lack of material Vance thought he would find, there proved to be an abundance of items to review.

My search quickly became an adventure in itself. Because of the large numbers of items to locate and the often unconventional nature of the publications, I had to be methodical in my search for material. The most available and obvious avenues were pursued at first—the card catalogs of regional public and university libraries and their *National Union Catalog*, the *Cumulative Book Index*, the OCLC computer network, the *Union List of Serials*, and others. The cumulative indexes of many publications, especially those such as the *Missouri Historical Review*, the *Arkansas Historical Quarterly*, the *Journal of American Folklore*, *Mid-America Folklore*, and *Western Folklore*, were particularly valuable not only for the occasional Ozarks article but also because the book review sections provided some titles. Indexes were not available for many of the smaller publications, such as news bulletins from rural electric and farm co-ops, so it was necessary to leaf through them page by page.

The material reviewed was kept within the boundary of the printed word. We examined many works that had the word *Ozark* in their title or had a title that suggested Ozarks folklore content but were of little or no value to the folklorist. Many of those writings are nonetheless included in the bibliography, with annotations explaining their value or lack of it. Movies and recordings are not included because each warrants a separate bibliography.

Another prime source were the footnotes and bibliographies of the many folklore-related publications that appeared in the 1960s and 1970s. Many a long-forgotten dissertation or manuscript that had been gathering dust for decades suddenly surfaced through the research of a present-day folklorist.

Privately printed works are a most important source of information, and many were located through local newspapers and historical societies and particularly periodicals like the *Ozarks Mountaineer*. Book-review sections and classified advertisements sent me to many books of this sort that I might not otherwise have found. I believe a brief definition of this type of publication is necessary. They are written mostly by persons in their "golden years" who wish to leave some record of their lives and their times. They are practically all reminiscences in the format of memoirs. They are written in the vernacular, just as the author might tell his story to the reader in person. It is the only work the author will ever publish, and most of them definitely lack the literary skills and polish of the professional writer. I once knew an old fiddler who was quite a storyteller. He always ended his "windies" with the expression "Hit's the truth, poorly explained!" and I guess this could be as good a definition as could be given for vanity-press publications. It is especially important to list them because they quickly become scarce; often only one or two hundred copies are printed, just enough for family and friends.

I found that personal follow-ups with a visit or phone call to some of these authors or with members of local literary societies (a number do still exist in the Ozarks) often led to the discovery of yet more titles. But sadly I was unable to obtain copies of a number of them. I was surprised to discover in my explorations that these items are practically ignored by public and academic libraries. Sometimes the author sends them a copy, but it seems little effort is made to search them out.

Between May 1975 and October 1980, I sent or took to Vance almost eight hundred items, mostly books and manuscripts, the majority of which he read and reviewed. After the success of *PITS* (as he referred to *Pissing in the Snow*), he began to get attention from some publishers and authors, and they frequently would send him copies of their work. The 1972 bibliography contained 2,643 entries; this supplement has 1,654 and could have many more, but bibliographers have to stop somewhere and prepare their product for publication. It seemed that 1982, a decade after the publication of the first volume of this bibliography, was a good place to stop and make the information available to the public. I have therefore included publications up to and including that year.

In his last years the acclaim Vance received for *Ozark Folklore: A Bibliography*, the enormous success of *PITS*, the republication of two of his previous works, and the knowledge that the one-volume edition of the folksongs and the second volume of the bibliography were forthcoming boosted his spirits considerably. He was elected a Fellow in the American Folklore Society, only the second non-Ph.D. to be so honored. But he longed for the days when he roamed the Ozark hills visiting with the old-timers and listening to their ballads and tall tales. This was made evident to me one spring day when I visited Vance while he was in the V.A. hospital in Fayetteville for a checkup. We were talking about spring in the Ozarks and the folk beliefs concerning the first plants and trees to bloom when I suddenly noticed tears in his eyes, and with his voice breaking he said, "I know that I shall never again see the dogwood bloom or the redhorse shoal."

Vance Randolph was the greatest folklorist the Ozarks will ever know and one of the greatest regionalists this country has ever had. But for his meticulous observations and his dedication in collecting and recording every bit of information about the Ozark people, a way of life that can never exist again would have been lost.

Vance's good friend and fellow folklorist Herbert Halpert, now professor emeritus at Memorial University of Newfoundland in St. Johns, said in his tribute to Vance in the *Journal of American Folklore* (July-September 1981), "Randolph probably came as close to becoming accepted as a native Ozarker as any 'furriner' ever could. He liked the Ozarkers for their pride, independence, and dignity. Like them he was a 'loner'; like them he also enjoyed sociability and leisurely talk, as well as camping, hunting, fishing, riding, gambling, drinking, and dancing. But in addition he was intensely interested in learning about all aspects of the Ozark folk culture and could convince people of the genuineness of his interest. A magnificent observer, gifted with a good ear and a fine memory, he was the perfect participant-observer collector." Halpert ended his eulogy by paraphrasing *Hamlet*: "He was a man, take him for all in all, we shall not look upon his like again."

A Note on Organization

Of necessity some changes have been made from the format used in Volume 1 for the division of sections. The first section has been renamed "Ballads and Songs" and has been divided into four categories: Songs, Instrumentals, Dance, and Personalities. The Instrumentals category became necessary because the revival of interest in folk music these past twenty years has resulted in much more being written about acoustical stringed instruments, notably the fiddle, banjo, guitar, mandolin, dulcimer (both lap and hammer), and a host of lesser-known variations. The Dance category covers the same topics as did "Backwoods Dances" in the first volume, mainly square dance and square dance calls. The Personalities category has been introduced for a reason similar to that of the Instrumentals category: so much attention has been given to the performers of folk music in recent decades that it seemed proper that this biographical material be given its own section.

A new section, "Foodways," concerns itself with Ozark cooking, recipes, wild foods, and food-related subjects. Vance said that the largest public response to the first volume concerned the subject of food, especially recipes.

"Biographies" is another new section that has been created to hold the large number of autobiographical and biographical works about Ozark personages. Hopefully this new section will facilitate research for those readers interested in character studies.

Finally, the new section titled "Folklife" contains material pertaining to lifestyles or everyday customs typical of life in the Ozarks.

1. Ballads and Songs

A. Songs

1. Anderson, Clay. "Treasures of the Ozarks Wilderness." *The Ozarks Mountaineer* 24:8 (September 1976): 21, 24–25.

    This article is about harvesting ginseng and wild honey, but it begins with one stanza from a ballad composed in the early 1970s. "My People All Came Here Before You," sung to the tune of "Old Rosin the Beau," was written by Bob and Kay Blair, residents of Mountain View, Arkansas. Blair is a lifelong hunter and trapper, and this song voices his frustration with the changing life-style in the Ozarks.

2. Anderson, John Q. "Ballad of a Badman." *Western Folklore* 31 (1972): 103–15.

    A Texas variant of the Cole Younger ballad, with a discussion of Younger and his association with Frank and Jesse James.

3. Baldwin, Jim. "Playing the Mountain Dulcimer." *Bittersweet* 1:2 (Winter 1973): 42–50.

    This article includes a sound sheet featuring dulcimer player Bill Graves of Laclede County, Missouri. He sings a six-stanza version of the ballad "Jesse James," somewhat different from those collected by Randolph (*Ozark Folksongs* [entry 66], 2:17–24), Belden (*Ballads and Songs* [entry 8], p. 402), and Cohen (*Long Steel Rail* [entry 26], pp. 104–5). He also sings two other songs on this recording, "Turkey in the Straw" and "I Saw the Light."

4. Baldwin, Jim. "Singing With So-Fa Syllables: Learning to Sing by Shape Notes." *Bittersweet* 2:1 (Fall 1974): 4–16.

    An excellent piece of work about singing schools, which have all but disappeared from the Ozark scene. This one, teaching shape-note or So-Fa syllables, is at the Lee's Summit Church of Christ near Lebanon, Missouri. The section entitled "A Singing School Education" (pp. 11–16) is a detailed explanation, with diagrams, of the shape-note method, its history, the scale, pitching, the voice parts, key signatures, and timing and breathing. All in all this is one of the most informative articles about this subject I've seen in print.

5. Baldwin, Rebecca, and Patsy Watts. "We've Got a Pig in the Parlor." *Bittersweet* 6:1 (Fall 1978): 49–61.

    Words and music to sixteen Ozark play-party games collected in southwest Missouri.

6. Banes, Marian Tebbetts. *The Journal of Marian Tebbetts Banes*. Fayetteville, Ark.: The Washington County Historical Society, 1977. 159p.

See p. 64 for stanzas of "Frog Went A Courting" and p. 65 for a seldom-heard version entitled "Kitty Alone and I," which the author says was sung in a minor key. On p. 67 is a version of "Juba" that she learned from a young Negro slave who could "crack the bones" and could do a " 'Jim Crow' shuffle, head hanging and arms devitalized."

7. Barbeau, Marius. "Voyageur Songs of the Missouri." *Bulletin of the Missouri Historical Society* 10:3 (April 1954): 336–50.

An informative article about the voyageur songs brought to Missouri by the early French explorers and settlers. He mentions many titles and gives the words, with translation and musical notations, to ten or so of them. Of definite regional interest are "Dans l'Mississippi," "Je Suis Des Bords De L'Ohio," and "Aux Illinois." Some of the songs he mentions are still sung in the Old Mines area of Washington County, Missouri.

8. Belden, H. M. *Ballads and Songs: Collected by the Missouri Folk-Lore Society*. Columbia: University of Missouri Press, 1973. 532p.

This is a reprint of the 1955 second edition. It is identical to the first edition published in 1940 but with the addition of a foreword by Edward Weatherly and a photo of Belden. The foreword is a biographical sketch of Belden and a tribute to his efforts and accomplishments in this field. Belden died in 1954.

9. Berry, Earl. *History of Marion County* (Arkansas). Little Rock: Marion County Historical Association, 1977. 523p.

Chapter 7, "Amusements, Entertainment and Recreation," tells of the emergence and popularity of the summer chautauqua. Music was a major part of these gatherings, and songs that lent themselves to vocal harmonizing became household favorites: "In the Gloaming," "Down by the Old Mill Stream," "Silver Threads Among the Gold," etc. See pp. 52–53, 56–60, for more about gospel singing, singing schools, and singing conventions.

10. Boulson, C. E. "Blind Boone and the Marshfield Tornado—Disaster Set to Music." *Webster County Historical Society Journal* 14 (April 1980): 6–8.

Blind Boone was a popular composer and pianist in the late nineteenth century. Hearing of the Marshfield tragedy of 1880, he composed a piece entitled "The Marshfield Tornado." It is said that when the piece was performed in Marshfield, it was so graphic in its tempo and its simulation of the tornado that many in the audience rushed outside, thinking another storm had struck. Boone never put it down on paper nor recorded it, so it remains only in the memories of any still living who heard it played.

11. Bridges, Percy. "Origins of a Missouri Rural Teacher." *White River Valley Historical Society Quarterly* 1 : 10 (Winter 1963–1964): 6–12.

The author, born in 1892, tells of his early years growing up in a log cabin in Christian County, Missouri. He talks about the songs his parents sang and gives five stanzas of the song "Bill Stafford" as sung by his father. He says he has never seen it in print, but both Randolph (*Ozark Folksongs* [entry 66], 3:27) and Belden (*Ballads and Songs* [entry 8], pp. 424–26) show several versions.

12. Brisco, Mary S. "Sister Sooky's Story: The Autobiography of Mary A. Brisco," with an introduction by Mary Celestia Parler. *Mid-South Folklore* 5 : 3 (Winter 1977): 77–99.

This is the manuscript that Sister Sooky gave Parler shortly before her death in 1958. William M. Clements, editor of *Mid-South Folklore*, calls it a folk-autobiography: he has shortened it a bit and improved the punctuation but preserved Mrs. Brisco's spelling and grammar. See pp. 94–96 for the texts of four old songs, including "Lord Boatman."

13. Brumley, Albert E. *All-Day Singin' and Dinner on the Ground*. Camdenton, Mo.: Albert E. Brumley and Sons, 1972. 64p.

A popular paperback with the subtitle "A Collection of Favorite Old Time Songs and Hymns and Choice Recipes From the Days of Yesteryear." The first thirty-one pages are devoted to shape-note songs, including "A Tramp on the Street," "Life's Railway to Heaven," "Shake Hands with Mother Again," etc. Albert Brumley was raised and lived his life in the southwest Missouri community of Powell. In his lifetime he claimed to have written more than seven hundred songs. He achieved national fame with "Jesus Hold My Hand" and "I'll Fly Away." He was inducted into the Country Music Hall of Fame in 1970 and into the Gospel Music Hall of Fame in 1972. With his family he operated a music publishing house until his death in November 1977.

14. ———. *The Best of Albert E. Brumley*. Powell, Mo.: Albert E. Brumley & Sons, 1966. 160p.

This is an all Brumley gospel songbook (one hundred songs) and contains some of his most famous compositions: "I'll Fly Away," written in 1931 (p. 3), "Jesus Hold My Hand," 1933 (p. 6), "I'll Meet You in the Morning," 1936 (p. 8), "If We Never Meet Again," 1945 (p. 14), and "Turn Your Radio On," 1938 (p. 46). All the music is in shape-note with four-part harmony.

15. ———. *Book of Radio Favorites—America's Favorite Songs of the Air with Four Part Harmony*. Powell, Mo.: Albert E. Brumley and Sons, 1966. 126p.

All gospel songs, set down in shape-note. Includes 126 Ozark favorites, such as "We Shall Meet Someday," "Looking for a City," "Gathering Flowers for the Master's Bouquet," and many others that are Bible Belt standards. Brumley knew as well as anybody the religious music of these hills.

16. ———. *A Collection of Folk Songs*. Dallas: Stamps-Baxter Music Corporation, 1972. 80p.

This is a commonplace shape-note songster, reprinted from Brumley's *Log Cabin Songs*, first issued in 1944.

17. ———. *Lamplitin' Songs and Ballads*. Powell, Mo.: Albert E. Brumley and Sons, 1977. 60p.

A greatly condensed version, only fifty-seven selections from the 1966 edition of *Lamplitin' Songs*, with no mention of M. Lynwood Smith (see entry 22).

18. ———. *Log Cabin Songs and Ballads*. Powell, Mo.: Albert E. Brumley and Sons, 1974. 64p.

The title is a bit misleading. There are more than fifty songs in this book; except for a half-dozen patriotic pieces such as "The Star-Spangled Banner," most of them are hymns, gospel songs, and sentimental pop songs—no ballads. Too many Stamps-Baxter songs, and Brumley plugs several regrettable compositions of his own. It seems to me that this opus is definitely inferior to the other Brumley collections.

19. ———. *Olde Time Camp Meetin' Songs*. Powell, Mo.: Albert E. Brumley and Sons, 1971. 64p.

A fine collection of old hymns and gospel songs, including "Bring Back to Me My Wandering Boy," "Farther Along," "The Great Speckled Bird," "Put My Little Shoes Away," "Will There Be Any Stars in My Crown?" and "When the Saints Go Marching In." Many of these songs are set in shape-notes and the book is a favorite for use with college students who have never seen the old "buckwheat" notation.

20. ———. *Songs of the Pioneers*. Camdenton, Mo.: Albert E. Brumley and Sons, 1970. 64p.

This unpaged paperback contains fifty-eight old songs including "Two Little Girls in Blue," "Casey Jones," "Flow Gently Sweet Afton," "Home Sweet Home," "Sweet Bunch of Daisies," and "The Old Oaken Bucket." Note pp. 32–33, "Folk

Music History in Song," by Gene Gideon of Taney County, Missouri, a regional musicologist and songwriter.

21. ————. *Songs of the Pioneers—Book No. 2*. Powell, Mo.: Albert E. Brumley and Sons, 1973. 64p.

More of the same as the first *Songs of the Pioneers* (1970). Number 36 is "Drink to Me Only with Thine Eyes," with the label "Arr. Copyright by Albert E. Brumley," without any mention of Ben Jonson.

22. Brumley, Albert E., and M. Lynwood Smith, compilers. *Lamplitin' Songs*. Wesson, Miss.: M. Lynwood Smith Publications; Powell, Mo.: Albert E. Brumley and Sons, 1966. 135p.

A mixed bag of what the preface calls "Cabin, Mother, Memory, and Reflection" songs, 137 of them. Mostly nineteenth-century tearjerkers, religious and music-hall songs, with a few of Brumley's thrown in. There are even a couple of well-known ballads, "Barbara Allen" and "Babes in the Woods." I know nothing of Smith other than the Brumley family says he was a "friend and coworker" of Albert's. There is an introduction by Gene Gideon.

23. Burt, Olive Woolley. *American Murder Ballads and Their Stories*. New York: Oxford University Press, 1958. 272p.

Pages 163–65 give the text and tune of the "Baldknobber" song. This is actually the song of a counter group, the Anti-Baldknobbers. She says that this version was given to her by one Cliff Coggburn in Ogden, Utah, some years before. None of the Coggburns still living in Taney County, Missouri, seem to know who this fellow was. The second verse, the mother's plea to her son to flee, is one I have never heard before.

Another incident (pp. 231–36) that produced two ballads was the murder of the Meeks family by the Taylor boys. This occurred near the town of Browning in Linn County, Missouri, in the 1880s. The first ballad, entitled the "Meeks Massacre" (or "Meeks Murder"), is well known. The second is a first-person account, said to have been sung for many years by Nellie Meeks as she traveled about with a carnival in the 1890s. Nellie, who was assumed dead by the Taylors, escaped and identified them as the murderers.

24. ————. "Ditties of Death in Deseret." In *Lore of Faith and Folly*, pp. 153–73. Salt Lake City: University of Utah Press, 1971.

She has a variant of the "Mountain Meadows" ballad (pp. 157–58), so much discussed by the Fancher clan in northwest Arkansas a few years ago. She also gives two stanzas of a little-known ballad about the execution of John D. Lee, one of the participants in the atrocity.

25. Cameron, Bill. "Star School in New Setting." *The Ozarks Mountaineer* 27:6–7 (July-August 1979): 22–23.

This article is about a schoolhouse that has been moved to the campus of the School of the Ozarks near Hollister, Missouri. But included are the words to a Civil War ballad commemorating an incident that took place at the Battle of Wilson's Creek in 1861. The author is a fine old Irishman, a retired salesman of miller's supplies, who has been active in the restoration of many old mills in the region.

26. Cohen, Norm. *Long Steel Rail: The Railroad in American Folksong.* Urbana, Ill.: University of Illinois Press, 1981. 710p.

A big book, listing over nine hundred song titles with lengthy discussions of eighty-five of them. This magnum opus is the culmination of fifteen years of exhaustive research by the author. For the song "John Henry" alone, he lists nearly six hundred published and recorded references. The reader might expect to be mired down with this much accumulation of data but such is not the case. Cohen presents a complete provenience for each of the eighty-five: the historic, social, and folkloristic events that contributed to its popularity and its establishment as a bona fide American folksong. All this along with a complete discography and listing of published sheet music.

See pp. 97–116 for the ballad "Jesse James." A thirteen-stanza version, as recorded in 1928 by Harry "Haywire Mac" McClintock, is given. Cohen hypothesizes that the "E" version found in Randolph's *Ozark Folksongs* (2:17) is probably the closest to the original. An equally interesting discussion of the ballad "Cole Younger" is on pp. 117–21. Cohen justifies the inclusion of both ballads in this particular book by citing the tremendous part the railroads played in determining the careers these two desperadoes pursued.

Norm Cohen is executive secretary of the John Edwards Memorial Forum at UCLA, an organization devoted to the study of American folk music on commercial recordings. He edits their quarterly and has authored numerous articles and essays on folk and early country music. His brother, David Cohen, a professional guitarist, is the music editor of that quarterly.

27. Cohen, Norm, ed. *Vance Randolph: Ozark Folksongs.* Urbana: University of Illinois Press, 1982. 590p.

This is an abridged edition of the four-volume set published 1946–1950 by the State Historical Society of Missouri. Cohen has selected some two hundred fifty songs out of the more than sixteen hundred that appeared in the original edition. His introduction should be read very carefully. In it he sets forth his guidelines used in selecting the songs. Also, he fully explains any revisions made and certain liberties he has taken in order to emend the material presented. In anticipation of criticisms that might arise pertaining to a condensed version of such a major work as *Ozark*

Folksongs, he states that for one thing, with today's prices, the single-volume selection makes it more economically available to students, scholars, and the public in general. Anyway, the original was not Randolph's complete collection by any means. One long chapter composed of bawdy songs was "blue penciled" by the publishers, and approximately two hundred texts were withheld by Randolph and offered to another scholar for possible use in a later publication. He has rearranged and regrouped a few of the songs, some with respect to their sequence within a chapter, others from one chapter to another. This has been done to better present a song with regard to the theme of a particular chapter, and to make the material easier to locate. Cohen has also reset some of the musical transcriptions, not to change the tune as set down by Randolph, but rather to make the transcriptions conform more to the rules of musical "calligraphy." Cohen's own headnotes, inserted between those of Randolph and the tune transcriptions, are a most valuable contribution. With these he has complemented Randolph's headnotes by updating the information and by citing other recorded and printed versions that have come about in the ensuing thirty years. Lest the reader be confused by geographic improprieties, on p. xviii of the introduction, in delineating the boundaries of the Ozarks, it should read *eastern* Oklahoma instead of *western* as stated. Overall, it appears to me a fine job, one I am certain Randolph would have found acceptable.

28. Commager, Henry Steele, ed. *The Blue and the Gray.* New York: Bobbs-Merrill Co., 1950. 1,201p.

Story of the Civil War as told by the men who fought. It is all good stuff, especially about the war in the West. For Ozark references see pp. 380–94. I like chapter 16, "Songs the Soldiers Sang."

29. Cowan, J. E. *Life in the Powell-Cyclone Community of McDonald County, Missouri.* Noel, Mo.: McDonald County Press, 1973. 160p.

See pp. 27–28 for the words and music of a song titled "My Brave Laddie Sleeps" as sung by Everett Craighead, a resident of this southwest Missouri county. It is a somewhat altered version of one written by John Hugh McNaughton in 1865 entitled "The Faded Coat of Blue."

30. Croce, June. "Froggie Is Still A-Courtin'." *The Ozarks Mountaineer* 27:8–9 (September-October 1979): 52–53.

A nostalgic discussion by the author about ballad singing in her family. A couple of stanzas of "Babes in the Woods" are given, and also of "Billy McQue," a version of the British broadside often called "The Old Woman of Slapsadam."

31. Dalton, Captain Kit. *Under the Black Flag.* Memphis: Lockard Publishing Company, 1914. 252p.

The author says he was with Quantrill's guerrilla band during the Civil War. After the war, he claims to have been a member of Jesse James's gang. In the chapter entitled "To Old Mexico. Unfortunate Affair at a Dance" (pp. 165–68), he tells the story of Jesse's encounter with a Mexican who provokes a fight by stepping on Jesse's foot. This incident became the theme for a ballad printed with the title "A Missouri Ballad" in *University Missourian* (16 February 1909). But G. Malcolm Laws doubts its currency in oral tradition. See p. 267 of his *Native American Balladry* (Philadelphia: American Folklore Society, 1964).

32. Dougan, Michael B. "Two Manuscript Folksongs from Civil War Arkansas and Their Background." *Mid-South Folklore* 2:3 (Winter 1974): 83–88.

The first manuscript tells the troubles of a Union sympathizer in northwest Arkansas harassed by both "Rebels" and "Kansians" and driven into the hills near Cassville, Missouri. The second reflects the Confederate point of view and is found in a manuscript of S. C. Turnbo, a collector of folklore who may have authored the verses denouncing the Yankee guerrillas. This manuscript is entitled "History of the Twenty-Seventh Confederate Regiment." The Turnbo typescript is in the *Arkansas Gazette* Foundation Library at Little Rock. Dougan is an assistant professor of history at Arkansas State University, a specialist in the culture and history of Arkansas.

33. Dugaw, Dianne. "The Dugaw Collection of Ozark Folk Songs." Master's thesis, University of Colorado, 1973. 175p.

There is a bound typescript of this thesis in the University of Colorado Library at Boulder, Colorado, and a copy at the Ozark Folk Center, Mountain View, Arkansas. The first part is all discussion and analysis, but the second section contains excellent transcriptions of seventy-eight songs and instrumental pieces, collected by the author in Searcy County, Arkansas, in August 1973. A revised version of the thesis appeared in *Mid-America Folklore* 11:2 (Fall 1983).

34. Emrich, Duncan. *Folklore on the American Land*. Boston: Little, Brown and Co., 1972. 707p.

Emrich devotes a whole chapter to Professor Kittredge of Harvard, one of his old teachers. Beginning on p. 541 is a full text and tune of "The Brazos River," "a rare and beautiful song" about Texas, which has been collected only once—in Fayetteville, Arkansas, as sung by Irene Carlisle in 1942. Recorded for the Library of Congress by Vance Randolph, of course. Emrich was head of the Folklore Section of the Library of Congress for many years.

35. Fuller, Michael J. "Origins of the Ballad of the Mountain Meadows Massacre." Typescript, Southwest Missouri State University, Springfield, Mo., April 1976. 12p.

An attempt to identify the composer of this ballad telling of the massacre of 120 members of the Fancher wagon train at the hands of Indians and Mormons in Utah in 1857. The train was made up of northwest Arkansans and southwest Missourians and began its journey from Harrison, Arkansas. Fuller thinks that it may have been composed by two members of the Mormon church who had firsthand knowledge of the tragedy.

36. Gregory, Fern Denise. "Selected Child Ballad Tunes in the Max Hunter Collection of Ozark Folksongs." Typescript, Warrensburg, Mo., 1979. (Copy in Springfield–Greene County Public Library.) 36p.

This is an abstract of a Master's thesis, Central Missouri State University at Warrensburg, 1979. Gregory has transcribed forty tunes from Max Hunter's large collection of tapes housed in the Springfield Public Library. It seems to us that she has done an excellent job. Her introductory discussion (pp. 1–14) is very impressive.

37. Haden, Walter Darrell. "Round the Jolly Pool." *The Ozarks Mountaineer* 25:9 (October 1977): 36.

The author quotes three stanzas of a song he collected in Douglas County, Missouri, in the late 1940s. It is clearly a variant of the "Johnny Fool" song, which I reported (*Ozark Folksongs*, 3:200–201).

38. Harwell, Richard B. "The Star of the Bonnie Blue Flag." *Civil War History* 4:3 (September 1958): 285–90.

An article about Harry Macarthy, an entertainer who, though he never lived there, billed himself as "The Arkansas Comedian." His composition "The Bonnie Blue Flag" (written 1861) gained equal popularity with "Dixie" in the South during the Civil War and is still well known in the Ozarks today. (See Randolph's *Ozark Folksongs*, 2:261–62). He also wrote another wartime favorite, "Missouri: or, A Voice from the South." An interesting description of one of his "Personation Concerts" is in this article.

39. Haworth, John J. "Taney County Baldknobbers." Typescript, [1937]. 11p.

This paper is about a vigilante organization formed in the early 1880s ostensibly to bring law and order to this area of southwest Missouri. As with most groups of this nature, they soon got out of hand, and their counterparts, the Anti-Baldknobbers, came into being. These "Anti-Knobbers" composed a song, the public singing of which resulted in a number of killings. See p. 3 for the story of one such incident and one verse of the song. Haworth was an Anti-Baldknobber.

40. Henigan, Julie. " 'I'm Old but I'm Awfully Tough': The Making of a Great Record." *Come For To Sing* 6:3 (Summer 1980): 5–9.

From the idea to the finished product, the step-by-step process in the making of the folk album *I'm Old but I'm Awfully Tough*, produced by the Missouri Friends of the Folk Arts (MFFA). There is much on field collecting techniques and problem solving in this article. When finished (1977) the album and its companion booklet featured the talents of seventeen traditional Missouri folk musicians and story-tellers. It was nominated for a Grammy Award in 1978.

The final pages carry the words and music to two traditional songs as sung by Lee Finis "Tip" McKinney, an original member of a 1920s stringband, Pope's Arkansas Mountaineers. "I'm Old but I'm Awfully Tough," a humorous song, first recorded on Victor in 1902, and, "Gipson Davy," a variant of a Child ballad (no. 200). A photo of McKinney appears on the cover of this issue.

41. Hudgins, Mary D. "Arkansas Traveler—A Multi-Parented Wayfarer." *Arkansas Historical Quarterly* 30:2 (Summer 1971): 145–60.

The author is a collector of Arkansas sheet music. She has covered the litera-ture of the whole field. In this paper she gives us everything that is known about the Arkansas Traveler. Miss Hudgins is a long-time resident of Hot Springs, Arkansas, and author of many valuable papers on Arkansas history and folklore.

42. ———. "A Musical Note on an Old Arkansas Song." *Arkansas Gazette*, 25 September 1966.

A fine photograph of the famous DeMoss Family, who claimed both words and music of "My Happy Little Home in Arkansas," which they launched at the Colum-bian Exposition in Chicago in 1893. The picture shows two Middle-European fid-dlers in white tie and tails, with wives dressed in formal wear to match. Like a Böhemischer group from south Chicago, they must have laid 'em in the aisles in Little Rock.

43. Hudson, Arthur Palmer. "A Ballad of the New Madrid Earthquake." *Journal of American Folklore* 60:236 (April-June 1947): 147–50.

Fourteen stanzas of this ballad, "A Call to the People of Louisiana," about the great cataclysm of 1811–1812. The only printed text known was discovered in the Duke University Library as "Song No. 222" in the rebound copy of a hymnal. Though its title page and other front matter are missing, it appears to be an 1832 publication entitled *A New Selection of Hymns and Spiritual Songs for Camp-Meetings*.

44. Hunter, Max Francis. "Songs from the Ozarks." Max F. Hunter Collection. Springfield–Greene County, Mo., Libraries. 1956–1980.

This collection, possibly the largest of Ozark folksongs in existence, is con-tained in forty-four volumes. Four are index data (one an alphabetical listing of the

260 singers with their songs, and the other three the alphabetical listing and location of the nearly twelve hundred different songs). Each volume contains a reel-to-reel recording of its contents. The songs are identified by their Max Hunter (MFH) number and their locations within the collection. If the singer used an alternate title, it is also indicated. There are also notations to show the locations of songs included in Francis Child's *The English and Scottish Popular Ballads*, in Vance Randolph's *Ozark Folksongs*, in Henry Belden's *Ballads and Songs*, and in Frank Brown's collection of North Carolina songs.

45. Jahoda, Gloria. *The Trail of Tears: The Story of the American Indian Removals, 1813–1855*. New York: Holt, Rinehart & Winston, 1975. 356p.

Much Indian lore throughout. The author gives a few words and the noted music to three Indian songs or chants: "Seminole Removal Song" on the title page of the foreword, the Mandan "Song to the Rayven" (p. 173), and the Seminole "Song of the Removal to Oklahoma" (p. 243).

46. Johnston, James J. "Two Historical Incident Ballads from North Arkansas." *Mid-South Folklore* 5:1 (Spring 1977): 25–29.

"Old Ben Taylor" was a poem about B. F. Taylor, a deputy United States marshal killed by a moonshiner in Searcy County, Arkansas, in 1897. Johnston prints a text "composed by some of Taylor's neighbors, collected from Dorsey Whitlow, a fiddler from Snowball, Arkansas." It was known by many local people, but there is no evidence that it was ever sung.

"The Garrett Ballad" according to Johnston "is a formal poem, never intended to be sung" written by the widow of a Confederate guerrilla, Temple Garrett, killed by the Yankees in 1864.

This paper is not very well written. It is not clear to me that either of these texts had any significant oral circulation.

Johnston is a native of Marshall, Arkansas, and is now an administrative officer of the American Embassy in Guatemala.

47. ———. "Two Ozark Civil War Ballads." *Mid-South Folklore* 5:3 (Winter 1977): 113–15.

A good text of a Yankee "Prairie Grove" song, and one stanza of a Confederate piece about the Battle of Wilson's Creek.

48. McIntosh, David Seneff. *Folksongs and Singing Games of the Illinois Ozarks*. Carbondale: Southern Illinois University Press, 1974. 119p.

An amateurish collection, but it seems to be quite authentic—an honest piece of work. Something comparable to my own folksongs from Missouri and Arkansas. Part I (pp. 1–52), devoted to local songs and ballads, is especially valuable, containing material concerning crimes, floods, railroad wrecks, etc., little known elsewhere. Most of the older songs are of British origin, mostly similar to those collected in Missouri and Arkansas. The singers are clearly identified and the documentation is adequate.

49. McNeil, W. K. "Ballads About Jesse James: Some Comments." *Mid-America Folklore* 8:1–2 (Spring-Fall 1980): 44–52.

McNeil discusses three separate ballads, analyzing the content of each and its relevance to the James legend. He cites two important questions neglected by collectors: (1) what influence has the media had upon the ballad, and (2) why have the James ballads remained alive in tradition while those of other well-known "badmen" have been forgotten? McNeil came to the Ozark Folk Center in Mountain View, Arkansas, as folklorist in 1976. A native of North Carolina, he received his Ph.D. in folklore from the University of Indiana, where he studied under greats like Richard Dorson, Henry Glassie, and Warren Roberts. He came to Arkansas from the Smithsonian Institution, where he had been director of the Regional America section of the Festival of American Folklife; his areas of expertise include folk music and song.

50. ———. "Ozark Folksongs." *The Ozarks Mountaineer* February 1977–December 1982.

The following list gives in alphabetical order the names of a series of articles about folksongs McNeil found still being sung in the Ozark region: "After the Ball" (April 1977): 32–33; "Around My Old Arkansas Homestead Sing the Bullfrogs" (March-April 1979): 16; "The Babes in the Woods" (April 1981): 55; "The Bald Knobbers" (February 1978): 8; "Beaver Cap" (August 1980): 16–17; "The Bridge Was Burned at Chatsworth" (February 1982): 56–57; "The Brooklyn Prisoner" (October 1977): 8; "Come, Take a Trip in My Airship" (October 1980): 62–63; "The Creole Girl" (December 1977): 34; "The Dark Eyed Sailor" (January-February 1979): 65; "The Decision in the Gypsy's Warning" (April 1982): 12–13; "The Drunkard's Dream" (March 1978): 36; "Fair Lady of the Plains" (June 1978): 19; "Fingers and Thumbs" (October 1982): 55; "The Girl That Wore a Waterfall" (August 1981): 16–17; "Go Wash in that Beautiful Pool" (May-June 1979): 12; "Golden Dagger" (September-October 1979): 20–21; "The Golden Vanity" (March 1977): 32–33; "The Gypsy Laddie" (August 1978): 26; "The Gypsy's Warning" (April 1982): 12–13; "I'll Remember You, Love, in My Prayers" (April 1978): 32–33; "In the Baggage Coach Ahead" (first in the series) (February 1977): 8; "The Iron Mountain Baby" (July 1977): 10–11; "Lee Mills" (July-August 1979): 48–49; "Life's Railway to Heaven" (April 1980): 10; "Little Blossom" (August 1977): 13; "Little Marian Parker" (November-December 1979): 19; "Little Mary Phagan" (June 1980): 60–61; "Little Shirt That Mother Made for Me" (February 1980): 49; "Lucky Jim" (November-December 1978): 58–59; "The Meeks Murder" (September 1977): 10–11; "The Old Elm Tree" (June 1981): 12–13; "Old Judge Duffy" (July-August

1979): 48–49; "The Old Maid and the Burglar" (July 1978): 27; "On the Banks of the Wabash" (March-April 1979): 16; "Peek-a-Boo" (August 1982): 18; "Peg and Awl" (December 1980): 16–17; "Plantonio" (May 1977): 30; "Rosewood Casket" (October 1981): 64–65; "The Shadow of the Pines" (December 1982): 12–13; "The Tie That Binds" (February 1981): 14–15; "Two Little Boys" (December 1981): 63; "The Wandering Cowboy" (June 1982): 16–17; "The West Plains Explosion" (May 1978): 34–35; "When Carnal First Came to Arkansas" (August 1978): 26; "The Wreck of the C. & O." (November-December 1978): 58–59; "The Young Farmer" (June 1977): 28.

51. ———. "A Preliminary Jesse James Discography." *Mid-America Folklore* 8:1–2 (Spring-Fall 1980): 93–96.

Twenty-one commercially released recordings, as complete a list as McNeil was able to discover, although he says there are undoubtedly more. No other criminal in American history has been sung about as much as Jesse James. Since this article was published a more extensive discography of ballads about Jesse James has appeared in Norm Cohen's *Long Steel Rail* (see entry 26), pp. 110–16. Unfortunately, Cohen's discography is not annotated as is McNeil's.

52. ———. "Songs, Poems, and Comments from the Papers of Thomas F. Mason." *Heritage of Stone* 3:2 (Fall 1979): 23–34.

About songs, mostly religious, that were written down around the turn of the century by this resident of Mountain View, Arkansas. McNeil gives the texts of eight of them along with comments about each. Of particular interest is "The White Pilgrim Song." There are four versions of this in vol. 4 of Randolph's *Ozark Folksongs*. *Heritage of Stone* is the publication of the Stone County, Arkansas, Historical Society.

53. Mahnkey, Douglas. "A Slave Song from Taney County." *The Ozarks Mountaineer* 26:4 (May 1978): 28.

Mahnkey gives the words to a ballad about an escaped slave. He heard his wife's family sing it sixty years ago in southwest Missouri. It is not found in any of the printed works on Ozark folksongs.

54. Martin, Roxie. "Songs of Bygone Days." *Arcadian Magazine* 1:9 (October 1931): 39.

Ozark ballad collecting by much the same methods Max Hunter used so successfully twenty years later. The texts of two ballads are given. "Proud Lady Margaret" is an altogether different song from the Child ballad of the same name (Child no. 47). It is actually a variant of Child no. 68, "Young Hunting" (see Randolph's *Ozark Folksongs*, 1:90). The second text he calls "The Lady of the North Countree" is a variant of Child no. 79, "The Wife of Usher's Well" (see Randolph's *Ozark Folksongs*, 1:122).

55. Messick, Mary Ann. *History of Baxter County: 1873–1973*. Little Rock: Mountain Home Chamber of Commerce, 1973. 506p.

This county history is good reading. Messick has interspersed her historical facts with lots of folksy information that is written much like those articles by neighborhood correspondents on the rural newspapers. Although professional historians will dispute many of her historical assumptions, there's no doubting that the folks who live in north-central Arkansas find this book interesting and entertaining. There is some discussion of songs, but they are mostly religious in nature. She says (p. 190) that "The Old Rugged Cross" was not sung in Baptist churches for many years due to Protestant fears that the symbol of the cross represented a foreign power.

56. Mullen, Patrick B. "Folk Songs and Family Tradition." In *Observations and Reflections on Texas Folklore*, edited by F. E. Abernathy, pp. 49–63. Austin: Texas Folklore Society, 1972.

This paper is based on a manuscript written by Benjamin Harrison Mullen, the author's grandfather. The manuscript turned up in Beaumont, Texas, but Ben Mullen was born on White Rock Mountain, near Fayetteville, Arkansas, where he taught school for many years. Ben told many tales of his life in the Arkansas Ozarks, with frequent mention of his Grandmother Faubus, a name well known in Arkansas. Ben Mullen wrote down the words of several old songs he had learned in the Ozarks, and that's what Patrick Mullen's paper is about. And a fine paper it is, too, with good texts of "The Dying Soldier" and "The Charge at Confederatesburg"—both Civil War songs. Also, such songs as "Barney McCoy," "The Blind Child," and the one called "Train Talk," which begins "Life is like a crooked railroad," and mention of many others.

57. "Musicians Compose Ballad about Cryts." *Springfield Daily News*, 28 June 1982.

In 1981 a Puxico, Missouri, farmer named Wayne Cryts broke the court-ordered locks on the grain elevators of a bankrupt elevator company and retrieved his impounded soybeans. His subsequent arrest and trial gained him national attention, and his plight became a rallying call for farmers across the nation. Two Jonesboro, Arkansas, musicians wrote a song about his exploits, "The Ballad of Wayne Cryts," and issued it on a forty-five r.p.m. record.

58. Ohrlin, Glenn. *The Hell-Bound Train: A Cowboy Song Book*. Urbana: University of Illinois Press, 1973. 290p.

A collection of one hundred songs with a foreword by Archie Green. Ohrlin sang all the songs himself, and Judith McCulloh transcribed the tunes from his tapes. He lives near Mountain View, Stone County, Arkansas. His informants are rodeo performers, professional musicians, bull riders, bronco busters, ropers, and the like. The same kind of pop singers that Margaret Larkin used to work with. The book is a good job.

59. Parker, A. E. "The Iron Mountain Baby." *The Shannon County Historical Review* 4:2 (July 1967): 2.

This is the story of the infant William Moses Gould Helms, who was thrown from a train near Irondale, Washington County, Missouri, in 1902. A text of the ballad is given, " . . . as composed by J. T. Barton to the tune of 'The Blind Child.'" He died in Texas in 1953 (this article incorrectly says 1957) and was returned for burial over the same rails from which he had been thrown fifty-one years previously. There is also a photo of Helms as a young man.

60. Parler, Mary Celestia. *An Arkansas Ballet Book.* Norwood, Penn.: Norwood Editions, 1975. 59p.

The texts of forty-three folksongs from the Parler Archive, assembled with no classification or headnotes, from a mimeographed outline used in Professor Parler's folksong seminar in 1963. The students were required to identify each item, compare it with printed collections in the University of Arkansas Library, and write a headnote for each song. It was very successful as a teaching device, a way of getting students to use the folksong literature. Most of the songs are well known, found in many American folksong publications, but two of them—"Alleghanies" (p. 1) and "Drumendoo" (p. 15) are new to me.

61. Pennington, John. "Song Book of Old Ballads." Fayetteville, Ark., ca. 1952. Mimeograph copy. 25p.

From the title-page: "Composed of songs of the Seventeenth, Eighteenth, and Nineteenth Centuries. Songs of Romance, Love, Adventure. Songs that were learned by the writer at a very early age and were retained in his memory for a period of approximately fifty-five years before being published."

Contains texts of twenty-one songs, including "Darling Black Mustache," "Man Who Wouldn't Hoe Corn," "Frog Went A Courting," "My Old Beaver Cap," "The Little Mohee," "The Boys That Go Courting." Pennington, a retired preacher when this was published, lived in Fayetteville for nearly seventy years. I knew him in the 1940s.

62. Peyton, Green. *America's Heartland, the Southwest.* Norman: University of Oklahoma Press, 1948. 286p.

See pp. 236–40 for a discussion of southwestern folksongs and other music. He claims the most active music capitol in the Southwest is the University of Oklahoma. Pages 144–54 deal with Arkansas, mostly about Hot Springs and Eureka Springs (which he calls one of the oddest cities in the United States). Pages 155–68 are about Oklahoma. The author's real name is G. P. Wertenbaker and he resides in San Antonio, Texas.

63. Pollan, Loy. "Provenience of Certain Cowboy Ballads." Master's thesis, University of Oklahoma, 1938. 119p.

Discussion of the texts only, no tunes, of nine cowboy ballads collected in Oklahoma: "When the Work's All Done This Fall," "The Dying Cowboy," "The Tenderfoot Song," "The Old Chisholm Trail," "The Cowboy's Lament," "Git Along Little Dogies," "The Cowboy's Dream," "Oh, Bury Me Not on the Lone Prairie," and "Old Paint." They are compared with variants found in published collections, most notably those of John A. Lomax, Carl Sandburg, Jules Verne Allen, Margaret Larkin, and Louise Pound. Of the nine, Pollan says only three were found to be based upon earlier ballads.

64. Rainey, Leo. *Songs of the Ozark Folk*. Branson, Mo.: The Ozarks Mountaineer, 1972. 56p.

Texts and tunes of forty-three songs, taped by Rainey from the singing of Ollie Gilbert, Noble Cowden, Benson Fox, Mable Daughtery, Jimmy Driftwood, and others. A paperback book dedicated to John Quincy Wolf, Jr. (1901–1972). Photographs of some twenty singers. No headnotes or references to other collections. But he does give the singer's name and address, with the date of his singing.

65. Rainey, Leo, Orilla Pinkston, and Olaf Pinkston. *Songs of the Ozark Folk*. Branson, Mo.: The Ozarks Mountaineer, 1976. 80p.

A reprint of the 1972 edition but with the addition of ten new songs and more photographs of the performers. Rainey has written the text. He collected the songs on tape and the Pinkstons transcribed them. This edition, in paperback also, contains many references to other collections. It is intended for the tourist trade, of course, but it's a good job.

66. Randolph, Vance. *Ozark Folksongs*. Vol. 1, *British Songs and Ballads*, 450p. Vol. 2, *Songs of the South and West*, 436p. Vol. 3, *Humorous and Play-Party Songs*, 399p. Vol. 4, *Religious Songs and Other Items*, 455p. Columbia: University of Missouri Press, 1980.

This reprint of the four-volume work, originally published by the State Historical Society of Missouri from 1946 to 1950, is a good job. A few of the songs that appeared in the original edition have been eliminated but, other than these, it's all here. This is a monumental work, unparalleled in its scope by any other collection from a particular region. A valuable addition to this reprint is the introduction by W. K. McNeil, folklorist with the Ozark Folk Center in Mountain View, Arkansas. McNeil presents a sensible synopsis of Randolph's work and its important contribution to our knowledge of oral tradition. McNeil is knowledgeable, and a careful study of this introduction is important for the serious student of Randolph and the American folksong.

67. Reynolds, John Hugh. *Makers of Arkansas History.* New York: Silver, Burdett and Company, 1905. 294p.

Pages 275–78 are devoted to proving that the "Arkansas Traveller" does not convey a proper and adequate description of the Great State of Arkansas.

68. Rowlett, Luther. "It Was April the Eighteenth 1894." *The Ozarker* 6 : 8 (September 1969): 6.

About the cyclone that hit Summersville, Missouri, in 1894, most of it taken from files of a newspaper called *The Current Wave.* Includes the text of a song, "The Summersville Cyclone," which the author thinks was written by J. T. Barton, the same country preacher who wrote "The Iron Mountain Baby" and "The Search for Little Alice Summers."

69. Schappes, Morris U. "An Anti-Semitic Anti-Folk Ballad." *Jewish Currents* 28 : 3 (March 1974): 20–21.

This is "The Jew's Garden" (Child no. 155) and is supposed to refer to the murder of young Sir Hugh of Lincoln in 1255, whom Chaucer says in the *Canterbury Tales* was "slayne also with cursed Jews." It is common in America and is found in most of the major collections. This poor fellow Schappes had apparently never heard of it until 1973, and was horrified to learn that an Ozark folksinger (eighty-one-year-old Mrs. Ollie Gilbert, of Mountain View, Arkansas) was singing it for local collectors. Those of us who know Mrs. Gilbert know that she learned the song from her mother, who sang many English ballads. If I were a betting man, as the saying is, I would wager a substantial sum that neither Mrs. Gilbert nor her mother ever heard of anti-Semitism. People of her generation here know nothing of Jews and have no prejudice either for or against them. *Jewish Currents* is a top-quality monthly published in New York, devoted to political subjects and Jewish propaganda.

70. Schroeder, Rebecca B. "Unprintable Songs from the Ozarks: Forgotten Manuscripts." *Missouri Folklore Society Journal* 4 (1982): 43–50.

These unprintable songs reside in the Joint Collection, University of Missouri Western Historical Manuscript Collection–Columbia and State Historical Society of Missouri Manuscripts. Randolph noted in the 1972 bibliography only three locations for this material: the Institute for Sex Research at Indiana University, the Delta File at the Library of Congress, and, on microfilm, the UCLA Library in Los Angeles. He had forgotten that any were on deposit at the University of Missouri. Schroeder goes on to describe the contents of the University of Missouri collection in some detail.

71. Settle, William A., Jr. *Jesse James Was His Name, or, Fact and Fiction Concerning the Careers of the Notorious James Brothers of Missouri*. Columbia: University of Missouri Press, 1966. 263p.

Settle says that the balladry about Jesse James "is both a result of and a factor in creating the figure of Jesse James as a modern Robin Hood." He says no printed versions can be found predating 1900 but that they undoubtedly appeared shortly after Jesse's death. Cited are stanzas collected by Randolph (*Ozark Folksongs*, vol. 2, 1948), and H. M. Belden (*Ballads and Songs*, 1940).

72. Shamel, H. Harold. *Seeds of Time, A Story of the Ozarks*. N.p.: Published by the author, n.d. 278p.

See p. 236 for the texts of eleven old songs, not folksongs but popular songs of the 1880s. "Christine Leroy," "Remind Me Not," and "Too Late" are still sung in the Ozarks.

73. Shepherd, Mark. "Saving the Songs." *Columbia Daily Tribune*, 5 June 1980.

The first few paragraphs talk about Randolph and his ballad collecting, but mostly it's about the workings and goals of the University of Missouri Press and the reprinting of Randolph's four-volume *Ozark Folksongs*.

74. Sherrer, Dwayne. "We Play a Little Music." *Bittersweet* 8:4 (Summer 1981): 54–64.

Tunes and words to thirteen songs and ballads collected near the village of Linn in Osage County, Missouri.

75. Silber, Irwin, ed. *Songs of the Civil War*. New York: Bonanza Books, 1960. 385p.

I was delighted with this collection. On pp. 198–200 is a fine ten-stanza version of the "Brass Mounted Army." I published a shorter text of this in volume 2 of my *Ozark Folksongs*, pp. 273–74, but could not find any headnote material and never saw it in any collection other than my own until I read Silber's book in 1975.

76. Simmons, Tommy, and Jean Simmons. *Simmons Family Songbook*. Mountain View, Ark.: The Stone County Leader, 1974. 40p.

A paperback with the Mountain View versions of thirty-three songs and fiddle tunes. See p. 4 for a portrait of Mrs. Ollie Gilbert, nationally known folksinger. This pamphlet is designed for the tourist trade, and is quite without documentation, but there are some good songs in it. I like the text and tune of "Rose Connelly" (p. 12). See the discussion of dulcimer tunings (pp. 39–40). The Simmons family is one of the most popular groups in the Mountain View area. They play autoharp, fiddle, guitar, and dulcimer, and have cut six commercial albums.

77. *Stamps-Baxter's Book of Brumley's Favorite Sacred Songs*. Dallas: Stamps-Baxter Music Publication, 1972. 98p.

This is a reprint of an earlier publication, *Albert E. Brumley's Book of Sacred Songs* (1944). This book contains ninety-eight songs, shape-note with four part harmony, all of which have appeared in other Brumley publications.

78. Vandeventer, W. L. "Justice in the Rough." Typescript, Springfield, Mo., 1952. (Copy in Christian County Library, Ozark, Mo.) 197p.

See p. 46 for an eight-stanza text (no tune) of the Anti-Bald Knobbers song, which I published in 1948 (*Ozark Folksongs*, 2:114–17) from B. F. Carney, Crane, Missouri, and W. T. Moore, Hollister, Missouri. Vandeventer says it was attributed to Coggburn.

79. Wallace, Jenell. "Rogers Resurrection Try Lives on in Song." *Springfield Daily News*, 7 July 1978.

In February 1978, Gladys Rogers of Harrison, Arkansas, died of pneumonia at age eighty. Her son, a self-ordained preacher, declared that by prayer he could bring her back to life. He put her body in a deep freeze, packed her in dry ice, and began a prayer vigil that lasted for six weeks. Because of the legal complications that arose in Arkansas, she was taken to a mortuary across the state line, in Reeds Spring, Missouri. All this attracted the attention of the national news media. Two local musicians, who thought "it's really something that was historical," composed a ballad titled "Resurrection Sunday" and recorded it on a forty-five r.p.m. record. The first stanza:

In a little town way down in the Ozarks
Came a man to raise his mother from the dead
She was setting all alone in a deep freeze
Just waiting for the Lord to raise the lid.

80. Westphal, June, and Catharine Osterhage. *A Fame Not Easily Forgotten*. Conway, Ark.: River Road Press, 1970. 224p.

A history of the town of Eureka Springs, Arkansas. Material drawn from published writings rather than oral legend. Pretty dull stuff, badly written. But it has some value for the student of local history. See pp. 104–5 for the words to the song "Ode to Eureka Springs" that used to be sung by the Tourist Social Hour Club.

81. White, Mahlon N. *The Legend of Keel Boat Kate*. Clinton, Mo.: The Printery, 1975. 30p.

Sung to the tune of "Turkey in the Straw," the author gives the words to a song, "The Ballad of Keel Boat Kate," he says he heard sung in the Osage River region of central Missouri. I have never heard of this "ballad" before, nor can I find any documented evidence of it in folklore archives. I suspect it is of far more recent origin than he infers in this book.

82. Wolf, John Quincy. "Who Wrote Joe Bowers?" *Western Folklore* 29:2 (April 1970): 77–89.

Wolf lists a great many men who have been credited with this piece—all carefully documented in footnotes. But the fact is that nobody knows who wrote the song.

83. Zemach, Harve, and Margot Zemach. *Mommy, Buy Me a China Doll*. Chicago: Follett Publishing Company, 1966. 32p.

A book for the very young using the text of this ballad along with full-page color illustrations. The title page says "adapted from an Ozark children's song" (see Randolph, *Ozark Folksongs*, 3:46; and Roger D. Abrahams, *A Singer and Her Songs* [entry 132], p. 47).

84. Ziff, Larzer. "Songs of the Civil War." *Civil War History* 2:3 (September 1956): 7–28.

Many songs that were favorites of both the North and South during the war, "Lorena," "Annie Laurie," "Juanita," "Lilly Dale," "Sweet Evalina," "The Girl I Left Behind Me," and a host of others, are still familiar and popular today in the Ozarks. It is not at all uncommon to hear these sung and/or played at music parties or "jam" sessions throughout the area. He also tells about Harry Macarthy, a Southern entertainer who was called "The Arkansas Comedian." On p. 21 there is a verse of "I Goes to Fight Mit Sigel." This bit of Confederate satire was directed at the Union troops under Gen. Franz Sigel. They were, for the most part, recent German immigrants who spoke little or no English at all and began the war in the trans-Mississippi campaigns in Missouri and Arkansas. To the Confederate Ozarker and likewise his Union counterpart, these were strange beings indeed.

B. Instrumentals

85. Baldwin, Jim. "Playing the Mountain Dulcimer." *Bittersweet* 1:2 (Winter 1973): 42–50.

This article gives instructions in both the traditional and the modern methods of tuning and playing this instrument, each quite different from the other. The traditional is described by Bill Graves, a native of Laclede County, Missouri, who learned the art from his grandfather. All about turkey quill picks and noters, and strumming, thumbing, and whipping the "Indian Walking Cane," as the mountain dulcimer is sometimes referred to in the Ozarks. The modern method, instructed by Lynn McSpadden and Elliott Hancock of Mountain View, Arkansas, talks about double-thumbing, three-fingered picking, and chording. A diagram showing various chords is shown, as is a tablature for the tunes "Skip to My Lou" and "Barbary Ellen." Good photographs. There is also a sound sheet with performances by Graves.

86. Burford, Jo. "Our Fiddlin' Forefathers." *The Ozarks Mountaineer* 25:8 (September 1977): 34–35.

Good piece about backwoods music. The miners in eastern Missouri remembered some old French pieces, but most of their fiddle tunes were ancient hoedowns derived from British pipers' tunes.

87. Christeson, R. P. *The Old-Time Fiddler's Repertory*. Columbia: University of Missouri Press, 1973. 208p.

A fine collection of old fiddle tunes, over two hundred of them. Christeson left out many of the most common tunes, "the ones that everybody knows," like "Soldier's Joy." He was raised in the Ozarks, and now lives in Auxvasse, Missouri. A lot of his stuff was collected in Missouri, from such characters as the Bell Family of Howell County, Jesse Cain of Dixon, in Pulaski County, Bill Driver of Miller County, and Tony Gilmore of Jefferson City, who could dance a jig and play his fiddle at the same time, and many other well-known Missouri fiddlers—the sort that win old-time fiddler's contests. There are only seventy-five or so tunes by Missouri fiddlers in this book. About two-thirds are by non-Missouri fiddlers (117 by one Nebraska fiddler alone). But it's all good. Christeson is a fiddler himself, not a folklorist or a musicologist, but a real old-time fiddler. This is a mighty good book. It is mostly dance music, of course—breakdowns, hornpipes, quadrilles, polkas, and waltzes, and about fifty miscellaneous items that he calls "pieces." Christeson began to collect fiddle music in 1933; since 1947 he has devoted himself entirely to field recording. He wrote me many years ago that he was having great difficulty in getting his tapes properly transcribed. The University of Missouri Press did a beautiful job with this book; the format facilitates use on a music stand, and metronome speed markings are featured throughout. An album of two LP records containing forty-one of the tunes recorded in the field by Christeson is available.

88. Curtis, Maxine. "Playing the Musical Saw." *The Ozarks Mountaineer* 25:6 (July 1977): 28.

Musical saws are three inches longer than conventional saws and are played using a regular fiddle bow. Mrs. Curtis and her husband are directors of a Bible camp near Dora, Missouri.

89. Emrich, Duncan. *Folklore on the American Land.* Boston: Little, Brown, and Co., 1972. 707p.

Years ago I wrote a piece, "Names of Ozark Fiddle Tunes," for *Midwest Folklore.* Files of *Midwest Folklore* are hard to come by now, but Emrich reprints the whole thing (pp. 128–35) with comments of his own: "I have put all these names here to further preserve them and make them more widely known," he says. "They should never be lost . . . go back and read them every so often. . . . Listen to your people and your country." (See vol. 1 of this bibliography, p. 315.)

90. Gage, Allen. "Old-Time Fiddling." *Bittersweet* 9:3 (Spring 1982): 48–53.

A discussion of Ozark fiddling and a very good one. The author is a musician himself and his father and grandfather are fiddlers. He has been very observant and makes some knowledgeable comments about fiddlers and their music. This is definitely worth reading and will be of value to anyone interested in the proprieties and idiosyncrasies of old-time fiddling. There is a sound sheet accompanying this article, thirteen tunes as rendered by three southwest Missouri fiddlers.

91. Galbraith, Art. "The Devil's Own Box." *Bittersweet* 9:3 (Spring 1982): 58–60.

This title is very similar to that of a previous article written by Galbraith (see the following entry), but this is a transcription from a taped interview by the *Bittersweet* staff. He tells of people who condemned the fiddle and square dancing as wicked and the work of the Devil. These same people would then have play-parties with singing only, no musical instruments, but would execute the same configurations as the square dancers and that was all right.

92. ———. "The Devil's Own Instrument." *The Ozarks Mountaineer* 25:9 (October 1977): 21.

The fiddle has either been revered or vilified in most parts of the country, but nowhere more so than in the Ozark Mountains. The author, a performer on the "devil's own," talks about these prejudices and about fiddling in general over the years, to its present-day popularity in the bluegrass style.

93. Gilbert, Joan. "Country Fiddlin'." *Missouri Life* 3:5 (November-December 1975): 40–47.

All about R. P. Christeson's work, with liberal mention of Thomas Hart Benton. A good paper with pictures. A good deal about square dancing and even jigging.

94. Gourd, Wayne. "Mountain Music Heritage." *Ozark Mountainwood Express* (1981): 1–2.

A very brief discussion of old-time music in the Ozarks. Of value is the listing of more than two dozen north Arkansas musicians, mostly fiddlers. *Ozark Mountainwood Express* is published in Harrison, Arkansas, for the tourist trade.

95. Green, Archie. "A Suggested Museum Show." *JEMF Quarterly* 15:55 (Fall 1979): 157–65.

Green says that museums should use more "folk music visuals" to depict our heritage. He thinks the art of Thomas Hart Benton would be more than adequate to fulfill such an undertaking. Among the Benton illustrations shown in this article is one entitled "Missouri Musicians," showing three Ozarkers on fiddle, guitar, and accordion. Tom Benton met these fellows in 1931 at a music party of his brother, Nat Benton. They were two brothers and a cousin from near Republic, Missouri. This interested me as I know their families and they all still make a lot of music in this part of the Ozarks.

96. ———. "Thomas Hart Benton's Folk Musicians." *JEMF Quarterly* 12:42 (Summer 1976): 74–90.

A good piece about Benton's love of Ozark music, and his use of it in his art. His grandfather was an old-time fiddler, and Benton himself played the harmonica and guitar. In 1942 he recorded a 78 rpm three-record-set for Decca entitled *Saturday Night at Tom Benton's*. Five illustrations depicting musical scenes are shown.

97. Hunter, Max Francis. "Fiddle Tunes from the Ozarks." Max Hunter Collection. Springfield–Greene County, Mo., Public Library.

Features fourteen fiddlers (eight from Arkansas, five from Missouri, and one from Oklahoma) and 122 tunes.

98. Krohn, Ernest C. *Missouri Music*. New York: Da Capo Press, 1971. 380p.

A republication of the 1924 edition. Concerns itself mostly with operas, symphonies, and chorales. It does mention two tunes pertaining to the Ozarks in a section entitled "Missouri State Songs" (pp. 56–58): "The Old Ozark Hills" and "The Ozark Song." The latter was composed by J. Breckenridge Ellis, author of *The Little Fiddler of the Ozarks* (see vol. 1 of this bibliography, p. 362).

99. McCulloh, Judith. "Uncle Absie Morrison's Historical Tunes." *Mid-South Folk-lore* 3:3 (Winter 1975): 95–104.

McCulloh prints sixteen careful transcriptions of Absie's best fiddle tunes, with his comments on the historical background of each. Such titles as "Bunker Hill," "Stony Point," "Bonaparte's Retreat," "The Eighth of January," "Richmond," and "Marching Through Georgia." I knew Absie Morrison and heard him play these pieces. Absie was a good fiddler, and I never fail to be impressed with McCulloh's skilled transcriptions of his music.

100. McNeil, W. K. "A Discography of Folk Music from the Ozark States." *Mid-America Folklore* 7:3 (Winter 1979): 83–86.

This is the first of what is to be a continuing series and will concern itself solely with LP recordings of the traditional music found in the states containing the Ozark region. In this issue McNeil discusses fifteen instrumental and/or vocal recordings. His comments are primarily intended to evaluate this material for teachers who might wish to use it in the teaching of folklore classes. McNeil is dedicated to his cause and will call things as he sees them.

101. ———. "Ozark Dance Tunes." Column in *Arkansas Country Dancer*. Little Rock: Arkansas Country Dance Society, 1980– .

This column appears periodically in this quarterly devoted to traditional dancing. To date the following tunes have been discussed with fairly extensive discographies included: "The Arkansas Traveler" (October-December 1981): 13–21; "Black-Eyed Susie" (April-June 1982): 5–9; "Flop-Eared Mule" (July-September 1982): 12–14. The quarterly is edited by Neil Kelley, an accomplished amateur dancer herself.

102. McSpadden, Lynn. *Mountain Dulcimers in the Ozarks*. Mountain View, Ark.: The Dulcimer Shoppe, 1977. 17p.

This is just a slick-paper booklet issued by a group of people who make and sell dulcimers, but it contains more information and better pictures than many pretentious volumes. It has the finest photographs of these instruments I have seen, and a long list of books about dulcimers and other folk instruments and how to play them.

103. Massey, Ellen Gray. *Bittersweet Country*. Garden City, N.Y.: Anchor Press, 1978. 434p.

The chapter "Singing with So-Fa Syllables" (pp. 357–73) is a fine description of the singing school and learning the So-Fa syllables by shape-notes. All about scale, pitching, voice parts, and rhythm.

104. Morton, Joseph W., Jr. *Sparks from the Campfire; or, Tales of the Old Veterans.* Washington, D.C.: The National Tribune, 1899. 469p.

See pages 142–45, "Story of a Little Drummer Boy," about the Civil War battle of Wilson's Creek that took place just southwest of Springfield, Missouri. Of interest is the part about the regimental fifer and a Scottish air, the "Flowers of Edinburgh," a tune still played by the old-time fiddlers in this part of the Ozarks.

105. Mulrenin, Karen, with Rita Saeger and Terry Brandt. "Old-Time Ozark Square Dancing." *Bittersweet* 2:1 (Fall 1974): 22–36, 58.

Instructions and calls for sixteen dances with a glossary of terms and careful explanations for many of the figures: circle eight, balance eight, promenade, etc. There is also a lengthy discussion of Ozarks square dancing in general. All in all this is one of the best articles on this subject I have seen. A sound sheet with five calls by a veteran Ozark caller is included. On p. 25 of this article is a drawing of the outline of a fiddle, filled with the names of eighty-eight authentic old-time fiddle tunes. About two dozen or so of these, including "Diddle on the Ground," "Old Aunt Sukie with Her Night Cap On," and "Corn Shucking Sally," I have never heard and hope to get to Laclede County someday to do so.

106. Patrick, Michael. "Bluegrass in the Ozarks." *The Ozarks Mountaineer* 29:2–3 (April 1981): 32–33.

This article gives some idea of a transition that has taken place in recent years. Although he mentions a few of the old traditional tunes and ballads, it's easy to see that such bluegrass favorites as "Foggy Mountain Breakdown," "Roll in My Sweet Baby's Arms," and other similar tunes now dominate the music scene. The author seems to infer that bluegrass is just another form of the old traditional music, but he fails to note what is distinctive about it and why it is a departure from the music of past generations in the Ozarks. He refers to two elements of the bluegrass festival, "pickers and crowds." The pickers are, as always, the musicians, but the crowds he speaks of are now content to sit and listen rather than take a more active part as they once did. This is partly a result of the very fast tempo of bluegrass. It's doubtful you'll ever see a square dance or a jig done to the breakneck time of "Dueling Banjos."

107. Pyles, Lida Wilson. "It Happened in the Ozarks." Manuscript, Carthage, Mo., 1982. 197p.

Descriptions of a number of what might be called supporting instruments that have all been used at one time or another in some parts of the Ozarks to accompany and help keep time for the lead instrument, which in most instances was the fiddle. These instruments (some musicologists might question their being called such) included knitting needles, gourds, jugs, jaw bones, and the musical saw. She also presents an interesting discussion about square dances and the square and jig dancers. The only copy of this manuscript is in the author's possession.

108. Seay, Sarah. "Modernizing a Mountain Art." *Bittersweet* 1:2 (Winter 1973): 36–41.

Bill Graves tells of his Cherokee grandfather, who he claims first thought of and constructed the dulcimer, or, as he called it, the "Indian Walking Cane." This happened during the Civil War. He kept his pattern "notched down" on a stick and made them as gifts for his friends. The rest of the article follows the assembly line creation of the modern dulcimers in the shop of Lynn McSpadden in Mountain View, Arkansas, that are sold complete or as do-it-yourself kits to all points in the United States. Contrary to what present-day proponents of this instrument would have the public believe about its use by Ozark pioneers, I had seen very few previous to their appearance at folk centers, theme parks, and other tourist attractions started in the 1960s and 1970s. Note Seay's statement on p. 36, "There has never been an abundance of dulcimers (in the Ozarks). This is probably why so little common knowledge is available about them."

109. Sherrer, Dwayne. "We Play a Little Music." *Bittersweet* 8:4 (Summer 1981): 54–64.

This is an exceptional article, done by the *Bittersweet* class of the Lebanon, Missouri, High School. Words and musical transcriptions, no less, of twenty tunes and songs collected from three elderly brothers who live near Linn in the central Missouri Ozarks. Six of these appear to be of local origin and I find no record of them in published collections. The rest are a mixture of traditional fiddle tunes, ballads, and songs of later vintage.

110. Thede, Marion. *The Fiddle Book*. New York: Oak Publications, [1967]. 160p.

I don't know what musicians would have to say about what Thede says about bowing, unorthodox tunings, etc., but she has collected more than 150 traditional fiddle tunes, mostly from Oklahoma fiddlers, and there are some good photographs of the old-timers. She has certainly been acquainted with a lot of fiddlers. She knows the jargon.

111. Thomas, Rosemary Hyde. *It's Good to Tell You: French Folktales from Missouri*. Columbia: University of Missouri Press, 1981. 246p.

Several of these tales mention music, especially the fiddle. See pp. 226–27 for discussions of Old Mines square dances, bouillons, and balls.

112. Wilgus, D. K. "On the Record." *Kentucky Folklore Record* 4:4 (October-December 1958): 184.

Praises a Jimmie Driftwood record, *Jimmie Driftwood Sings Newly Discovered Early American Folksongs* (Victor LPM 1635), as containing "performances on the mouth or picking-bow, which seems otherwise unreported from American White tradition." It includes "the rare 'Battle of New Orleans.'"

C. Dance

113. Adams, Emmett. "To Dance and Pay the Fiddler." *The Ozarks Mountaineer* 21:10 (November 1973): 20–21.

This article is well worth reading. Adams was born at the turn of the century and grew up in the wilds of Taney County, Missouri. As a young man he says that from 1914 through 1922 he danced three nights a week, nine months out of the year. His reputation as a square and jig dancer was such that he earned the nickname of "Rag Foot." And he knows all the old squares and fiddle tunes and names many of them. He says he would dance all night and then doze off walking behind the plow the next day. When in his seventies I have seen "Rag Foot" cut a jig that would test the endurance of a man half his age.

114. Draper, Cena Christopher. *Ridge Willoughby*. Austin, Tex.: The Steck Company, 1952. 119p.

See p. 112 for the words to an obscure square dance call that I had not heard before called "Swing the King."

115. Duncan, Robert S. *History of the Baptist in Missouri*. St. Louis: Scammell & Company, 1882. 937p.

See pp. 248–49 about the "dancing Baptists."

116. Fitzhugh, Jewell Kirby. "Play Parties and Square Dances." *The Ozarks Mountaineer* 22:5 (June 1974): 38–39.

Sensible discussion, with many fragments of song texts and several dance calls.

117. Galbraith, Arthur. "Music Parties in the Ozarks." *The Ozarks Mountaineer* 28:6–7 (August 1980): 35, 50.

An accurate, to-the-point article with none of the misconceptions seen in so many writings on this subject. The author is an old-time Ozark fiddler himself and speaks from firsthand knowledge.

118. Gerstäcker, Friedrich. "Women in the Backwoods." Trans. Ralph Walker.
     Early American Life 13:6 (December 1982): 14–16, 19–23.

On p. 16 is a brief account of a frontier dance that takes place in the Arkansas
Ozarks, ca. 1840. He says that these pioneers knew nothing of the German waltzes
or glides but did only lively jigs and reels.

119. Grover, James R. "Ralph Hughey: Northwest Arkansas Storyteller." *Mid-South
     Folklore* 3:1 (Spring 1975): 3–11.

On pp. 4–5 is the story of a ruckus that took place at "the New Year's Dance at
Elkins" in 1966 as told to the author by this storyteller from Madison County.
Grover collected this and other stories while he was a student at John Brown University in Siloam Springs, Arkansas.

120. Lyon, Marguerite. "Lady of the Hills." Unpublished manuscript, Forsyth,
     Mo., 1948. 234p.

Good accounts of early square dances, dance halls, and fiddling in the southwest Missouri Ozarks on pp. 69–70, 101, and 114.

121. Massey, Ellen Gray. *Bittersweet Country.* Garden City, N.Y.: Anchor Press,
     1978. 434p.

In the chapter entitled "Old-Time Ozark Square Dancing" (pp. 393–421) are
instructions and calls to over twenty-five dances. One set called to finish out the
evening is " 'Wind That Waterbury Watch' . . . and wind it tight, Or we'll be here
till broad daylight." There is also a helpful glossary of terms.

122. Parks, Celeste. "Square Dancing—Beginning, and Now." *Ozark 71* 2:1 (January-February 1977): 13, 24, 26.

An informative article tracing square dancing from its beginnings in the seventeenth-century "country dances" of the British Isles to its present-day popularity in
the Ozarks. Pretty good reading, which is unusual for a tourist publication. *Ozark
71* is a guidebook published in Bentonville, Arkansas, for the Joplin, Missouri–Fort
Smith, Arkansas, section of U.S. Highway 71.

123. Patrick, Michael D. "Ozark Music Parties." *The Ozarks Mountaineer* 26:3
     (April 1978): 26–27.

Patrick thinks these gatherings are somehow derived from play-parties. But the
play-party was just a square dance without instrumental music, while the music parties he describes normally consist entirely of instrumental music without much
dancing. Meetings of fiddlers and guitarists and banjo pickers have always been
common in the Ozarks, but they have nothing to do with play-parties.

124. ———. "Traditional Ozark Entertainment." *Missouri Folklore Society Journal* 3 (1981): 47–57.

Patrick talks about play-parties and music parties but apparently is still unaware of the difference in the two. Again he says that today's music parties are direct descendants from the play-parties of a couple of generations ago. In reality, today's music parties are descendants from yesteryear's music party, not the play-parties, which had no instrumental music. He also tells of shivarees and square dances. One banjo player said the reason there were so many musicians in his county was because the bandstand was the safest place to be when the fighting started.

125. Stephens, H. Page. "The Case of the Missing Folk Music: A Study of Aspects of Musical Life in Stone County, Arkansas, from 1890–1980." *Mid-America Folklore* 10:2–3 (Fall-Winter 1982): 58–69.

The author did his preliminary research between 1967 and 1969, in the midst of a very formative time in the life of this county. The article begins with biographical sketches of four natives and the comparison of their musical achievements within the community. He then goes on to discuss the folk music and the folk festival revivals of the 1960s and 1970s, a period when this county gained national recognition and prominence for its folk music and traditions and saw the establishment in the county seat, Mountain View, of the Ozark Folk Center, then a federally funded city project—now a state park. Aside from these facts and developments, the interesting parts of this article are the discussions of the serious repercussions that arose from this sudden fame and new tourist industry (with its dollars) that had unexpectedly intruded upon the lives of the local inhabitants of this relatively isolated region of north-central Arkansas.

126. Stone, Lloyd. "Across the Big Piney to the Square Dance." *The Ozarks Mountaineer* 24:3 (April 1976): 18.

The story, as it was told to the author by his father, of a dance he attended in Texas County, Missouri, in 1901 that lasted until dawn. One stanza of a square dance call is given.

127. Stong, Phil. *Hirum, the Hillbilly.* New York: Dodd, Mead & Company, 1951. 104p.

Chapter 5, "A Square Dance" (pp. 68–87), has some minor errors in Stong's description of the dance, but what he says about the musicians (p. 77) is definitely a truism.

128. White, Kathleen K. *True Tall Tales from Missouri.* Clinton, Mo.: The Printery, 1976. 70p.

Page 63 tells of the very early square dances and fiddlers. Folks either stood or danced all night. Favorite tunes were "Chicken Pie" and "Buffalo Gals."

129. Williams, Leonard. "An Early Arkansas 'Frolic': A Contemporary Account." *Mid-South Folklore* 2:2 (Summer 1974): 39–42.

Charles Noland, under his pseudonym of "Pete Whetstone," gives this account of a frolic or party (Williams refers to it as a play-party but it is generally accepted today that this term applies only to gatherings with no instrumental music). It first appeared in *The Spirit of the Times* in 1837. The titles of three fiddle tunes are mentioned: "All Night There," "She Wouldn't and She Couldn't," and "My Roaring River," none of which are familiar today to any of the old-time fiddlers I mentioned them to.

130. Wolf, John Quincy [Sr.]. "A Country Dance in the Ozarks in 1874." *Southern Folklore Quarterly* 29:4 (December 1965): 319–21.

This account, written in 1931, is the same one that appears later in *Life in the Leatherwoods* (see entry 180), edited by his son, John Quincy Wolf, Jr.

131. Worthen, Mary Fletcher, compiler. *Matters and Things in General.* Little Rock: Arkansas Territorial Restoration Foundation, 1974. 59p.

Excerpts that were published in Arkansas newspapers during the territorial period, 1819 through 1836. Page 30 is an interesting diatribe on the evils of dancing that appeared in the *Arkansas Gazette*, 14 December 1824.

D. Personalities

132. Abrahams, Roger D. *A Singer and Her Songs: Almeda Riddle's Book of Ballads.* Baton Rouge: Louisiana State University Press, 1970. 191p.

This story of her life was dictated into a tape recorder by Mrs. Riddle and revised very cautiously by Abrahams. It is forthright and good. Her people were farmers in Missouri and Arkansas. It was John Quincy Wolf who "discovered" her as a folk singer. This book has the texts and tunes of about fifty songs. Almeda Riddle is a pleasant, elderly country woman, who says she is related to Frank and Jesse James. She visited us several times at Fayetteville and my wife recorded many of her songs. Many of her texts are conflated, like the elder Lomax's. She learned a few stanzas as a child. Later on, if she found a good stanza in print, or in a commercial recording, she adopted it to fortify her own text. Compare Jimmy Driftwood and May Kennedy McCord. Abrahams is a professor of English and anthropology at the University of Texas in Austin.

133. Albin, Edgar A. "Almeda Riddle: Folk Singer of Arkansas." *Ozark Highways* (Winter 1972): 17–21.

A visit with well-known ballad singer "Granny" Riddle at her home near Greer's Ferry, Arkansas. This is a good biographical sketch of Almeda and her career. Note the account of the church meeting held nearby at the Lone Pine Community House. The final page of this article is her version of Gussie L. Davis's nineteenth-century tearjerker, "In the Baggage Coach Ahead." This was a "Special Hill-Folks Issue," no designation as to volume or number.

134. Anderson, Clay. "A Chunk of Driftwood." *The Ozarks Mountaineer* 19:3 (April 1971): 19, 26.

About James "Jimmie Driftwood" Morris, his music and his career.

135. Barton, Cathy. "Max Hunter, Ozark Song Collector." *Missouri Folklore Society Journal* 1 (1979): 18–32.

Max Hunter is a Springfield, Missouri, salesman who travels through the Ozarks and collects folksongs and tales as a hobby. Starting in 1956, he has made tape recordings of over one thousand songs and three hundred sixty fiddle tunes, besides a great number of dialect samples and "fifteen hours of jokes." Every tape is carefully labeled with informants clearly named and identified. I know Hunter and I have seen him work. His collection is certainly the largest and perhaps the most valuable ever assembled in this region. Much of it has been deposited in the Library of Congress, the University of Arkansas–Fayetteville, the University of Missouri–Columbia, and the public library in Springfield. Cathy Barton's paper is the best account of Max Hunter that I have seen.

136. Bowen, Elbert R. "Negro Minstrels in Early Rural Missouri." *Missouri Historical Review* 47:2 (January 1953): 103–9.

Fascinating paper, with names, dates, anecdotes, handbills, and other illustrations. Some valuable references to old-time songs and rhymes.

137. Braswell, O. Klute. "The Stephen Foster of the Ozarks." *Carroll County Historical Society Quarterly* 24:1 (Spring 1979): 1–8.

About James Thomas Braswell (1873–1947), musician and native of Carroll and Newton counties, Arkansas. He organized bands in Ozark communities and wrote songs, mostly with Ozark themes—"My Dear Old Ozark Home," "I'm Glad I'm a Hillbilly," "Camping in the Ozark Hills," to name a few. He claimed to have written "Everybody's Got to Have Somebody Sometime," which achieved national prominence.

138. Cansler, Loman D. "He Hewed His Own Path: William Henry Scott, Ozark Songmaker." *Studies in the Literary Imagination* 3:1 (April 1970): 37–63.

The story of a fellow at Bennett Springs, Missouri, who wrote verses, and sometimes sang them to old familiar melodies like "The Wearing of the Green." It seems that none were ever published, and none found its way into the oral tradition of the region.

139. ———. "Walter Dibben, an Ozark Bard." *Kentucky Folklore Record* 13:4 (October-December 1967): 81–89.

An old man in Long Lane, Dallas County, Missouri, used to make up little rhymes about neighborhood affairs and even national politics. He sang them himself sometimes, to nondescript tunes. Most of these crossroads poets publish their verses in weekly newspapers, but Walter Dibben did not. According to this article, his tunes were reminiscent of "Sweet Betsy from Pike." Cansler, who is a teacher in a high school in North Kansas City, collected thirty-nine of Dibben's songs, but prints only five in this paper. Walter Dibben died in 1967 at the age of eighty.

140. Cardwell, Nancy. "Max Hunter—Ozark Folklore Field Collector." *Bluegrass Unlimited* 16:1 (July 1981): 27–29.

Max talks about some of his adventures in ballad collecting. Of value is his discussion of the field methods he used that enabled him to compile what is possibly the most extensive collection of Ozark balladry on record.

141. ———. "Mountain Music—Family Style." *The Ozarks Mountaineer* 28:8–9 (October 1980): 19.

The Cardwells, father, mother, son, and two daughters, are typical of the family groups that entertained in communities around the Ozarks forty or more years ago. Hopefully there is a trend back to this practice.

142. Casteel, Gussie. "Thelma & Lonnie." *The Ozarks Mountaineer* 30:2–3 (April 1982): 34.

Thelma and Lonnie Robertson, both natives of Ozark County, Missouri, were local musicians who "made good" and for almost thirty years entertained by radio and road show throughout the Midwest. Lonnie was one of the very best of what we now call "traditional" fiddlers. His repertoire was astounding. It became a mixture of Ozark hoedowns, reels, and blues, which he had learned growing up in southern Missouri, with hornpipes and waltzes he had acquired from the early days of his career in north Missouri. He died in 1981. Thelma, who sang with Lonnie, grew up only a few miles from his homeplace. She was a rural schoolteacher and rode bareback to teach in the Barefoot School northwest of Gainesville before she and Lonnie began their careers.

143. Cochran, Michael. "Say Hello to the Real Speck Rhodes: An Interview with the Ozarks' Favorite Funnyman." *West Plains Gazette* 10 (January-February 1981): 11–21.

Conducted by the editor with this native son of Howell County, Missouri, who made it good as a member of one of the nation's most popular country music groups. This is a good insight into the role of the comic or clown, who is a vital member of such groups. Note the similarities of this character to his earlier counterparts of the vaudeville and minstrel shows.

144. Curtis, James R. "Woody Guthrie and the Dust Bowl." *Places* 3:2 (July 1976): 12–18.

Excerpts from Woody's songs, and quotes from the writings of Steinbeck, Alan Lomax, Pete Seeger, and others. John Greenway wrote, "Guthrie will, in my opinion, grow to a high rank even among sophisticated American poets."

145. Deane, Ernie. *Ozarks Country*. Branson, Mo.: The Ozarks Mountaineer, 1975. 191p.

"Willie Laid Down His Bow," pp. 101–2, is about Willie Morrison of Fox, Arkansas, one of the finest of the old-time fiddlers in the Arkansas Ozarks. Pages 110–12 are about "Bill Baker, Folk Musician," of Madison County, Arkansas, who, along with his brother Toby, was a member of the Weaver Brothers and Elviry. This was a popular country-music group in the 1930s and 1940s. They were from the Missouri Ozarks. Pages 77–79 tell of the singers and songs he found in Mountain View and Eureka Springs, Arkansas. Pages 102–3 are about ballad singer Almeda "Granny" Riddle.

146. Downs, Joan. "The Living Roots of Country Music." *Life* 72:25 (30 June 1972): 60–70.

Lots of good photos of traditional musicians from the Carolinas to Louisiana, including two pages on square dancing on the courthouse grounds in Mountain View, Arkansas. On p. 70 is an editorial entitled "Battle of the Hootenannies." This is about the schism that developed in Mountain View between the purists who wanted only the "old timey" music performed and those who wanted the modern sound. Some residents of that part of the Ozarks may take issue with the author's statement that Jimmie Driftwood's "pitch" in Washington, D.C., got the money for the Ozark Folk Center located in Mountain View.

147. Ellis, Larry. "That Fiddler from Adak." *Missouri Life* 3:3 (July-August 1975): 18–23.

This is an autobiography of the author's life and his fiddle. It's a pretty typical story of many of the younger fiddlers today in the Ozarks. He was raised near

Marshall, Missouri, and, like most fiddlers of his generation, he began with the "old timey" tunes but is now deep into bluegrass. The title refers to a town not in the Ozarks, but Alaska, where he was stationed while in the Navy.

148. Foreman, Diana. "Fiddlin' Around." *Bittersweet* 5:2 (Winter 1977): 62–69.

About fiddler and fiddle maker Violet Hensley of Yellville, Arkansas.

149. Gage, Jimmy. "A Green County Boy on the Radio." *Bittersweet* 9:3 (Spring 1982): 63–65.

A Laclede County, Missouri, fiddler tells about playing on a small-town radio station in the 1940s. He speaks of the different instruments that have seconded (accompanied) his fiddling over the years.

150. Glenn, Wayne. "It Was in the Summer of 1936." *Springfield News and Leader*, 29 June 1975.

Sidney Robertson, WPA agent, came to Springfield and recorded Ozark folk ballads. She recorded songs from May Kennedy McCord, Paul Holland, a father-and-son team named Rice, Slim Wilson, the Ray Denoons, and others. I met Mrs. Robertson at that time, and everything was as Glenn tells it except that my (notoriously unreliable) memory would have dated it 1934 instead of 1936. This article was reprinted in *The Ozarks Mountaineer* (December 1975, pp. 18–19).

151. Godsey, Helen, and Townsend Godsey. "Queen of the Hillbillies." *The Ozarks Mountaineer* 25:10 (November 1977): 14–15, 26–27.

Raised in Galena, Stone County, Missouri, May Kennedy McCord was a close friend of Vance and one of his most valuable informants in all matters pertaining to the Ozarks. Her knowledge of folksongs alone contributed almost seventy-five entries for *Ozark Folksongs*. This is an important article.

152. Guthrie, Woody. *Bound for Glory*. New York: E. P. Dutton, 1943. 428p.

Woody's own story, and he didn't pull any punches. Illustrated by his own fantastic drawings. In 1969 Dutton brought out a "new edition," with a good photo of Woody by Robin Carson and a fine foreword by Pete Seeger. I knew Woody and always wished I could have known him better. I thought he was a great man, and I still think so. His "This Land Is Your Land" is a better song than the mindless "God Bless America" that the TV singers plug so relentlessly nowadays.

153. Henigan, Julie. "Max Hunter: The Traveling Salesman Who Rescued a Folk Heritage." *Springfield Magazine* 2:5 (October 1980): 40–42.

A good article about Max in which he explains his methods of collecting. Also a fine photograph of him taken in the Springfield library where a large segment of his collection is stored.

154. Holt, Bob. "My First Love Is These Old Tunes I Learned from My Dad." *Bittersweet* 9:3 (Spring 1982): 54–58.

Holt is a native of Douglas County in southwest Missouri. He is one of the best of the old-time square-dance fiddlers in this part of the Ozarks. He talks about his style of fiddling and of the tunes he plays.

155. Hunter, Max. "Ozarks Folklore Field Collector." *Just for the Record* 1:5 (August 1977): 7, 18.

Brief account of a ballad hunt in the Missouri Ozarks. Max helps a farmer get in his hay, collects thirty old songs. *Just for the Record* is a slick-paper monthly published in Springfield, Missouri.

156. Jarvis, Peggy. "R. P. Christeson: Sage of the Ozarks." *Pickin'* 6:2 (March 1979): 8, 10.

About Bob Christeson, whose book, *Old-Time Fiddler's Repertory: 245 Traditional Tunes* (see entry 87), has sold more than three thousand copies. Christeson tells of his years of collecting, the first recordings being with an early wire recorder in the 1940s. He holds fast to one requirement for old-time fiddling: "If you can't dance to it, why play it?" He laments that old-time fiddling has declined and that today, "People have turned themselves into consumers of entertainment instead of providing their own."

157. Jennings, Ron. "Ragtime Struts Back Home." *Missouri Life* 2:6 (January-February 1975): 47–52.

All about Scott Joplin and the "Maple Leaf Rag," the beginning of ragtime. It all happened in Sedalia, Missouri, in 1899, according to Jennings. He doesn't mention the town of Joplin, Missouri, at all. Well, there's no denying that the disreputable Maple Leaf Club was in Sedalia and that the famous "Maple Leaf Rag" was first published in Sedalia. Jennings says it was "written and performed" there, and there's nobody alive now who can prove it ain't so.

158. Johns, Paul W. *Unto These Hills: True Tales from the Ozarks.* Ozark, Mo.: Bilyeu-Johns Enterprises, 1980. 104p.

This little book concerns itself mostly with the area around Christian County, Missouri. Pages 22–24 tell of Sam Weatherman, probably the best remembered of all the old-time fiddlers in that part of the Ozarks. When asked by a young guitar player who was going to accompany him at a fiddle contest what key his tune would be in, Sam replied, "It don't make a damn bit of difference, young man, you jest keep up!"

159. Johnson, Claude E. "Singing Schools of Today." *Arkansas Gazette*, "Sunday Magazine," 15 June 1941, pp. 9, 14.

Tells of schools still in existence in some Arkansas communities. Also much about Albert Brumley of Powell, Missouri, and his popular gospel song, "Turn Your Radio On."

160. Kantor, MacKinlay. *Missouri Bittersweet*. Garden City, N.Y.: Doubleday and Company, 1969. 324p.

See the account of the fake folksong that fooled Carl Sandburg (pp. 265–66). Kantor seems surprised that Sandburg was "miffed" when he realized that he had been fooled.

161. Lindley, Helen C. "The Hoss-Hair Pullers and Hillbilly Quartet." *Izard County Historian* 5:2 (April 1974): 9–13.

In the 1920s, a group of Calico Rock, Arkansas, men under the direction of a local doctor organized two musical groups, the Hoss-Hair Pullers and the Hill-Billy Quartet. Their first and subsequent broadcasts were from Hot Springs, Arkansas, and they received wide acclaim in the Midwest. There is an amusing story of their imprisonment by a county judge and then being required to sing their way out of jail. A discography is included.

162. McKowen, Carol. "An Interview with Jimmy Driftwood, the Arkansas Minstrel." *Ozark Highways* (Winter 1972): 34–47.

This is a good narrative of a visit with James Corbett Morris, whose historical ballads achieved fame for himself and the Stone County, Arkansas, Rackensack Society. In spite of some views to the contrary, there's no doubt that Driftwood's popularity with the American public was instrumental in drawing national attention to the folk culture of northern Arkansas in the 1960s. Lots of good, informal photographs of Jimmie and his wife, Cleda.

163. "Max Hunter Hunts for Folk Songs in the Ozarks." *New Seasons* 6:2 (April 1978): 8–9.

Brief article about Max Hunter and his astounding collection of Ozark folksongs.

164. Olin, James, Julia Hager, and Barry Bergey. "Old-Time Fiddling: An Interview with R. P. Christeson." *The Devil's Box* 10:3 (September 1976): 14–20.

This interview with Bob Christeson, author and compiler of *The Old-Time Fiddler's Repertory* (see entry 87), was conducted in his home at Auxvasse, Missouri. He speaks about the past and present of old-time fiddling in Missouri. Christeson is a fiddler himself, one of the best. He has observed his avocation very carefully over the years, and his conclusions about its future are not encouraging.

165. Parrish, William. "'Blind' Boone's Ragtime." *Missouri Life* 7:5 (November-December 1979): 17–23.

From 1880 until his death in 1927, John William "Blind" Boone was one of the most popular and foremost practitioners of ragtime in the Midwest. Many musicologists credit Missouri as the birthplace of ragtime and cite "Blind" Boone's contributions along with those of Scott Joplin and Tom Turpin. He is especially remembered in the Ozarks for his composition "The Marshfield Tornado," which so upset the audience in Marshfield when he performed it there that many ran for cover, fearing another "cyclone" was approaching. Though one of his most famous numbers, he never wrote this piece down.

166. Pirtle, Caleb, III. "An Ozark Man Keeps His Music Alive." *St. Louis Post-Dispatch*, "Sunday Magazine," 18 July 1982.

A patronizing piece about Jimmie Driftwood of Timbo, Arkansas, who achieved national fame as a performer of traditional Ozark music, and about the Ozark Folk Center, established in Mountain View for the preservation of Ozark folkways.

167. Reuss, Richard A. "Woody Guthrie and His Folk Tradition." *Journal of American Folklore* 83:329 (July-September 1970): 273–303.

Biographical detail. Reuss sees Woody as the rustic minstrel, "comedian-sage," a kind of proletarian Will Rogers.

168. Rice, Don. "Teacher, Historian, Balladeer: He Teaches Us Our Heritage in Music and Song." *Best Years* 5:1 (Winter 1981): 20–24.

In 1936 Jimmy Driftwood was a rural teacher in Timbo, Arkansas. In the tradition of balladry, he set words to an old fiddle tune, "Eighth of January," in order to teach his students history. In 1958 it became a hit song, and the fame he received did much to focus national attention on the music and crafts of the Ozarks. The cover is a fine color photo of Jimmy and his wife, Cleda. *Best Years* is a quarterly published for senior citizens by the National Association of Mature People.

169. Richmond, James T. *Newton County, Arkansas, in Song and Story.* Jasper, Ark.: Jasper Informer Printing Company, 1936. 102p.

This title and description appeared in several lists and bibliographies, but the book was never published; J. Milam of the Informer Printing Company writes me

(18 July 1955) that "it was never gotten beyond the talk stage." Richmond once operated a lending library in Newton County (see Hartzell Spence, "Modern Shepherd of the Hills," *Saturday Evening Post*, 8 November 1952, pp. 26–27, 130–33). But I don't think he ever wrote or published any books. For the local reaction to Spence's story see the "Ozark Outlook" editorial by Tom Dearmore (*Baxter Bulletin*, Mountain Home, Arkansas, 20 November 1952), reprinted in *Ozark Guide* (Winter 1953, pp. 7–8). Otto Rayburn knew Ted Richmond as well as anybody; he told me that Richmond was "completely unreliable." Richmond died November 1975 in Texarkana, Texas, at age ninety-two.

170. Rickman, Glen. "A Fiddler Will Never Be Worth a Damn." *Bittersweet* 9:3 (Spring 1982): 61–63.

Reminiscences of seventy years of fiddling. Much about the square dances he played for in his youth. He says he never took a girl to a dance where he was to play because if trouble started, all he would have to worry about was his fiddle. Rickman has lived his life in Stone County in southwest Missouri. He thinks he can play close to two hundred tunes.

171. Schroeder, Rebecca B. "Vance Randolph and Ozark Folksongs." *Missouri Folklore Society Journal* 2 (1980): 57–67.

A review of the reprint of the 1980 edition of Randolph's *Ozark Folksongs*. But Schroeder covers far more than just critical comments on the work itself. She pretty well tells it as it was about the academic community's attitudes toward Randolph's collection, recounting the many problems and disappointments he encountered from the 1920s until its publication by the State Historical Society of Missouri in four volumes, 1946–1950, and finally its republication just six months before his death. Aside from *Ozark Folksongs*, the writer discusses other folksong collections of Randolph's yet to be published.

172. Smittle, Delilah. "Violet Hensley: The Fiddle Maker from Yellville, Arkansas." *Ozark Highways* (Summer 1974): 30–33.

Violet was born and raised in Montgomery County, Arkansas. As a girl she plowed and did all kinds of farm chores. She also learned to play the fiddle, and at fifteen she made her first one. Now, forty-three years later, she's still involved in making and playing the fiddle. She says her repertoire is "about one hundred and fifty tunes." In 1971 she represented Arkansas at the Smithsonian Institution's Festival of American Folklife in Washington, D.C.

173. Stephens, H. Page. "The Case of the Missing Folk Music: A Study of Aspects of Musical Life in Stone County, Arkansas, from 1890–1980." *Mid-America Folklore* 10:2–3 (Fall-Winter 1982): 58–69.

Biographical sketches of four Stone County folk musicians and the differences in the development of their musical contributions to the community.

174. Stone County 4-H Council, ed. *The Faces of Rackensack*. Mountain View, Ark.: Stone County Leader, 1972. 80p.

Brief biographical sketches with photographs of more than one hundred members of this organization that originated in Stone and the surrounding counties in north-central Arkansas. Its objectives were the preservation and perpetuation of Ozarks traditions, principally music. The biographical notes include the musical talents of each member (many played more than one instrument), and the breakdown is interesting: guitar, 49; dancing (square and jig), 32; singing, 31; mandolin, 22; banjo, 20; fiddle, 19; autoharp, 10; dulcimer (lap), 9; harmonica or French harp, 5; bass fiddle, 2; juice harp, 1; square-dance caller, 1; wash-tub bass, 1; piano, 1; dancing dolls, 1; dobro, 1; pickin' bow, 1; organ, 1; and tamborine, 1. They make good music in Stone County!

175. Vaughn, Jerry. "That Ozark Playboy: Red Murrell." *JEMF Quarterly* 17:63 (Fall 1981): 119–22.

About a successful country music star and his band, Red Murrell and His Ozark Playboys, among the top western swing entertainers on the West Coast during the 1940s. Red was born (1921) and reared in Willow Springs, Missouri.

176. Waldo, Terry. *This Is Ragtime*. New York: Hawthorn Books, 1976. 244p.

See pp. 127, 129 about Percy Wenrich. This Joplin native was influenced by the music he heard as a child around the old House of Lords. He composed such ragtime standards as "Put On Your Old Grey Bonnet," "Dixie Blossoms," and "When You Wore a Tulip," to name a few.

177. Wixson, Douglas. "The Oral Tradition of Fiddle Music in the Early Days of Radio: Uncle Jim Haley of Pulaski County." *Missouri Folklore Society Journal* 1:1 (1979): 2–17.

An excellent article about an old-time fiddler in Pulaski County, Missouri. A good insight into the importance these backwoods virtuosos played in the lives of the early Ozarkers before radio or TV. Uncle Jim would play over the early telephone, and the party lines would be open for miles around. Some folks hung the receiver in a milk pail to amplify the sound. The author uses good sources, especially the quotes from John Quincy Wolf, Thomas Hart Benton, and Emmett Adams. This same article was reprinted in *Mid-America Folklore* (Fall 1979) under the title "Bacchus in the Backwoods: Uncle Jim Haley, Ozark Fiddler." Wixson teaches at the University of Missouri–Rolla.

178. Wolf, John Quincy [Jr.]. "Aunt Carolyn Dye: The Gypsy in the 'St. Louis Blues.'" *Southern Folklore Quarterly* 33:4 (December 1969): 339–46.

All about Carolyn Dye of Newport, Arkansas. She was a famous seer and fortune-teller and finder of lost objects. W. C. Handy told Dorothy Scarborough that Carolyn was the Gypsy in his "St. Louis Blues." Wolf says that she was "one of the most celebrated women who ever lived in the mid-South." Born in slavery, the date of her birth is unknown. She died in 1918, and the tombstone at Newport gives her age as one hundred eight, but some of her friends thought she was not more than ninety. I never met Carolyn Dye, but everybody I knew in Arkansas seemed to have heard all about her. In 1930 the Memphis Jug Band recorded "Aunt Carolyn Dye Blues" (Victor 23347).

179. ———. "Folksingers and the Re-Creation of Folksong." *Western Folklore* 26:2 (April 1967): 101–11.

After many years of collecting in "the White River country of the Arkansas Ozarks," Wolf discusses the ways in which folksingers change (consciously or unconsciously) the songs as they sing them. The quotations from such informants as Neal Morris of Mountain View, Jimmy Driftwood of Timbo, Fred High of Berryville, Barry Sutterfield of Marshall, Almeda Riddle of Heber Springs, and other Arkansas folksingers are all required reading. His conclusions are worth reading, and show he has common sense.

180. Wolf, John Quincy [Sr.]. *Life in the Leatherwoods*. Memphis: Memphis State University Press, 1974. 159p.

On pp. 119–22 Wolf gives a good account of a square dance he attended in Izard County, Arkansas, in the 1880s. Especially note his description of the jig dancer (pp. 121–22). Wolf gives us some of our best views of the nineteenth-century Arkansas Ozarks. He comments (p. 148) that in the isolation of that region, "I learned to look at commonplace things large and small and see whatever was special about them. And because people were scarce, everyone I saw was important."

181. Wolfe, Charles. "Caney Mountain Fiddler: The Lonnie Robertson Story." *The Devil's Box* 12:3 (1 September 1978): 34–48.

An interview with one of the most accomplished old-time fiddlers of Missouri. Lonnie learned his early fiddling while growing up in Ozark County, Missouri. As a young man he moved to St. Joseph, Missouri, and was influenced by north Missouri and Nebraska fiddling, resulting in a unique style that was to foster a professional career on radio for the next forty years. His popularity in the Ozarks had a substantial effect upon fiddling in the region. Robertson died in February 1981. The author writes extensively about the early music of radio and records. He currently teaches at Middle Tennessee State University in Murfreesboro, Tennessee. *The Devil's Box* is a quarterly publication of the Tennessee Valley Old-Time Fiddler's Association.

182. Womack, Tom. "Collecting Folk-Music of the Ozarks." *Columbia Daily Tribune*, 30 July 1977.

A fine front-page story about Max Hunter of Springfield, Missouri, collector of folksongs in the Ozarks. Not a professional folklorist, Max is a businessman who collects folklore as a hobby. He has taped more than twenty-two hundred folksongs in Missouri and Arkansas since 1956, also a great number of fiddle tunes, folktales, backwoods jokes and anecdotes, pioneer reminiscences, and the like (see entry 1213). I think he is the best folklore collector who has worked in the Ozarks since the death of Prof. H. M. Belden of the University of Missouri. This is a good newspaper story about Max with two good photographs.

2. Folk Speech

183. Adams, Emmett. " 'Pon Honor." *The Ozarks Mountaineer* 26:3 (April 1978): 10.

Some intelligent and penetrating comments on the Ozark dialect. He says he has heard the pronoun *you'ens* all his life, but has never heard a hillbilly say *we'uns*. A *poke*, he says, is a brown paper bag. He worked as a clerk in a country store, "but never did I hear anyone ask for a *poke* of flour or a *bag* of flour. It is always a sack." "A *tow sack*, a *burlap sack*, and a *gunny sack* were always one and the same to me."

184. ———. "Sayings and Such in the Ozarks." *The Ozarks Mountaineer* 26:6 (July 1978): 36.

Sixty sayings and wisecracks collected by a veteran foxhunter in Forsyth, Taney County, Missouri.

185. *American Folklore and Legend.* Pleasantville, N.Y.: Reader's Digest Association, 1978. 448p.

Under the heading "Ozark Lore" is a shortened and respectable version of "Change the Name of Arkansas? Hell No!" (pp. 160–61).

186. Batson, Larry. "The Ozarks." *Picture* (Sunday supplement of the *Minneapolis Tribune*), 21 June 1981, pp. 4–7, 15.

About the changing Ozarks. Some discussion of dialect on p. 7. Batson was raised in the Ozarks and is the author of *The Hills Are Theirs: Tales from the Ozarks* (entry 382).

187. Berry, Earl. *History of Marion County.* Little Rock: Marion County Historical Association, 1977. 523p.

See pp. 47–48 for sayings and metaphors collected in this north-central Arkansas county.

188. Beveridge, Tom. *Tom Beveridge's Ozarks.* Pacific Grove, Calif.: Boxwood Press, 1979. 85p.

At the Springfield, Missouri, Court of Appeals in 1960, Judge Justin Ruark ruled on a case that involved the use of the word *hillbilly*. His statement is presented here in its entirety (p. 71). "Cap" Ruark was a native of Newton County, Missouri, and a keen observer of the Ozarker. Ruark's comments should be studied carefully. There is more on Ozark speech under the chapter headings "Ozark Redundancies,"

"Idioms and Accents," and "Speech Patterns" (pp. 56–61), in which he puts forth some observations of his own. Other speech notes are found on pp. 1–3, 19, and 22.

189. Bowen, Iris O'Neal. *Hully-Gully, How Many?* Mabelvale, Ark.: Foreman-Payne Publishers, 1971. 56p.

Memories of the author's childhood as the daughter of a preacher in rural Arkansas. Her parents were prudish in speech beyond any hillfolk I have ever known. Children were punished for using such words as *golly*, *gee whiz*, and *gosh* because these terms were suggestive of profanity, and a preacher's children must avoid the least appearance of evil (pp. 6–7).

190. Carlson, Al. "College Jive Is Still Alive." *The Springfield News-Leader*, 22 March 1981.

This article contains a word list of 119 college slang terms compiled by the United Press International (sources unidentified). A local reporter takes it to some Ozark campuses for comparison and comments by the students.

191. Clements, William M. "The Rhetoric of the Radio Ministry." *Journal of American Folklore* 87:346 (October-December 1974): 318–27.

A careful study of backwoods evangelists and their methods. Clements's research was carried out in northeastern Arkansas, mostly in Craighead and Poinsett counties, but what he says applies pretty well to the entire Ozark region. The author is a professor at Arkansas State University at Jonesboro.

192. Dark, Harry, and Phyl Dark. *The Greatest Ozarks Guidebook.* Springfield, Mo.: Greatest Graphics, 1979. 240p.

Just as the title states, this is a guidebook to the various tourist attractions and points of interest in the Missouri-Arkansas Ozarks. Beautiful photos of beautiful places, but little folklore. See pp. 11–18 for the discussion of "Ozarker vs. Ozarkian" (much in the same vein as the "Missour-ee vs. Missour-uh" controversy) and other Ozark terms.

193. Deane, Ernie. "All Things Changing Ozark Folk Speech." *Proceedings of the Conference on Ozark In-migration.* Eureka Springs: Arkansas Humanities Committee, 1976. 124p.

A discussion of the Ozark dialect as described by novelist Donald Harington at a "Conference on In-migration" at Eureka Springs in June 1976. He compares the folk speech reported by Randolph and Wilson in 1953 with that which Harington found in 1976, showing the effect of radio, television, etc., on Ozark speech. Deane is a native of south Arkansas, a freelance feature writer, and a former professor of journalism at the University of Arkansas, Fayetteville. This article is cited as being a reprint from *The Grapevine* (5 June 1976), a weekly tabloid printed in Fayetteville, Arkansas. It appears in an unpaginated appendix of selected newspaper and magazine articles pertaining to the conference and to regional growth.

194. ———. *Ozarks Country*. Branson, Mo.: The Ozarks Mountaineer, 1975. 191p.

For more than twenty-five years Ernie has been a keen observer of the Ozarks. On pp. 26–30 are various definitions of the term *hillbilly*. Also see the chapter "Hill Talk Is Fading Fast" on pp. 45–46.

195. Dumas, Bethany K. "The Morphology of Newton County, Arkansas: An Exercise in Studying Ozark Dialect." *Mid-South Folklore* 3:3 (Winter 1975): 115–25.

Should be read in connection with Dumas's Ph.D. dissertation (see next entry). It is easier reading for laymen like me, not familiar with the technical jargon of modern dialectology.

196. ———. "A Study of the Dialect of Newton County, Arkansas." Ph.D. dissertation, University of Arkansas at Fayetteville, 1971. 228p.

This dissertation is based on a questionnaire adapted from the *Dialect Atlas* program, answered on tape by twenty carefully selected informants resident in Newton County, with particular attention to the Ben Hur–Moore area in the southeastern part of the county, which seems to be an important relic area. The work is the first fruit of the Arkansas Language Survey (ALS), begun by Gary N. Underwood at the University of Arkansas in 1970. I knew Dumas and other ALS workers at the University of Arkansas and was much impressed by their dedicated and painstaking methods of collecting and evaluating data, very different from the fanatic zeal and "isogloss madness" of some of the *Dialect Atlas* people. However, it is a sober fact that the future study of the Ozark dialect is in the hands of university-trained specialists like Underwood's workers, mostly students of Hans Kurath, now at the University of Michigan. Their terminology and methods are too technical for me to deal with, and I can only advise my readers to study the ALS material as fast as it reaches publication.

197. Duncan, Robert S. *History of the Baptist in Missouri*. St. Louis: Scammell & Company, 1882. 937p.

In the brief biographical sketches of the many preachers and deacons who served in the church districts are found the usual variety of nineteenth-century journalistic euphemisms for death. Instead of simply saying a person died we find that Reverend So-and-So "fell asleep in Jesus," "fell in the harness," "now rests from his labors," and so on. One that seemed to say it best was "he died of a general relaxation." What more could you say? Also see p. 38 for an interesting explanation of the term *bushwhacked*.

198. Faubus, Orval Eugene. *Down from the Hills*. Little Rock: Pioneer Press, 1980. 510p.

On pp. 494–95 are editorials written by six different Arkansas reporters in rebuttal to the caustic article by Charles Morrow Wilson that appeared in the *Reader's Digest* (February 1959), "Orval Faubus—How Did He Get There?" To add ridicule to his criticism, Wilson presented Faubus speaking in a backwoodsey, stereotyped Ozark dialect: this was far from the truth, as these editorials explain.

199. Freeman, Dale. *How to Talk Pure Ozark in One Easy Lesson*. Springfield, Mo.: H-F Enterprises, 1961. 16p.

This little paperback sells to the tourists and they must enjoy it. In 1982 it was in its eighteenth printing and has sold over 135,000 copies. But Freeman has written some good articles about the Ozarks. He is a former editor of the *Springfield Leader & Press*, in which he wrote a weekly column titled "The Ozarker."

200. Gibson, Arrell M. *Wilderness Bonanza: The Tri-State District of Missouri, Kansas, and Oklahoma*. Norman: University of Oklahoma Press, 1972. 362p.

This book is a history of the mining operations in this region, but it also is practically a lexicon of local mining terms and slang. These are scattered throughout but especially see pp. 197–98.

201. Gideon, Gene. "All-Day Singin' and Dinner on the Ground." In Albert E. Brumley, *All-Day Singin' and Dinner on the Ground*, pp. 32–34. Camdenton, Mo.: Brumley and Sons, 1972.

An interesting explanation of this very common Ozark expression. Gideon has lived all his life in the hills of Taney County, Missouri, and is especially knowledgeable about the religious music of the region.

202. Harington, Donald. "Should the Migrants Learn the Language?" *Proceedings of the Conference on Ozark In-migration*. Eureka Springs: Arkansas Humanities Committee, 1976. 124p.

An interesting and amusing discussion of the traditional folk speech of the old-timers (pp. 38–41) contrasted with the dialect of the newcomers from the cities. Harington is a native Arkansan, the author of *The Architecture of the Arkansas Ozarks* (1975) and several novels about the Ozark region.

203. Huddleston, Duane. "Sweet Lips Has Spoken." *Independence County Chronicle* 14:4 (July 1973): 45–50.

"Sweet Lips" was the name of a gun used in a well-known murder that occurred in the 1820s in the White River Valley near Calico Rock, Arkansas. Upon shooting the victim, the murderer said "Sweet Lips Has Spoken." This expression is still used by elderly residents to denote finality, the ultimate end of a situation.

204. Hunt, Robin Larkey. *Ozarkian Philosophy*. Silver City: New Mexico Western College Print Shop, 1957. 60p.

A paperback pamphlet with many proverbs and wisecracks. Hunt says he is from the Ozarks. He taught at New Mexico Western, and this pamphlet was sold at the college bookshop.

205. Hunter, Max Francis. "Sayings from the Ozarks." Max Hunter Collection. Springfield–Greene County (Missouri) Libraries.

This section of the Hunter Collection is contained in six volumes. The index lists the sayings by a key word only, not the complete saying, e.g. "like a toad in a hail-storm" is indexed simply as "toad," and then where it can be found. The material is in five volumes, each with its own tape. There are a total of 1,040 sayings. The complete sayings are listed in these volumes. On the tapes, Max himself reads many of the sayings, while others are read by the informant; each is defined and discussed, a valuable contribution to the material. Max's interpretations and his dialect are authentic. He is a life-long resident of the Ozarks, as are most of his informants. (For a description of the entire Hunter Collection, see entry 1213.)

206. Jeffery, A. C. *Historical and Biographical Sketches of the Settlement of the Valley of White River, Together with a History of Izard County*. Richmond, Va.: The Jeffery Historical Society, 1973. 70p.

This slick-paper booklet, edited by Dale Hanks, is made up of newspaper stories that Jeffery wrote in Izard County, Arkansas, more than one hundred years ago. Hanks has preserved Jeffery's exact wording, which is fine for students of the Ozark speech of the period. See p. 32 for an example: *stout* is used in the dialect sense. A man is described as "six feet and one inch high, weighed 175 pounds, very stout, dark skin, black eyes, etc." *Stout* does not mean obese but strong, muscular, just as it does in the backwoods today. On p. 59 old Jonathan Magness is called "desperately *wicked*," meaning only that he used many cuss words. On p. 30 is the tale of the two old men who "fell out" and were so old and frail that their friends would not let them fight so they agreed to *curse each other out*: "the corruption of your damned old heart, sir." This ended the affray and "they were soon drunk again."

207. Kennicutt, Wally. *Ozark Nature Gallery*. Paragould, Ark.: White Printing Company, 1979. 114p.

See p. 22 about the razorback hog and Hernando de Soto, and about Hugo Bezdek, who in 1908 referred to his University of Arkansas football team as "a fighting bunch of razorback hogs from the Ozark hills." Nowadays, there are football fans in Arkansas who look upon Mr. Bezdek's simile as divine revelation.

208. King, Johnny. *Johnny the Country Boy*. Springfield, Mo.: Roberts & Sutter, 1973. 140p.

This book began as a series of talks the author gave over radio station KGBX, Springfield, Missouri, in the 1960s. These are reminiscences by the author of his boyhood in an Ozark community fifty years ago. See the chapter about "Old Sayings" (pp. 69–72).

209. Kottler, Barnet, and Martin Light, eds. *The World of Words: A Language Reader*. New York: Houghton, Mifflin Company, 1967. 471p.

Some quotes from *Down in the Holler* (1953) under the chapter heading "Backwoods Grammar" on pp. 164–68.

210. Krause, Bonnie, and Kay Carter, eds. *Folk Sayings and Beliefs of the Illinois Ozarks*. Carterville: Illinois Ozarks Craft Guild, 1978. 36p.

This is designated book 2 of a three-book series covering the folkways of five southern Illinois counties. Book 1, *Home Remedies of the Illinois Ozarks* (entry 646), and book 3, *Tall Tales, Ghosts and Omens of the Illinois Ozarks* (entry 347), describe practices that are very similar to what would be encountered in the Missouri and Arkansas Ozarks. But this volume, book 2, offers more unique findings in regard to sayings and beliefs that appear to be specific to this particular region. All three of these publications offer an interesting look at an area that some folklorists are hesitant to accept as having a cultural kinship with the Missouri-Arkansas region.

211. Lawson, Marvin. *By Gum, I Made It*. Branson, Mo.: The Ozarks Mountaineer, 1977. 128p.

See the appendix (pp. 115–26) for lists of "Colloquial Words, Phrases, and Sayings."

212. Lee, Robert. "The Tragedy of Our Country." *The Ozarker* 6:1 (February 1969): 8.

This is a long and thoughtful paper about current problems in the Ozarks, but it was the final paragraph that held my interest. Speaking of Roscoe Stewart, founder of a fine monthly magazine published in Branson, Missouri, Dr. Lee says, "Mr. Stewart disliked the word *Ozarker*"; he liked *Ozarkian* better. Lee might have wondered why Stewart called his own magazine the *Ozarks* Mountaineer, a form which offends professors of English and other sticklers for "correct" English.

213. McAtee, W. L. "Some Folk and Scientific Names for Plants." *Publications of the American Dialect Society* 15 (April 1951): 3–25.

 Cf. Bessie Reid's "Vernacular Names of Texas Plants," pp. 26–50 in the same issue of *PADS*.

214. Massey, Ellen Gray. *Bittersweet Country*. Garden City, N.Y.: Anchor Press, 1978. 434p.

 See the chapter entitled "This Speech of Ours" (pp. 206–12) for lists of more than two hundred words and sayings collected in and around Laclede County, Missouri.

215. Messick, Mary Ann. *History of Baxter County: 1873–1973*. Little Rock: Mountain Home Chamber of Commerce, 1973. 506p.

 Many references to local sayings, wisecracks, and rhymes of this north-central Arkansas county are found in the chapter titled "Cross Questions and Silly Answers" (pp. 493–506).

216. Miles, Kathleen White. *Annals of Henry County . . . . Vol. I, 1885–1900*. Clinton, Mo.: The Printery, 1973. 491p.

 Death notices and biographical sketches, brief tidbits about community life in this Missouri county, an interesting look into nineteenth-century middle America. If nothing else the reporters on the local newspaper, *The Clinton Eye*, must be given credit for creativity with the language. There were noted over fifty different ways to announce a person's death. One that laid it on the line: "He was born; he is dead!"

217. [Miles, Kay White.] *The Ozark Dictionary*. Clinton, Mo.: The Printery, n.d. 15p.

 This pamphlet is unsigned, but it is pretty much like Zinderman's *Hill Latin*. Several similar paperbacks are found in the newsstands and roadside taverns for the tourist. Of no great value, but serious students of the dialect should leaf through them. This one is subtitled "How to Talk Right Around Hyar."

218. *Missouri Folklore Society Journal: Special Issue*. 4 (1982). 116p.

 This is a special issue dedicated to the life and works of Vance Randolph. Along with articles about Vance or his writings, there are some interesting excerpts from *Down in the Holler: A Gallery of Ozark Speech*, first published in 1953: "Monsters and Dangerous Creatures in Ozark Lore," p. 42, a listing with definitions of twenty-three mythical creatures found in the Ozarks; "Taboos and Euphemisms," p. 50, concerning sexual topics; and "Ozark Vocabulary," p. 110, a listing of archaisms, direction words, and twenty-one synonyms for hillbilly.

219. Monaghan, Jay. "Civil War Slang and Humor." *Civil War History* 3:2 (June 1957): 125–33.

Interesting article. Missouri and Kansas references scattered throughout. For one of the best books written on the Civil War in the Ozarks region, see Monaghan's *Civil War on the Western Border, 1854–1865* (Little, Brown & Company, 1955).

220. Moore, Sally, Gina Hilton, Jenny Kelso, Caryn Rader, Tracy Waterman, and Patsy Watts. "This Speech of Ours." *Bittersweet*, various issues, 1974–1980.

Approximately 275 old-time figures of speech and picturesque phrases collected by members of the *Bittersweet* staff in Laclede and surrounding counties in southwest Missouri. See the following issues: Spring 1974, p. 42; Summer 1974, p. 4; Spring 1975, p. 26; Fall 1975, p. 54; Spring 1976, p. 49; Winter 1976, p. 13; Summer 1977, p. 2; Winter 1977, p. 2; Winter 1978, p. 29; Summer 1979, p. 31; Spring 1980, p. 26.

221. Nothdurft, Lillian. *Folklore and Early Customs of Southeast Missouri*. New York: Exposition Press, 1972. 77p.

A juvenile account of village life in the early 1900s. The chapter entitled "Picturesque Speech" (pp. 13–19) is a list of over two hundred commonplace metaphors. The author, a native of Cape Girardeau, has taught for some years in the Joplin Public Schools.

222. O'Dell, Kathy. " 'C' Sound, 'S' Sound Make Cuss Words Cuss." *Springfield Daily News*, 25 June 1981.

Ethel Strainchamps of Springfield tells of her theory of "phonetic symbolism." She contends that certain words are the result of male chauvinism, that our language "is a put-down to women, and men made the language." Ms. Strainchamps was a newspaper columnist and is a recognized authority on the Ozarks dialect. See her *Don't Never Say Cain't* (entry 236).

223. Parler, Mary Celestia. "Proverbs from Arkansas: Adjectival Comparisons." Typescript, University of Arkansas at Fayetteville, 1961. 415p.

Material gathered by students in Parler's folklore classes at the University of Arkansas during the years 1955 to 1961. There were two versions of this manuscript;

the one deposited in the official university archive was expurgated—the expressions that seemed a little too coarse for an Arkansas college in the 1950s and 1960s were cut out. The volume she gave me was not expurgated—although I saw nothing in it to shock an undergraduate, even in Arkansas. The book is a bit more interesting and lively than the maxims. The three big volumes of maxims (see next entry) were a little dry and tedious.

224. ————. "Proverbs from Arkansas—Maxims." Typescript, University of Arkansas at Fayetteville, 1962. 3 vols., pp. 1–365, 366–569, 570–760, continuous pagination. Bound typescript in University of Arkansas Library.

These three volumes (760 pages) contain more than 2,900 items collected from oral sources in Parler's folklore classes, during the years 1955 to 1961 inclusive. Each item was written on an index card with the student's name and the date, and usually a note about when and where the student heard it. Where it seemed necessary, the student explained the meaning of the proverb, and sometimes he added some bit of background material.

Other than the elimination of duplicates, Miss Parler and her associates did no editing at all. The material was typed always *verbatim* but not necessarily *literatim*; if a word was misspelled but still recognizable, the typists did not bother to correct it.

225. Pennington, Eunice. *Ozark Folkways*. Piedmont, Mo.: Piedmont Printers, 1978. 56p.

On p. 51 there is a good list of "Folkwords: Glossary of Ozark Terms and Expressions." Mrs. Pennington was formerly librarian for the Current River Regional Library in Van Buren, Missouri.

226. "Put Out a Fleece." *Ark/Ozark* 2:1 (Fall 1969): 32–35.

An old saying based on a story found in the sixth chapter of Judges. Old timers "put out a fleece" when important decisions were to be made.

227. Pyles, Lida Wilson. "It Happened in the Ozarks." Unpublished manuscript, Carthage, Mo., 1982. 197p.

The chapter entitled "The Hill-Billy Has a Word for It," pp. 1–11, discusses backwoods grammar and speech; dropping final *g*'s, wrong tenses, etc. She cites numerous expressions and phrases. Of special interest are some very localized metaphors, where an expression or phrase uttered by some individual in the past has become part of the local vocabulary. The only copy of this manuscript is in the author's possession.

228. Quigley, Martin. "And the case for Missour-ee." *The Midwest Motorist* 47:4 (April 1976): 7–8.

Quigley, a former newsman, now editor of *The Midwest Motorist*, cites numerous rationales and rules for the "-ee" pronunciation. In his rebuttal to columnist Bill Vaughan's arguments for "-uh" (see entry 246), he contends that Vaughan's error is due to snobbery and tin ears and asks, "Why ain't it the Miss-iss-ipp-uh River?" Included is a questionnaire entitled "Missour-uh vs. Missour-ee" for the readers to voice their opinions.

229. ———. "The Score: Missour-ee 59, Missour-uh, 41." *The Midwest Motorist* 47:5 (June 1976): 8–10.

Results of the questionnaire that appeared along with the Vaughan-Quigley debate in the April issue. A map, designating preferences by postal zip code regions, shows that today the central and western Ozarks lean towards the "-ee" ending.

230. Randolph, Vance, and George P. Wilson. *Down in the Holler: A Gallery of Ozark Folk Speech*. Norman: University of Oklahoma Press, 1979. 320p.

Unaltered reprint of the work originally published in 1953 by the University of Oklahoma Press.

231. Rayburn, Otto Ernest. "Ozark Customs." *Arkansas Historical Quarterly* 18:2 (Summer 1959): 73–77.

He tells of men hard as "bearfoot bread" who would issue a harvesting challenge to their neighbors by the noise they made when they sharpened the blade on their scythe. It was called "to whet a banter."

232. Shamel, H. Harold. *Seeds of Time, A Story of the Ozarks*. No place of publication, publisher, or date given. 278p.

The author's family moved from Kansas to the Missouri Ozarks in the 1890s. They stayed only a few years and finally gave up trying to make a living from the poor farmland and moved on to greener pastures. But while there they were much impressed by the Ozark dialect. "I suppose there never was a region with more colloquialisms in the everyday language" (p. 65); the children laughed aloud to hear the natives say *you-uns* and *we-uns*. They traded livestock for a little farm with a log house on a hilltop, which they named Mount Where-You-At. Someone remarked, "They got airy cow," and a little girl from Kansas asked her mother, "What is an airy cow?" (p. 75).

233. Starr, Fred. *High Hills, Deep Hollows, and Tall Tales of the Ozarks*. Fayetteville, Ark.: Southwest Printing Co., 1968. 24p.

Similar to Dale Freeman's dialect book. Works such as these do have their place in the study of dialects.

234. Steele, Pauline Davis. *Hill Country Sayin's and Ozark Folklore*. West Fork, Ark.: Hutcheson Press, 1976. [40p.]

This paperback contains a great amount of information, not classified, but set down alphabetically. There are over 175 definitions of folk speech and sayings as well as songs, tales, riddles, jokes, games, play-parties, dances, local history, arts and crafts, place-names, all the familiar categories and more.

235. ———. *Hill Country Sayin's and Ozark Folklore*: *Book Two*. West Fork, Ark.: Hutcheson Press, 1977. [41p.]

This book gives even more examples of folk speech and sayings, over two hundred, than did its predecessor (see preceding entry). Neither book presents a systematic study of mountain speech or Ozark dialect. But they are both mighty good reading. Book 3 was ready to go to press at the time of the author's death in 1979. Hopefully someday it will be printed.

236. Strainchamps, Ethel Reed. *Don't Never Say Cain't*. Garden City, N.Y.: Doubleday & Co., 1965. 168p.

Autobiography of a girl brought up in a most backward part of the Missouri Ozarks. She went to college, became a schoolteacher and a journalist. She went in for linguistics and worked with Porter G. Perrin on his usage textbook. She has collected items for a long time and published some good papers in the *American Mercury* and elsewhere. Clay Anderson writes a nasty review of this book in *The Ozarks Mountaineer* (December 1965, p. 12), but what she says about Ozark speech is well worth attention.

237. Switzler, William F. "Missouri—The Meaning of the Word and How To Pronounce It." *Boonville Missouri Democrat*, 22 October 1897.

Under the title "The Real Meaning of the Word Missouri" this article was reprinted in the *Kansas City Star*, 27 August 1922, and also in the *Missouri Historical Review* 17:2 (January 1923): 231–32.

238. Thomas, Rosemary Hyde. *It's Good to Tell You: French Folktales from Missouri*. Columbia: University of Missouri Press, 1981. 246p.

From the first settlers—miners brought into this lead-rich region of the Missouri Ozarks by Phillippe François Renault in 1723—until the mid-twentieth century, these communities enjoyed an isolation that exceeded that of their Anglican neighbors by more than a hundred years. Before the 1920s a majority of the children knew no English. They considered their 250-year-old dialect to be a "degraded patois." But observations made by Clyde Thogmartin, Jr. (*The French Dialect of Old Mines, Missouri*, 1970), corroborates those made by Henry Brackenridge in 1814, that "all things considered, their language is more pure than might be suspected."

The twenty-one tales presented in this book appear in both English and Old Mines French. To comprehend the French versions of these tales, the reader needs a better-than-high-school familiarity with the language, but Thomas says that anyone fluent in standard French can understand 75 percent of the Old Mines dialect.

239. ———. "Traditional Types of Nicknames in a Missouri French Creole Community." *Missouri Folklore Society Journal* 2 (1980): 15–25.

A discussion of French "dit" names collected in the Old Mines region of Washington County, Missouri. The author classifies these into five categories: names of humorous intent, names of denigration, place of origin, plant names, and terms concerned with physical appearance. She says this practice has all but disappeared today, due in part to the dependence of business transactions upon written documents rather than oral communication.

240. Thomas, Roy Edwin. *Authentic Ozark Stories About . . . .* Green Forest, Ark.: Larimer Publications, 1972. 48p.

This is a series of six pamphlets "collected, transcribed, and edited" by Dr. Thomas, stories about hunting and trapping that he has collected in interviews with old-timers in the Arkansas Ozarks. Each pamphlet ends with a glossary of words and phrases that he has transcribed in "Ozarks dialect."

241. ———. *Popular Folk Dictionary of Ozarks Talk.* Little Rock: Dox Books, 1972. 96p.

This is a paperback for the tourist trade, not a serious study of Ozark speech. Authentic as far as it goes, but it's pretty dull going. Thomas says it is based on 248 tape recordings of interviews with old residents. He is a native of Morganton, Van Buren County, Arkansas, and was educated at the University of Arkansas and the University of Texas. He is the author of several other booklets about Ozark customs, pioneer hunting stories, and the like.

242. Tidgwell, Flo M. "Genteel Speech Seems Ever More Desirable." *The Ozarks Mountaineer* 22:6 (July 1974): 32–33.

A couple of generations back, says Tidgwell, "it was a brazen affront" to say "boar, jackass, or bull," although buck, rooster, drake, and stallion were freely used. It would not do to say backhouse or privy; the correct term was *Mrs. Jones.* A lady's leg was always a limb, and the word *guts* was not used at all. Tidgwell spins two mildly amusing anecdotes, but thinks that the old prudish speech was on the whole a good thing. She still flinches a little at the indelicacy of modern speech.

243. Underwood, Gary N. "Razorback Slang." *American Speech* 50:1–2 (Spring-Summer 1975): 50–69.

Material collected on the Fayetteville campus of the University of Arkansas in 1970–1972, while the author was a member of the English faculty. This article contains a glossary of 448 terms.

244. ———. "Some Characteristics of Slang Used at the University of Arkansas at Fayetteville." *Mid-South Folklore* 4:2 (Summer 1976): 49–54.

A condensed version of the article cited in the preceding entry. The article summarizes the unusual mixture of rural or "redneck" and urban or "hip" slang, which he contends is the result of students from rural backgrounds coming into a university environment.

245. Van Doren, Ruth Fitch. "The Ozark Hill People." *Missouri Life* 1:3 (July-August 1973): 46–51.

This author's treatment of the speech of the hillfolk is full of errors and misunderstandings. Her knowledge of the people is superficial to say the least, but the photographs by Townsend Godsey are so good that they more than make up for the deficiencies in the text.

246. Vaughan, Bill. "The Case for Missour-uh." *The Midwest Motorist* 47:4 (April 1976): 6–7.

More of the endless wrangling over the correct pronunciation of the state's name, this one a humorous debate between two veteran Missouri newspapermen (see entry 228). Bill Vaughan, a syndicated columnist for the *Kansas City Star*, defends the "-uh" faction, but admits that he has voted for men who have said "Missouree."

247. Walpole, Sherlu. "Linguist Ethel Strainchamps: Battling Sexism in the Language." *Springfield Magazine* 2:6 (November 1980): 26–29.

An interview with Ms. Strainchamps, who is primarily known for her theory of "sound symbolism." As a reviewer of language books and dictionaries she says she believes she is the only person who has reviewed every dictionary published since 1961. Along with this achievement she has amassed an astounding collection of over half a million "cites" on English usage. This article also includes biographical information about this etymologist from the hills of Polk County, Missouri.

248. Webber, Everett, and Olga Webber. "In Them Hills." *Holiday* 1:7 (September 1946): 27–29.

Descriptive piece about Ozark resort towns. Some references to dialect and folk culture. I knew these people at Eureka Springs in the 1950s.

249. White, Alice Melton. "A 'Good Scald' on Colloquialisms." *The Ozarks Mountaineer* 25:7 (August 1977): 31.

Explanation of the vernacular references to *a good scald*, *haw-bushing*, and others. A brief note, but interesting to the student of dialect.

250. Williams, Leonard, ed. *Cavorting on the Devil's Fork: The Pete Whetstone Letters of C. F. M. Noland.* Memphis: Memphis State University Press, 1979. 281p.

See appendix 2, "Glossary of Proper Names" (pp. 216–38), and appendix 3, "Glossary of Words and Phrases" (pp. 239–45), the latter defining more than 175 used by Noland in these "letters" published between 1835 and 1856.

251. Wilson, Charles Morrow. "Orval Faubus—How Did He Get That Way?" *Reader's Digest* 74:442 (February 1959): 78–84.

An article attacking Gov. Orval Faubus of Arkansas, written during the nationally publicized integration problems in Little Rock in the late 1950s. This article, full of sarcasm and ridicule, quotes Faubus in an exaggerated Ozark dialect. I have heard Faubus many times but never heard him speak as Wilson portrays him. Wilson, born in northwest Arkansas, was a reporter on the *Arkansas Gazette* and a writer of some merit. Many of his works are cited in the first volume of this bibliography.

252. Wolf, John Quincy [Sr.]. *Life in the Leatherwoods.* Memphis: Memphis State University Press, 1974. 159p.

Some pleasant comments by Wolf on local phrases and sayings (pp. 106–7) remembered from his youth in Izard County, Arkansas. He tells of the incident that spawned the expression "Jake, get a big un," which became part of the folk speech of that region. For another similar circumstance that produced a traditional saying see the article "Sweet Lips Has Spoken" by Duane Huddleston (entry 203).

253. Zinderman, Zeek. *Hill Latin: Ozark Hillbilly Lingo Dictionary.* Cabool, Mo.: Hickoryville Publications, 1967. 44p.

Another comic rube paperback, with cartoons. Better than most such books, it is a bestseller at gift shops and tourist traps. Mostly just bad re-spelling, but there are two or three sensible sentences in the introduction. How can we criticize the old timer's "tawk," he asks; they "butchered up the language in one way, the educated outer world butchers it in another, so what's the diff?" Some of their words, he admits, may be local or even neighborhood words, some of them "may be only two or three holler words." This "Zeek Zinderman" is a writer by trade. He publishes a kind of newspaper called the *Hickory Prevaricator.* Though this dictionary is just a joke, there's some good stuff in it.

3. Place Names

254. Abner, Vannie. *Heir to These Hills: A Story of a Magnificent Land and Its People*. Hicksville, N.Y.: Exposition Press, 1978. 95p.

This novel is about the town of Hahatonka, located in Camden County, Missouri. The original settlement was called Gunter's Big Spring. Tradition had it that the nearby spring and the Niangua River had been a favorite recreation haunt of the early Osage Indians. Around 1895 the name was changed to Ha-ha-tonka, supposedly an Indian word meaning "laughing waters." But, more than likely, it is the onomatopoeic creation of some early settler (see p. 13).

255. Angus, Fern Joyner. "The Hog Eye Picnic." *The Ozarks Mountaineer* 26:6 (July 1978): 28–29.

Hog Eye is a widely used nickname for the village of Charity, in Dallas County, Missouri, some thirty-five miles northeast of Springfield. The name was derived from a brand of bourbon whiskey made in a local distillery.

256. *Arkansas Geographic Names*. Reston, Va.: U.S. Geological Survey, 1981. Vol. 1, pp. 1–220; vol. 2, pp. 221–449.

These publications (there eventually will be one for each state) are available through the Geographic Names Information System (GNIS) of the U.S. Geological Survey. Every geographic name that appears on the maps issued by this government agency is listed. The names are in alphabetical order in the first column of each page. The next column identifies their feature—locale, stream, church, cemetery, school, etc. (Pages one through four define the terms used for these identifications). Then the county where it is located, followed by its location by longitude and latitude. These two volumes for Arkansas alone list over twenty-two thousand place names, an invaluable source of information. Those for Missouri and Oklahoma are soon to be issued.

257. Baker, Ronald L. "Folk Legends in Place-Name Research." *Journal of American Folklore* 85:338 (October-December 1972): 367–73.

He thinks the study of place names can help to separate historical "facts" from migratory legend.

258. Berry, Earl. *History of Marion County (Arkansas)*. Little Rock: Marion County Historical Association, 1977. 523p.

Chapter 20 (pp. 331–37) deals with the names of all known post offices in the county. Chapter 22 (pp. 342–405) tells the story of all the towns, how they were named, and some good tales about many of them.

259. Beveridge, Thomas R. *Geologic Wonders and Curiosities of Missouri*. Rolla, Mo.: Missouri Division of Geology and Land Survey, 1978. 451p.

This is a wonderful book, full of color photos and drawings depicting the places and phenomenons described by the title. Beveridge has taken his subject out of the realm of academia with its scientific jargon that one normally finds in a work of this nature, and presents it in a straightforward manner easily understood by the layman. There is a wealth of place-name material throughout, but especially see chapter 15 (pp. 405–14), "The Devil in Missouri," listing eighty natural geologic features named in some manner for "his Satanic Majesty." Beveridge says this testifies to the pioneer Calvinistic Missourians' preoccupation with the Devil.

260. ———. *Tom Beveridge's Ozarks*. Pacific Grove, Calif.: Boxwood Press, 1979. 85p.

See pp. 1, 3, 34, 45, and 47. Beveridge was Missouri state geologist for a number of years and later an instructor at the University of Missouri–Rolla.

261. Black, J. Dickson. *Beaver Lake Area—Past and Present*. Rogers, Ark.: Timberwolf Publishers, 1979. 76p.

The author is a resident of Rogers, having moved here from Chicago in the 1950s. But he has done his homework with this little book, just as he did with his previous work, *History of Benton County* (see following entry). There are many place-name references throughout; see pages 1, 7, 10, 12, 14, and especially 74–76 for the story of the Lost Bridge.

262. ———. *History of Benton County (Arkansas), 1836–1936*. Little Rock: International Graphics, 1975. 496p.

Probably the most valuable sections of this book are those concerned with place names. Three chapters are worth looking at: chapter 7, "Post Offices"; chapter 13, "Schools"; and chapter 24, "Towns and Villages." Some specialists in local history can see little merit in this book because it lacks scholarly documentation. They didn't think much of Sally Stockard in 1904, either, or Henry Miller in 1945. But nonacademic readers sometimes see values that the scholars miss. To me, the *History of Benton County* carries a kind of zany charm and a lot of not-too-obvious Arkansas humor. I think it's a damn good book and I wouldn't have missed it for a farm in Texas.

263. Bogan, Jim. "Missouri Litany." In *Ozark, Ozark: A Hillside Reader*, ed. Miller Williams, pp. 154–55. Columbia: University of Missouri Press, 1981.

Seventy-five unusual Missouri place names were used in the composition of this poem.

264. [Boulson, Charles E., compiler.] *The Postoffices of Webster County (Missouri) 1839–1979*. Marshfield, Mo.: Webster County Historical Society, 1979. 48p.

This special publication by the society lists in alphabetical order all seventy-two of the post offices that have existed in Webster County. This is a detailed and valuable piece of work.

265. Brown, Miriam Keast. *The Story of Pierce City, Missouri, 1870–1970*. Cassville, Mo.: Litho Printers, 1970. 128p.

See p. 47 for changing the "ei" to "ie" in Pierce City. A similar "Post Office" theory is given for the naming of Snowball, Arkansas. Also see "Pierce or Peirce, Please" in the *Springfield Daily News* (19 July 1982).

266. Caldwell, Erskine. *Afternoons in Mid-America*. New York: Dodd, Mead and Company, 1976. 276p.

About his tour through the Middle West. I was interested in what he says about Tulsa, Oklahoma. The name is from a Creek word, he was told, meaning small village. Maybe so, but that ain't the way I heard it when I lived in Sapulpa.

267. Carney, George O. "Bug Tussel to Slapout: Place Names on the Oklahoma Landscape." *Places* 3:2 (July 1976): 30–36.

Discusses place names of French, Indian, folk, and out-of-state origins. He concludes, ". . . by reconstructing the past landscape of Oklahoma through place names, one can diagnose the particular cultural penetration into an area . . . ." Mostly taken from previously printed material. The author is a member of the Geography Department of Oklahoma State University in Stillwater. (See Charles Gould's *Oklahoma Place Names* [1933] and George H. Shirk's work by the same title [1965].)

268. Cohen, Gerald Leonard, ed. *Interesting Missouri Place Names*. Rolla, Mo.: Published by editor, 1982. 76p.

This is the first in a series of monographs about Missouri place names that Cohen plans to issue at three-year intervals. He has dedicated this project to the memory of Robert L. Ramsay and his monumental works in this field, notably *Our Storehouse of Missouri Place Names* (1952; rpt. University of Missouri Press, 1973). The introduction (pp. 1–21) is a very thorough synopsis and chronology of the formal studies of this subject in Missouri, written by Adolf Schroeder, a German professor and etymologist at the University of Missouri–Columbia. Following are detailed and well-documented investigations of twenty-two unusual place names. Besides citing previously printed materials, Cohen also includes additional information he has compiled through personal correspondence and interviews. A bibliography and index are found on pp. 67–76.

269. Cook, Blanche, and Cheryl Cook. *The History of Goodman, McDonald County, Missouri.* Pineville, Mo.: McDonald County News-Gazette, 1978. 126p.

Lots of place-name information throughout but especially see the story of Splitlog, Oklahoma, on pp. 7–12.

270. Cotrel, Chris. "Oxly, Hawk Point and Other Interesting Missouri Place Names." *Bittersweet* 7:2 (Winter 1979): 43.

Discusses some interesting Missouri place names with local explanations of their origins.

271. *The Dallas County, Missouri Story (1841–1971).* Buffalo, Mo.: Dallas County Historical Society, 1974. 434p.

Page after page of names, must be practically every man, woman, or child who has ever lived in Dallas County since its beginning. But there is an abundance of place-name information scattered throughout. Especially see pp. 128, 184–85, and 264–65.

272. Deane, Ernie. *Ozarks Country.* Branson, Mo.: The Ozarks Mountaineer, 1975. 191p.

Most of the material for this book was first seen in Ernie's "Ozarks Country," a popular column carried by many newspapers in the Ozarks region. Each chapter is a reprint of one of these with the title and date it appeared. See p. 15, "Why We Say 'Arkansas'"; p. 18, "How Yellville Was Named"; p. 21, "Missouri Place Name Origins"; p. 22, "The Cap'n Named Pro Tem, Missouri"; p. 24, "No Gas at Gassville"; p. 148, "Unusual Italian Settlement"; p. 149, "There Is a Real Noel"; p. 186, "Points of Note on the White River"; p. 188, "Rivers in Arkansas Ozarks"; and p. 189, "The Alabamians Moved West."

273. Gibson, Arrell M. *Wilderness Bonanza: The Tri-State District of Missouri, Kansas, and Oklahoma.* Norman: University of Oklahoma Press, 1972. 362p.

See chapter 3, "District Developments since 1865" (pp. 27–40). It is filled with fascinating place-name information. He lists over 150 names of towns, camps, and mines. He says that of the 85 or so camps that existed at one time or another, only 30 remained by 1950.

274. Goolsby, Elwin L. *The Teeth on the Bradley-Rushing Building and Other Stories*. Sheridan, Ark.: Grant County Museum, 1978. 73p.

This book is described on the title page as a "collection of legends, tall tales, exaggerations, and factual lore of Grant County, Arkansas." That pretty well describes the content. It only remains to say that these items are all very brief, and there are one hundred of them. There is some good stuff on place names, see pp. 3, 29, 33, 34, 40, 52, 57, and 61.

275. Griffith, Cecil R. *The Missouri River: The River Rat's Guide to Missouri River History and Folklore*. Leawood, Kans.: Canfield and Sutton, 1974. 96p.

Griffith lists every river town by name, and tells how the name was acquired. Some of these place-name stories are documented in official records, old books, and newspaper files. But many are just traditions—memories of the old men who sit on benches in front of the courthouse (p. 10). They are good stories, anyhow.

276. Hardaway, Billie Touchstone. *These Hills My Home: A Buffalo River Story*. Republic, Mo.: Western Printing Company, 1980. 179p.

The chapter entitled "Some Creeks Along the Buffalo," pp. 138–47, tells the stories of the names of twenty-two that flow into this National Scenic River located in northwest Arkansas.

277. Harris, Barbara. "A Trademark of Missouri Caves." *The Ozarks Mountaineer* 22:4 (May 1974): 22–23.

Worth reading if only for the great number of picturesque names. Some of these are "developed" caverns, open to tourists, but many are "wild" caves on private property, known only to the Missouri Geological Survey workers and to a few local spelunkers.

278. Ingenthron, Elmo. *Indians of the Ozark Plateau*. Point Lookout, Mo.: School of the Ozarks Press, 1970. 182p.

Though not a professional archaeologist, Ingenthron seems to know a lot about the Indians who have lived in the Ozarks. There are scattered references to their influence upon the folklore of the Ozarks throughout, but practically everything of folkloristic interest is in the last chapter. Page 157 lists place names of Indian origin.

279. "In Relation to the Pronunciation of the Name 'Arkansas.'" *Arkansas Historical Association* 2 (1908): 462–77.

Reprint of an 1880 pamphlet by the Arkansas Historical Society.

280. "Interesting Letters Received from Authority on Friedrich Gerstaecker." *Independence County Chronicle* 2:1 (October 1960): 47–48.

Letters from Prof. Clarence Evans of Northeastern Oklahoma State University, Tahlequah, concerning Gerstaecker's use of Oiltrove instead of Oil Trough as the name of this old Ozarks community. Evans's conclusions are based upon a literal translation from the German and are very different from those accepted today as to the origin of this name.

281. Johns, Paul W. *Unto These Hills: True Tales from the Ozarks.* Ozark, Mo.: Bilyeu-Johns Enterprises, 1980. 104p.

Pages 100–102 have a list of fifty-five place names with discussions of the origins of many. Lake Taneycomo was named for its location in Taney County, Missouri. Interesting also are the explanations for Peculiar, Avert, Protem, and Slapout.

282. Johnston, James J. "Needmore and Push." *The Ozarks Mountaineer* 19:3 (April 1971): 31.

Discussion of the naming of these two early Searcy County, Arkansas, settlements.

283. Keay, Glen. "From *Enough* to *Barely-Do.*" *The Ozarks Mountaineer* 22:6 (July 1974): 40.

Brief treatment of eye-catching place names in both Missouri and Arkansas. Keay lists most of the best ones.

284. Keesee, Irene. "Strickler's Heritage." *The Ozarks Mountaineer* 25:10 (November 1977): 21, 28.

See p. 21 for an amusing "legend" about how Hog Eye, Arkansas, got its name. The place was known as Moffett until one day the gamblers got to shooting at each other, and "a hapless hog ran into the fire and a bullet entered its eye. Someone said that Moffett's name should be changed to Hog Eye. The name stuck." Miss Keesee got this story from Charlie Sherry of Prairie Grove, Arkansas. It will not be accepted by the place-name experts, of course. They have a very different explanation of the name. But even if Charlie Sherry knew the scholarly theory, he might not care to tell a lady about it.

285. Lee, Linda. "Daisy, Defiance, Solo, and Other Unusual Missouri Place Names." *Bittersweet* 6:3 (Spring 1979): 45.

Note the story of how the town of Cooter, Missouri, was named. Miss Lee says the post office was first called *Coutre*, French for *turtle*, "due to the many turtles in the area." But after a few years it was Americanized to Cooter. Maybe so, but many Missourians tell another story. (Note: This issue incorrectly printed as vol. 7).

286. Leighly, John. "Biblical Place Names in the United States." *Names: Journal of the American Name Society* 27:1 (March 1979): 46–59.

Author says, "Most of the names are east of the Mississippi; the appeal of biblical names evidently diminished with time. . . ." He says Missouri has only twenty-six compared to much higher numbers in the East. I'm afraid Leighly's informants have shortchanged him. In most four or five county areas in the Missouri-Arkansas Ozarks one can discover far more than this number.

287. Leland, J. A. C. "Indian Names in Missouri." *Names: Journal of the American Name Society* 1:4 (December 1953): 266–73.

A long list of Missouri place names from Ramsay's monumental work. Leland says, "I have attempted to give the etymology of the Indian names, thus supplementing Ramsay's excellent study." I do not know anyone who is familiar with all of these Indian languages, or who is competent to evaluate Leland's etymology. It is interesting reading, anyhow.

288. McGinnis, A. C., ed. *A History of Independence County, Arkansas. Independence County Chronicle* 17:3 (April 1976): 1–119.

Much about early settlers, the Civil War, the White River and steamboats, Batesville, Oil Trough, Sulphur Rock, etc., lots of names, facts, and figures but little folklore. A few place-name references. See pp. 21, 27, 29, 76, and 83.

289. ———. "Notes on Poke Bayou." *Independence County Chronicle* 11:1 (October 1969): 25–31.

Although occasionally called "Poke," this river was named for a species of heron, the sitepoke. The author presents a thorough investigation of this name. It is now generally spelled *Polk*.

290. Maddux, Theresa. Articles in various issues of *Bittersweet*.

Brief discussions of some unusual Missouri place names: "Peculiar, Bourbon and Competition" (Winter 1976): 2; "Romance and Blackwater" (Fall 1977): 38; "Forty Four, Nail and Cotton Plant" (Spring 1978): 2.

291. Messick, Mary Ann. *History of Baxter County, 1873–1973*. Little Rock: Mountain Home Chamber of Commerce, 1973. 506p.

See chapter 11, "Other Towns and Places—Then and Now" (pp. 77–96), about the towns and post offices, and chapter 19, "In the Sweet By and By" (pp. 194–208), about names of churches and cemeteries. Other place-name references on pp. 10, 43, 66–67, 109, and 192.

292. Miller, E. Joan Wilson. "The Naming of the Land in the Arkansas Ozarks: A Study of Culture Processes." *Annals of the Association of American Geographers* 59:2 (June 1969): 240–51.

Worth reading. A few minor errors. The author is mistaken in assuming that Allsopp was a native of Arkansas. I knew him well, and I think he was an Englishman. A valuable study of Arkansas place names.

293. Morgan, Gordon D. *Black Hillbillies of the Arkansas Ozarks: A Report of the Department of Sociology, University of Arkansas.* Fayetteville, Ark.: University of Arkansas, 1973. 165p.

See pp. 66–67 under the heading "Naming the Town" for the black contributions to place names in the Ozarks.

294. Morris, John W. *Ghost Towns of Oklahoma.* Norman: University of Oklahoma Press, 1977. 229p.

A valuable work about towns that have "bloomed, boomed, and busted." For those located within the Oklahoma Ozarks see Bernice, Cayuga, Hanson, Mayes, Nicksville, Park Hill, Picher, Piney, and Tahlonteeskee.

295. Moser, Arthur Paul. "A Directory of Towns, Villages, and Hamlets: Past and Present of Counties of Missouri." Typescript, Springfield, Mo., 101 vols., 1958–1981.

In 1958, Moser, a retired salesman, began compiling a directory of Missouri counties, making an effort to record the names of every town and village that has ever existed within their boundaries. He does not include the larger cities.

In 1982 he completed his task, all 114 counties of Missouri. These are deposited in the Springfield–Greene County Library in Springfield, Missouri. With each town Moser gives all the information he has gathered and designates every source. He even gives the township, range, and section location of most. Besides the printed sources used, he had many personal interviews with "old-timers" and identifies each informant. Along with this data pertaining to the place names, he gives additional information about the present status of the town, if it still exists. Though Moser and his work may lack the scholarly credentials of the academic, there is no denying the value of this extraordinary compilation to future researchers in this field.

This work has much more detail and is better workmanship than Ramsay's great studies done at the University of Missouri (see volume 1 of this bibliography, pp. 87–89). Of course, the Ramsay collection includes all kinds of Missouri place names, while Moser confines his attention to "settlements." There must be considerable overlapping and duplication, but Moser's studies are really something! It's a pity that he and Professor Ramsay didn't get together somehow.

296. Mottaz, Mable Manes. *Lest We Forget—History of Pulaski County, Missouri, and Fort Leonard Wood.* Springfield, Mo.: Cain Printing, 1960. 81p.

See place-name information on pp. 1–4, 22–23, and 31. She persists in referring to the "Weir Road," as if it was named after a person (it's now Highway 66), instead of the Wire Road, so named because of the telegraph lines that followed it.

297. Nickel, Wally. *From These Beginnings: Ozarks Past, Book One.* Camdenton, Mo.: Lake of the Ozarks Council of Local Governments, 1981. 54p.

This book is full of interesting vignettes about places in a five-county area in the central Missouri Ozarks. Each story is accompanied by a photo of the subject. Lots of place-name data throughout, places like Passover, Lover's Leap, Hahatonka, Orla, Ball School, etc. In Laclede County a new town of Lebanon was laid out parallel to the just-completed railroad, which ran in a southwesterly direction. It is said that there have been people who have been born, lived their lives, and died in Lebanon who never knew where north really was.

298. Nuwer, Hank. "So, Uh, What's Buffalo Like?" *Oui* 10:2 (February 1981): 104–19.

The author visited the fifteen towns in the United States with the name *Buffalo* and gives a ludicrous account of his experiences. He labeled each with descriptive names such as "friendliest," "coldest," "most beautiful women," etc. Buffalo, Missouri, was designated as the toughest, "where there are still a few good ol' boys who'd rather carve flesh than wood." The *Springfield Daily News* (14 January 1981) interviewed residents for their reactions to the article and found some had thought Nuwer and his photographer were doing a story for a "We" magazine, which they assumed was a human-interest type of publication. In this Dallas County town "where churches outnumber taverns 10 to 2," there were some raised eyebrows when it was discovered that *Oui* was actually a girlie magazine, part of *Playboy* publications.

299. Parkes, Darla. "I See the World in Missouri." *Show-Me Libraries* 32:5 (March 1981): 25–28.

The author lists over one hundred Missouri towns with names reflecting the multinational origins of the pioneer settlers. Though she classifies Oronogo in Jasper County as being American Indian, the commonly accepted, but not proven, source is that it was coined from a miner's saying "Ore or no go!" (see Livingston, *History of Jasper County*, 1912, p. 79).

300. Penprase, Mike. "Businessman Faces Piercing Questions." *Springfield News and Leader*, 23 November 1978.

Pierce City, Lawrence County, Missouri, was named in 1870 for a Frisco official named Peirce. But for a long time now citizens have been spelling it Pierce. They are still wrangling about the spelling.

301. Pfister, Fred. "What's in a Name?" *Ozark Highways* (Summer 1975): 29–30.

Brief discussion of over twenty place names in the Missouri-Arkansas Ozarks.

302. Phillips, George H. *Handling the Mail in Benton County, Arkansas, 1836–1976.* Siloam Springs, Ark.: Benton County Historical Society, 1979. 136p.

Lots on place names. The section entitled "Instructions Relative to Names of Post Offices" (pp. 22–25) gives brief definitions revealing the origins of many.

303. Rennick, Robert M. "The Role of Oral History in Place-Name Research." *Indiana Names* 3:1 (Spring 1972): 19–26.

The techniques of the folklore collector and the oral historian are substantially the same, says Rennick.

304. Saults, Dan, ed. *Rivers of Missouri.* Columbia, Mo.: M.F.A. Publishing Co., 1949. 100p.

There are many place-name references throughout this book. He says that if the explorers of the Mississippi River had come from the South instead of the North, the Mississippi above the mouth of the Missouri River would have been a tributary of another name. This work is a publication of the Missouri Conservation Commission.

305. ———. "The State of Ozarkia." *The Ozarks Mountaineer* 25:9 (October 1977): 28–29.

Saults suggests that southern Missouri and northern Arkansas should have been formed according to cultural and geographic similarities rather than by political decree. He names the state *Ozarkia* and defines the boundaries as encompassing a land "that would grow corn badly, trees fairly well, and rocks in abundance."

306. Schell, Joe C. *Big Sugar Creek Country.* Goodman, Mo.: McDonald County Historical Society, 1969. 95p.

Much about McDonald County, Missouri, place names; Boone Hollow, Cyclone, Mail Hollow, Rocky Comfort, Penitentiary Bend, Granny's Branch, and many others. This is an interesting little book.

307. Schon, Jon. "The Name Is Hog Scald." *Ark/Ozark* 1:4 (Summer 1969): 2–3.

Some interesting accounts about this beautiful spot located three miles south of Eureka Springs, Arkansas.

308. Schroeder, Walter A. "Panther Hollow and Dead Elm School: Plant and Animal Place Names in Missouri." *Missouri Historical Review* 73:3 (April 1979): 321–47.

Well documented with maps showing the geographic distribution of place names of specific flora and fauna. Many little anecdotes, comments on legends, values of place-name study, and so on. A thoughtful and valuable paper. Schroeder is a teacher of geography at the University of Missouri–Columbia.

309. Shannon, Karr. *A History of Izard County, Arkansas*. Little Rock: Democrat Printing Co., 1947. 158p.

A superior county history, with a great deal of valuable information about place names and pioneer customs. Even the biographies of prominent citizens (pp. 113–58) are well written and sensible, without the extravagant praise so common in books of this kind. Shannon was for many years a columnist and feature writer on the *Little Rock Democrat*.

310. Shirk, George H. *Oklahoma Place Names*. Norman: University of Oklahoma Press, 1965. 233p.

Except for Gould's book of the same title, published in 1933, this is the only treatment of the subject that I have seen. There are several Master's theses in the University Library—Shirk mentions two of them on p. 233—but they have not been printed so far as I know. Shirk's treatment of Indian names is always interesting. On p. 209 he says that *Tulsa* is named for "an old Creek town in Alabama." But many of the old-timers do not accept this interpretation.

311. Smith, Kenneth. *The Buffalo River Country*. Fayetteville, Ark.: The Ozark Society, 1967. 176p.

This is a wonderful book about the most scenic river in the Ozarks region. It was designated a National Wild River in 1972 and Smith's impressive photos, many in full color, attest to the importance of its preservation. This book is not just another photo essay but is complemented by a fine text. The first part entitled "The River" (pp. 10–73) covers the Buffalo mile by mile from its source to the mouth. The second part, "The Land," takes a good look at its history and the people. The entire work abounds in interesting place names.

312. Smith, Maggie Aldridge, ed. *Hico, A Heritage—Siloam Springs History*. Cassville, Mo.: Willard Burton, 1976. 447p.

This was produced by the Benton County, Arkansas, Bicentennial Committee as part of its contribution to the celebration of the nation's two hundredth anniversary. Hico is the original name of Siloam Springs. This book is a kind of scrapbook, a history of Benton County and the people who have lived there. Place-name references throughout. See pp. 236–38 for the story of Trail of Tears Baptist Church.

313. Smollen, Dot. "Quiet Days for Oronogo." *The Ozarks Mountaineer* 21:5 (June 1973): 26.

Good story, about Oronogo, Missouri, a lead-mining camp formerly called Minersville. Gives two "legends" about the origin of the new name. There are other tales not mentioned in this article.

314. Stone, Elizabeth. "In Search of Slave Graves." *Izard County Historian* 11:2 (April 1980): 22–24.

One of the graves located is that of a young Baxter County, Arkansas, slave who was killed by a storm. There was a new post office opening in the neighborhood and some wanted to name it "Little Joe" in his memory. As his clothes had been blown off by the storm, "Naked Joe" was suggested. They finally selected "Old Joe."

315. Thompson, Henry C. *Our Lead Belt Heritage*. Flat River, Mo.: News-Sun, 1955. 187p.

This is about the old mining region in Ste. Genevieve, Madison, Washington, Jefferson, and St. Francois Counties in the eastern Missouri Ozarks. Mining operations by white men began with the French in the mid-eighteenth century here. Thompson says that Old Mines in Washington County is probably older than Ste. Genevieve. This is local history, well written. Place-name information is found on pp. 90–97.

316. Van Cleef, A. "The Hot Springs of Arkansas." *Harper's New Monthly Magazine* 56 (January 1878): 193–210.

On p. 206 there is a picture showing a group of crude shacks that is labeled "Ral, the City on the Mountain." *Ral* is a dialect term for syphilis.

317. Vickery, Margaret Ray. *Ozark Stories of the Upper Current River*. Salem, Mo.: The Salem News, [1967?]. 97p.

Lots of stories about the upper Current River country, mostly in Shannon County, Missouri. Some thought the Ozark region got its name from the osage orange or the bodarc (French: *bois d'arcs*) tree, usually called a hedge apple tree. There are many more place-name references throughout. See pp. i–iii, 16, 45, 57, 68, 87.

318. Vineyard, Jerry, and Gerald L. Feder. *Springs of Missouri*. Rolla: Missouri Geological Survey and Water Resources, 1974. 267p.

A big book with fine pictures, maps, tables, graphs, etc. Sections on geology, water analysis, flora and fauna, commercialization. Everything I want to know about springs in Missouri, with good bibliographies and descriptions of individual springs—all the big springs, and a great many of the smaller ones. Incidentally, there is quite a bit about place names throughout.

319. Weaver, H. Dwight, and Paul A. Johnson. *Missouri the Cave State*. Jefferson City, Mo.: Discovery Enterprises, 1980. 336p.

The introductory chapters tell, in a general nature, about the use of caves by the Indians, early explorers and settlers, civil war guerrillas, outlaws, and, into modern times, their use during prohibition and World War II for storage, and their development as tourist attractions. The rest of the book deals with these same subjects as they pertain to specific caves. The names, past and present, of each cave are discussed. This is a valuable book for the toponymist.

320. "Who Named the Ozarks and When?" *Missouri Historical Review* 32:4 (July 1938): 523–33.

The State Historical Society carried out extensive research and read everything from the early explorers to the best modern scholars and mapmakers. The Indians around Arkansas Post called themselves Quapaws, but other tribes (and white explorers) called them Arkansas, after the river on which they lived. The French used *aux Arkansas* to refer to the country of the Arkansas tribe. *Ozarks* is "an anglicized version of *aux Arcs*, a French abbreviation for *aux Arkansas*." The first man to call the hills of south Missouri and north Arkansas "the Ozarks" was Stephen R. Long, between 1817 and 1820. This paper is fully documented, and contains also a discussion of the Masserne Range, another early name for the Missouri-Arkansas hills.

321. Wood, Larry E. "Wide Places in the Road." *The Ozarks Mountaineer* 24:6 (July 1976): 22, 43.

An appreciation of small settlements. Even the names of tiny villages seem more colorful than those of larger towns. He lists many eye-catching place names in Missouri and Arkansas.

322. Wylie, John. "Devil's Jump Off . . . ." *Missouri Conservationist* 40:7 (July 1979): 8–9.

A tongue-in-cheek continuation of Washington Irving's "The Legend of Sleepy Hollow" bringing Ichabod Crane to the Ozarks, where an encounter with the devil results in a sinkhole in Perry County, Missouri, being called "Devil's Jump Off."

4. Tall Tales

323. Adams, Emmett. " 'Pon Honor." *The Ozarks Mountaineer* 25:7 (August 1977): 32–33.

See p. 33 for the tale of the old woman who cut down a big tree to keep the cat from getting in through a hole in the roof. Just shows how ingenious we hill people are!

324. Aman, Reinhold, ed. "Change the Name of Arkansas?: Senator Johnson's Great Speech." *Maledicta* 2:1–2 (Summer-Winter 1978): 229–30.

This is my text from *Pissing in the Snow* (see entry 515), without the annotations. See also Aman's reference on p. 295.

325. *American Folklore and Legend.* Pleasantville, N.Y.: Reader's Digest Association, 1978. 448p.

Some well-known tall tales on pp. 161–62. "The Belled Buzzard," hoop snakes, the saw hog, and others.

326. Black, J. Dickson. *Beaver Lake Area—Past and Present.* Rogers, Ark.: Timberwolf Publishing, 1979. 76p.

Pages 24–25 tell of a mysterious "devil fish" caught in the 1860s by one J. H. Van Hoose of Fayetteville, Arkansas, in the White River. Black states that he has found the writings of Van Hoose to be truthful and that he believes this story.

327. Bradford, Samuel James. *Legends of the Ozark Hills.* Lebanon, Mo.: Ozark Publishers, 1971. 26p.

A small paperback containing short stories, three being regional legends of the Lebanon, Missouri, area. Two are Indian lore: Bennett Springs being tears of the Great Spirit, and drums sounding from a sinkhole. The third is of a folk hero, "Jed Hollister, Big Liar of the Ozarks." I have found no evidence of this story elsewhere in Laclede County nor anyone having knowledge of a hero so named. It may be these tales are family stories or a figment of the author's imagination. Bradford was a retired minister-educator who had returned to Lebanon where he was raised. This booklet was to have been the first of a series on regional folklore material but he died shortly after it was published.

328. Carr, Suzanne, with Ronnie Hough and Sarah Seay. "Big Windies." *Bittersweet* 2:2 (Winter 1974): 4–7.

A visit with Lebanon, Missouri, resident Sam Bradford. He tells five more tales about his own Paul Bunyan–type folk hero, Big Jed Hollister (see preceding entry).

329. Cochran, Michael. "Say Hello to the Real Speck Rhodes: An Interview with the Ozarks' Favorite Funnyman." *West Plains Gazette* 10 (January-February 1981): 11–21.

Rhodes is a native of West Plains, Missouri, who made it big in radio and television for over fifty years as a comic on the country music circuits. He talks about his career and his comedy routine. On p. 18 he tells about the fellow who goes to the doctor's office and says he has the shingles.

330. Coleman, James W. *Experiences of an Arkansas Backwoodsman.* New York: Vantage Press, 1976. 158p.

Some tallish tales—on p. 46 he tells us that wild ducks were so abundant "you could not see the sky, and the sound of their wings was deafening"; in fact, "shooting did not disturb them in the least, because they could not hear the noise of your gun." All worth reading is in the first sixty pages; the rest of the book is about Coleman's adventures as a football coach and a soldier in World War II. He came out of the army a lieutenant colonel with a Bronze Star. Coleman is now retired and lives in Reno, Nevada.

331. Cowan, J. E. *Life in the Powell-Cyclone Community of McDonald County, Missouri.* Noel, Mo.: McDonald County Press, 1973. 160p.

This is a good book. I especially like the chapter titled "Wildlife in McDonald County," pp. 114–19. Concerning the vast number of passenger pigeons, a hunter would never waste powder and shot by firing into a flock overhead, for there would be so many birds flying below those killed that they would carry them off on their backs. Many more tales about bear, deer, bobwhite, and the like.

332. Davis, Lowell. *The Ozark Hillman's Handbook.* N.p.: Lowell Davis Publications, 1969. 98p.

Short essays on a variety of Ozark subjects, mostly about folklife and crafts. There are a few familiar anecdotes. See pp. 41–42 for the one entitled "Eph Carlton's Talkin' Dog."

333. Deane, Ernie. *Ozarks Country.* Branson, Mo.: The Ozarks Mountaineer, 1975. 191p.

Pages 54–55, "Beware the Gowrow," are about the giasticutus, the fillyloo, sometimes called the gillyloo bird, and the gowrow, all mythical monsters reported mostly in the Arkansas Ozarks.

334. Findley, J. W. *A Voice from the Ozark Hills*. Springfield, Mo.: Roberts & Sutter, 1982. 221p.

Some tallish tales on pp. x, 38, 39, 74, 82, and 150. A new one was transplanting the hoopsnake and the rooster head (p. 70).

335. Flynn, Mike. "The Role of Women in Bawdy Ozark Folktales: A Content Analysis Study." Unpublished paper, University of Arkansas at Fayetteville, 1979. 12p.

The author, a student at the university, used stories from Randolph's *Pissing in the Snow* (see entry 515) as the source of his study.

336. Freeman, Dale. "When the Moon Fell." *Springfield News-Leader*, 9 March 1975.

Two stories, the first occurring in 1939. A resident of eastern Greene County, Missouri, wrote to Springfield's well-known weatherman, C. C. Williford, that he had seen the moon "fall" a few nights before and wondered if anyone else had reported it. (See Williford's *Letters to the Ozarks Weatherman*, 1948 [annotated in volume 1 of this bibliography, p. 534], and also entry 344 in this volume). The second story is about the old moonshiner and his cigar-smoking hound.

337. Gerstäcker, Friedrich. "Women in the Backwoods." Trans. Ralph Walker. *Early American Life* 13:6 (December 1982): 14–16, 19–23.

For the most part Gerstäcker's accounts of frontier life in the Arkansas Ozarks have been confirmed by scholars as trustworthy. But in this article, published in a German magazine in the 1840s, he tells, as a matter of fact, the old tale of the young couple (in this case Missourians) who take a night's shelter in an abandoned cabin. The husband starts a fire and during the night, when he arises to get their baby a drink, steps upon poisonous snakes that have been attracted by the warmth of the fire. His wife discovers his corpse the next morning.

338. Goolsby, Elwin L. *The Teeth on the Bradley-Rushing Building and Other Stories*. Sheridan, Ark.: Grant County Museum, 1978. 73p.

There are no songs or ballads in the collection, and few references to dialect or superstition, but there are a lot of good stories. Especially see pp. 41 and 59, both concerning a dog's cold nose, and p. 47 for the title story. Many more stories throughout. Also much about pioneer customs, place names, and buried treasures. Goolsby has done a good job of compiling and editing. He has shown that there is more than one way to write a county history.

339. Hardaway, Billie Touchstone. *These Hills My Home: A Buffalo River Story*. Republic, Mo.: Western Printing Company, 1980. 179p.

Chapter 9, "Tall (and not so tall) Tales . . . ," pp. 148–52, tells three stories from Newton County in northwest Arkansas.

340. Harrell, Mary Frances. *History and Folklore of Searcy County, Arkansas.* Harrison, Ark.: New Leaf Press, 1977. 481p.

The first ninety pages, labeled "Oral History," consists of interviews with old settlers; all good stuff, without too much editing. The body of the book is the usual genealogy and biographical hokum, with pictures of the prominent citizens. But the final section, "Tall Tales and Folklore," contains lists of household remedies, common superstitions, and traditional wisdom of a sort.

341. *Hillbilly Laugh Book.* Amarillo, Tex.: Baxter Lane Company, 1972. No pagination.

Though the word *Ozarks* is mentioned a few times, this is just another paperback of the same old jokes, but with the word *hillbilly* inserted, that have been in print for years.

342. Hubert, Renee, ed. *Ozark Country Sunshine—History of the Blue Eye School District.* Blue Eye, Mo.: Blue Eye High School, 1976. 32p.

See p. 8 for the story of the trunk that knocked to foretell death and p. 26 for the cave that "grew itself shut." This little book was printed as "Vol. 1: No. 1 (Spring 1976)" and was hoped to be the first of a regularly issued journal much in the same manner as Lebanon High School's *Bittersweet*, but this was the only one ever published.

343. Hughes, Marion. *Three Years in Arkansas.* Hatfield, Ark.: The Looking Glass, 1979. 100p.

A reprint of this controversial publication (first published in 1904; see entry in vol. 1 of this bibliography). In his foreword, the current publisher lauds it as "the state's most important heirloom." Still, a few sentences later, he feels it necessary to make an appeal to Arkansas "to throw off the yoke of false pride, to dispell the unfounded fears, and to put aside the needless hostility."

344. "It Wasn't the Moon." *Ark/Ozark* 2:1 (Fall 1969): 6–7.

Reprinted is a letter received by well-known weatherman/philosopher C. C. Williford of Springfield, Missouri. The letter, sent in the late 1930s, tells of seeing the moon fall (see entry 336).

345. Jackson, Thomas W. *On a Slow Train Through Arkansas.* Forrest City, Ark.: Marshall Vance, 1982. 96p.

Subtitled *Funny Railroad Stories, Sayings of the Southern Darkies, All the Latest and Best Minstrel Jokes of the Day*, this is a reprint of Jackson's best-selling joke book, first published in 1903. It contains an excellent twenty-eight-page introduction by Harlan Daniel, a native of Fox, Arkansas, who now resides in Memphis, Tennessee. He says that previous to the publication of this edition, *On a Slow Train* had been in print fifty-six consecutive years and sold more than three million copies (a fact still held in much chagrin by many Arkansans).

346. Kennicutt, Wally. *Ozark Nature Gallery*. Paragould, Ark.: White Printing Co., 1979. 114p.

On pp. 104–5 Kennicutt tells of the White River monster that resides in the vicinity of Newport, Arkansas, and of the lesser known Camden County sea serpent. More tales about giant rattlesnakes and hoop snakes on pp. 87, 91–92.

347. Krause, Bonnie, and Kay Carter. *Tall Tales, Ghosts and Omens of the Illinois Ozarks*. Carterville: Illinois Ozarks Craft Guild, 1978. 36p.

This book covers a wide spectrum of tall tales and stories, but with a few exceptions, they differ little from those encountered elsewhere in the Ozarks.

348. Lair, Jim. "Tall Tales Big Part of Ozark Mountain Lore." *Carroll County Tribune* (Berryville, Arkansas), 30 September 1981.

This article tells a story about when the "champeen" fistfighter of Missouri meets the "champeen" fistfighter of Arkansas. Lair got this from Doug Mahnkey of Forsyth, Missouri.

349. McNeil, W. K., and Kathy Nicol. "Folk Narratives of Jessie Hubert Wilkes." *Tennessee Folklore Society Bulletin* 48:3 (Fall 1982): 68–82.

Jessie Hubert Wilkes lives near Cave City, Arkansas. He is seventy-seven-years old and is the accepted storyteller "par excellence" in his community. This article contains eighteen of his best, taped and transcribed by the authors, both professional folklorists. Each story has been annotated, if possible, by type and motif as indexed by Ernest W. Baughman in his *Type and Motif Index of the Folktales of England and North America* (The Hague: Mouton, 1966). Much of this material has been featured in a film titled *They Tell It for the Truth: Ozark Mountain Storytellers*, produced by Pentacle Productions, Kansas City, Missouri, and on an album, *Not Far from Here: Traditional Tales and Songs Recorded in the Arkansas Ozarks* (Arkansas Traditions, 1981).

350. Manning, Walter. "McDonald County Saga Recalled." *Joplin Globe*, 28–30 September 1977.

This man lives near Southwest City, Missouri, on a farm his family has occupied for more than one hundred years. In this article, and in two succeeding issues of the *Globe*, he tells the story of the "great beast" that gave the Manning family so much trouble at the turn of the century. The Mannings were corn-and-hog farmers, but they kept a small flock of sheep in Massengill Hollow, and the "great beast" was killing too many of them. Frank Manning, Walter's grandfather, finally killed the beast in the fall of 1900. It was identified as a mountain lion at the time, but in later years some local storytellers spoke of it as a "lobo"—which means a gigantic wolf. All agree, however, that it was seven feet long, and hell on sheep.

351. Messick, Mary Ann. *History of Baxter County, 1873–1973*. Little Rock: Mountain Home Chamber of Commerce, 1973. 506p.

This is more an informal narrative about the people and their customs, religion, politics, social doings, and such, than it is a history. She tells some good stories. On p. 98 is the one about the old timer who came to the White River to see where the new railroad was going to cross. The tracks were laid to the river's edge and the tunnel on the opposite side was started, but no bridge work had begun. He said, "You might make me believe that with a good running start the train can jump the river but you'll never make me believe that it'll hit that hole every time." More tales are on pp. 58, 110, 186, and 494. Messick is postmistress at Gassville, Arkansas.

352. Nothdurft, Lillian. *Folklore and Early Customs of Southeast Missouri*. New York: Exposition Press, 1972. 77p.

The selection of "Tall Tales" (pp. 28–35) is perhaps worth reading.

353. Pyles, Lida Wilson. "It Happened in the Ozarks." Unpublished manuscript, Carthage, Mo., 1982. 197p.

In the chapter "Liars and Yarn Spinners" the author tells five tales, most of which are common in the Ozarks, but of interest is the one about black powder, which I have only heard around the mining region of Joplin and Webb City. The only copy of this manuscript is in the author's possession.

354. Randolph, Vance. "Folklore." *The Ozarks Mountaineer* 26:10–11 (November-December 1978): 16–17.

Three brief tales: "Where Did That Dollar Go?," "It Was a Different Bear," and "Howell Free State."

355. ———. "Folklore." *The Ozarks Mountaineer* 27:2–3 (March-April 1979): 56–57.

More stories collected by Randolph: "Dividing Up the Steers" as told by Otto Ernest Rayburn, "Piled High and Deep" by George Milburn, and—one of Vance's favorites that he heard in southwest Missouri in the 1920s—"The Barber Wasn't Scared."

356. ———. "The Oldest Inhabitant." *The Ozarks Mountaineer* 26:8–9 (September-October 1978): 18.

This story originally appeared in my *Sticks in the Knapsack* (New York: Columbia University Press, 1958), pp. 8–10.

357. ———. *We Always Lie to Strangers*. Westport, Conn.: Greenwood Press, 1974. 309p.

This is a reprint of my collection of tall tales, first published under the same title by Columbia University Press in 1951. As far as I can see, it's an exact reprint, including the drawings by Glen Rounds.

358. ———. "The White River Monster." In *Ozark Guide Yearbook*, pp. 2–4. Reeds Spring, Mo.: Gerald Pipes, 1961.

About the river monster seen near Newport, Arkansas. Reprinted from *Funny Stories from the Ozarks* (Little Blue Book no. 1897).

359. Rayburn, Otto Ernest. "Ozark Fish Stories." *Ozark Guide* (October 1958): 7–8.

Three stories: a cross-eyed catfish caught when it runs into a bridge trying to escape; training ducks to fish; and a tale, which he says is true, of a 1913 flood washing the contents of a saloon into a river, and for weeks afterward drunk fish were caught by hand.

360. Richardson, Ellen Earle. *Early Settlers of Cane Hill*. Fayetteville, Ark.: Washington County Historical Society, 1968. 63p.

Of interest chiefly to descendants of the early settlers. Written in 1940, first published in 1955. This is one of a series of booklets edited by Prof. W. J. Lemke, of the University of Arkansas. See p. 14 for the story about the fast-growing pumpkin vine.

361. Ring, Bill. *Tall Tales Are Not All from Texas*. Point Lookout, Mo.: School of the Ozarks Press, [1980]. 91p.

The author was an entertainer on radio and television in the Ozark region for many years. Recently he hosted a radio program devoted primarily to fishing reports. He conducted a tall tales contest, and this book is a collection of seventy-seven of those submitted, mostly about giant fish, snakes, hunting dogs, and the like. Anyone who floated the rivers back in the forties and fifties will appreciate "The Peck Bait" story on p. 13. Ring always signs off with a quote from fishing guide Jim Owen of Branson, Missouri: "If you're too busy to go fishing, you're too busy."

362. Saults, Dan. "Save Our Karkhagne." *The Ozarks Mountaineer* 26:8–9 (September-October 1978): 16–17.

A tongue-in-cheek plea for the karkhagne, which Saults says is an endangered species. The karkhagne was a science-fiction monster invented by two newspapermen in the 1950s, described by Paul Greer (*The Ozarks Mountaineer*, November 1955, p. 9). It has no connection with oral tradition and must not be taken seriously as folklore. Compare the yarns of Col. W. J. Zevely and John Park Cravens.

363. Townsend, Will. *Not By a Jugfull: Ozarks Tall Tales*. Branson, Mo.: The Ozarks Mountaineer, 1979. 38p.

This is just a pamphlet for the tourist trade, but it contains many of the classic whoppers, and several that are new to me. The author is a newspaper writer from north Missouri, but he has lived in the Ozarks for a long time and knows a lot of the old-timers.

364. ———. "Poets of the Tall Tale Tradition." *The Ozarks Mountaineer* 25:11 (December 1977): 18–19.

A fine collection of old James River windies. There are related stories in the Ozarks, and some of them have been printed many times, but they are still mighty good yarns.

365. Turrentine, Gloria Hale. "Visiting Grandma in the Ozarks." *The Ozarks Mountaineer* 26:2 (March 1978): 34–35.

Speaking of wild turkeys (p. 35) an old woman says, "In early summer the dew would be so heavy and sticky that turkeys couldn't fly. They called this the Honey Dew. Grandpa would come in with a big gobbler, or maybe two or three young ones, frying size." May Kennedy McCord told me something like this years ago, but I never quite believed it. Turrentine lives near Ozark, in Christian County, Missouri.

366. White, Kathleen K. *True Tall Tales from Missouri*. Clinton, Mo.: The Printery, 1976. 70p.

News stories, mostly taken from county histories published in the 1880s. See p. 18 for an account of Thomas Benton Young of Audrain County, who climbed a grapevine and cut it off *above* his head. Note also the tale (p. 65) of Sam Cole, whose only garment was a long shirt. But he went to a dance anyhow, riding a bull since he had no horse.

367. White, Mahlon Neill. *Stories about Old Blue, Osage River Fish, Too Big to Catch*. Warsaw, Mo.: Benton County Publishing Co., 1967. 68p.

Tales of the giant catfish called Old Blue, who has cruised around in the Osage River and the Lake of the Ozarks since prehistoric times. He never talks to anybody save Skunk Hide Turner, the old trapper of Pecan Valley.

368. Wolf, John Quincy [Sr.]. *Life in the Leatherwoods*. Memphis: Memphis State University Press, 1974. 159p.

Several tall stories from north-central Arkansas heard by Wolf during his youth between the 1870s and 1890s. See pp. 71–72 for Aunt Polly and the Devil; p. 74 about using "spring lizards" in place of a forked stick to "witch" for water; pp. 81–82 about how hawks tricked roosting chickens; and pp. 84–85 for weather stories.

5. Stories and Anecdotes

Ackerson

369. Akerson, Calvin C. *Seneca*. Seneca, Mo.: Seneca News-Dispatch, [c. 1977].
47p.

This pamphlet is a pretty good history of Seneca in southwest Missouri. The
people of Seneca today seem to know nothing of Akerson or his book. There is some
internal evidence that the concluding chapter (which may have been written by another hand than Akerson's) might be dated as early as 1965. See pp. 37–38 for a
description of the nine-day ceremony that he calls the "Indian Dog Dance," credited
to the Seneca and Modoc tribes. "A dog was killed on the first day of the feast and
hung up on a pole 'in a crucified position,' on the ninth day, it was cut down and
burned in a slow fire on a 'special altar,'" while the Indian orators stood in the
smoke and made speeches.

370. Albin, Ed. "Vance Randolph: 'The Damned Fools Are a Gainin' on Us.'"
Springfield Magazine 2:7 (December 1980): 22–23.

The author met Randolph in 1948 when Albin joined the faculty of the University of Arkansas at Fayetteville. He reminisces about their friendship over the ensuing years. Albin now lives in Springfield, Missouri. The title refers to Randolph's
thoughts concerning "progress" in the Ozarks.

371. "Alf Bolen: The Meanest Ozarker of 'Em All." In *Ozark Guide Yearbook*,
pp. 6–9. Reeds Spring, Mo.: Gerald Pipes, 1961.

About the infamous Ozarks bushwhacker. This first appeared in the *Springfield
News-Leader*.

372. Allen, Earl "Chick." *Capt. William Allen, Civil War Veteran of Missouri*.
Cassville, Mo.: Litho Printers, 1974. 48p.

Some parts of this book are so full of factual errors pertaining to the Civil War
in the Ozarks that it could be considered under the category of "tall tales." But this
in itself makes it of interest to the folklorist as a good example of the fallibility of
oral history.

373. ———. *Ozark Indian History*. Cassville, Mo.: Litho Printers, 1974. 32p.

This is Allen's own interpretation of the history of the Indians who have lived in
the Ozarks: Osage, Delaware, and Cherokee. It differs substantially from accepted
versions.

374. Allen, Eric. *Tales and Legends of the Ozarks*. Muskogee, Okla.: Hoffman Printing Co., 1974. 102p.

Paperback booklet of six sensational stories set in the Arkansas Ozarks, no folktales or legends. Just short stories of the sort we used to see in the pulp magazines. Lots of shooting and gunfighter's talk. Of no great value for the folklorist.

375. *American Folklore and Legend*. Pleasantville, N.Y.: Reader's Digest Association, 1978. 448p.

Aside from some familiar tall tales, the rest of the Ozarks section of this book is made up of brief articles covering well-known stories and anecdotes, all pertaining to Arkansas. The editors have condensed their material to the point that there is no mention of the Missouri Ozarks.

Under the subtitle of "Ozark Lore: Hillbillies and Razorbacks" (pp. 160–62) are excerpts from Pete Whetstone. Pages 164–65 are a condensation of Thomas B. Thorpe's well-known *Big Bear of Arkansas*.

376. Anglin, Melvin D. *The Civil War: From Hearsay*. Berryville, Ark.: Published by the author, [c. 1975]. 32p.

Born just after the turn of the century in rural Tennessee, the author grew up listening to the stories of old Civil War veterans as they refought the war. His principal informant was his grandfather, an unreconstructed Rebel. Most of the events take place in Tennessee but as he entered his teens, the family moved to Berryville in Carroll County, Arkansas. The last third of the book relates to events in the northwest Arkansas Ozarks, mostly concerning the atrocities committed by the bushwhackers who terrorized the Missouri-Arkansas border area. This little book isn't very well written, but I'm confident he has recorded these tales pretty much the way he heard them, the way old-timers on town "whittlin' benches" used to tell such stories.

377. Banes, Marian Tebbetts. *The Journal of Marian Tebbetts Banes*. Fayetteville, Ark.: The Washington County Historical Society, 1977. 159p.

On pp. 65–66 she recounts a story, in the form of a refrain, as told by a slave named John about the devil and a boy who went fishing on Sunday called "Pull Me Out Simon." Another one she remembers, p. 67, that was popular among the children, carried the first line "An old woman, all skin and bo-o-ones," with the last word of each line pronounced with a low groan. The final line ended with a loud shout, designed to give a good scare to any newcomers. Throughout this journal Ms. Banes gives the reader a personal and pleasant glimpse of childhood among the well-to-do in antebellum Arkansas.

378. Barrick, Mac E. "The Migratory Anecdote and the Folk Concept of Fame." *Mid-South Folklore* 4:2 (Summer 1976): 39–47.

A discussion of the continuation of certain anecdotes originally attributed to a particular historical character but then perpetuated by assigning it to a different central figure contemporary to succeeding generations. One example taken from Vance Randolph's *Hot Springs and Hell* is "The Governor Said Manure." Originally told about Jeff Davis, it is now attributed to Harry Truman. Barrick teaches Spanish at Shippensburg State College in Pennsylvania.

379. Barry, Clara Reasoner. *Off the Square in Springfield*. Springfield, Mo.: Elkins-Swyers Co., 1947. 29p.

The author is a newcomer in Springfield. She didn't get here until 1907, but she has collected some fine gossipy tales from the old-timers; some date back to Civil War days. Many of the great names are here. Mrs. Barry is a very good writer. The tales are charming, but not too important for any but local historians.

380. ———. *The Pie on the Square*. Springfield, Mo.: Elkins-Swyers Press, 1946. 45p.

More charming bits about the history of Springfield, which she gathered in casual talks with the old residents. The people in Springfield today know little about the Barry pamphlets, and nobody seems to remember much about Mrs. Barry, except that she was a "nice old lady."

381. ———. *The Square*. Springfield, Mo.: Published by author, 1945. 22p.

This is another nice little pocket-size booklet. It is well written and I enjoyed reading it, but as with Mrs. Barry's other works, it is of interest mainly to long-time residents of Springfield.

382. Batson, Larry. *The Hills Are Theirs: Tales from the Ozarks*. Minneapolis: Minneapolis Tribune Publishers, 1978. 155p.

Batson lives in Minneapolis now, where he does a column for the *Tribune*, but he was born and raised in the Missouri Ozarks. He writes reminiscently of his boyhood and writes very well, too. Not much folklore, but some good anecdotes.

383. Bell, J. H. "Pining Away for Gaddo County." *Frontier Times* 42:2 (March 1968): 10–13, 62, 64.

On p. 64 the author says that one of his children was "treed by a wild boar" near Washburn, Missouri. He does not use the word *razorback*, but that's probably what it was.

384. Bentley, R. C. "The Farmington Papers." Unpublished manuscript, Fayetteville, Ark., 1978. 47p.

A handwritten collection of bawdy tales collected in the village of Farmington, Arkansas, in the 1930s and 1940s. The original is deposited in the Special Collections Library at the University of Arkansas, Fayetteville. There are fifty-three brief stories, with little editing and less expurgation. The manuscript suffers from inadequate documentation, but it contains a lot of valuable material. Prof. Robert Cochran, who obtained the manuscript for the university, tells me that he is sending a machine copy to the Kinsey Institute at Indiana University.

385. Berry, Earl. *History of Marion County* (Arkansas). Little Rock: Marion County Historical Association, 1977. 523p.

Pages 65–70 tell the story of the Tutt-Everett War, one of the most famous of Ozark feuds. Civil War stories on pp. 80–82.

386. Berry, Evalena. *Time and the River: A History of Cleburne County*. Little Rock: Rose Publishing Company, 1982. 392p.

This is mostly a conventional county history, but chapters 3, "Pete Whetstone of Devil's Fork" (pp. 34–43), 14, "Family Life" (pp. 274–94), and 16, "Recreation and Entertainment" (pp. 303–28), will be of interest to students of Ozark folklife. The book is profusely illustrated and has numerous anecdotes collected from local residents.

387. Bettelheim, Bruno. *The Uses of Enchantment: The Meaning and Importance of Fairy Tales*. New York: Alfred A. Knopf, 1976. 328p.

This is delightful reading for anybody, but is also full of sound scholarship, with valuable notes and adequate bibliography. His analysis of the familiar stories places a great emphasis on the psychoanalytic approach, which seems a bit old-fashioned today, but I enjoyed reading it. Many of these tales are still in oral circulation in Missouri and Arkansas.

388. Biggs, Wallace R. "A Man Is Hanged." *American Mercury* 49:193 (January 1940): 37–41.

Detailed story of the hanging of Sonny McDaniel at Springfield, Missouri, in 1935. "A true account of an execution that made a holiday down in the Ozarks," says the editor. McDaniel was a convicted murderer, and it was a legal hanging.

389. Black, J. Dickson. "Fort Sill's Ghosts." *Visions* 2:1 (Fall 1979): 22–24.

Two short ghost stories from old Fort Sill, Indian Territory. The tales date back to 1874. As late as the 1920s there were still people living around the fort who claimed to have seen the ghosts told about in both stories. Black lives in Rogers, Arkansas. He is the author of a fine anecdotal history of Benton County (see entry 1330). *Visions* is published biannually by the creative writing classes of the Rogers Center North Arkansas Community College.

390. Boulson, C. E. "The Marshfield Tornado." *Webster County Historical Society Journal* 2 (April 1976): 2–7.

Account of the great storm that desolated Marshfield, Missouri, in 1880. Compare *Marshfield and Her Cyclone*, by M. A. Wilson (see entry 1523).

391. Boyd, Don. *Treasure Hunting in the Ozarks*. Springfield, Mo.: Published by the author, 1975. 120p.

This is a "quality paperback," well printed on good paper, with substantial stiff pasteboard binding, good maps, three-page bibliography, good index. Plenty of good pictures, many old photographs, including the only good picture I ever saw of Pony Boyd. "He was widely known as the loudest hollerin' lawyer in the Ozarks" (p. 78). Clear account of the Indian, French, and Spanish legends and enterprises clear down to Mathias Splitlog (p. 13) in McDonald County, Missouri. Reproductions of many old drawings and photographs.

392. Brewer, Wanda Eve. *Roaring River Realities*. Kansas City, Mo.: Lowell Press, 1962. 60p.

A fine booklet with good photos and adequate treatment of Dr. Sayman, the soapmaker who owned the whole park area and deeded it to the State of Missouri. The only other interesting person here is Jean Wallace, the witch—I knew her, she was just a fortune teller. Her log shanty finally burned, with the "Mountain Maid" inside. This booklet was reprinted in 1973.

393. Brisco, Mary S. "Sister Sooky's Story: The Autobiography of Mary S. Brisco." With an introduction by Mary Celestia Parler. *Mid-South Folklore* 5:3 (Winter 1977): 77–99.

Dr. William M. Clements, editor of *Mid-South Folklore*, edited this a bit for publication, but it reads pretty much like the original longhand manuscript, which I have seen. There are a good many anecdotes in this paper.

394. ———. "Sister Sooky's Story." *Carroll County Historical Society Quarterly* 23:1 (Spring 1978): 14–29.

This is the identical story, edited by Mary Celestia Parler, that appeared in *Mid-South Folklore* (Winter 1977), but minus the valuable reference notes.

395. Bristow, Joseph Quayle. *Tales of Old Fort Gibson*. New York: Exposition Press, 1961. 247p.

A collection of short pieces about old Fort Gibson, in what is now Muskogee County, Oklahoma, where the author lived in the early 1900s. These are enjoyable tales, especially "Balloon Ascension" (pp. 31–34), "An Ozark Vignette" (pp. 63–67), "Longhorns" (pp. 75–78), "Timmie Jack" (pp. 85–90), "Albert Pike and Fort Gibson" (pp. 102–6), and "Judge Parker" (pp. 110–23). I heard many of these stories as a child, and knew some of the characters. Much on local history and pioneer legend. Bristow was born in Baldwin, Kansas, in 1884 and grew up during the "Great Run" in Oklahoma. In his early years he worked with surveying parties in the West. He retired from a career in federal service in 1954.

396. Brown, Forrest. *Kiver Up the Still, Ma—Thar's a Stranger Comin'! Fun in the Ozarks*. New York: Exposition Press, 1965. 119p.

A collection of hillbilly jokes and anecdotes, of little interest for the folklorist. The author was born in Chillicothe, Missouri, where he "worked his way through his last two years of high school" and later "put himself through nine years of university and sixteen correspondence courses," according to the jacket of his book. The same jacket blurb says he earned four degrees, including a Ph.D. He attended Missouri Wesleyan, Boston University, Harvard, and the University of California, where he was a Guggenheim Fellow in 1947. He is now a commander in the Naval Reserve and lives in Springfield, Missouri. He does not write well, however, and his book has little value to the serious student of the Ozark scene.

397. Brunvand, Jan Harold. *The Vanishing Hitchhiker: American Urban Legends and Their Meanings*. New York: W. W. Norton & Company, 1981. 208p.

This is a study of over thirty of these legends, fully documented. For Ozark references, see p. 31, a vanishing hitchhiker story collected by Vance Randolph in Mountain Home, Arkansas, in 1941.

398. Burns, Cherie, ed. "Tell It for Truth." *Bittersweet* 9:4 (Summer 1982): 4–19.

Douglas Mahnkey tells over thirty of his best stories. After almost fifty years as a practicing lawyer in Taney County, Missouri, he understands the Ozark people as well as anyone now living. His mother was Mary Elizabeth Mahnkey, the closest the Missouri Ozarks ever came to a poet laureate.

399. Canby, Courtlandt, and Nancy E. Gross, eds. *The World of History*. New York: Mentor Books, 1954. 224p.

A popular anthology issued by the Society of American Historians. See p. 113 for a reprint of the "Johnny Appleseed" story from my *Who Blowed Up the Church House?* (1952).

400. Clayton, Joe. "Magic Barrel of 1950 Makes Town Glad for Quiet." *Springfield News-Leader*, 7 September 1981.

Remembering the mysterious self-filling barrel on the Orr family farm in Texas County, Missouri. One Labor Day weekend an estimated ten thousand skeptical visitors overran the farm. Shortly after this incident Farmer Orr reported the disappearance of the barrel.

401. Coffin, Tristram, and Hennig Cohen. *Folklore from the Working Folk of America*. Garden City, N.Y.: Anchor Press, 1973. 464p.

"A Traveling Salesman Story," pp. 37–38, was collected by Randolph in Galena, Missouri, in the 1930s. It first appeared in *Southern Folklore Quarterly* in June 1950 in an article entitled "Tales from South Missouri."

402. Coleman, James W. *Experiences of an Arkansas Backwoodsman*. New York: Vantage Press, 1976. 158p.

The first sixty pages include the author's memories of life on a farm in southern Arkansas, with many good anecdotes. See especially "Trip to Bucksnort" (pp. 15–17), "New Hunting Ground" (pp. 24–26), "Charley Goliath and the Alligator Gar" (pp. 34–36), "A Duck Hunting Trip" (pp. 44–46), and "John H. Coleman and Henry Benford" (p. 49).

403. Condon, Frank. "Local Ghost Makes Good." *Collier's* 102:22 (26 November 1938): 14, 44, 46.

All about the filming of *Jesse James* at Pineville, Missouri. Contact of the hillfolk with the aliens from Hollywood. Cf. the *Jesse James* booklet by Poindexter and Fitzpatrick, two local men (Pineville, Missouri, 1938, 31p.) For additional comments see also "Preliminary Filmography of Jesse James" by W. K. McNeil (entry 1075).

404. Cooke, Thomas D. "Two Ozark Analogues to Two Old French Fabliaux." *Southern Folklore Quarterly* 44 (1980): 85–91.

Two tales from Randolph's *Pissing in the Snow* are closely related to old French literary tales written in the thirteenth century. Dr. Cooke is a professor of English at the University of Missouri–Columbia.

405. Dalton, Captain Kit. *Under the Black Flag*. Memphis: Lockard Publishing Company, 1914. 252p.

He tells of his adventures with Belle Starr (pp. 143–56), whom he describes as ". . . a Venus in beauty, a Minerva in Wisdom, a thief, a robber, a murderer, and a generous friend." He obviously employed the services of a ghost writer who wrote his tales in a romantically adventurous style. The reader should not take Dalton seriously.

406. Darnell, Gerry. "Bald Knobbers: The Ozark Vigilantes." *Bittersweet* 6:4 (Summer 1979): 20–30.

Based upon Lucille Morris Upton's *Bald Knobbers* (1939), but includes interviews with several old residents. Quotes Elmo Ingenthron, who is inclined to defend the Knobbers, especially the Taney County group headed by "Captain" Kinney. A good article, with several photographs I had not seen before.

407. Deane, Ernie. *Ozarks Country*. Branson, Mo.: The Ozarks Mountaineer, 1975. 191p.

Ernie did me the honor of asking me to write a foreword for this book. I wrote him one paragraph: "Ernie might stretch the blanket sometimes, but when he tells you something for the truth you'd better believe it. If he says that a chicken dips snuff, you'll find a snuff box under its wing and that's telling it like it is." Ernie has roamed the hills in search of material for his column and knows most of his informants firsthand.

The article entitled "He Was Really Snakebit" (pp. 56–57) contains the old one about the fellow who was chased into a hole by a bull but kept coming back out, only to be chased back again. When asked why he didn't stay in the hole, he said, "There's a bear down there!" See pp. 113–14 in *The Hell-Bound Train: A Cowboy Songbook* by Glenn Ohrlin (entry 58) for the song "Jake and Roanie," which tells this same story. Pages 183–84 of *Ozarks Country*, "When Senators Met in a Cave," tell of the special session of the Arkansas General Assembly that met in 1931 in a cave at Bella Vista. They passed some unusual resolutions. Other good stories on pp. 66, 71, and 112.

408. Downs, Robert B. *The Bear Went Over the Mountain: Tall Tales of American Animals*. Detroit: Singing Tree Press, 1971. 358p.

This is a reprint of a book first published by Macmillan in 1964. See the section entitled "Ozark Ozone" (pp. 115–42), which includes eight animal tales from my folklore books, and a long quote about "Fabulous Monsters" from my *We Always Lie To Strangers*.

409. Drago, Harry Sinclair. *Wild, Woolly & Wicked: The History of the Kansas Cow Towns and the Texas Cattle Trade*. New York: Clarkson N. Potter, 1960. 354p.

The chapters entitled "Wild Bill Takes Over" and "Abilene in Its Tarnished Glory" (pp. 88–111) concern Hickok's tenure as sheriff of Abilene. Page 96 tells of the famous Hickok-Tutt duel that took place in Springfield, Missouri. There are chapter notes and a bibliography.

410. Draper, William R., and Mabel Draper. *Old Grub Stake Days in Joplin.* Girard, Kans.: Haldeman-Julius Publishing Co., 1946. 32p.

Some interesting material about the mining camps of southwest Missouri. Mabel Draper was a native of Joplin and knew many of the old-timers. Cf. Dolph Shaner, *The Story of Joplin* (1948; see volume 1 of this bibliography, p. 206).

411. Field, Roswell Martin. *In Sunflower Land, Stories of God's Own Country.* Chicago: Schulte and Co., 1892. 257p.

Kansas is the Sunflower State, but there is a lot about Missouri in this book. The author was a brother of Eugene Field of St. Joseph, Missouri.

412. Findley, J. W. *Experiences of a Walking Preacher.* Springfield, Mo.: Roberts & Sutter, 1980. 156p.

Some memories of a Church of God preacher who, now in his eighties, tells of his life and ministry in the southwest Missouri Ozarks. All this is interspersed with a liberal helping of Bible quotes and religious testimony. But it is good reading and an interesting look at the Ozarks during his lifetime, especially his comments on the 1930s and the Great Depression. The author has a fine sense of humor and there are a great many stories and anecdotes. On p. 102 he tells of the woman whose husband was sick. The doctor leaves some powdered medicine with the instructions to measure the doses by just what would "lay on a dime." On the next visit the man is worse. When the doctor asks the wife if she followed the directions, she says yes, but she didn't have a dime so she used two nickels. Also see pp. 20, 45, 62, 89, 94, 97, 102, 117, and 147.

413. ———. *A Voice from the Ozark Hills.* Springfield, Mo.: Roberts & Sutter, 1982. 221p.

As with Reverend Findley's first opus, this book abounds in Ozark stories, brief anecdotes, dialect jokes (see p. x for Dutch, p. 163 for black; his interpretation of these dialects is as outlandish as the stories themselves), and countless one-liners. Some of the better ones are found on pp. 10, 38, 41, 69, 74, 78, 124, 135, 147, and 177.

414. Fletcher, John Gould. "Education Past and Present." In *I'll Take My Stand: The South and the Agrarian Tradition,* by Twelve Southerners, pp. 92–121. New York: Harper and Brothers, 1930.

This dull book is worth reading if only because of Fletcher's contribution. I also enjoyed John Wade's "The Life and Death of Cousin Lucius" (pp. 265–301).

415. Fletcher, Philip Cone. *The Story of My Heart*. San Antonio: Alamo Printing Co., 1929. 344p.

The autobiography of a Methodist preacher, who had churches at Siloam Springs (pp. 13–19), Fort Smith (pp. 21–27), Eureka Springs (pp. 29–35), Fayetteville (pp. 45–61), and Little Rock (pp. 97–107, 121–83). Many amusing anecdotes. Compare the biography by Silas Wesley Rogers, *The Radiant Philip Cone Fletcher* (Cedar Rapids: Torch Press, 1923).

416. Flowers, Paul. *How to Wean a Compact (and Other Ozark Goodies)*. Batesville, Ark.: White River Press, 1975. [50p.]

The author is a well-known Memphis newspaperman who has a wide acquaintance in Arkansas. About a hundred modern "hillbilly" jokes and anecdotes, with some amusing scraps of dialect, and fine recipes for pot liquor and muscadine leather. See also the famous bull cincher, which country blacksmiths make to fool credulous tourists. I know Flowers from way back, and I read everything he writes. But students of folklore can't get much out of him. He has been known to tell a windy, and must not be taken too seriously.

417. Ford, Gary D. "Away in the Arkansas Ozarks." *Southern Living* 17:8 (August 1982): 66–71.

The usual travel article with pretty pictures, some of the Folk Center at Mountain View. He tells about the old Ozarker who moved to Kansas. After a brief stay he told his wife they were going back. "I'd rather be in jail in Arkansas than a rich man here!"

418. Ford, Jean Elizabeth. *Fish Tails and Scales*. N.p.: Ford Enterprises, 1982. 86p.

A collection of thirty-five tales, yarns, and stories remembered by the author about her father. Mitch Ford, who died in 1969, lived in Branson, Missouri, and worked for the late Jim Owen and his famous float service. Mitch guided many a fisherman down some of the most beautiful water that ever existed in this part of the world—the White River, the lower James, and the Kings. All are now inundated by Corps of Engineers lakes. He was a member of a select group of colorful rivermen: Little Horse Jennings, Charlie Carr, Emmett Adams, Leather Standridge, and Tom Yocum, to name but a few. The life these fellows knew can probably never be again. The foreword is by Jim Owen.

419. Fountain, Sarah. *Arkansas Voices: An Anthology of Arkansas Literature*. Little Rock: Rose Publishing Company, 1976. 258p.

This book offers much more traditional material from oral sources than most literary anthologies. See pp. 106–27 for Ozark folktales, and pp. 136–48 for Negro tales that Richard Dorson collected at Pine Bluff.

420. Fox, Leland. *Tall Tales from the Sage of Cane Hill*. Greenfield, Mo.: Vedette
     Printing Co., 1971. 172p.

This is not the Cane Hill I know best, which is in Washington County, Arkansas. Fox's Cane Hill is in Missouri, between Stockton and Dadeville. This book
seems to be a series of factual stories, with photographs, such as a chapter devoted
to Bill Akard, a champion trick shot, and another chapter to Dr. L. E. Meador, a
professor at Drury College in Springfield, Missouri. The whole book is fascinating
reading for me, because I know many of the people that Fox writes about. The
whole thing is well written, with good glimpses of rural Missouri in the early part of
the century. Chapter 12 (pp. 65–69), entitled "Corn Belt Squeezin's," tells the fine
points of illegal moonshining that emerged with the Eighteenth Amendment. The
author says, "These operators had one thing in common with their more sedate,
church-going neighbors. They all voted against repeal." But most of the book is not
of much interest to folklorists. Long on local history. Fox died in 1976.

421. Freeman, Dale. "A Little More Cider." *Springfield News-Leader*, 29 June
     1975.

Part of my tales from *The Talking Turtle* (1957) is reprinted with pleasant commentary in Freeman's "The Ozarker" column in the Sunday paper. After a few kind
words about my *Ozark Folklore* bibliography, he describes my methods of collecting folklore material. "Good ol' Vance Randolph," says he, adding that "there
should be more nice guys like that around to collect such stories and preserve
them!" Only a few years ago Freeman's town was full of people who regarded "good
ol' Randolph" as Public Enemy Number One, "dragging up that old hillbilly stuff,
that we had better forget just as soon as we can."

422. Gaskins, John. *True Tales of an Old Bear Hunter: The Life and Adventures of
     John Gaskins*. Eureka Springs, Ark.: Eureka Springs Historical Museum,
     1980. 41p.

A reprint of the scarce 1893 edition (see vol. 1 of this bibliography, p. 162).
This is worth reading, many good stories of the early days in the Eureka Springs
area. Introduction by Lida Pyles.

423. Gibbons, Robert H. "Shootout at Springfield." *Missouri Life* 1:5 (November–
     December 1973): 46–51.

Wild Bill Hickok and Dave Tutt staged a duel in the public square in 1865.

424. Gideon, Gene. "Folklore." *Ozark Highways* (Winter 1972): 48–49.

This article includes another story of the self-filling barrel in Texas County,
Missouri. The barrel kept itself full all through the 1950s until the family who owned

it got tired of curious visitors and chopped it to pieces. Gideon lives in Forsyth, Missouri, where he composes gospel songs.

425. Green, Rayna. "Magnolias Grow in Dirt: The Bawdy Lore of Southern Women." *Southern Exposure* 4:4 (1977): 29–33.

A fine article, mostly about middle-class women in east Texas, which Green describes as "a Southern enclave in the Southwest." She tells several good stories, quite without expurgation, some of them attributed to her mother and her grandmother. Dr. Green was born in Texas and once taught folklore at the University of Arkansas. *Southern Exposure* is a quarterly published by the Institute of Southern Studies at Chapel Hill, North Carolina.

426. Green, Robert L. "The Outlaw Henry Starr." *Northwest Arkansas Merchandiser*, Bentonville, Ark., 8 June 1977.

Detailed account of the Bentonville bank robbery in 1893, with a photograph of Henry Starr, and some facts about Starr that I had not seen in print before. This is a fine story, based upon interviews with old-timers. Green was born and raised in Benton County. He graduated from high school at Pea Ridge and now lives at Gravette.

427. Greenway, John. *Folklore of the Great West*. Palo Alto, Calif.: American West Publishing Co., 1969. 453p.

This is a very fine anthology, all pieces selected from the files of the *Journal of American Folklore*. Greenway served as editor of the *Journal* for four years (1964–1968), and his main interest is in western songs and stories. His great West includes parts of Missouri, Arkansas, and Oklahoma, with occasional excursions across the Rio Grande. Items from the Ozarks are scattered through the text. It ends with my paper "Nakedness in Ozark Folk Belief" (*Journal of American Folklore* 66 [1953]: 333–39), which is here reprinted for the first time so far as I know. Not the least valuable part of this big book is Greenway's comments and discussions, totaling about fifty thousand words—all well done. *Folklore of the Great West* is required reading for all serious students. Greenway is a professor of anthropology at the University of Colorado, Boulder.

428. Gregory, Jack, and Rennard Strickland. *Cherokee Spirit Tales*. Fayetteville, Ark.: Indian Heritage Association, 1969. [44p.]

Twenty oral legends from Cherokee mythology. Illustrated with charcoal drawings by Willard Stone, well-known Cherokee woodcarver. These tales were collected in Oklahoma.

429. ———. *Sam Houston with the Cherokees, 1829–1833*. Austin: University of Texas Press, 1967. 206p.

About Sam Houston's marriage to Talihina (Diana Rogers), a Cherokee girl from near Muskogee, Oklahoma. The authors teach at the University of Arkansas at Fayetteville. Gregory is part Cherokee, and he grew up near Muskogee, hearing all the Talihina tales and traditions.

430. Griffith, Cecil R. *The Missouri River: The River Rat's Guide to Missouri River History and Folklore*. Leawood, Kans.: Canfield and Sutton, 1974. 96p.

The material in this book was assembled by C. R. Griffith, a river pilot who was born in Kansas and spent his entire life on the Missouri. After his death in 1970, the book was edited by Kenneth R. Canfield and Richard L. Sutton, Jr. They also wrote a brief biography of Griffith (pp. 87–93). The book traces the whole course of the Missouri from Three Forks, Montana, to its juncture with the Mississippi eighteen miles above St. Louis. During his many years on the river, he recorded legends and anecdotes about towns and geographic features along the way and tells many of them in this book. "Old Griff" was a great man and will be long remembered by all who love the river.

431. Grover, James M. "Ralph E. Hughey: Northwest Arkansas Storyteller." *Mid-South Folklore* 3:1 (Spring 1975): 3–11.

Ralph Hughey is a well-known storyteller of Siloam Springs, Arkansas. The author prints eight tales that he collected "several years ago," including "The New Year's Dance at Elkins," "Willard and the Mayor's Dog," "Bank Robberies," "The Farmer and the Wolf," "D. C. Bruster and the Hershey Bars," "The Klansman and the Pope," "Fire at the Gobson Ranch," and "Labon Jacob and George Kess." These tales are supposed to be descriptions of recent local events, and are known to a great many people around Siloam Springs. As Grover points out, they are very like some of the stories Dorson collected years ago along the Maine coast.

432. Gusewelle, C. W. "A Continuity of Place and Blood." *American Heritage* 29:1 (December 1977): 96–108.

Page 106 has the story about the tourist who wants to see a still in operation. He finds a young boy to guide him to one but the boy wants his money in advance because, he tells the tourist, "You ain't coming back." Gusewelle is an editorial writer for the *Kansas City Star*.

433. Haden, Walter Darrell. *The Headless Cobbler of Smallett Cave*. Nashville, Tenn.: The Kinfolk Press, 1967. 109p.

Tale of a ghost in Douglas County, Missouri. Local tradition of a shoemaker who used the cave in Civil War times. Ghost has a bunch of shoes where his head should be. Book has bibliography and notes, along with pen-and-ink drawings by the author, who is described as "a professor of English at the University of Tennessee, Martin." Reviewed by E. W. Baughman (*Journal of American Folklore* 81 [October-December 1968]: 360–61).

434. Hair, Mary Scott. "Lest We Forget." *White River Valley Historical Quarterly* 5:8 (Summer 1975): 7–8.

Story about Memorial Day, or Decoration Day, with some interesting remarks about the Short family of Stone County, Missouri. Mention of a boy who died at fifteen "from eating a wild parsnip which he thought was ginseng." Mrs. Hair lives in Hurley, Missouri. (The cover of this issue is mistakenly shown as "Fall" 1975).

435. Hale, Preston Orin. *Tales of the Ozarks*. Topeka, Kans.: Published by the author, [c. 1963]. 32p.

Eighteen brief anecdotes from the life of a boy from northern Illinois who in 1893 came to a farm in Howell County in the southern Missouri Ozarks. He was very young, too young to attend school. Mostly about chores, farm work, and hunting small game. All seems true enough, except perhaps the tale about "Wild Hogs" (pp. 28–31). He talks about wild razorback sows that weighed about eighty pounds, and pigs "hardly as large as a squirrel." Hale died in 1971.

436. Halpert, Herbert, and Violetta M. Halpert. *Neither Heaven Nor Hell*. St. John's, Newfoundland: Memorial University of Newfoundland, Department of Folklore Reprint Series, no. 5, 1979. 19p.

See pp. 7–11 for the Ozark tale of Fiddler's Green. The Halperts spent the years 1960–1961 in Fayetteville, where Herbert was visiting professor of folklore.

437. Harington, Donald. "Bawdy Ozark Tales." *Grapevine* 8:18 (19 January 1977): 10.

This is ostensibly a review of my *Pissing in the Snow*, but Harington, a native of Little Rock, discusses his old neighbors. The old-time Ozarkers, says he, ". . . male and female alike, were the horniest creatures in the history of Western Civilization." That's taking in a lot of territory. *Grapevine* is a weekly, published in Fayetteville, Arkansas.

438. ———. *Lightning Bug*. New York: Delacorte Press, 1970. 212p.

There are not many folklore references in this work of fiction, but those that do appear are authentic—see the anecdotes on pp. 17–18, 39, 47, 58–59, and 181. Harington is a native Arkansan and he knows what he's talking about.

439. Harris, Robert L. "Politician Extraordinary." *The Ozarks Mountaineer* 25:11 (December 1977): 16–17.

Several good anecdotes about Archibald Yell.

440. Harris, William. "The White River Monster." *Mid-South Folklore* 5:1 (Spring 1977): 3–23.

A careful study of the monster reported from Jackson County, Arkansas, in 1937. Mostly taped interviews with twenty-two persons in and around Newport, Arkansas. The author, a native of Newport, teaches English in a high school at Greer's Ferry, Arkansas. He is interested in "what has happened to a legend as it has wandered through oral and popular tradition." The paper ends with a long list of references in regional newspapers: the *Arkansas Democrat* and *Arkansas Gazette* of Little Rock, the *Memphis Commercial Appeal*, the *Newport Independent*, and the *Jackson County Democrat* of Newport.

441. Haswell, A. M. "The Story of the Bald Knobbers." *Missouri Historical Review* 18:1 (October 1923): 27–35.

A well-written account, but must not be taken too seriously. Haswell was an honest man; I knew him well. But, he was credulous. He was born in Burma of missionary parents and never saw the Ozarks until he was twenty-one years old. I don't think he ever understood the Ozark people.

442. Hays, Brooks. *Hotbed of Tranquility: My Life in Five Worlds*. New York: Macmillan, 1968. 238p.

A collection of good stories, loosely strung together in an autobiography. The author was for many years a congressman, and at the time of this book's publication lived in Russellville, Arkansas. Many of his best stories have Ozark references. A most entertaining book. Hays died in October 1981.

443. Hinton, Ted. *Ambush: The Real Story of Bonnie and Clyde*. Austin, Tex.: Shoal Creek Publishers, 1979. 211p.

This is the story, as told to Larry Grove, of the pursuit and killing of Bonnie Parker and Clyde Barrow, who terrorized the Midwest during a two-year crime spree (1932–1934) that left twelve persons murdered. Hinton was one of the six officers who took part in the fatal ambush near Gibsland, Louisiana, on 23 May 1934. Due to the illegal tactics employed by these lawmen in gunning down the duo, it was agreed by all concerned that the true story would only be divulged by the last surviving officer, who became Ted Hinton. Hinton, a member of the Dallas County, Texas, Sheriff's Department, had known the Barrow family personally, and even though he was determined that they had to be stopped, ". . . genuinely admired the extraordinary courage, skill, and loyalty that made Bonnie and Clyde stand out almost as heroes in the public imagination." Well, maybe so, but Gordon McCann had an uncle, a detective on the Joplin, Missouri, police force, who took part in the April 1933 shootout in that town when the Barrow Gang escaped and left two fellow officers dead. He and lots of other folks around there never quite shared Hinton's "admiration" for the two. But it's a good story and traces their violent career from beginning to end. Hinton died in 1977. Larry Grove is a free-lance writer and a member of the journalism department at Southern Methodist University in Dallas.

444. Hoenshel, E. J., and L. S. Hoenshel. *Stories of the Pioneers*. Point Lookout, Mo.: School of the Ozarks Press, 1974. 72p.

A collection of interviews with old settlers. Aside from the preface by Dan Saults, this is a reprint of the 1915 edition (see vol. 1 of this bibliography, p. 108).

445. Hoffmann, Frank. *Analytical Survey of Anglo-American Traditional Erotica*. Bowling Green, Ohio: Bowling Green University Popular Press, 1973. 309p.

The only scholarly book on the subject that I have seen—a very valuable work. The best material is probably in the annotated bibliographies, in the detailed descriptions of the literature, and in the "Type-Index" and the "Motif-Index" of erotic folk literature (pp. 160–288), both of which contain many Ozark references.

In the section on "Field Collections" (pp. 69–78), I was surprised to learn that the Ozark collection of erotic folklore is recognized as the largest and best in the United States, although it is only a small part of our large collection of general folklore. It is also surprising to find Vance Randolph characterized as "unquestionably the foremost American collector of erotic folklore" (p. 70). We had not realized that this minor segment of the Ozark collection (most of it still unpublished) was so highly regarded by specialists in traditional erotica.

446. [Horner, Irene, ed.] *Keepsake Stories of the Ozarks*. Cassville, Mo.: Litho Printers, 1972. 96p.

A paperback with a gaudy cover, contents "compiled from local news stories," the sort of thing that used to be sold on trains. It contains eleven feature stories. "Roaring River Old Maid a Witch?" about Jean Wallace, with photos by local men. "The Connecting Link," the world's shortest standard-gauge railroad, from Exeter to Cassville. "Roaring River Gift of Soap King," about T. M. Sayman. "The Day They Hung Clumb," a Berry County hanging in 1887. "Devils' Hole Near Eagle Rock," a cavern. "Confession of a 'Hot Check' Artist," a local criminal named Sutcliff. "The 'May Never Arrive' Saga," about the Missouri and North Arkansas Railroad. "A Wild Thing in Both Men and Dogs," from the *Kansas City Star*. "Civil War Days in Berry County," by local staff, unsigned. "Double Slaying a Century Ago," from the *White River Valley Historical Quarterly*. "Fresh from the Hills," by Marge of Sunrise Mountain (*Chicago Tribune*).

447. Horner, Irene. *Roaring River Heritage*. Cassville, Mo.: Litho Printers, 1978. 55p.

The most complete story I've seen about what is now a Missouri state park. Lots of good stuff throughout. An especially fine account of Jean Wallace, the Mountain Maid of Roaring River, who possessed the power of clairvoyance. The last private owner of the park, Dr. Thomas Sayman, a millionaire soap manufacturer, donated it to the state in 1928. Many photographs.

448. Huddleston, Duane. "Sweet Lips Has Spoken." *Independence County Chronicle* 14:4 (July 1973): 45–50.

Three different stories of a fatal shooting that took place in the early days of Izard County, Arkansas. "Sweet Lips" was the name given to the rifle by the murderer. Another account of this incident is found in *Life in the Leatherwoods* by John Quincy Wolf (entry 584), pp. 68–69.

449. Hudgins, Mary D. "Note from '74: The Two Great Stage-coach Robberies." *Arkansas Gazette*, 8 November 1970.

There were two stagecoach robberies near Hot Springs in 1874. Hudgins gives the facts and the anecdotes. All about the James brothers and the Younger boys.

450. Hulse, Edgar E. *The Ozarks: Past and Present*. Springfield, Mo.: Irwin Printing Co., 1977. 292p.

There is some good material in this book, especially in the section devoted to tales and anecdotes (pp. 159–96). The writing is much better than in Hulse's novels.

451. Hultsch, E. *Claude Piersol, the Kidnapper*. Springfield, Mo.: Privately printed, 1918. 94p.

A hastily written paperback account of the kidnapping on 30 May 1917 of Lloyd Keet, the infant son of Mr. and Mrs. J. H. Keet, who lived in a modest bungalow on Pickwick Street in the southeast part of Springfield, Missouri. Such crimes were not so common then, and this kidnapping attracted national attention. The ransom demanded was only $6,000, and Keet made every effort to pay, but failed to get in touch with the kidnappers. On 9 June the body of the child was found in an old cistern. This book describes the case and the police work and the trials in great detail. Several men were imprisoned, and Piersol was convicted of murder and hanged. There are numerous references to Missouri customs and local history.

452. Hunter, Max Francis. "Jokes from the Ozarks." Unpublished manuscript, Springfield–Greene County (Missouri) Public Library.

This collection consists of seven volumes, each with its own tape. There are a total of seventy jokes. Each volume lists the titles of the stories only, no transcriptions or documentation, and their sequence on the tapes. Max has placed a "B" following the titles of any that are bawdy (there are thirty-two) and advises the listener, "You are forewarned!" Some of the jokes are told by Max, others by the informants. Depending upon the nature of the joke, many did not wish to be identified.

453. Hynd, Alan. "The Case of the Deadly Landlord." *True, the Man's Magazine* 36:226 (March 1956): 44–45, 74–77.

A highly colored story of the Benders, accurate in the main, except for the ending. Hynd has a posse under Colonel York capture the Benders and hold a kangaroo court in a field near Thayer, Kansas. They shot all four Benders to death, and threw the bodies in an old well.

454. Ihrig, B. B. *History of Hickory County, Missouri, 1970.* Warsaw, Mo.: The Printery, 1970. 419p.

In the 1840s a feud between two families living in Hickory County soon spread to include the entire population of this northwest part of the Missouri Ozarks. It became known as the "Slicker War" due to the practice of one faction who tied their victims to a tree and whipped or "slickered" them with hickory withes. The area became divided into Slickers and Anti-Slickers, and things got so bad the governor sent the state militia in to restore order. This story is covered on pp. 32–36.

455. Ingenthron, Elmo. *The Land of Taney, A History of an Ozark Commonwealth.* Point Lookout, Mo.: School of the Ozarks Press, 1974. 523p.

This is really just a county history, but it is much better than most such books that have come out of Missouri and Arkansas. The author has been a teacher and a school administrator much of his life, and has more book-learning than most of the people who write county histories. He knows how to use libraries, and the mechanics of scholarly research. Also, he was married to one of the Keithley girls, and thus allied himself with a clan, the members of which knew all about the unwritten and traditional lore of the whole region—Taney County was once a lot bigger than it is now.

456. Ingenthron, J. H. *A Fictitious Love Affair and Other Short Stories.* Forsyth, Mo.: Published by the author, 1945. 49p.

The title story and the fourth (about the army camp) may be fiction, but the other tales are well known to me. Everybody in Taney County, Missouri, remembered Uncle Dave and Uncle John, and we all heard about the old sow. Probably these stories are true in every essential detail. Ingenthron was a lawyer in Forsyth, Missouri.

457. Jahoda, Gloria. *The Trail of Tears: The Story of the American Indian Removals, 1813–1855.* New York: Holt, Rinehart and Winston, 1975. 356p.

A big book, covers in great detail the whole subject of the Indian Removal, the attempt to drive all the tribes from their eastern homes into the territory west of the Mississippi. There is much about the Ozarks, especially northwest Arkansas. It tells of other tribes, besides the Cherokee and Seminole, already living in Missouri and Arkansas that were deprived of their lands and experienced their own "Trail of Tears." A savage, brutal book—it could not be otherwise. It is well researched, with maps, elaborate notes, and an adequate bibliography. The author began her work at the University of Wisconsin and now lives in retirement at Tallahassee, Florida.

458. Jansen, William Hugh. "A Folktale——On Paper?" *Mid-South Folklore* 3:3 (Winter 1975): 83–87.

A discussion of the difficulties one encounters in reducing oral narrative to print. Professor Jansen is the only man I know who seems to understand the problem as I see it from the Ozarks—his first paragraph on p. 84 has warmed my damned old heart. Jansen, a professor of English at the University of Kentucky and former student of Stith Thompson, died in 1979.

459. Jeffery, A. C. *Historical and Biographical Sketches of the Early Settlement of the Valley of White River, Together with a History of Izard County.* Richmond, Va.: The Jeffery Historical Society, 1973. 70p.

On p. 8 is a revealing anecdote. Robbers came in the night and stole a man's wagon. They "rolled it off a few hundred yards and burned it, and carried off the iron to shoe their horses." I had not realized that metal was so hard to get on the frontier.

460. Jeffries, T. Victor. *Before the Dam Waters: Story and Pictures of Old Linn Creek, Ha Ha Tonka and Camden County.* Springfield, Mo.: Midwest Litho and Publishing Company, 1974. 58p.

Old Linn Creek in Camden County, Missouri, was located on the Osage River; its site was inundated in 1931 by the waters of the Lake of the Ozarks. See pp. 23–24 for a "Lover's Leap" legend attributed to the Osage Indians.

461. Johns, Paul W. *Unto These Hills: True Tales from the Ozarks.* Ozark, Mo.: Bilyeu-Johns Enterprises, 1980. 104p.

This is a collection of stories covering a variety of subjects, mainly concerned with Christian County, Missouri, and neighboring counties. It is a good selection and although a few have appeared previously in other publications, there are some I have never seen in print before.

On pp. 35–39 he tells of the Baldknobbers, a vigilante organization that got out of hand, the end result of which was the public hanging of four members in Ozark, Missouri, in 1889. It's interesting that even now, ninety-two years later, the author finds it prudent to omit the names of those involved. See pp. 39–40 for the story of the Hickok-Tutt duel fought in Springfield, Missouri, that began the legend of Wild Bill. On pp. 41–43 are short accounts of some of the well-known outlaws that have frequented the Ozarks, including Alf Bolen (the Civil War bushwhacker), Belle Starr, Pretty Boy Floyd, Ma Barker and her boys, and Clyde Barrow and Bonnie Parker.

The author, a native of the region, is currently curator of the Christian County Museum.

462. Jones, Evelyn Milligan. *Tales about Joplin . . . Short and Tall.* Joplin, Mo.: Harragan House, 1962. 148p.

This is really a conventional history, but contains more humorous anecdotes than most local histories. The material is presented in forty short chapters or tales. See especially "The Coming of the Bee-Gum," "Light from God's Egg," "The Little Forked Stick," "Split Log and His Iron Horse," and "The House of Lords." The book is full of esoteric allusions fully understood only by the old-time residents of Joplin.

463. Jordan, Philip D. "Humor of the Backwoods, 1820–1840." *Mississippi Valley Historical Review* 25:1 (June 1938): 25–38.

A valuable and amusing paper, with good bibliographical data in the footnotes. Jordan's writings are always richly documented, always entertaining. The *Mississippi Valley Historical Review* was changed to the *Journal of American History* in the mid-1960s.

464. Junas, Lil. *Cadron Creek: A Photographic Narrative.* Little Rock: The Ozark Society Foundation, 1979. 96p.

A fine hardback book about the Cadron River and its environs, located in north-central Arkansas. This is done in much the same manner as Kenneth Smith's *The Buffalo River Country* (see entry 1485). Lots of photos along with text. Local lore says Jesse James visited the area frequently. One such story supposedly caused the failure of an 1880s health spa known as Pinnacle Springs when it was told Jesse had used it as a hideout (p. 42).

465. Kantor, MacKinlay. *Missouri Bittersweet.* Garden City, N.Y.: Doubleday and Co., 1969. 324p.

Although written as a travelogue, this is really a personal portrait of the whole state, and a remarkable piece of writing. There are many old tales. See the one about Jesse James and the old woman's mortgage (pp. 90–91). Also the blind horse and the mule that was not blind, but did not give a damn (p. 100). On pp. 157–58 he tells the old tale with the punch line "Leave her lay where Jesus flang her."

466. Kennicutt, Wally. *Ozark Nature Gallery*. Paragould, Ark.: White Printing Company, 1979. 114p.

This is the revised edition of the original 1972 printing. It is about the animals that inhabit the Ozarks, their habitat and characteristics. All written in an informal manner, minus the scientific jargon usually accompanying these surveys. He includes much local lore and stories about many of the subjects.

467. Kirk, Elmer B. *Four Days with the Dead*. Marionville, Mo.: Marionville Press, 1953. 39p.

The author lives at Buffalo, Missouri, and calls himself "Ozark Pete." But of the nine fantastic tales in this book only one (pp. 35–39) has any real connection with the Ozark region; it contains a few backwoods words and locutions.

468. Krone, May. *Ozark Trail of Poetry*. Osage Beach, Mo.: Distributed by Herman Krone, 1971. 48p.

Mostly religious verse but see pp. 22–23 for the poem entitled "Indian Burial Cave." About the legend of an Osage princess and the caves along the Osage River in the Missouri Ozarks.

469. Lamb, Arthur H. *Tragedies of the Osage Hills*. Pawhuska, Okla.: Osage Printing Company, 1935. 206p.

Accounts of violent crime in Oklahoma, with discussions of several outlaws.

470. Lambert, Roger. "Drought Letters." *Mid-South Folklore* 3:1 (Spring 1975): 21–23.

In the late summer of 1930, a distressed farmer wrote President Hoover: "I call on you to stop all radios and airplanes and all unnecessary electricity immediately before we all burn up and starve to death. There is enough unnecessary electricity used over the radios by indecent music and jazz alone to give some relief for they are going from the time you get up till long after you go to bed with nothing fit to listen to. I have been watching the clouds for the last two weeks and every time a cloud gets in the sky and it looks like rain somebody starts their radio and/or an airplane goes over till we can see the clouds no more and I think it is time such things stop."

Lambert teaches history at Arkansas State University, Jonesboro.

471. Lawson, Marvin. *By Gum, I Made It: Life in the Ozark Hills of Arkansas, 1900–1925*, ed. Ernie Deane. Branson, Mo.: The Ozarks Mountaineer, 1977. 128p.

The success story of a very intelligent farm boy who put himself through the University of Arkansas. He educated all his children, too. He wrote this book, and it's a good one, full of details about rural life, and it's been skillfully edited by Ernie Deane. See pp. 35, 49, 67, 89, 98, 101, for amusing anecdotes and wisecracks. The book ends with a ten-page wordlist and discussion of dialect. Marvin Lawson retired to Conway, Arkansas.

472. Leath, Sam A. "Courtships and Marriages Among Ozark Indian Tribes." *The Ozarks Mountaineer* 4:6 (March 1956): 4.

Leath claims he has translated these tales from picture-writing on rocks; he tells us just where these inscriptions are located, and discusses them at length.

473. ———. "Indian Tales of Adventure." *Carroll Courier*, Eureka Springs, Ark., 5 January 1933, p. 4.

Leath's adventures in the Ozarks, with some discussion of his "picture-writing."

474. Legman, Gershon. *No Laughing Matter: Rationale of the Dirty Joke*. (Second Series). New York: Breaking Point, 1975. 992p.

There are numerous Missouri and Arkansas references, including several of my hitherto unpublished Ozark folktales from a manuscript in the Library of Congress. See pp. 179–80, 217, 439–40, 648, 682, 823, 853–54, and 954–55.

Legman has written many other books and papers on related subjects; the one I like best is *The Horn Book: Studies in Erotic Folklore* (1964). Born in Scranton, Pennsylvania, in 1917, he has lived in the south of France for many years. His point of view is essentially that of a psychoanalyst, an orthodox Freudian of the old school. The late Archer Taylor told me in 1958 that Dr. Legman knows more about erotic literature than anybody else in the world, and I believe that Professor Taylor spoke the truth. There is a full-page review of this book by R. Z. Sheppard in *Time* magazine, 10 November 1975.

475. *The Life Treasury of American Folklore*. New York: Time Inc. Book Division, 1961. 348p.

This originally appeared as a series of articles in *Life* magazine from August 1959 to August 1960. That material was rewritten and added to, as were the fine color paintings by artist James Lewicki, and was published as this collection of 150 stories, legends, and sayings. Though the publishers have taken some liberties with a few of the stories to make it "good reading," all in all it's a good job. Those that concern themselves with the Ozarks are "Jesse James and the Widow" (pp. 189–90), "The McCanles Fight as Hickok Told It" (pp. 202–5), "The Talking Turtle" (pp. 270–71), "High Winds and Funny Weather" (pp. 276–77), "A Little Piece of Thread" (pp. 282–83), and "Snipe Hunters" (pp. 289–90).

476. Littledale, Freya, ed. *Ghosts and Spirits of Many Lands*. Garden City, N.Y.: Doubleday, 1970. 164p.

Littledale has long been concerned with juveniles, and there is a strange teen-age air about this book. Most of the stories were first published in England. Many are literary rather than anthropological or folkloristic—people like Lafcadio Hearn, Lady Wilde, and Moritz Jägendorf. Jägendorf does not write as well as he talks, but he is still the best storyteller I ever met. The Ozark archive is represented in this anthology by one folktale, "Blood on His Forehead" (pp. 135–38), which I collected from Ethel Strainchamps, Springfield, Missouri, in 1952. Mrs. Littledale lives in Roosevelt, New Jersey.

477. Lomax, John A. "Stop-Over at Abilene." *Southwest Review* 25:4 (July 1940): 407–18.

A long poetic speech made by Judge Parker, Fort Smith, Arkansas, in sentencing a Mexican for murder. Reprinted in James N. Tidwell, *Treasury of American Folk Humor* (see entry 560), pp. 363–64.

478. Lyon, Peter. "The Wild, Wild West." *American Heritage* 11:5 (August 1960): 32–48.

In the last of the nineteenth century, legends were created about the western frontier by the pulp magazines and sensation-seeking reporters who were constantly searching for superheroes to interest and excite their readers. This author compares the facts with the fictions, and his conclusions are interesting. Among those he examines are three familiar to the Ozarks, Wild Bill Hickok, Jesse James, and Belle Starr.

479. McCall, Edith. *English Village in the Ozarks*. Branson, Mo.: n.p., 1969. 114p.

A history of Hollister, Missouri. The hotel bears the sign "Ye Old English Inn." This book is not well written, but the facts are there—all that one cares to know about Hollister, Missouri. Of special note is the story of the Hollister bank robbery in 1911 and of the events that took place at the new jail in Branson (pp. 66–70). Old-timers still tell this one. I was interested to learn that Dr. Townsend Godsey, author of *These Were the Last* (see entry 1377), was mayor of Hollister in the 1940s. Profusely illustrated with photographs.

480. McGilvry, Wilma. "Ozark's Hoots and Haunts." *Springfield Daily News*, 30 October 1981.

Regional ghost stories as told by students at Southwest Missouri State University at Springfield. Same old standard stories but in contemporary settings.

481. McKennon, C. H. *Iron Men: A Saga of the Deputy United States Marshals Who Rode in the Indian Territory*. Garden City, N.Y.: Doubleday and Company, 1967. 224p.

About the deputy U.S. marshals who policed western Arkansas after the Civil War. All the great names are there. A good account of Ned Christie, Cherokee outlaw.

482. Mahnkey, Douglas. *Bright Glowed My Hills*. Point Lookout, Mo.: School of the Ozarks Press, 1968. 158p.

Reminiscences and old stories about Taney County, Missouri. The author is a lawyer in Forsyth, Missouri. Though he is not a professional writer, his story is well worth reading.

483. ———. *Hill and Holler Stories*. Point Lookout, Mo.: School of the Ozarks Press, 1975. 232p.

This is a collection of brief anecdotes, a few genuine folktales, and ancient jokes and wisecracks. It is a much better book than Mahnkey's *Bright Glowed My Hills* (see preceding entry). I enjoyed it because I have lived among the people he writes about, and knew many of them personally. His mother was Mary Elizabeth Mahnkey, one of the few authentic poets who ever lived in the Ozarks. I have heard most of the stories he tells, but they are good stories and he sets them down in good unpretentious language. But his interest is always in local history, not folklore. He doesn't write as well as his mother did, but neither do any of the rest of us.

484. ———. "A Slave Song from Taney County." *The Ozarks Mountaineer* 26:4 (May 1978): 28.

Besides discussing the song, Mahnkey tells four stories about slaves told among families in Taney County, Missouri.

485. Messick, Mary Ann. *History of Baxter County, 1873–1973*. Little Rock: Mountain Home Chamber of Commerce, 1973. 506p.

The author is the fifth generation of her family to live in this north Arkansas county. She is not a trained historian and has just set the facts down as she and her informants have found them. There is no scholarly documentation of her data and it lacks an index, but it does contain a lot of interesting material. It is done in the manner of Earl Berry's later work about the neighboring county, *History of Marion County* (entry 385). See pp. 27–30 for the story of "Old Morg," the Civil War bushwhacker, and pp. 229–33 about the Denton-Twiggs feud in Gassville. Page 186 tells of mischievous boys who in the summer during church meetings would switch babies sleeping in wagon beds while their parents were inside the church. Many a poor parent didn't discover the exchange until already home.

486. Miles, Kathleen White. *Annals of Henry County . . . Vol. 1—1885–1900*. Clinton, Mo.: The Printery, 1973. 491p.

Full of brief stories and anecdotes, taken from the files of *The Clinton Eye*, the local newspaper. On p. 222 is a notice about Bald Knobbers in this northwest Ozark county. This is interesting as I have never seen references to this vigilante group so far north. Their activities had always been confined to counties in the southwest part of the state, principally Christian, Stone, Douglas, and Taney. Henry, and neighboring Benton County, had their problems with these organizations in the 1840s, an incident referred to as the "Slicker Wars."

487. Miles, Kathleen White, and Kathleen Kelly White. *Tattle-tales: Bits and Pieces About the Golden Valley*. Clinton, Mo.: Democrat Publishing Co., 1967. 107p.

Facts, figures, dates, and pictures of Clinton, Missouri, and its past. Not much folklore, but see pp. 34–48 for stories of the Younger and the James brothers, and a woman outlaw by the name of Chinese Dot.

488. Miller, E. Joan Wilson. "The Ozark Culture Region as Revealed by Traditional Materials." *Annals of the Association of American Geographers* 58:1 (March 1968): 51–77.

Uses Ozark folk tales "to test the hypothesis that folk materials, if documented, may be used by the cultural geographer." An elaborate study, with maps and graphs, lists of informants, etc. Some very penetrating observations. The material studied is all from my four folktale books published by the Columbia University Press.

489. Monaghan, Jay. *Civil War on the Western Border, 1854–1865*. Boston: Little, Brown and Co., 1955. 454p.

A fine book, with many army jokes and wisecracks. See especially the accounts of Wilson's Creek, Pea Ridge, and Prairie Grove.

490. Moody, Claire Norris. *Battle of Pea Ridge, or Elkhorn Tavern*. Little Rock: Valley Printing Co., 1956. 40p.

A pamphlet sold to tourists who visited the battlefield, mostly a rehash from old books and newspapers, but a few lively anecdotes. Includes a description of conditions after the battle, from A. W. Bishop's *Loyalty on the Frontier*.

491. Morgan, Arthur E. "New Light on A. Lincoln's Boyhood." *Atlantic Monthly* 125 (February 1920): 208–18.

The author, a civil engineer, found a son of Sophie Hanks living in the Ozarks. Sophie grew up with Abe Lincoln and recalled many tales and anecdotes about him, which she passed on to her family. Morgan heard these items from Sophie's son and wrote them down as best he could.

492. Morgan, Deidra. "I Can't Hear the Music for Those Dogs." *Bittersweet* 9:1 (Fall 1981): 48–56.

Foxhunting along the Niangua River in Laclede County, Missouri. The title is the punch line from the old one about the fox hunter who takes his preacher on a hunt. The fox hunter asks the preacher if he can hear that beautiful music (the hounds), whereby the preacher replies, "I can't hear the music for those dogs."

493. Morton, Joseph W., Jr., ed. *Sparks from the Camp Fire, or Tales of the Old Veterans*. Washington, D.C.: The National Tribune, 1899. 469p.

Stories of the Civil War, told by 150 anonymous Union veterans. For those that took place in the Ozarks see pp. 53, 57, 114, and 142. All edited by Morton, no documentation. Mostly tales of combat, but some humorous anecdotes.

494. Mottaz, Mable Manes. *Lest We Forget—A History of Pulaski County, Missouri, and Fort Leonard Wood*. Springfield, Mo.: Cain Printing, 1960. 81p.

Several good stories about this north-central Ozarks county. On pp. 72–73 is the legend of the cave and the lost violinist whose playing can still be heard. See my *The Talking Turtle* (Columbia University Press, 1957), pp. 27–29.

495. Mullins, David W. *History of Sharp County, Arkansas*. Master's thesis, University of Colorado, 1934. 126p. (Typescript at the University of Colorado.)

It is a very fine county history, but not much folklore. See p. 40 for a splendid tale about a settler who had been cheated out of his home, and came back at night to kill the new owner. He was bitten by a snake just as he was about to fire. The shooting was called off!

Dr. Mullins is a native of Sharp County, later president of the University of Arkansas. He once told Ernie Deane that he had a great quantity of notes discarded from this thesis, later lost when his mother's cabin burned. He thinks this lost material may have contained many folktales and dialect notes.

496. Napier, Claude E. *Ozark Men*. N.p.: Published by the author, 1971. 125p.

This paperback is mostly about Taney County, Missouri, especially the town of Forsyth. Rambling narrative with no system or organization. I liked it because I knew so many of the people he mentions. Also, he drags in his soldiering on the Mexican border in 1916—he was a corporal under Pershing when they were chasing Villa. Compare his "The Banter's Lick" (pp. 34–36) with O. E. Rayburn's story "Whetting the Banter" (see entry 231).

497. Nelson, Buck. *My Trip to Mars, the Moon, and Venus*. Mountain View, Mo.:
Published by the author, 1956. 44p.

Buck Nelson lived on a farm on the Texas-Howell county line just north of
Mountain View, Missouri. In July 1956 he was visited by a flying saucer. It was
commanded by "Little Bucky of Venus," and he took Buck on the first of what was
to become many trips into outer space and to the planets. Buck said that "Little
Bucky" was actually an earthling taken to Venus years ago to teach English. This
little book tells of the author's travels and adventures. (My copy came with a
postcard picture of a flying saucer, a counterfeit Confederate one-hundred-dollar
bill, and a notice that I could become a life member of Buck's Saucer Club for one
dollar). Buck got his story into the newspapers and soon began going about the
country lecturing about his experiences and in 1956 also held his first "Space Con-
vention" on his farm. Folks from all over who had also traveled in space showed up.
It became an annual event for a number of years. But by the mid-sixties Buck
claimed that the U.S. Armed Forces radar network had scared the spacemen away
and had also disrupted his telepathic communications with them. "My mind's a
blank," he said (see the *Springfield Leader & Press*, 29 June 1964). Shortly thereafter he pulled up stakes and moved—to California.

498. Neville, A. W. *The Red River Valley, Then and Now*. Paris, Tex.: North Texas
Publishing Co., 1948. 278p.

A great collection of anecdotes, mostly about Texans and Oklahomans. But see
the section "Outlaws Visited the Valley" (pp. 47–62) for tales of Jim Reed, Belle
Starr, John Middleton, Frank James, and others well known to the Ozark hillfolk.
The book is based on the author's daily feature "Backward Glances," which appeared in the *Paris News*.

499. Neville, H. Clay. "A Missouri Vendetta: History of the Famous 'Slicker War' in
the Ozarks." *St. Louis Globe-Democrat*, 6 June 1896.

About the vigilante group who administered their own brand of "justice" in
Hickory and Benton counties in the 1840s, harbingers of the Bald Knobber and Regu-
lator groups that were to appear in the post–Civil War Ozarks. Neville says "slick-
ing" or whipping a person with switches, usually hickory boughs, came from Tennessee and Kentucky.

500. Noe, Fay. *All in a Lifetime*. Chicago: Adams Press, 1965. 112p.

The story of a woman who spent most of her long life in the Missouri Ozarks.
She writes very well of rural adventures, with many humorous anecdotes. See pp.
69–70 for an account of the magic self-filling rain barrel near Houston, Missouri.

501. Nunn, Bill. "Fox Hunting: 'That Heavenly Music.'" *St. Louis Globe-Democrat*, 19 December 1981.

Another account of the "I can't hear a thing for those blasted dogs" tale (see entry 492). This same joke is used by several narrators interviewed in a movie, *They Tell It for the Truth: Ozark Mountain Storytellers* (Pentacle Productions, 1979).

502. Owen, Jim M. *Hillbilly Humor*. New York: Pocket Books, 1970. 124p.

Brief paragraphs, mostly gags and anecdotes. The author lived in Branson, Missouri. I knew him for many years. He was a guide for fishermen—got rich running a float-trip company and selling foxhounds and fighting cocks. Owen died in 1972.

503. Page, Tate C. *The Voices of Moccasin Creek*. Point Lookout, Mo.: School of the Ozarks Press, 1977. 446p.

This is the second edition, revised and enlarged. The first edition appeared in 1972. Started as a chronicle of the Page family and their kinfolk and connections; the book grew into a description of pioneer life in the wildest part of the Boston Mountain section of the Ozarks, some thirty miles north of Russellville, Arkansas. The old settlers—the Pages, the Tates, the Howards, the Cromwells, and the rest— are long gone now, their cabins have crumbled into dust, and even the stone chimneys are fallen down. Most of the region is now included in a Federal Forest Reserve.

Dr. Page spent most of his life as a teacher and school administrator. For some years he was dean of the School of Education, Western Kentucky University. After retirement he returned to his old stomping ground in Russellville, Arkansas, where he died in 1984. He had served as a former president of the Arkansas Folklore Society.

Page's first interest is genealogy, and he is inclined to get a little sentimental in old graveyards sometimes, but he's earthy enough in his detailed description of the backwoods life. See pp. 125–54 for a fine series of old-time anecdotes.

504. Parler, Mary Celestia. "Collecting Folklore on Campus." *Arkansas Alumnus* 12:2 (November 1958): 6–7.

Pleasant paper about collecting in one's spare time—between classes as it were. Mostly sayings and wise cracks, but there are several tales of the supernatural. "Folklore is not entirely a thing of the past; it is still being made."

505. Patterson, Robert. "A New Town in Arkansas." *New York Spirit of the Times* 14:2 (9 March 1844): 13–14.

This piece is signed "Concordia" but Masterson (*Tall Tales of Arkansaw*, 1943, p. 415) has identified the author as Patterson. The story of a frontier real-estate fraud, since the town consists of one house, one family. Scattered bits of dialect, some reference to backwoods customs.

506. Pearson, Edmund L. *Murder at Smutty Nose, and Other Murders*. Garden City, N.Y.: Doubleday, Page & Company, 1926. 330p.

See "Hell Benders, the Story of a Wayside Tavern" (pp. 263–90). See also the valuable Bender bibliography on pp. 329–30.

507. Pennington, Eunice. *Ozark Folkways*. Piedmont, Mo.: Piedmont Printers, 1978. 56p.

This book begins with an "Introduction to Folklore" (pp. 3–6), but the author knows nothing about folklore as the term is used by the professional folklorists. Her book is full of fake "legends" about Indians, undocumented local history, foolish discussion of Nashville country music, and poorly written verse. However, it is still worth reading for a few revealing items like "The Legend of Carry Nation" (p. 24). Mrs. Pennington, the author of several successful juveniles, lives on a farm in Carter County, Missouri.

508. Phelan, Robert. "Stories of Ghost Mountain." *Flashback* 30:3 (August 1980): 9–11.

These stories were collected by one Ardys Crapo, a relative of the narrator. All about spook lights and mysterious sounds that occurred on a mountain in the vicinity of Greenland, Arkansas, in the 1890s. *Flashback* is published quarterly by the Washington County (Arkansas) Historical Society.

509. Pipes, Gerald. "Outlaws and Pettycoats." In *Ozark Guide Yearbook*, pp. 29–36, 61–68. Reeds Spring, Mo.: Published by the author, 1961.

Stories of eight well-known and some not-so-well-known desperadoes who have roamed the Ozark hills and have firmly established themselves in the regional folklore: "Trail of the Bloody Barrows" (pp. 29–31), Bonnie and Clyde; "Bandit Queen of the Ozarks—Belle Starr" (pp. 32–34); "Shantyboat Girl" (pp. 34–36, 61–62), the story of Helen Spence and murder on the White River in Arkansas; "'Ladykiller's' Fight with the Hillbillies" (pp. 62–64), the Hickok-Tutt duel in Springfield, Missouri; "The Hill Folk Plus 'Nice Walter Cook'" (pp. 64–65), about bank robber Jake Fleagle; "The Last Stand of Henry Starr" (pp. 65–66), who was Belle's nephew but gained a reputation by his own exploits; "The Phantom Terror" (pp. 67–68), about 1930s bank robber/killer Charles "Pretty Boy" Floyd from the Cookson Hills of Oklahoma; and "Historic Last Hanging" (p. 68), about the last official hanging in the state of Missouri, when murderer Red Jackson was hanged on the square in Galena, Missouri, May 1937.

510. "Polly and the Cyclone." *Webster County Historical Society* 15 (August 1980): 5–6.

This story appeared in the *West Plains* (Missouri) *Quill* newspaper, date unknown. Polly was a bilingual parrot brought to Marshfield, Missouri, in the 1870s by a local doctor. She had lived her first years in Cuba and spoke Spanish as well as English. She prayed, sang hymns, and repeated the local gossip. It is said she survived the tornado of 1880 by calling for help from the wreckage.

511. Pride, John F. *Bald Knobbers and Other Humorous Tales of the Ozark Mountain Hillbilly*. N.p.: Published by the author, 1926. 113p.

Four short stories in thick dialect. The author can't write, but he has been in the Ozarks. See p. 108 for a mention of *Hookrum*, as a place name. On the title page he says he is "author of *Three Years in the Arkansas Ozarks*" but I haven't been able to trace that one. *Bald Knobbers* is a cheap red paperback, but I paid ten dollars for it at a book shop near Branson.

512. Quesenbury, William. "Fishing in Arkansas." *New York Spirit of the Times* 15:28 (6 September 1845): 327.

Yarn about catfish, frogs, and mosquitoes in a "slue" near Prairie Grove, Arkansas. The author, also known as Bill Cush, was once editor of the *Southwest Independent* at Fayetteville, Arkansas.

513. Randolph, Vance. "Folk Tales from the Hills." *The Ozarks Mountaineer* 26:6 (July 1978): 12.

Two brief anecdotes, "Holes in Her Stockings" and "He Didn't Get No Cash."

514. ———. "Goose Flesh from Heaven." *The Ozarks Mountaineer* 25:9 (October 1977): 22–23, 26.

Account of the wild geese killed by lightning at Galena, Missouri, in 1943. Estimates of the number killed ranged from 150 to 500, and the story made the national headlines.

515. ———. *Pissing in the Snow and Other Ozark Folktales*. Urbana: University of Illinois Press, 1976. 153p.

One-hundred-one bawdy tales. This is one of the "unprintable" collections deposited in the Library of Congress in 1954. In 1975, Dr. Rayna Green, then a professor of English at the University of Massachusetts at Amherst, dusted it off and sold it to the University of Illinois Press.

This was reprinted in paperback (Avon Books, 1977). See review by Richard Tallman (entry 551).

516. ———. "The Plumed Knight from Arkansas." *The Ozarks Mountaineer* 26:2 (March 1978): 26–27, 29.

The saga of Allen McQuary and his fantastic pilgrimage.

517. ———. "Three Tales." *Mid-America Folklore* 7:1 (Spring 1979): 5–7.

"They Skinned Him Alive," collected 1941 in Fayetteville, Arkansas; "The Traveler and the Baby," collected 1941 in Farmington, Arkansas; and "They Seen the Elephant," collected 1956 in Berryville, Arkansas.

518. ———. *Vance Randolph in the Ozarks.* Branson, Mo.: The Ozarks Mountaineer, 1981. 90p.

A reprint of sixteen of Randolph's stories that previously appeared in *Wild Stories from the Ozarks* (Haldeman-Julius, 1943), *A Reporter in the Ozarks* (Haldeman-Julius, 1944), and in four issues of *The Ozarks Mountaineer* (October, November 1977; March, May 1978).

519. ———. *Who Blowed Up the Church House?.* Westport, Conn.: Greenwood Press, 1975. 232p.

This is a hardcover reprint. The original was published by Columbia University Press in 1952.

520. ———. *Wild Stories from the Ozarks.* Girard, Kans.: Haldeman-Julius Publisher, 1943. 60p.

This is Little Blue Book no. 1848. It contains four stories: "The Henley-Barnett Feud" that took place in Searcy County, Arkansas, in the 1930s; "The Case of Helen Spence," murder and tragedy down along the lower White River; "Pearl Fishin' Ain't Romantic," about the mussel harvesters on Ozark rivers; and "To Hell With Honey," Randolph's personal experiences as a beekeeper. Of special note is the introduction, in which Randolph describes his first visit to the Ozarks in 1899. These stories have all been republished as part of *Vance Randolph in the Ozarks* (see entry 518).

521. Randolph, Vance, and Gershon Legman. "The Magic Walking Stick." *Maledicta* 3:2 (Winter 1979): 175–76.

A bawdy tale, here printed for the first time, about an ensorcelled genital and a magic walking stick. Randolph collected this story in Eureka Springs, Arkansas, in 1958. Following is a letter of explanation about the folktale motif of this "vagina loquens" by Legman, a noted authority on obscene folklore. *Maledicta* is a paperback published twice a year specializing "in uncensored studies and collections of 'offensive' words and expressions."

522. Rayburn, Otto Ernest. "Ozark Customs." *Arkansas Historical Quarterly* 18:2 (Summer 1959): 73–77.

An unusual story about "feather grafters" who went about the country cheating folks out of the feathers used in their bedding. Also describes "barking" squirrels and "noodling" fish.

523. Rich, Carroll Y. "The Autopsy of Bonnie and Clyde." *Western Folklore* 29 (1970): 27–33.

Discussion of the public interest and the many misconceptions that arose during Clyde Barrow and Bonnie Parker's crime spree, begun in 1932 and ending in a fusillade of gunfire two years later in western Louisiana. The author says that after their deaths they were forgotten until public concern about the violence of the late 1960s and then a popular motion picture (*Bonnie and Clyde*, 1967) renewed interest in their escapades. This may have been true about the rest of the country during this thirty-five-year interim, but was not the case in the tri-state corners of the Ozarks (Missouri, Arkansas, Oklahoma). Stories continued to abound not only about this infamous duo, but also about Ma Barker and Pretty Boy Floyd. Just as it used to be that every native Ozarker seemed to have a grandfather who had watered Jesse James's horse, now everyone has a grandfather who put gas in Bonnie and Clyde's car. The last part of the article tells of the events of the day of the ambush and the confusion at the combination furniture store and morgue in Arcadia, Louisiana. The coroner's reports are given verbatim.

524. Roper, William L. "When the Clock Struck Twelve." *Ozark Guide* 14:50 (Autumn 1956): 7–10.

Another account of the duel between Dave Tutt and Wild Bill Hickok, at Springfield, Missouri, shortly after the Civil War. Nothing new.

525. Ross, Edith Connelley. "The Bloody Benders." In *Collections of the Kansas State Historical Society: 1926–1928*, pp. 464–79. Topeka: Kansas State Printing Plant, 1928.

Though the atrocities committed by the Benders occurred in southeastern Kansas, stories about them and their disappearance have circulated throughout the southwestern Missouri Ozarks for generations. Also see *Kate Bender: The Kansas Murderess* by Allison Hardy (Haldeman-Julius, 1944).

526. Rubrecht, August. "An Arkansas Folk Tale—Old Ben." *Southern Folklore Quarterly* 30:4 (December 1966): 342–43.

Story of a coon hunt, collected in Seligman, Missouri, in 1960. Confused hunters, working in the dark, skinned Old Ben the dog instead of the coon. Dick Simpson, a banker in Eureka Springs, Arkansas, told me a similar tale in 1953, which I published as "The Banker Eats Coon," in a collection called *Sticks in the Knapsack* (Columbia University Press, 1958).

527. Sackett, Sam. "Jesse James as Robin Hood." *Mid-America Folklore* 8:1–2 (Spring-Fall 1980): 38–43.

This is a discussion of the factors the author feels have contributed to the persistence of the James legend. Of the principal reasons mentioned, he says that if he were to select one over all others that he feels has sustained the legend, "I would select the dramatic irony of the fact that it was one of his own confederates and comrades who killed him," thus making him a martyred hero. This paper was originally presented at the annual meeting of the American Folklore Society in 1969. Sackett is a retired educator who now lives in Clinton, Oklahoma.

528. Schell, Joe C. *Big Sugar Creek Country*. Goodman, Mo.: McDonald County Historical Society, 1969. 95p.

Tells of the family that went to Joplin, Missouri, on an overnight trip. Not being familiar with electricity, they tried to blow out the light at bedtime, finally ended up covering it with a sock (p. 19).

529. Schon, Bill. "There Was a Razorback Hog!" *Ark/Ozark* 1:1 (Fall 1968): 39–40.

The author claims to have seen one about the turn of the century in Craighead County, Arkansas. He says they are red-brown, weigh three hundred to five hundred pounds, and have curved tusks with knifelike edges. Some say they are descendants of those brought by De Soto's soldiers, others that they are just domestic hogs that have reverted to the wild. Whatever their genealogy, I have seen the damage alleged to have been done by one on a farm near Cassville, Missouri, in the 1960s. Razorbacks are not to be taken lightly.

530. Scott, Victor. *Legends and Stories of Happy Hollow*. N.p.: n.p., 1959. 60p.

Happy Hollow was a Bible camp north of Strafford, Missouri. These legends and stories are a mixture of spurious Indian legends and Bible quotes. There is no serious folklore content.

531. Shannon, Karr. *Hillbilly Philosophy*. Little Rock: Parke-Harper Co., 1932. 180p.

Twenty-nine pleasant little essays or sermons, like Shannon's column in the *Arkansas Democrat*, a few anecdotes, old-time expressions, references to folk beliefs and the like.

532. Sherrer, Dwayne. "We'll Treat You So Nice You Can't Help but Like Us." *Bittersweet* 8:4 (Summer 1981): 36–53.

A visit with three elderly brothers near the community of Linn, Missouri, living much as did their parents a century ago, with none of the modern conveniences of the twentieth century. They tell some interesting stories of their early days.

533. Shirley, Glenn. *Six-gun and Silver Star*. Albuquerque: University of New Mexico Press, 1955. 235p.

Factual stories of Oklahoma outlaws, 1889 to 1907. Much about the Daltons, the Doolin gang, and the Cherokee Strip.

534. Skinner, Charles Montgomery. *Myths and Legends of Our Own Land*. Philadelphia: J. B. Lippincott Company, 1896, vol. 2. 335p.

See "How the Crime Was Revealed," pp. 182–83, about an apparition and murder near Lebanon, Missouri, in the 1850s. On pp. 316–17 there is a silly "Indian legend" about Mammoth Spring, Arkansas.

535. Smith, Maggie Aldridge. *Siloam: Legend of 28 Springs*. Siloam Springs, Ark.: Published by the author, 1972. [32p.]

Fake "Indian legends" with poor pen drawings by Ralph Lawson. All about the usual chief's daughter named Star Berry Bright, who renounced the Osage religion and worshiped Jesus, and thus lived happily ever after. No documentation. Paperback pamphlet. Badly written.

536. Snow, Thad. *From Missouri*. Boston: Houghton Mifflin Co., 1954. 341p.

This book is mostly concerned with agriculture and economics, but there are some good stories. See p. 27 for the tale of James Whitcomb Riley shouting all night on a gravel bar, "Jess, let me see your ass." For a hilarious tale of Snow's religious conversion, see p. 33. Then there's the old "Horse Hollow" story on p. 45. Snow cured his corns and planter warts by walking barefoot in the snow, and says his feet did not get cold (p. 89). Chapter 14 (pp. 113–22) is the best story about mules I ever read. I hope it's true.

537. Spector, Jerry. "When the Hanging Judge and the Lady Outlaw Ruled the Roost in Old Fort Smith." *The Midwest Motorist* 54:4 (March-April 1983): 9–11.

The first part of this article is about Belle Starr as portrayed by Speer Morgan in his novel *Belle Starr* (Little, Brown and Company, 1979). The rest is interesting anecdotes as told by the park ranger at the Fort Smith (Arkansas) National Historic Site about "Hanging Judge" Isaac Parker and his executioner, "The Prince of the Hangmen," George Maledon. This last part is worth reading.

538. Spickard, Betty. *Prunella Tittletop from Spit 'N Missit*. Branson, Mo.: The Ozarks Mountaineer, 1982. 72p.

Brief humorous stories about imaginary people and happenings in a small town in the Ozarks. The author lives in Springfield, Missouri, and has been a regular contributor to *The Ozarks Mountaineer* for a number of years.

539. Starr, Emmet. *History of the Cherokee Indians and Their Legends and Folk-lore*. Oklahoma City: The Warden Company, 1921. 680p.

Page 143 tells about the secret Keetoowa Society. During the Civil War they identified themselves by crossed pins on their lapel and were called "Pin Indians."

A large part of this book is devoted to genealogy and tribal records, but pp. 143–63 are fascinating reading about the Cherokee Nation and their alliance with the Confederate States of America during the Civil War. Much about John Ross, Stand Watie, John Drew, Gen. Albert Pike, and their subsequent military engagements. The author was a Cherokee, born in what is now Adair County, Oklahoma. He died in 1930.

540. Starr, Fred. *Gifts from the Hill*. Boston: Christopher Publishing House, 1960. 88p.

This is a little book of cracker-barrel philosophy, meditations about life and love, birth and marriage, death and taxes, somewhat in the manner of the late Edgar Guest. But there is a fine humorous anecdote on p. 12, and several references to folk belief on p. 53, and a mildly amusing wisecrack on p. 70. Starr was a retired teacher who wrote Ozark humorous tales for local newspapers. We were good friends for many years, and he told me a lot of good stories. He died in November 1973.

541. Steckmesser, Kent Ladd. "The Oklahoma Robin Hood." *American West* 7:1 (January 1970): 38–41.

Good account of Pretty Boy Floyd and his neighbors in the Ozarks. The author is in the Department of History at California State University at Los Angeles.

542. Steele, Phillip. *Hearth Tales of the Ozarks*. Springdale, Ark.: Published by the author, [c. 1968]. 25p.

Ten familiar tales, retold in a kind of high school English. No attempt at dialect or local color. The yarns are mere outlines or summaries or story treatments. They are not as widely known or as generally believed as Steele thinks, but six of them are common in one form or another. This booklet is of little value to the serious reader because of complete lack of documentation. His informants are not named nor directly quoted. Nevertheless, this book is worth reading. The author lives near Springdale, Arkansas.

543. ———. *War Eagle: Its Legend, History, and Fair*. Springdale, Ark.: Published by the author, 1979. 12p.

The first pages tell the legend of the young Indian maiden, Se-quah-dee and her lover, War Eagle, the son of a Cherokee chief. Steele notes that when the first surveyors entered the area before 1820, the river already was named War Eagle River. The rest of the book tells the history of the War Eagle mill (built c. 1835) and of the arts and crafts fair that is held on the grounds each October.

544. Stekert, Ellen Jane. "Pissing in the Snow." *Appalachian Journal* 6 : 1 (Autumn 1978): 62–64.

Ostensibly a review of my *Pissing in the Snow*, this article contains some perceptive reflections about folklore in the Appalachians and the southern mountains generally, where Dr. Stekert has extensive collecting experience. A past president of the American Folklore Society, she is now a professor of English at the University of Minnesota.

545. Stevens, D. W. *Jesse James, the Midnight Horseman, or, The Silent Rider of the Ozarks*. New York: Frank Tousey, [c. 1894]. 65p.

This is no. 522 of the New York Detective Library series of dime novels. William A. Settle, Jr., argues in *Jesse James Was His Name* (see entry 1630), p. 188, that this was written by John R. Musick, who often used the name Stevens. Musick (1849–1901) was born in St. Louis and had lived in north Missouri during the 1870s.

546. Stewart, Clinton. *60 Selected Tales from Jake's Barber Shop*. N.p.: Published by the author, [c. 1965]. [64p.]

Short, short stories. Some of these anecdotes may be traditional, but they are presented as fiction. Fact or fiction, they are entertaining small-town stuff.

547. "Stories of Stone County." Mimeographed copy, Mountain View, Ark., 1972. 30p.

Most of these are genealogy, but one student's grandfather may have housed the James Boys (p. 22). Another (p. 27) tells it as it is about an uncle, whom he "really admired in a certain respectful way," who was a "wizard moonshiner." This same uncle, though illiterate, also did a "pretty respectable job of counterfeiting."

548. Street, James, Jr., ed. *James Street's South*. Garden City, N.Y.: Doubleday & Co., 1955. 282p.

A collection of Street's writings, edited by his son. Rambling story of the race riot at Elaine, Arkansas, floods in the Arkansas River, and a fantastic murder story from Marked Tree, Arkansas. On pp. 239–56 is a fine tale about the *Arkansas Gazette*, where Street once worked as a reporter.

549. Sutter, Archibald. *American Notes: 1881*. Edinburgh: William Blackwood & Sons, 1882. 118p.

Sutter was a Scotsman, a civil engineer, who came to America to report on the holdings of the Missouri Land Company, which had a lot of real estate in Barry County, Missouri. Working out of St. Louis, he investigated Barry County, all right, where he did not bathe in the Roaring River Spring due to reports of the deadly poisonous yellow water snake that swam there. But he also made side trips to Vinita, Oklahoma (then in the Choctaw Nation), and Fayetteville and Eureka Springs, Arkansas. What he says about the Ozark region, and indeed the United States in general, is interesting and amusing. This is enjoyable reading, but it has few folklore references.

550. Tait, Samuel W., Jr. "Missouri." *American Mercury* 8:32 (August 1926): 481–88.

With all their faults, says Tait, Missourians are still better than the people in adjoining states. Some rambling tales about political history and Missouri politicians. Tait was educated at Washington University in St. Louis.

551. Tallman, Richard S. "Vance Randolph. Dirty Words and Obscenity: A Review Essay." *Mid-South Folklore* 5:2 (Summer 1977): 67–72.

This paper begins as a review of my *Pissing in the Snow*, but it is really a thoughtful and penetrating discussion of the whole subject of traditional erotica, its collection and publication. The author was a professor at Arkansas College at Batesville and is now a free-lance writer in Toronto, Ontario, Canada.

552. Taylor, W. O. *Seventy Years in the Ministry*. Orlando, Fla.: Daniels Publishing Co., 1978. 181p.

The story of a Baptist preacher who worked the small-town churches in the Ozarks from 1907 to 1976. The book contains several amusing anecdotes. Taylor will be long remembered as the author of *The Old Timers Did It This Way* (see entry 1496).

553. Tebbetts, Diane, compiler. "Legend Texts of Jesse James." *Mid-America Folklore* 8:1–2 (Spring-Fall 1980): 53–85.

These are transcriptions of interviews with seventy-one informants, divided into the following categories: "How Jesse's Career Began," "Jesse's Hideouts," "Jesse's Buried Treasure," "Jesse and the Widow," "Other Good Deeds," "The Notorious Jesse James," "They Didn't Know It Was Jesse," "Jesse's Death," and "The Real Story." These were selected from the archives of six universities and each text is identified by informant, where and when collected, collector, and location of the collection. These informants represented ten states. Of the seventy-one texts, Kentucky contributed the most with thirty-three. Next was Arkansas with thirteen, then, in declining order, were Indiana, Michigan, Utah, Illinois, Oregon, and finally, with one text each, were Maine, Tennessee, and Missouri. It is somewhat ironic that even though Tebbetts tried to locate texts from Missouri, she was able to find only one item. As Tebbetts says in the preface to this issue, this situation "surely indicates only the lack of collecting and not the lack of materials to be found in the field."

554. Thayer, William Makepeace. *A Youth's History of the Rebellion*. New York: Thomas R. Knox and Co., 1865. 336p.

See chapter 8 (pp. 136–49) for a lively account of the battle at Pea Ridge. Several good anecdotes. The author was a Unionist.

555. Thomas, George B. *True Tales of the Old Ozarks: The Story of a Missouri Mountain Boy after the Civil War*. New York: Exposition Press, 1963. 54p.

The jacket tells us that the author was born and raised in the "heart of the Missouri Ozarks," but went to Baker University in Kansas and got his Ph.D. from Boston University in 1913. He was a Methodist preacher, became president of Carleton College in Farmington, Missouri, and is now retired in Florida. These tales are memories of his youth. He remembers when the men sat on one side of the church, and the women and girls on the other side. See pp. 21–22, "The Explosive Egg," for the tale of the village jokers who, with wax and acid, etched a fake "prophecy" on a hen's egg, that the world would come to an end on a certain date, only a few days distant. The villagers were hysterical with fright, but the two miscreants finally "divulged the trickery." Upon which "the prayer-meeting language went on as vehemently as before, but with a shift of spirit from the reverential to the irreverential." There are some good stories in this book. See pp. 28–30 for "Jesse James Passes By," also pp. 36–37 for "Escape from a Wolf Pack." Another good one is "The Headless Ghost" (pp. 47–48). "Hunting for Hidden Treasure" (pp. 52–54) is also worth reading. Dr. Thomas's tales are probably true, just as the title of his book indicates. This is a scarce item now, already out of print.

556. Thomas, Rosemary Hyde. *It's Good to Tell You: French Folktales from Missouri*. Columbia: University of Missouri Press, 1981. 246p.

Texts in French and English of twenty-one folktales collected over a three-year period in the Old Mines region of Washington County, Missouri. These were compared with those collected by Ward A. Dorrance (*The Survival of French in the Old District of Ste. Genevieve*, 1935), and Joseph Mèdard Carriére (*Tales from the French Folklore of Missouri*, 1937). Thomas notes that only three or four stories collected in the 1970s were not among those collected in the 1930s. They also found that the most popular of that period were still the favorites. Thomas is an English teacher at St. Louis Community College. There are some unusual illustrations by Ronald W. Thomas.

557. Thomas, Dr. Roy Edwin. *Book One: Authentic Ozarks Stories About Big Varmits: Bears, Wolves, Panthers. Book Two: Authentic Ozarks Stories About Bee Huntin' and Stingin' Insects. Book Three: Authentic Ozarks Stories About Bird Hunting and Trapping: Quail, Ducks, Turkeys, Geese, Passenger Pigeons. Book Four: Authentic Ozarks Stories About Fox-Huntin' and Fox Dogs. Book Five: Authentic Ozarks Stories About Coon-Huntin'. Book Six: Authentic*

Ozarks Stories About Hunting and Trapping: Possums, Skunks, Mink, Bobcats. Green Forest, Ark.: Larimer Publications, 1972. 48p. each.

These six items are paperback pamphlets comprised of interviews with old-timers whose ages averaged eighty-four, all presented in "authentic" Ozark dialect. The pamphlets are sold by Dox Books in Little Rock. Thomas lists two more on the back cover: *Catching Fish, Frogs, and Turtles,* and *Chicken Peddling and Buying and Selling Pelts.* I have been unable to locate either of these and assume they were never published. He says he collected the stories with a tape recorder, and "transcribed and edited" them himself. I do not doubt this, but I should like to hear the tapes to see how much "editing" was done. I believe many of these stories are actual interviews with old-timers, but there is no real documentation. I hope Dr. Thomas is a good editor and transcriber, as he is obviously a good collector. He was formerly a professor of business administration at Appalachian State University and now lives in Conway, Arkansas.

558. Thompson, George. *Prison Life and Reflections.* Hartford, Conn.: A. Work, 1849. 377p.

Mostly about slave stealers, men sent to the Missouri Penitentiary "for attempting to aid some slaves to liberty." Life on the Missouri frontier, from an abolitionist's point of view. The author ends his book (p. 377) with "Reader, farewell, till we meet at the Judgement."

559. Thurman, Robert S. "'Twas Only a Joke." *Tennessee Folklore Society Bulletin* 35:3 (September 1969): 86–94.

Practical jokes in southwest Missouri, especially in the mining region around Joplin.

560. Tidwell, James N., ed. *A Treasury of American Folk Humor.* New York: Bonanza Books, 1956. 620p.

A collection of over 350 humorous American folk tales containing many edited or authored by Ozark writers such as Fred Allsopp (p. 63), Col. Sandy Faulkner (p. 38), Vance Randolph (pp. 33, 59, 215), and Mary Parler (p. 533). Tidwell was a professor of English at San Diego State College.

561. Tilghman, Zoe Agnes. *Oklahoma Stories.* Oklahoma City: Harlow Publishing Corporation, 1955. 230p.

Tales from Oklahoma history, from 1536 to 1907. Designed for use in schools. Many fine photographs of Indians and whites, with description of frontier crafts and customs. The author was the widow of a celebrated deputy United States marshall.

562. Trachtman, Paul. *The Gunfighters.* New York: Time-Life Co., 1976. 238p.

This beautiful book was first published in 1974—this is the latest revision. Several paintings by Charles Russel are printed in full color, and there are hundreds of splendid photographs. All about Frank and Jesse James, the Youngers, the Dalton brothers, Roy Bean, Judge Parker of Fort Smith, the Doolins, Belle Starr, and many lesser outlaws—many of them from Oklahoma. The finest factual book about gunfighters I have ever seen.

563. Tuck, Clyde Edwin. "The Bowie Knife: Its Inventor, Hero of Alamo, Once an Ozarkian." *The Ozarks Mountaineer* 5:11 (September 1957): 10.

The old story of James Black, who made the first Bowie knife at Washington, Arkansas, a story told by Gov. Daniel W. Jones. The interesting thing about this version is that Tuck says he got it from Opie Read.

564. Tudor, Maurice. *Pictorial Crackerbarrel*. Marshall, Ark.: Marshall Mountain Wave, 1977. 64p.

This is a special souvenir edition of "some of the better told tales of Searcy Countians and news scenes as they appeared in the *Marshall Mountain Wave* newspaper, 1972–1976." It is full of good stuff, over two hundred photographs and articles about life in this north-central Arkansas county. Especially see "The Peckerwood Point Story" (pp. 34–35), "The Point Peter News" (pp. 51–53), and "More on the Searcy County Art of Letting Well Enough Alone" (pp. 55–56). Tudor is a writer and photographer for the *Wave*.

565. Turilli, Rudy. *I Knew Jesse James*. Stanton, Mo.: Published by the author, 1981. [69p.]

The title page says this edition is a "renewed copyright and published by Francena Turilli, 1981." Francena is Rudy's widow and runs the Jesse James Museum on the highway a few miles north of Meramec Caverns. With the exception of a different title and cover and a few changes in the photographs, there is no difference in the text of this edition from that of the 1965 version sold at the caverns (see next entry).

566. ———. *The Truth About Jesse James*. Stanton, Mo.: Published by the author, 1966. [75p.]

In 1948 Lester Dill, owner of Meramec Caverns near Stanton in Franklin County, Missouri, and his son-in-law, Rudy Turilli, a promotion and publicity man from New York, claimed to have discovered Jesse James still living in Lawton, Oklahoma, under the alias of J. Frank Dalton. He was 101 years old at the time, and the cave owners lost no time in moving him to Meramec Caverns. They immediately began court proceedings to have him legally declared the real Jesse James. The court declined, but the trial gained Dill and Turilli a million dollars worth of publicity. Turilli compiled this book, which is still being sold to the tourists.

Although the title page says *The Truth About Jesse James*, inside the title page it is called *I Knew Jesse James*.

567. Turnbo, Silas. *Fireside Stories of Early Days in the Ozarks*, part 2. Pontiac, Mo.: n.p., [c. 1910]. 87p.

Most of the items are hunting yarns, all about desperate fights with panthers and bears. Some tales about deer, wolves, elk, and buffalo. But on pp. 32–33 he tells the "falling stars" tale of 13 November 1833 (a meteor shower reported nationally), when folks thought it was the end of the world and sat up all night, expecting to see the dead rise out of their graves! And on p. 82 he says that Marshall, Arkansas, was formerly called Burroughville, which I did not know before. The stories are the same general type as those in Turnbo's *Fireside Stories*, part 1 (see volume 1 of this bibliography, pp. 211–12). Turnbo never had much luck selling either part 1 or part 2. In their later years "Clab," as he was known, and his wife Matilda moved to Broken Arrow, Oklahoma, where a son lived. He died in 1924 and rests in a cemetery near there.

568. ———. *The Turnbo Papers*. Unpublished manuscript, 28 vols., ca. 1900–1910.

A handwritten collection of happenings in the south-central Missouri and north-central Arkansas Ozarks covering a period from the earliest settlers to the 1880s. Although he published two paperbacks entitled *Fireside Stories of the Ozarks*, few of the stories from this manuscript were used. After moving to Broken Arrow, Oklahoma, Turnbo sold his writings to the Kansas State Historical Society shortly before his death. There they gathered dust until sold to a Kansas City, Missouri, rare book dealer, who in turn sold them to the Springfield Art Museum in 1954. They were typed and put into twenty-eight volumes (notebooks) of approximately seventy-five pages each. Here again, aside from an occasional excerpt appearing in local historical bulletins, they have been little used. In 1977 they were presented to the Springfield–Greene County Libraries, and again there was talk of publishing them, just as there had been twenty-three years previously.

569. Turner, George. *George Turner's Book of Gun Fighters*. Amarillo, Tex.: Baxter Lane Co., 1972. 64p.

This is reminiscent of the Haldeman-Julius paperbacks of the thirties and forties that were sold on passenger trains and in bus stations. These are brief sketches of the more notable gunfighters of the Old West, many of whom contributed to Ozark folklore and legend: Jesse James, the Younger brothers, Bob and Charles Ford, Wild Bill Hickok, the Dalton gang, and Belle Starr. Pretty good reading to while away the time even though Turner makes some statements that are new to me and deviate from the accepted accounts.

570. Tyler, Virginia. "Ozark Personalities." *Ark/Ozark* 1:2 (Winter 1969): 16–18.

A visit with Cobb Gaskins, White River guide from Beaver, Arkansas. His great-grandfather was John Gaskins, a famous bear hunter (see volume 1 of this bibliography, p. 162).

571. Van Buskirk, Kathleen. "Capture of an Outlaw." *The Ozarks Mountaineer* 29:1 (February 1981): 38–39, 62–63.

The folks around Hollister, Missouri, knew them as the Cook brothers, Walter and Lee. These peaceful farmers, as their neighbors referred to them, were in reality Jake Fleagle and his brother Lee, wanted for bank robbery and murder. The law caught up with them in October 1930, and Jake was killed. Lee got away but was captured a few months later. Tens of thousands of dollars in bank loot was never accounted for. (People say that the day of Jake's killing, Lee was seen driving at high speed near their cabin south of Hollister. He stopped at a road crew, where he knew some of the workers, and yelled, "Jake's dead, there's trouble ahead, and I'm a'rollin'." With that he sped off and was never seen in those parts again.)

572. ———. "A Civil War Tale: Nightmare on the Doorstep." *The Ozarks Mountaineer* 24:8 (September 1976): 19, 27.

A white cotton spread, pictured with its owner, is practically all that survived a bushwhacker's raid in 1863. Still in the possession of a granddaughter who resides in Protem, Missouri. There is an all-too-common story of murder and pillage surrounding this tattered heirloom.

573. Vandeventer, W. L. "Justice in the Rough." Typescript, Springfield, Mo., 1952. (Copy in Christian County Library, Ozark, Mo.) 197p.

Chapter 9, "The Christian County Legions," gives much detail about ceremony and ritual, etc., which was not taken so seriously back in Taney County, details of how to make and wear masks, and how a man was initiated, with a noose around the neck and the muzzle of a gun at his breast while he took the oath (printed in full on p. 87). Chapter 13, pp. 121–39, describes the trials of the Christian County Bald Knobbers in great detail. The following chapter is a painfully detailed account of a last desperate jailbreak, and all about how most of them were recaptured. Then comes a long account of the final appeals, a letter printed in full from Governor Frances denying clemency, tear-jerking statements by Pony Boyd and other celebrated defense lawyers, and the story of one young murderer who was baptized in an old bathtub that had been carried into the jail.

The sheriff had never even seen a legal execution, but he did the best he could. He hanged three men at once, on one homemade three-holer gallows. It was a terrible botch, and Vandeventer describes every detail. The burial was a mess, too, and it also is described in great detail. His manuscript ends with a statement the sheriff later received from a professional hangman, describing equipment and procedure to prevent such distressing blunders as spoiled the Christian County hanging.

574. Vickery, Margaret Ray. *Ozark Stories of the Upper Current River*. Salem, Mo.: The Salem News, n.d. 97p.

See pp. 35–38 for the story of Missouri governor Herbert S. Hadley's float on the Current from Welch's Cave to Round Spring in 1909. He did it up right with an entourage of politicians and reporters from all over the state going along with him. It was headlined "Hadley's Exploration Expedition of the Ozarks." There's a good foldout photograph of all of them taken at the end of the float.

575. Viitanen, Wayne. "Folklore and Fakelore of an Earthquake." *Kentucky Folklore Record* 19:4 (October-December 1973): 99–111.

About the New Madrid earthquake of 1811–1812. Folktales and folk history, also many phoney "Indian legends" and fake anecdotes. Some documentation in footnotes. Several good Reelfoot Lake stories.

576. Ward, Dorys, and Joe Senn. *Historical Sketches of the Warm Fork Hill Country*. Point Lookout, Mo.: School of the Ozarks Press, 1973. 70p.

This is a beautifully executed work, a folio-size book with text supplemented by good charcoal drawings done by a Ms. Anita Caldwell. It's all about the Thayer, Missouri/Mammoth Spring, Arkansas, area of the Ozarks. But, it is mostly a history of the region, about the Indians, the white settlers, the development of the towns, their economy, the coming of the railroads, etc. Not much folklore, with the exception of some Civil War tales that may still be heard today in the oral history of the region. See pp. 27–29 for the exploits of the northern Jayhawker, Col. William Monks, and pages 29–34 for those of his counterpart, Sam Hildebrand, the southern bushwhacker.

577. Weaver, H. Dwight, and Paul A. Johnson. *Missouri the Cave State*. Jefferson City, Mo.: Discovery Enterprises, 1980. 336p.

This is a wonderful book, full of photographs, drawings, and maps. The text not only tells the geological facts of each cave, but also any legends or historical matter worth mentioning. It is all done in the same manner Beveridge did in his *Geologic Wonders and Curiosities of Missouri* (see entry 259) that concerned itself with the surface features of Missouri. Interesting stories and legends abound throughout. Especially see pp. 47, 55, 92, 96, and 209. For Jesse James lore see pp. 130, 146, 169, 179, and 266.

578. Wellman, Paul I. *A Dynasty of Western Outlaws*. Garden City, N.Y.: Doubleday and Company, 1961. 384p.

One of the best books about outlaws. Nearly all of the well-known characters who worked in Missouri, Arkansas, and Oklahoma are represented. Valuable bibliography. For many years, Wellman did features for the *Kansas City Star*.

579. White, Kathleen K. *True Tall Tales from Missouri*. Clinton, Mo.: The Printery, 1976. 70p.

Stories taken from various central and southern Missouri county histories of the 1880s, mostly the Goodspeed type of publications. On p. 7 is the story of the Hickok-Tutt duel on the Springfield public square in 1865, and on p. 23 the story of Saline County legislator Morton Palmer, who called himself "the ring-tailed painter" and staged free-for-alls at legislative sessions, even flattening the governor on one occasion.

580. White, Mahlon N. *The Legend of Keel Boat Kate*. Clinton, Mo.: The Printery, 1975. 30p.

Tales about this female "Mike Fink" and her adventures along the river. The author claims to have "13 tattered water soaked pages" from her diary. He thinks that in the early 1800s she actually operated a boat on the Osage River in central Missouri.

581. Wigginton, Eliot, ed. *I Wish I Could Give My Son A Wild Raccoon*. Garden City, N.Y.: Anchor Books, 1976. 366p.

Eliot Wigginton, editor of the successful *Foxfire* publications (six volumes), leaves the north Georgia locale and expands the coverage to stories and interviews from all corners of the United States, Maine to California to Alaska, and points in between. It's all good reading. Of Ozarks interest, two feature articles from the Lebanon, Missouri, High School project, *Bittersweet*: p. 204, "Change My Life? I Might Do Worse," and p. 241, "Friends Are Lots Nicer Than Money." Also see p. 165 for the story by a Clarksville, Arkansas, resident, "We Would Look Through Thick Catalogs and Wish for This and That."

582. Williams, Leonard, ed. *Cavorting on the Devil's Fork: The Pete Whetstone Letters of C. F. M. Noland*. Memphis: Memphis State University Press, 1979. 281p.

This book contains some of the best (sixty-three) of Charles Fenton Mercer Noland's "Pete Whetstone" letters, published between 1835 and 1856. Each is complemented by valuable footnotes. Equally important are the five appendixes that further examine and define the contents of the "letters." The introduction contains a biography of Noland. This book is a must for those interested in the development of southwestern humor in the frontier days of the Arkansas Ozarks.

583. Wilson, Francis. *John Wilkes Booth, Fact and Fiction of Lincoln's Assassination*. Boston: Houghton Mifflin Company, 1929. Rpt. New York: Benjamin Blom, 1972. 321p.

All about how Booth escaped and lived in Oklahoma under the name John St. Helen. Committed suicide at Enid in 1903. The story involved Albert Pike (p. 228). There are people in Arkansas today who say that Mrs. C. R. Banks of Lamar, Missouri, a niece of John Wilkes Booth, paid St. Helen's living expenses for many years. Cf. Allsopp, *Folklore of Romantic Arkansas* (1931), 2:264–69.

584. Wolf, John Quincy [Sr.]. *Life in the Leatherwoods*. Memphis: Memphis State University Press, 1974. 159p.

The chapter "Dreams and Characters" (pp. 67–74) has some good regional stories in it. Especially note the one about a well-known episode that occurred in the 1820s in Izard County, Arkansas, about revenge and murder and two guns named "Jack O' Diamonds" and "Sweet Lips." Even today the story of "Sweet Lips Has Spoken" can be heard around those parts. Also see pp. 106–7 for one entitled "Jake, git a big un!"

585. ———. "My Fifty Years in Batesville, Arkansas." Ed. Nancy Britton and Nana Farris. Parts 1, 2. *The Independence County Chronicle* 23:1–2, 3–4 (October 1981–January 1982; April 1982–July 1982): 1–49, 50–104.

In 1887, at age 23, Wolf left the Leatherwoods and moved fifty miles south to the river town of Batesville, county seat of Independence County, Arkansas. Here he lived until his death in 1949. In 1937 he wrote a series of articles for the *Batesville News-Review* describing the Batesville he had come to fifty years previously. As with most writings of this nature, the subject matter would be of interest primarily to the local inhabitants. But the wit and expertise of Wolf make these reminiscences interesting reading for outsiders as well. Numerous stories and anecdotes are found throughout. Especially see pp. 13, 17, 75.

586. Zinderman, Zeek. *A Pig in a Poke*. West Plains, Mo.: Quill Print, n.d. 80p.

Another comic paperback, full of cartoons, ridiculous photos, and even more ridiculous anecdotes, just the kind of stuff the tourists love to buy.

587. ———. *The Vanishing Outhouse*. Raynesford, Mont.: Janher Publishers, 1977. 60p.

Paperback about privies in the Ozarks. Crude jokes and comic pictures. Another good seller at the tourist traps along the highways in Missouri and Arkansas. See p. 23 for a real old-time backhouse anecdote.

588. Zink, Wilbur A. *From Bandit King to Christian*. Appleton City, Mo.: Westport Press, 1971. 8p.

This pamphlet tells about the reformation of a bank robber. He was at one time associated with Frank James in a Wild West Show, and I remember seeing him in Joplin about 1908. In his old age, after twenty-five years in prison, he settled in Lee's Summit, Missouri, and joined the church. He told reporters that he was brought up in a Christian home. "My folks were all Christians," said he, adding that his great-grandfather married a daughter of Light-Horse Harry Lee, a Revolutionary general, and that all of his brothers were good Christian boys, and were bank robbers only on the side, as it were. His name was Cole Younger.

589. ———. *The Roscoe Gun Battle: The Younger Brothers vs. Pinkerton Detectives*. Appleton City, Mo.: Democrat Publishing Company, 1967. 29p.

Roscoe is a small community located near the Osage River in St. Clair County, Missouri. A couple of miles to the north is the settlement of Monegaw Springs, in the nineteenth century the home grounds of the four Younger boys of bank robbery fame. In 1874 the Pinkerton Agency sent two detectives to try and apprehend the fugitives. They met up with John and Jim Younger just outside Roscoe, and in the ensuing gun battle one of the detectives, a local guide they had hired, and John Younger were killed. The author is a native of St. Clair County and knows as much about the Youngers as anybody.

6. Games and Riddles

590. Baldwin, Rebecca, and Patsy Watts. "We've Got a Pig in the Parlor." *Bittersweet* 6:1 (Fall 1978): 49–61.

A collection of sixteen Ozark play-party games. Texts, tunes, and brief descriptions of each game. No documentation, but apparently they were collected in the vicinity of Lebanon in Laclede County, Missouri.

591. Bowen, Iris O'Neal. *Hully-Gully, How Many?* Mablevale, Ark.: Foreman-Payne Publishers, 1971. 56p.

See the chapter entitled "Visiting the Cousins in Melbourne" (pp. 33–35) for a good version of the old "snipe hunting" joke.

592. Brandt, Terry. "Children's Games." *Bittersweet* 1:1 (Fall 1973): 40–44.

Description of twenty games, the kinds they played at recess in the rural Ozark schools.

593. Coffin, Tristram, and Hennig Cohen. *Folklore from the Working Folk of America*. Garden City, N.Y.: Anchor Press, 1973. 464p.

See "Spelling Riddles" on p. 163; of the nine shown, the first six were collected by Randolph. These originally appeared in the *Southern Folklore Quarterly*, December 1944.

594. Davis, Carl. "When It Came to Playing a Joke, They Were Ready." *Bittersweet* 10:1 (Fall 1982): 42–49.

With today's "sophisticated" sense of humor, the pranks reminisced by these oldsters may seem foolish and maybe a bit cruel, but in the days before we let radio and television furnish our entertainment, folks created their own, partly by practical jokes and pranks. Seldom was any harm done and it all was taken good-naturedly.

595. Emrich, Duncan. *The Hodgepodge Book*. New York: Four Winds Press, 1972. 367p.

A vast collection of folk beliefs, superstitions, riddles, nonsense jingles, children's rhymes, game songs, choosing-up rhymes, jumprope rhymes, ball-bouncing rhymes, proverbs, popular sayings, taunts, childish insults, and juvenile wisecracks generally. The book is addressed primarily to children, and there is little conventional documentation. But the general notes in the back of the book are useful, and the fifty-page bibliography is one of the best I have seen, with many Missouri and

Arkansas references. Emrich died in August 1977, at which time he was working on a book concerning the folklore of death.

596. Escott, George. *History and Directory of Springfield and North Springfield.* Springfield, Mo.: Patriot-Advertiser, 1878. 273p.

This is a rare book and the first part (pp. 1–165) is full of valuable information. For a good account of the amusements and early Ozark pranks among the practical jokers of the community in the 1830s see pp. 52–54.

597. Fitzhugh, Jewell Kirby. "Elderberry Legends and Uses." *The Ozarks Mountaineer* 25:7 (August 1977): 16.

The author says the elderberry found in the Ozarks (*Sambucus canadensis*) is the American or sweet elder. Also called the common elder, it is thought of mostly for its use as a jelly or wine. Because of its pithy stems, it was also one of the best plants for the making of whistles and flutes, pop guns, pea shooters, and many other homemade toys.

598. ———. "Play Parties and Square Dances." *The Ozarks Mountaineer* 22:5 (June 1974): 38–39.

Descriptions and words to some of the most popular play-party games. "Skip-to-My Lou," "The Girl I Left Behind Me," and "Thus the Farmer Sows His Seed." The author is a frequent writer on Ozarks subjects.

599. Gilmore, Robert Karl. "Theatrical Elements in Folk Entertainment in the Missouri Ozarks, 1885–1910." Ph.D. dissertation, University of Minnesota, 1961. 290p.

Baseball was the most popular and competitive game played between rural Ozark communities during this turn-of-the-century period, although Gilmore says that its importance seemed to fade around 1905. See pp. 176–80.

600. Huddleston, Duane. "In Days of Old, When Knights Were Bold." *Independence County Chronicle* 16:2 (January 1975): 35–45.

In the years immediately following the Civil War, knighthood flourished again for a brief period in north Arkansas. Knights took part in tournaments of tilting or jousting to bring honor to their home towns. Human opponents were replaced by rings suspended by wires as targets for the lance. It may all sound a bit silly to us nowadays—as it must have to some of their contemporaries—but from the description given by Huddleston, they sure had a good time. The author is a well-known authority on the White River region of Arkansas. He has written a most extensive work on steamboating in this region that has yet to be published.

601. Kettelkamp, Gilbert C. "Country-School Games of the Past." *Mid-America Folklore* 8:3 (Winter 1980): 113–23.

The author began his school years in 1909, attending Gopher Hill School near the town of Nokomis in south-central Illinois. He gives detailed descriptions of five of the most popular school games: "Blackman," "Darebase," "Hatball," "Sowhole," and "Longtown." Each is accompanied by a diagram showing the layout of the game.

This issue is mistakenly printed as "Fall 1981."

602. King, Johnny. *Johnny the Country Boy*. Springfield, Mo.: Roberts & Sutter, 1973. 140p.

The author gave a series of talks called "The Country Boy" over a Springfield, Missouri, radio station in the 1960s. He told of his boyhood on an Ozark farm some forty to fifty years earlier. The whole book is worth reading. The chapters called "Our Games and Equipment" (pp. 13–16), and "Games and Pastimes" (pp. 117–20) cover a large variety of those played on the schoolyards, with good descriptions of each.

603. Long, Kathy. "Poor Pussy, Going to Heaven on a Board and Other Parlor Games." *Bittersweet* 8:3 (Spring 1981): 43–50.

Descriptions of twenty-four parlor games played years ago that the author says are still popular today in her neck of the woods.

604. McGinnis, A. C. "Town Ball." *Independence County Chronicle* 9:4 (July 1968): 41–42.

This variation of baseball was the most popular among students of the one-room schools of north Arkansas. Because of the difference in rules, it was possible for a team to stay at bat for a week at a time. McGinnis lists these rules, as complicated as any you might find for our present-day sports.

605. McIntosh, David Seneff. *Folksongs and Singing Games of the Illinois Ozarks*. Carbondale: Southern Illinois University Press, 1974. 119p.

Part 2 (pp. 53–110) deals with play-party songs and children's games, detailed description of jumprope rhymes and chants, etc. McIntosh was a professor at the University of Southern Illinois at Carbondale, where he spent thirty-five years collecting folklore. Now deceased, he spent his retirement years in Makanda, Illinois. This book, which is worth careful study, was put together by Dale Whiteside, who contributed a valuable introduction.

606. McNeil, W. K. "Folklore from Big Flat, Arkansas, Part 1: Rhymes and Riddles." *Mid-America Folklore* 9:1 (Spring 1981): 9–21.

Nine riddles and thirty-two rhymes collected by students in an Ozark studies class at the Big Flat High School in Baxter County, Arkansas. In answer to some critics who question the value of material collected by high school students, McNeil points out some significant collections gathered by novices in past years.

607. ———. "Play-Party Songs Recalled." *The Ozarks Mountaineer* 25:10 (November 1977): 10–11.

A good piece about play-party songs with descriptions and words to five of them, "Buffalo Girls," "We'll All Go Down to Rouser's," "Shoot the Buffalo," "1860," and "Tidyo."

608. McReynolds, Douglas. " 'Mysterious Names' Riddles in the Ozarks." *Bulletin of the Missouri Historical Society* 30:3 (April 1974): 205–7.

McReynolds quotes a curious old riddle that Archer Taylor and I published (*Southern Folklore Quarterly*, March 1944, pp. 1–10) and adds a similar item he found in Stone County, Missouri, as recently as 1969. McReynolds is a professor of English at East Carolina University at Greenville, North Carolina.

609. Messick, Mary Ann. *History of Baxter County, 1873–1973*. Little Rock: Mountain Home Chamber of Commerce, 1973. 506p.

See the descriptions on p. xiii of candy breaking, on pp. 163–64 of baseball, on p. 493 of cross questions and silly answers, and on p. 495 of the old prank of tick-tacking.

610. "Moonshiner Haunts Lake." *Sun Scenes* 4:20 (August-September 1981): 15.

This article begins with the story of a mysterious houseboat that disbursed illegal liquor on the Lake of the Ozarks during Prohibition. What follows is an account of the moonshine trade in this central Missouri region. "Children up in Massachusetts played a 'shoot 'em up' game called 'Pilgrims and Indians,' in St. Louis it was 'Cops and Robbers.' In the Ozarks children called it 'Moonshiners and Revenuers.' "

611. Morrow, Gala. "Child's Play, Games and Amusements of Ozark Children." *Bittersweet* 4:4 (Summer 1977): 4–11.

Detailed description, with photos and diagrams, of fifteen jumprope games, with texts of songs and rhymes involved. Also hopscotch, mumblety-peg, and several marble games.

612. Nothdurft, Lillian. *Folklore and Early Customs of Southeast Missouri*. New York: Exposition Press, 1972. 77p.

See the chapter titled "Entertainment" (pp. 50–62) for the texts of six well-known play-party songs—no music, but brief descriptions for playing the games.

613. Ogilvie, Craig. "Conyer's Spring School." *Independence County Chronicle* 9:4 (July 1968): 33–40.

Good description of the activities of this one-room school in the early days of free schools. Tells of the games played at recess, and says that as public transportation was unheard of, everyone rode "Shank's Mare." An ancestor of the author taught here during the 1910–1911 session.

614. Owens, William A. *Swing and Turn*. Dallas: Tardy Publishing Co., 1936. 117p.

A fine collection of play-party songs—texts, tunes, and directions for playing the games. Not much source documentation. Most of the material was collected in Texas, but much of it is identical with that still popular in Arkansas.

615. Page, [Tate C.] Piney. "Homemade Toys and Playthings." *The Ozarks Mountaineer*, various issues, 1973–1974.

Tate C. "Piney" Page grew up in Pope County, Arkansas, an area of abounding beauty, now located within the confines of the Ozark National Forest. He became a teacher and at the time of his retirement was dean of the College of Education at Western Kentucky University. Much of the material in this series of articles appeared in Page's *The Voices of Moccasin Creek* (see next entry). See the following issues: "Fun with Wind and Water: Water Mills, Windmills, Bows and Arrows," 21:9 (October 1973): 30–31; "Pop Guns, Squirt Guns," 21:8 (September 1973): 30–31, 33; "Downhill on a Truckwagon," 21:10 (November 1973): 22–23; "Sleds and Lipity Dips," 21:11 (December 1973): 26–27; "Quill Whistle, Rolling the Hoop, Whizzers, Button on a String," 22:9 (October 1974): 12.

616. ———. *The Voices of Moccasin Creek*. Point Lookout, Mo.: School of the Ozarks Press, 1977. 446p.

An excellent description of pioneer life in this south-central part of the Arkansas Ozarks, an area now contained within the Ozark National Forest. Chapter 13 (pp. 174–93) is titled "Homemade Toys and Playthings"—popguns, squirt guns, windmills, watermills, bows and arrows, slingshots, corncob throwers, feather whistles, corn shuck dolls, see-saws, flying jennies, stilts, and dozens of other fascinating gadgets.

617. Parler, Mary Celestia. "More Riddles from Arkansas." Typescript, Fayetteville, Ark., 1962. (Copy in Special Collections, University of Arkansas Library, Fayetteville.) 261p.

Collected by Miss Parler's students at the University of Arkansas between February 1955 and August 1961. This volume contains groups labeled "Genealogical Riddles," "Spelling Riddles," "Catches," "Neck Riddles," "Fake Riddles," "Thought Problems," etc., everything except Archer Taylor's "True Riddle" category.

618. ———. "Riddles from Arkansas." Typescript, Fayetteville, Ark., 1962. 149p.

Gives 315 riddles, what Archer Taylor calls "True Riddles," some in many versions and variants. Miss Parler collected this material from her folklore classes at the University of Arkansas at Fayetteville between February 1955 and August 1961. There is a bound copy in the Folklore Archive, University of Arkansas Library.

619. Schmickle, Fred. "Ozarks Notebook: The Old Marble Game." *The Ozarks Mountaineer* 22:5 (June 1974): 12–13.

Marbles was once a man's as well as a boy's game. The author explains all about lagging, fudging, taws, "old boulder," all familiar terms at the "settoos." Many towns had a special "marble ground" either in town or between rival communities that provided a lot of excitement on weekends. He gives a detailed description of an old-time marble game, similar to the one we used to call "Hoss In."

620. Smith, Grace Hunt. *Buttermilk and Cracklin' Bread: An Ozarks Story.* [Republic, Mo.: Western Publishing Co., 1979.] 158p.

Pleasant memories of the author's life in southwest Missouri. See p. 51 about an old prank called "ticktacking." Mrs. Smith lives in Mt. Vernon, Missouri.

621. Stallcup, Helene. "Candy Breaking: Country Social." *The Ozarks Mountaineer* 24:11 (December 1976): 24.

Good article about one of the more common social activities of the Ozarks in the nineteenth century that has all but disappeared.

622. Steele, Pauline Davis. *Hill Country Sayin's and Ozark Folklore.* West Fork, Ark.: Hutcheson Press, 1976. [40p.]

Among the many references to games throughout, see the descriptions of "The Flying Dutchman," "The Needle's Eye," and "Pleased or Displeased." Also a good list of riddles, which the author says they called "guessing games." There is a wealth of folklore material presented in this and in a sequel, *Hill Country Sayin's and Ozark Folklore: Book Two* (1977). But this material will not be used or quoted by serious students because it is not indexed or even paginated. A great pity. The author, according to the publisher's blurb, is a graduate of the University of Arkansas, a teacher, and an ordained minister.

623. Williams, Leonard. "An Early Arkansas 'Frolic': A Contemporary Account."
Mid-South Folklore 2:2 (Summer 1974): 39–42.

Charles Noland, under his pen name of "Pete Whetstone," describes a game played at a party he attended in 1837.

7. Superstitions

624. Adams, Emmett. "'Pon Honor." *The Ozarks Mountaineer* 25:7 (August 1977): 32–33.

Adams says that if you "cut your potatoes up and soak them in sulphur a day or two before planting, the bugs will never bother them." Of course you must plant them when the moon is right. Also, when the potatoes are dug and put in storage, put a few apples in with them to prevent sprouting.

625. Aikman, Lonnelle. *Nature's Healing Arts: From Folk Medicine to Modern Drugs*. Washington, D.C.: National Geographic Society, 1977. 199p.

This book is packed with detailed information about medicinal plants, with splendid colored photographs of doctors and their patients in many parts of the world. But the first section (pp. 1–23) is devoted entirely to the Ozark region of Missouri and Arkansas. The author interviews Billy Joe Tatum of Melbourne, Arkansas, Monty Pope of Branson, Missouri, Ella Dunn of Walnut Shade, Missouri, Chick Allen of Silver Dollar City, Missouri, Robert Prewett of Spokane, Missouri, and other well-known Ozark herbalists. A beautiful book with magnificent photographs.

626. Allen, Earl "Chick." *Capt. William Allen, Civil War Veteran of Missouri*. Cassville, Mo.: Litho Printers, 1974. 48p.

See pp. 12–13 for a listing of herbs and roots the author says were used by troops in the Civil War.

627. ———. *Ozark Root Digger*. Branson, Mo.: School of the Ozarks, 1967. 18p.

Chick Allen was one of the "performers" at a "tourist attraction" called Silver Dollar City, near Branson. This paperback pamphlet is "wrote by Chick Allen and Evelyn Fullerton" (his daughter). The booklet, illustrated by very poor amateur photographs, is simply a list of herbs and what the authors think they are good for. Here is the list: wahoo, sassafras, gentian (jenshun), yellow root, may apple, sinicity, lady slipper, red root, black and white snake root, horsemint, hoarhound, catnip, gusleymoke, life everlasting, black haw, slippery elm, wild cherry, mullein, pokeroot, winter fern, paw paw. The book is very badly written, with no attempt to illustrate or identify the plants by any but their common regional names.

628. *American Folklore and Legend*. Pleasantville, N.Y.: Reader's Digest Association, 1978. 448p.

"Ozark Practices" (p. 163) lists various superstitions with many "offensive" words omitted; this is one of those articles that says *defecate* instead of *shit*.

629. Anderson, Clay. "Rural Americans at Work: 'You're called on to do anything.' "
Chapter 3 in *Life in Rural America*, edited by the National Geographic Society.
Washington, D.C.: National Geographic Society, 1974. 207p.

Clay visits farms in the Midwest. Page 76 tells of a Gainesville, Missouri,
banker who possessed power to remove warts.

630. Andrews, Elizabeth. "Trails in the Dust." *The Ozarks Mountaineer* 22:9 (October 1974): 23.

Around Gravois Mills, Missouri, the copperheads and rattlers make for high
ground before a rain. Andrews says the natives examine snake tracks in the dusty
road to see if the snakes were moving slow or fast. If fast, it means a rain is coming
very soon; if slow, there may be several hours to prepare for the storm. The two
kinds of tracks are described in detail. I have heard some talk of this snake-track
business, but know very little about it.

631. "Aunt Betty's Doctorings of Yesterday." *Izard County Historian* 7:3 (July
1976): 28–29.

A list of thirteen home remedies, all to be given with "TLC" (tender loving
care).

632. Austin, Violet. *The Sad and Happy Days of a Country Girl*. Cassville, Mo.:
Litho Printers, 1980. 123p.

Mostly a personal family history about living in the Ozarks in the first half of
the twentieth century. Very little folklore. There is a brief reference to the singing of
mocking birds after dark being a forecast of death (p. 112).

633. Ayensu, Edward S. "Passiflora." *The Anglican Digest* (January-March 1975):
3–5.

All about the Christian symbols in the flower of the maypop vine (*Passiflora
incarnata*), which is common in the Ozarks. "The bud of the flower represents the
Eucharist, the parts of the floral envelope, petals and sepals the ten faithful apostles
of Christ; the corona represents the crown of thorns; the five stamens represent the
wounds; the three stiles represent the nails, and the three bracts on the peduncle, the
Trinity . . . the lower surfaces of some *Passiflora* leaves have round spots, which
represent the thirty pieces of silver for which Christ was betrayed." All this panoply
of symbolism was invented by the Jesuits, and was particularly popular in Spain and
later in many Latin American countries. Protestants in the southern states have
similar notions about the flowers of the dogwood and judas trees, and it is not surprising that they were delighted with the maypop vine. I was surprised to see a very
complicated *Passiflora* design in a stained-glass window of St. Paul's Episcopal
Church in my home town of Fayetteville, Arkansas. This article in the Anglican

Church's quarterly is a condensation of a scholarly paper printed in the March 1975 issue of the *Smithsonian*, published by the Smithsonian Institution in Washington, D.C.

634. Barrett, Viola. "Ozark Profile." *Ark/Ozark* 2:2 (Winter 1970): 2–6.

This is about "Grandma" Prickett, who lived near Hog Scald in the Arkansas Ozarks. Her story, as told by Glen Swedlun, a retired artist from Chicago, is a brief but inspiring account of her life as a midwife. There are many references to superstitions pertaining to childbirth. The magazine cover is a painting by Swedlun of her barn.

635. Behymer, F. A. "Weird Omens of the Ozarks: Superstitions Which Governed the Hillbilly in Days Gone by and Which Still Prevail in Remote Regions." *St. Louis Post-Dispatch*, 29 June 1947.

This is actually a review of Randolph's *Ozark Superstitions* (Columbia University Press, 1947).

636. Bench, Vicki; Jenny Kelso; Genetta Seeligman; Jim Harrelston; Kathy Long; Beverly Barber; Lisa Mestan. "So They Say." *Bittersweet*, various issues, 1974–1983.

Lists of proverbs and folk beliefs, around two hundred in all, collected in southeast Missouri. They are humorous but not without merit. Several were new to me. They may be found as follows: Summer 1974, p. 26: Spring 1975, p. 53; Summer 1975, p. 10; Spring 1976, p. 69; Fall 1976, p. 24; Fall 1977, p. 10; Summer 1979, p. 53; and Summer 1983, p. 69.

637. Berry, Evalena. *Time and the River: A History of Cleburne County.* Little Rock: Rose Publishing Company, 1982. 392p.

See chapter 15, "Medicine, Midwives and Home Remedies," pp. 295–302.

638. Beveridge, Thomas R. *Geologic Wonders and Curiosities of Missouri.* Rolla, Mo.: Missouri Division of Geology and Land Survey, 1978. 451p.

Photos and drawings explaining over four hundred of these geological occurrences, all in a commentary easily understood. Aside from these geological explanations and descriptions, Beveridge goes a step further and tells the legends and stories associated with many. See pp. 8–9, 10, 29–30 for Indian legends; pp. 124–25, the Osage River monster; pp. 226–28, Murder Rocks in Taney County; pp. 342–44, the "Land of Uz" legend concerning the Grand Gulf in Oregon County (see also Rayburn's *Ozark Country*, 1941, pp. 314–16); and p. 397, the spook light on the Devil's Promenade (see also Randolph's *Ozark Superstitions*, 1947, pp. 233–35).

Beveridge was Missouri state geologist from 1955 to 1964. Following this he became a member of the faculty of the University of Missouri – Rolla until his death in 1978, shortly before the publication of this book.

639. Blanchard, Helen. "Great-Grandmother and the Ague Weed." *The Ozarks Mountaineer* 21:2 (March 1973): 28–29.

The common blue-flowered ague weed (*Gentiana*) is not only good for malaria, but also makes a fine general tonic for elderly people with rheumatism. Blanchard's grandparents make their medicine in an oak keg, using sixteen pounds gentian, with twelve pounds of orange peel and some saffron and sassafras and fennel and anise seed, also fifteen gallons of corn whiskey. This should be aged for a couple of months, then strained and bottled. I have tasted this stuff myself, and it doesn't taste very good. But it does make an old man feel better, and maybe it helps his rheumatism, too. The late Jim Owen, who lived in Branson, Missouri, thought very highly of gentian bitters. Helen Blanchard lives in Alaska now, but she must have lived in the Ozarks at some time or other.

640. Bowen, Iris O'Neal. *Hully-Gully, How Many?* Mablevale, Ark.: Foreman-Payne Publishers, 1971. 56p.

Quite a list of herb remedies and folk beliefs about healing on pp. 28–29.

641. Brandon, Jim. *Weird America: A Guide to Places of Mystery in the United States.* New York: E. P. Dutton, 1978. 257p.

The author, an investigative reporter, has visited every state looking into tall tales to find out if they have any factual bases. He is particularly interested in fabulous monsters, flying saucers, strange inscriptions on stones, and so on. His real name is William Grimstad and he is knowledgeable and intelligent. I have met him. It seems to me that he is a little credulous, too inclined to credit some honest farmer's tale rather than the testimony of established scientists. However, what he says about Arkansas (pp. 15–20), Missouri (pp. 120–25), and Oklahoma (pp. 184–87) is interesting reading.

642. Bryant, David E. "Observing Bird and Animal Behavior, He Predicts the Weather." *Today's Farmer* 62:7 (August 1970): 32–33.

Elba Pyles was raised in Carroll County, Arkansas, on a farm near Eureka Springs. He has been reading the behavior of nature's creatures to make his forecasts since his grandfather taught him the signs in his early youth. His wife, Lyda (an author of Ozark fiction and collector of tall tales), says he is 90 to 95 percent accurate and has bettered the U.S. Weather Bureau on many occasions. *Today's Farmer* is a publication of the Midcontinent Farmer's Association (MFA).

643. Buchanan, H. E. *My Life Story*. Ed. Jean Newhouse. Fayetteville, Ark.: Washington County Historical Society, 1972. 42p.

This was a limited edition of two hundred copies published by the society as bulletin no. 59. Buchanan was born 4 October 1881 on a farm somewhere near Prairie Grove, Arkansas. As a boy he cured his warts by cutting notches on a stick, then hiding it "where nobody could ever find it." He tells of plowing up a joint snake; its tail broke into several pieces, but the pieces did not join up as he had been told. He recounts the years spent acquiring an education, culminating with a Ph.D. in 1909 from the University of Chicago. From this point forward, Buchanan's story is that of a moderately successful college professor. The latter part of his chronicle is of no great value to the folklorist or the local historian.

644. Byler, Treva. "Home Remedies for Common Ailments." *Izard County Historian* 9:3 (July 1978): 29–33.

Ten ailments with various remedies given for each. The author lives in Melbourne, Arkansas.

645. Carrigan, Ann. "Nineteenth Century Rural Self-Sufficiency." *Arkansas Historical Quarterly* 21:2 (Summer 1962): 132–45.

Home remedies, herbs, etc., based on a manuscript book brought to Arkansas from North Carolina in the 1850s.

646. Carter, Kay, and Bonnie Krause. *Home Remedies of the Illinois Ozarks*. Carterville: Illinois Ozarks Craft Guild, 1977. 40p.

Over two hundred seventy remedies, listed under the headings of the afflictions they "cure." These were collected from informants who live in a five-county area of southern Illinois.

647. Chittum, Ida. *Tales of Terror*. Chicago: Rand-McNally and Co., 1975. 123p.

Eighteen tales of ghosts, haunted houses, apparitions, and mysterious happenings the author says she heard while growing up in the Ozarks. She doesn't say where she lived, but her geographic references place her stories in the eastern part of the Missouri Ozarks. Chittum is a writer of children's stories and now lives in southern Illinois.

648. Coffin, Tristram, and Hennig Cohen. *Folklore from the Working Folk of America*. Garden City, N.Y.: Anchor Press, 1973. 464p.

Pages 5–6, "Women Who Run with Wolves," originally appeared in *Midwest Folklore* 6:1 (Spring 1956): 38–39. Randolph collected it around Pineville, Missouri, in the 1920s.

649. Copp, Annie Claiborne. "The Haunted Log School House." *Izard County Historian* 7:2 (April 1976): 35–36.

The footsteps of a soldier who died a violent death in the schoolhouse during the Civil War could still be heard many years later by the local people.

650. Deane, Ernie. *Ozarks Country*. Branson, Mo.: The Ozarks Mountaineer, 1975. 191p.

See the articles entitled "Some Oldtime Remedies," p. 52; "Our Weatherman Is Mr. Groundhog," p. 58; "Hard Winter's a' Coming," p. 59; "To Keep Witches Away," p. 60; "Folklore About Hair," p. 61; and "Is It Superstition or Fact?," p. 62.

651. Findley, J. W. *Experiences of a Walking Preacher*. Springfield, Mo.: Roberts & Sutter, 1980. 156p.

Many references to superstition throughout this autobiography by a retired preacher from southwest Missouri. See p. 16 for a ghost story, p. 102 for folk medicine, and p. 156 about logs "riven" by lightning.

652. ———. *A Voice from the Ozark Hills*. Springfield, Mo.: Roberts & Sutter, 1982. 221p.

The chapter entitled "Hants" (pp. 161–74) is a mixture of humorous stories, strange happenings, and ghosts and apparitions, with the latter leaning heavily on "sweeping white things" and "balls of fire." Also see pp. 24, 76, and 82.

653. "Fish Folklore." *Ark/Ozark* 1:4 (Summer 1969): 16.

Superstitions and tales about fish and fishing.

654. Fitzhugh, Jewell Kirby. "Elderberry Legends and Uses." *The Ozarks Mountaineer* 25:7 (August 1977): 16.

This article tells the legend of the elder and Old Christmas Eve, which says that the elder, regardless of weather conditions, will send up its shoots on that particular night. (Also see Randolph's *Ozark Superstitions*, p. 78.)

655. Foldvary, Ron. "Ghost Hollow: A Living Museum." *Flashback* 29:1 (May 1979): 23–26.

Reports of a woman's ghost that runs through this hollow located within the town of Fayetteville, Arkansas. *Flashback* is a quarterly publication of the Washington County, Arkansas, Historical Society.

656. Frost, Gavin. *Witchcraft: The Way to Serenity*. Salem, Mo.: School of Wicca, 1974. 28p.

Put out by the now-defunct Coven of Boskendnan–School of Wicca, this Salem, Missouri, witches coven would, according to the form in this booklet, enroll one as a "student witch" and subsequently (to quote the enclosed diploma) as a "Doctor of Celtic Witchcraft," all for ten dollars. The author, an Englishman who claimed a Ph.D. from the University of London, pulled up stakes in 1977, three years after he and his wife arrived in this central Missouri Ozarks community, and headed for parts unknown. Because of this and other publications, Frost has been tagged the "mail order witch."

657. Gage, Allen. "Is the Sign Right?" *Bittersweet* 8:3 (Spring 1981): 51–53.

Three informants tell of various planting activities and other chores about the farm that must be carried out in compliance with rules pertaining to the phases of the moon and the signs of the Zodiac.

658. Gannon, Robert. "Balls o' Fire." *Popular Mechanics* 124:3 (September 1965): 116–19, 207–8, 211.

All about the spooklight near Joplin, Missouri. The local people say it is "a ghost, a miner with his lantern searching for children carried off by the Indians, a will-o-the-wisp, glowing minerals, or hoodoo." Gannon thinks it is caused by automobile headlights on U.S. Highway 66, ten miles distant.

659. Gideon, Gene. "Folklore." *Ozark Highways* (Winter 1972): 48–49.

Discussion of some folk medicines. The author believes madstones do cure rabid bites.

660. Godsey, Townsend. "Fading Ghosts of the Ozarks." *The Ozarks Mountaineer* 23:9 (October 1975): 16–17.

A good account of the decay of ghost-story telling in the Ozarks; many quotes from May Kennedy McCord's writings, and my own, on the subject. McCord always said the shortage of ghost stories was due to the fact that there are so few "lonesome places" nowadays, no deserted houses or old covered bridges or neglected burying grounds for ghosts to haunt. Godsey thinks our new electric lights are bad for ghosts. It is certainly true that the hillfolk do not devote whole evenings to telling tales of the supernatural as they did in the early days, or even within my own memory.

661. Hail, S. A. "A Short Story of My Long Life." *The Independence County Chronicle* 20:4 (July 1979): 4–37.

On pp. 10–11, Hail describes the Ozarker's reaction to the visit of the great comet of 1859 and to the display of the aurora borealis in 1860.

662. Hand, Wayland D. "A Few Unusual Folk Beliefs from the Ozark Country."
   Mid-South Folklore 3 : 3 (Winter 1975): 105–8.

Hand lists about thirty items collected from his students at UCLA, but all
brought to California by people from the Ozark region, south Missouri and north
Arkansas. Nearly all of them are represented in the Parler Archives at the University
of Arkansas.

663. Hardaway, B. Touchstone. *These Hills My Home*. Point Lookout, Mo.: School
   of the Ozarks Press, [1972?]. 95p.

About a family that lived in Low Gap in Newton County, Arkansas, the first
part of this century. See pp. 10–11, "The 'Sang Hunters," about the gathering of
ginseng.

664. Harral, Rex. "Grandma's Do-It-Yourself Doctoring Kit." *The Ozarks Mountaineer* 20 : 3 (April 1972): 26–27.

The "kit" referred to in this article was a half-full sack of fresh cow manure.
The author recalls suffering from that nemesis of all barefoot boys, the stone bruise.
Grandma's cure was to tie his foot in the sack overnight. By morning he claims the
bruise had erupted and after a cleansing application of lye soap and hot water,
he was cured. I've always considered this particular remedy as one of those where
the patient survived in spite of the cure. (Also see Ella Dunn's *Granny Woman of the
Hills* [see entry 879], pp. 23–24.)

665. Hassinger, Edward W., and Robert L. McNamara. *Family Health Practices
   Among Open-Country People in a South Missouri County*. Columbia, Mo.:
   Research Bulletin no. 699, University of Missouri College of Agriculture,
   1959. 25p.

A statistical survey, this one of 152 rural households in Laclede County, Missouri. See pp. 21–24 about home medications, listing the 92 commercial medicines
and the 42 "home-made remedies" found being used in these homes.

666. Hawk, Kathy. "Old Time Cures." *Bittersweet* 3 : 2 (Winter 1975): 21.

Old-time home remedies for what ailed the family horse, collected near
Lebanon, Missouri.

667. Holliday, Don R. *Autobiography of an American Family*. Ph.D. dissertation,
   University of Minnesota, 1974. 254p.

See pp. 92–98 for folk beliefs and superstitions about Ozark agriculture, herb
remedies, hunting, fishing, and other matters of interest to the folklorist.

668. Holman, Nancy. "Orenda: The Philosophy and Practices of a Modern Day Springfield Witch." *Springfield Magazine*—part 1: 2:5 (October 1980): 28–31; part 2: 2:6 (November 1980): 44–46.

A visit with a twenty-two-year-old high priestess of the Church of Wicca in which she explains her philosophy of "neo-paganism." The author attends a Wiccan ceremony complete with robes and hoods, candles and incense, incantations and ritual.

669. Horner, Irene. *Roaring River Heritage*. Cassville, Mo.: Litho Printers, 1978. 55p.

See chapter 4 (pp. 23–31) for a good account of Jean Wallace, the Witch of Roaring River, who was believed to possess the powers of clairvoyance. She lived alone for more than forty-eight years on a mountain overlooking Roaring River State Park. Folks visited her from all parts of the Ozarks hoping to make use of her "sixth sense." She died in the fire that destroyed her cabin in 1940. There are several photographs that I had not seen before.

670. ———. "Roaring River Old Maid A Witch?" In *Keepsake Stories of the Ozarks*, pp. 5–20. Cassville, Mo.: Litho Printers, 1975.

This article is essentially the same one that appears later in the author's *Roaring River Heritage* (see preceding entry).

671. Huddleston, Duane. "Sweet Lips Has Spoken." *Independence County Chronicle* 14:4 (July 1973): 45–50.

The vision or screech of an owl predicted death in this story of murder in the 1820s in Izard County, Arkansas. This omen is also mentioned in Randolph's *Ozark Superstitions*, p. 245.

672. Ihrig, B. B. *History of Hickory County, Missouri, 1970*. Warsaw, Mo.: The Printery, 1970. 419p.

Pages 44–45 tells of an affliction known as "old Missouri Ague" and its remedies. The author says it left the country when the wild turkeys vanished.

673. Ingenthron, Elmo. *Borderland Rebellion: A History of the Civil War on the Missouri-Arkansas Border*. Branson, Mo.: The Ozarks Mountaineer, 1980. 373p.

This is the most complete story to date of the conflict that all but depopulated this region during the Civil War. But Ingenthron is a historian, and he makes no reference to the many folktales spawned in the Ozarks by incidents of this period. For example, one such incident that later gave rise to a popular "headless ghost" tale can be found in the chapter entitled "Border Guerrillas and Bushwhackers," with its story of Alf Bolin, the Confederate guerrilla (pp. 285–89). Bolin, one of the most feared of all the border ruffians terrorizing the area around Taney County, Missouri, was ultimately killed and his decapitated head taken to Springfield, where it allegedly was displayed on a pole in public.

674. Jeffery, Wendell. "Ginseng . . . Ozark Gold." *Missouri Conservationist* 40:8 (August 1979): 12–13.

American ginseng (*Panax quinquefolium*) is the most valuable forest perennial harvested in Missouri. Its dried roots are now bringing up to $140 per pound, practically all of it going to the Chinese market. But it is close to being placed on the endangered species list. Reasons for this problem and instructions for its conservation are discussed.

675. Johns, Paul W. *Unto These Hills: True Tales from the Ozarks.* Ozark, Mo.: Bilyeu-Johns Enterprises, 1980. 104p.

The Ozarks have an abundance of springs, including many that were credited with curative powers, and these fostered short-lived towns. On pp. 67–69 Johns tells of two of these, Reno and Ponce de Leon. The latter was founded by a man with the appropriate name of Fountain T. Welch. On pp. 98–99 are listed fourteen "old-time" Ozark beliefs and superstitions.

676. Johnston, James J. "Haints on Bear Creek." *The Ozarks Mountaineer* 19:7 (August 1971): 29.

Haunted cabins near Marshall, Arkansas.

677. Kantor, MacKinlay. *Missouri Bittersweet.* Garden City, N.Y.: Doubleday and Co., 1969. 324p.

This is presented as a kind of travelogue, a series of brief essays about the places Kantor visited. There are many references to folk beliefs. Note the matter of the cattle kneeling on Christmas Eve, a story he got from Betty Love of Springfield, Missouri, who actually *saw* a whole herd of cows on their knees (pp. 83–89). *Missouri Bittersweet* is the most enjoyable book I have read in a long time.

678. Kennedy, Steele T. "Is There Gold Near Cass?" *Arkansas Democrat Magazine*, Little Rock, 20 July 1958.

About an elusive Spanish treasure of gold in Franklin County, Arkansas. One fellow "witched" for it with a three-pronged peach-tree switch. To not leave anything to chance he placed a silver coin in one prong, a gold one in the second, and a copper one in the third.

679. Kennicutt, Wally. *Ozark Nature Gallery*. Paragould, Ark.: White Printing Co., 1979. 114p.

Some superstitions about snakes, lizards, and sea serpents. See pp. 86, 95, 104–5.

680. King, Johnny. *Johnny the Country Boy*. Springfield, Mo.: Roberts & Sutter, 1973. 140p.

The chapters in this book are based upon scripts used by the author on a radio program he hosted in the late 1960s on KGBX in Springfield, Missouri. The chapter entitled "Aches, Pains, and Remedies" (pp. 29–32) is mostly about a salve the author's grandmother concocted from the bark of a "mysterious tree." He describes in detail how she made the salve but does not identify the tree. I also liked his treatment of "Superstitions and Prediction" (pp. 113–16). This is a good book.

681. Klomps, Virginia. "Herb Remedies." *Missouri Conservationist* 41:8 (August 1980): 12–15.

Tells of the *Doctrine of Signatures*, an ancient belief that every ailment had a specific remedy, and that an object's shape, color, and taste was a clue to the illness it could treat. Toothwort (*Dentaria laciniata*) has ivory-colored flowers, so it was used for problems of the teeth; bleeding heart (*Dicentra spectabilis*) has red, heart-shaped petals, so it was for heart disease, and so on. Some of those common to the Ozarks are discussed.

682. Koenig, Paul. "Madstones." *Missouri Conservationist* 42:11 (November 1981): 22–24.

Photographs of the "Nelson Madstone," over one hundred years old, that has reportedly treated more than fifteen hundred persons, of whom only one died. Other well-known Missouri madstones are discussed. According to this article, the correct term for this product of the rumen of a deer is *bezoar*, a Persian word meaning the expulsion of poison. The author is the associate editor for *Outdoor Life* magazine.

683. Krause, Bonnie. "The Legend of Dug Hill." *Mid-America Folklore* 10:1 (Spring 1982): 24–26.

Dug Hill is located in Union County in the southern Illinois Ozarks. For generations stories of the supernatural have been associated with this locale. The author relates five of these "haunts."

684. Lamp, Ann. "Pages from an Ozarks Herbal." *The Ozarks Mountaineer* 20:11 (December 1972): 34–35.

About the medicinal values of wild ginger, mayapple (which she calls American mandrake), burdock, and many others. A good paper.

685. ———. "Uses for Queen Anne's Lace, Mullein, and Wapatoo." *The Ozarks Mountaineer* 21:8 (September 1973): 20–21.

Queen Anne's lace for stimulants, diuretics, and carminatives; mullein for hay fever, croup, and asthma; wapatoo for diuretics and anticorbutics. Brief instructions for preparations of each.

686. Lyon, Marguerite. "Lady of the Hills." Unpublished manuscript, Forsyth, Mo., 1948. 234p.

The "Lady" in this biography was Mary Elizabeth Mahnkey of Taney County, Missouri, who received national acclaim for her writings and poetry about the Ozarks (see volume 1 of this bibliography, pp. 175–76, 224, 254–55, 296, 313, 334, 439–40). MEM was a hill woman in the true sense of the word. She harbored many superstitions and talks about many of them throughout this manuscript. See pp. 54–55 for a good account of a "dumb supper," pp. 76–77 for weather lore, pp. 182–83 about "haints." Other references are found on pp. 9, 97–98, 167–68, and 229. There is also much about folk medicine; see pp. 41–43, 116, 128–31. MEM believed in these cures, as did most of her contemporaries in the Ozarks, and used them with good results. She saw nothing unusual about them but considered them God's gift to the well-being of her family. Modern medicine has discovered that many of them are more fact than fiction.

687. McCoy, Max. "The Legend of the Spook Light." *The Ozarks Mountaineer* 26:8–9 (September-October 1978): 58.

Another article about the mysterious light that appears on a lonely road near Hornet, south of Joplin, Missouri. The author mentions three of the many legends associated with the phenomenon.

688. McGrath, Martha. "Marshfield's Medicinal Spring." *The Ozarks Mountaineer* 29:4–5 (June 1981): 29.

The great cyclone of 1880 devastated this Webster County, Missouri, town. It also caused the appearance of a spring, whose alleged curative powers gave rise to the town's reputation as a health spa. This interest soon dwindled, but its brief popularity contributed towards Marshfield's recovery from the storm.

689. McKay, A. F. "Eureka Springs, The Gem of the Ozark Mountains." *Daily Times-Echo*, Eureka Springs, Ark. September 1894.

Fine full-page article, apparently reprinted from *American Climates and Resorts*, published by the American Health Resort Association. Compares the mysterious curative powers of the waters of Eureka Springs with those of Hot Springs, with which "it is so often confounded in the minds of physicians and others." The author was a physician who had lived in Eureka Springs.

American Climates and Health Resorts, in which this article appeared in 1893, was a journal published in Chicago. It was edited by Dr. McKay, who visited health resorts all over America. This same article was reprinted in the *Eureka Springs Weekly Flashlight*, 16 June 1901.

690. Mahnkey, Doug. "The Madstone: Talisman of the Hills." *The Ozarks Mountaineer* 19:3 (April 1971): 20–21.

Four stories "authenticating" the power of madstones in the southern Missouri Ozarks. These accounts are based on personal interviews conducted by the author, a lawyer and life-long resident of Taney County, Missouri. Includes a good photograph of Mahnkey holding a piece of the York family madstone that was cut into sections and divided among the sons of the original owner upon his death.

691. Mason, Tom. "The Legends of Haunted Bridge." *Springfield Magazine* 2:5 (October 1980): 32–33.

Strange happenings on "Hatchet Man's Bridge," just north of Springfield, Missouri.

692. Massey, Ellen Gray. *Bittersweet Country*. Garden City, N.Y.: Anchor Press, 1978. 434p.

The chapter entitled "Old-Time Cures" (pp. 252–56) lists sixty home remedies collected by the *Bittersweet* staff in Laclede County, Missouri.

693. Masterson, Mike. "White River Monster Is a Part of Newport Legend and History." *Newport* (Arkansas) *Independent*. Centennial edition, 11 August 1975.

This is the same "Monster" that Bram Bateman saw in the summer of 1937. I wrote about him myself in *We Always Lie to Strangers* (1951, pp. 72–74), but Masterson brings the tale up to date. People around Newport and Jacksonport State Park still see the critter occasionally. Jimmy Driftwood has written a ballad about it, and Josephine Graham has painted a fine picture showing the monster captured with a lasso and dragged out on a sandbar, with a great crowd of Suggins standing around looking at it. Mrs. Graham saw the monster as a very large paddlefish, with a rope around its long nose. She thinks it broke loose from its captors and escaped into the river. Mike Masterson is the editor of the *Hot Springs Sentinel-Record* now, but he used to live in Newport and knows all the boys up the creek.

694. May, Leland C. "Old Fashion Remedies." *The Ozarks Mountaineer* 28:2–3 (April 1980): 54.

A dozen or so cures for colds, sore throats, earaches, boils, warts, measles, arthritis, appendicitis, and stomach aches.

695. Messick, Mary Ann. *History of Baxter County, 1873–1973*. Little Rock: Mountain Home Chamber of Commerce, 1973. 506p.

An interesting, relatively contemporary legend is that of a mysterious small plane that was allegedly shot down and crashed into the waters of Lake Norfolk during the lake's construction in the early days of World War II (p. 324). Divers found nothing beneath the waters, and neither the beating of drums nor the floating of loaves of bread upon the water produced any evidence of the pilot. Other superstitions are found on pp. 7, 203–4, and 208. On p. 134 Messick tells about persons called "blood-stoppers" who were believed to have the power to stop bleeding by prayer. Madstones are also discussed. A list of home remedies is given on pp. 335–36.

696. Middleton, Garland. *Spooksville Ghost Lights*. No publishing data given. 12p.

This is a little booklet sold to the tourists who come to see the mysterious light that appears nightly on a county road south of Joplin, Missouri. It is just a collection of newspaper articles and testimonial letters about the light and its legend. The author bills himself as the curator of the Spooksville Museum.

697. Miles, Kathleen White, compiler. *Annals of Henry County—Vol. 1, 1885–1900*. Clinton, Mo.: The Printery, 1973. 491p.

A collection of articles excerpted from the *Clinton Eye* newspaper, mostly obituaries, births, and social events pertaining to the Clinton and Henry County area. But there are occasional folklore references. See p. 194 about the "White Doe Madstone." Its reputation was such that the owner offered to sell shares in it. More about madstones on pp. 86 and 202. On p. 215 is the story of a girl with mysterious electric powers who picked up a cat and electrocuted it. On p. 311 a doctor advertises that he can straighten cross-eyes or remove a cataract in thirty minutes without pain and without the use of chloroform. This work contains a thorough index. No volume 2 of the *Annals* has yet appeared.

698. Miller, E. Joan Wilson. "Ozark Superstitions as Geographic Documentation." *Forum and Journal of the Professional Geographer* 24:3 (August 1972): 223–26.

A painstaking study of my *Ozark Superstitions* (1947). Dr. Miller selected 1,715 distinct items of belief for special attention, and prints a fine map to show their distribution. "Some folk material, when analyzed, may offer clues to the resources of the habitat in which they are effective. A traditional way of thinking and doing takes place in a specific locale, with such a resource base known, valued and used by the folk. A relationship may be deduced by the study of superstitions, the indices of items within the habitat." Miller is all for an interdisciplinary work in which the cultural geographer and folklorist "contribute to a further understanding of the dynamics of the regionalisms of man's occupance." Miller is an Englishwoman who got her geography in Europe, I think, and then came to Indiana University. Dorson sent her to me in Fayetteville. A very smart lady, and a very good writer.

699. Mills, Glenn. "An Interview with Chick Allen, Root Man of the Ozarks." *Ozark Highways* (Fall 1972): 22–27.

Chick Allen is a native Ozarker who runs a small tourist attraction near Branson, Missouri, called the Wash Gibbs Free Museum. His knowledge of folk medicine through the use of roots and herbs and his gift of gab have earned him appearances on national television and on the college circuit. A list of fourteen herbs and their medicinal uses is given.

700. "Moonshiner Haunts Lake." *Sun Scenes* 4:20 (August-September 1981): 15.

During the Depression of the early 1930s, a phantom moonshiner allegedly plied his trade along the shores and coves of the Lake of the Ozarks in central Missouri. As he was never caught by the authorities, his existence couldn't be contested, this being the determining factor in substantiating an apparition as fact. Phantoms abounded in the Ozarks during Prohibition. *Sun Scenes* is a publication given free of charge at motels and shops for the tourist trade.

701. Morris, James S. "The Shawnee's River Devil." In *Ozark Guide Yearbook*, pp. 10–11. Reeds Spring, Mo.: Gerald Pipes, 1961.

An Indian legend about the formation of Reelfoot Lake that resulted from the New Madrid earthquake in 1811.

702. Morson, Donald, Frank Reuter, and Wayne Viitanen. "Negro Folk Remedies Collected in Eudora, Arkansas, 1974–1975." *Mid-South Folklore* 4:1 (Spring 1976): 11–24.

Important not so much because it contains much new material (most of it is in Newbell Niles Puckett, *Folk Beliefs of the Southern Negro*, 1926), but because of long quotes directly from the field tapes—live, vivid, clear, a brief but stimulating paper.

703. Mottaz, Mable Manes. *Lest We Forget—A History of Pulaski County, Missouri, and Fort Leonard Wood*. Springfield, Mo.: Cain Printing, 1960. 81p.

Pulaski County is located in the north-central Ozarks. See pp. 41–42 for a list of fifteen local superstitions.

704. Nelson, G. Pepper. "Ozark Witchcraft Tradition Runs Deep in Them Thar Hills." *Springfield Magazine* 2:5 (October 1980): 20–23.

An interview with an elderly native of the south Missouri region whom the author calls "the oldtimer." Stories of a herblorist (he claims the late Chick Allen was the finest), power doctors, incantations, hexes, counterspells, and witches. He says that although there are still witches in the Ozarks, they are not of the older tradition.

705. Nothdurft, Lillian. *Folklore and Early Customs of Southeast Missouri.* New York: Exposition Press, 1972. 77p.

Includes a chapter on superstitions, with over two hundred listed under such subtitles as "Good Luck," "Bad Luck," "Signs and Omens," "Marriage Signs," "Weather Signs," etc., all collected in the southeast Missouri Ozarks. The author was born and lived her early life in Cape Girardeau County.

706. Owen, Mary Alicia. "Among the Voodoos." In *Proceedings of the International Folklore Congress*, pp. 239–48. London, 1891.

Discusses black traditions in Missouri, including a voodoo fire dance following a Christian revival and voodoo meetings in church buildings. The author was one of the founders of the Missouri Folklore Society and a friend of H. M. Belden. She later published an expanded treatment of this text under the title *Voodoo Tales, as Told Among the Negros of the Southwest* (see volume 1 of this bibliography, p. 186). See "Mary Alicia Owen, Collector of Afro-American and Indian Lore in Missouri" by W. K. McNeil (entry 1604).

707. Page, Piney. "From Moccasin Creek: Ozark Expressions." *The Ozarks Mountaineer* 30:6–7 (August 1982): 47.

The sage of Pope County, Arkansas, gives twenty-five folk beliefs. He quotes his grandmother's skepticism toward weather signs: "All signs fail in wet and dry weather."

708. Parler, Mary Celestia. "Folk Beliefs from Arkansas." Typescript, University of Arkansas–Fayetteville, 1962. 15 vols., no pagination.

This material was collected by students in Parler's folklore classes at the University of Arkansas from 1955 to 1961. The material is classified according to a system devised by Prof. Wayland Hand of UCLA. This classification was used in the *Brown Collection of North Carolina Folklore*, and will be used in Hand's forthcoming *Dictionary of American Superstitions and Folk Beliefs*, a monumental work that has occupied him for many years.

Besides these fifteen bound manuscript volumes, the Parler Archive contains all the items collected during the years 1956 to 1974, a vast collection on index cards, not yet typed into books for binding. This will amount to another fourteen big volumes—a total of twenty-nine volumes altogether.

Professor Hand has spent some time at the University of Arkansas and examined the material in these collections. It is my understanding that he has copied the Arkansas items so as to incorporate them easily into his *Dictionary*.

709. Pennington, D. D., Eunice Pennington, and Albert Pennington. *Ozark National Scenic Riverways*. Fremont, Mo.: Published by the authors, 1967. 79p.

Mostly a haphazard collection of facts and figures covering the Current and Jacks Fork rivers region of Carter and Shannon counties in Missouri. A lot of this is a rehash of material found in Eunice Pennington's *History of Carter County* (see entry 1462). In 1967 these two rivers had just been designated Ozark National Scenic Riverways. About the only items for the folklorist are found on pp. 20–21 under the heading "Harmful Plants and Weeds" and on pp. 44–45 in a section on Indian remedies.

710. Pompey, Sherman Lee. *Granny Gore's Ozark Medicine*. Kansas City, Kans.: Brake-Watson Printing Co., 1961. 15p.

This pamphlet is badly written and not too well printed. But I believe that the material concerning herb remedies and magical charms is authentic and genuine. I have collected many of these items in the same region where Mr. Pompey worked.

711. Price, Mary Sue. "Full House Has Good Luck; Doing Wash Brings Bad." *Springfield News-Leader*, 2 January 1982.

A dozen or so folk beliefs associated with the New Year.

712. Pyles, Lida Wilson. "Haunted Honeymoon and Collected Ozark Ghost Stories." Unpublished manuscript, 1980. 71p.

These are four stories collected by the author, a lifelong resident of Carroll County, Arkansas, and Jasper County, Missouri. She claims the first story, "Haunted Honeymoon," which takes up more than half of the manuscript, actually happened to her and her husband in the first house they lived in after their marriage. I know Mrs. Pyles personally, and in spite of the fact that some skeptics might call attention to her position as director of the tall tales contest held each year in Eureka Springs, Arkansas, I believe she is telling it as she saw it. The other three stories; "The Phantom Hitchhiker," "The Ghost of Grindstone Mountain," and "The Gaskins Ghosts" are all familiar types found in the Ozarks. The only copy of this manuscript is in the author's possession.

713. ———. "It Happened in the Ozarks." Unpublished manuscript, Carthage, Mo., 1982. 197p.

Under "Ozark Superstitions" (pp. 105–16) and "Of Weather Signs" (pp. 117–23), she discusses about twenty-four items collected from the southwest Missouri and northwest Arkansas Ozarks. The only copy of this manuscript is in the author's possession.

714. Randolph, Vance. *Ozark Magic and Folklore*. New York: Dover Publications, 1964. 367p.

Paperback reprint of *Ozark Superstitions* (Columbia University Press, 1947).

715. ————. "The Strange Woman of Green Forest, Ark." In *Ozark Guide Yearbook*, p. 16. Reeds Spring, Mo.: Gerald H. Pipes, 1965.

This article appears on p. 16, but it was first published as "The Witch on Bradshaw Mountain" in the *University Review*, summer 1936 (see volume 1 of this bibliography, p. 263). There is a drawing of the "witch" by Thomas Hart Benton.

716. Rees, Alwyn D. "The Measuring Rod." *Folk-Lore* (London) 65:1 (April 1954): 30–32.

Meaning of the stick used to measure the dead; in many countries, often buried with the corpse. For its use in the Ozarks, see Randolph's *Ozark Superstitions*, p. 314.

717. Rice, Will. "Accusing Flowers." *The Ozarker* 5:7 (October 1968): 3.

The Ozark tale of the flowers on Star Mountain, ten miles south of Marshall, Arkansas, which grew in such a fashion as to point out a murderer. This yarn is still told in rural Carroll County. Otto Rayburn once told me that he believed "there might be some truth in it." This same story appeared in the *Ozark Guide*, January-February 1944, p. 16. Will Rice lived in St. Joe, Arkansas. He wrote tall tales for newspapers all over Missouri and Arkansas for many years, usually headed "It Ain't Necessarily So."

718. Richard, Eugene. "Those Mysterious Animal Mutilations." *Arkansas Times* 6:2 (October 1979): 32–5, 38.

Sensational and highly colored, not much documentation. Richard attributes these outrages to a mad scientist, or to one of the Satanist groups. *Arkansas Times* is a slick-paper bimonthly published in Little Rock.

719. Richmond, Sue. "Herbal Remedies." *Ozarkia* 3:4 (December 1982-January 1983): 20, 29.

Medicinal uses for some of the old standbys: chemonile flower, golden seal, comfrey roots, cayenne powder, raspberry tea, peppermint, and catnip leaf. In this same issue see p. 35 about a new organization of midwives, The Midwives Alliance of North America (MANA).

720. Roberts, Carla, and Terri Jones. "Good for What Ails You." *Bittersweet* 5:4 (Summer 1978): 15–25.

About two yarb experts, Ella Dunn and Earl Stiles. How to use the following remedies: asafetida, August flower, balm of Gilead, black cohosh, butterfly root, catnip, comfrey, dogwood, elm, ginseng, golden seal, hickory, horehound, Indian turnip, Jerusalem oak, lily of the valley, mayapple, mullein, nerve root, pennyroyal, poke, red root, sarsaparilla, sassafras, wild cherry, wild ginger, wild grape, and witch hazel. Good drawings and photographs. Both vernacular and botanical names are given for each plant, as well as instructions on preparation and use. A very fine article. The back cover of this issue is a full-page color photograph of Ella Dunn.

721. Roberts, John W. "The 'Spook Light': A Missouri Parking Legend." *Mid-America Folklore* 7:2 (Fall 1979): 31–40.

Another look at the mysterious light that dances along an isolated road in Newton County, Missouri. As no acceptable scientific explanation has ever been given, legends of the supernatural continue to abound. Roberts compares eleven different accounts he collected from six informants who live in the area. He is especially interested in those associated with what he calls "teenage parking legends."

722. Sanders, Evelyn. "A Special Spooky Road." *The Ozarks Mountaineer* 28: 6–7 (August 1980): 40–41.

Another in a long succession of stories about the mysterious light that appears on a country road south of Joplin, Missouri. This one tells the legend of Indian lovers who eloped and, when capture seemed imminent, committed suicide. The light is said to represent their spirits, returning each night to resume their flight. There is a photograph of the Spook Light Museum.

723. Shelby, Kermit. "Legend of the Lonesome Valley." In *Ozark Guide Yearbook*, pp. 14–16, 79–82. Reeds Spring, Mo.: Gerald Pipes, 1962.

The story of a boy doomed to a life of misfortune and wanderlust because he was born with a caul or "veil" on his face. (See also Randolph's *Ozark's Superstitions*, p. 203.)

724. Shuck, Kenneth M. *Pioneer Potions and Lotions.* Springfield, Mo.: Intaglio Publications, 1976. 8p.

A thin paperback pamphlet, but it lists more than sixty old-time remedies—the author calls them "cures." There is some use of strange ingredients, such as wolf liver and deer bladders, but mostly common herbs and household stuff like lye, ammonia, whiskey, and vinegar. No dependence upon charms or amulets or magic. Shuck says he got most of these remedies from his mother's people, sensible pioneers from Kentucky. He is a former director of the Springfield Art Museum.

725. Snowden, Raymond B. Letter to the editor. *The Ozark Mountaineer* 22:4 (May 1974): 44.

Mr. Snowden writes from Salem, Missouri, to say that pokeberries are *not* poisonous, as so many people believe. He eats them raw, and cooked in pies, with no bad effects. "They are as good as blackberries," writes Mr. Snowden. Maybe so, says the editor, but the famous Euell Gibbons says "the seeds *are* very poisonous," and he (the editor) is not quite ready to eat pokeberries.

726. Soric, Peggy. "No Cauldrons Bubble for Today's Witch." *Springfield News-Leader*, 22 October 1978.

A Sunday feature story about the Shadow Coven in Springfield, Missouri. These people call themselves witches, but seem to be quiet, respectable citizens, who have nothing to do with Satanism. The author interviewed three members who complained of persecution and bad publicity. "We are tired of hiding," they said, but asked Peggy not to publish their names. "Witchcraft had a bad press for over two thousand years," said one. "Witchcraft is the oldest religion in the world. We do no evil, yet have always been criticized by the Christians, and often openly persecuted." One man said he had been fired at more than once, but the bullets missed. The reporter was invited to attend a "harmony ritual" at one of their Sabats, but declined.

727. Soric, Susan. "Devil's Fair Grove Visit Recalled." *Springfield News-Leader*, 15 November 1980.

An interview with Harold E. Goss, age ninety-one, who is probably the last living witness to this image that appeared on the wall of the Methodist Church in Fair Grove, Missouri, in 1895. (See Randolph's *Ozark Superstitions*, pp. 229–30.) The event panicked the small community. Goss presents his own deduction about its cause.

728. Southwick, Barbara Merrick. "The Saga of the Witches of Salem, Missouri." *Springfield Magazine* 2:5 (October 1980): 24–27.

In 1974 a pair of modern-day witches settled in this south-central Missouri community hoping the name *Salem* would help promote settlement of a family of witches. But stories of strange happenings and mysterious rituals soon spread among the residents, and the "witch hysteria" that followed forced this modern-day priest of Wicca to leave in 1977.

729. Spear, Denelle. "Medicinal Plants and Ozark Folklore." *Springfield Magazine* 1:10 (March 1980): 18–20.

A brief article about some of the more common medicinal species found in the Ozarks. Many quotes from Orpha Gazette, a herbalist who lives in Dunnegan, Missouri. The author is a student at Southwest Missouri State University in Springfield.

730. Steele, Phillip. "Legend of the Devil's Teakettle." *The Ozarks Mountaineer* 28:4–5 (June 1980): 19.

A wet-weather artesian spring located in northwest Arkansas leaves polished stones scattered about after its infrequent eruptions. These are referred to as "jewels of the devil" and much superstition surrounds them.

731. ———. "The Legend of Ginger Blue." *The Ozarks Mountaineer* 29:4–5 (June 1981): 19.

The tears of an Indian maiden mourning the loss of her brave form his image on a stone. This occurs in what is now called Mystery Cave, located near the town of Lanagan in the southwest corner of Missouri.

732. ———. "The Phantom Caboose." *The Ozarks Mountaineer* 29:1 (February 1981): 18.

Steele heard this story as late as 1980. A caboose, seen by respectable citizens as well as hobos, reportedly travels up and down the tracks with no engine.

733. Stewart, Melinda. "The Unusual and Unexplainable." *Bittersweet* 7:2 (Winter 1979): 32–33, 65.

Eight Ozark ghost stories, collected from students in a high school at Lebanon, Missouri.

734. ———. "The Unusual and Unexplainable." *Bittersweet* 7:3 (Spring 1980): 24–25.

Five more stories about ghosts, witches, and murder collected in Laclede County, Missouri. (This issue of *Bittersweet* was incorrectly printed as "volume 8.")

735. Stone, Elizabeth Woodcock. "The Woodcock Family." *Izard County Historian* 7:3 (July 1976): 27–29.

See on pp. 28–29 the section titled "Aunt Betty's Doctorings of Yesterday," which lists thirteen home remedies used by Margaret Yeary "Aunt Betty" Woodcock (1870–1947).

736. Tatum, Billy Joe. "A Country Doctor's Wife Takes a Look at ———." *The Ozarks Mountaineer* 20:6 (July 1972) to 24:11 (December 1976).

This series is all about ailments and the herbs and/or plants used to treat them. The author's husband is a general practitioner in Melbourne who prescribes some of these folk medicines for his patients. She begins the series discussing the ailments and the required curative plants. Later she places more emphasis on the individual plants themselves and their specific medicinal uses. The subjects may be located as follows: poison ivy, p. 11 (July 1972); hiccups, pp. 12–13 (August 1972); freckles, pp. 28–29 (September 1972); cures for warts, p. 40 (October 1972); cough remedies, p. 29 (November 1972); toothache remedies, p. 13 (December 1972); teas, pp. 36–37 (April 1973); tranquilizers, pp. 10–11 (June 1973); vitamins, pp. 34–35 (September 1973); hair care, p. 32 (October 1973); garlic, pp. 10–11 (February 1974); dangerous plants, pp. 10–11 (March 1974); rejuvenators, pp. 12–13 (April 1974); summer complaint, p. 29 (August 1974); wildflower medicines, pp. 24–25 (October 1974); pine tar making, p. 18 (November 1974); medicinal plants: mullein, pp. 10–11 (February 1975); ginseng, pp. 14–15 (March 1975); golden seal, pp. 8–9 (April 1975); comfrey, pp. 28–29 (May 1975); ginger, pp. 10–11 (June 1975); chamomile, pp. 8–9 (July 1975); Solomon's seal, p. 11 (August 1975); catnip, p. 10 (September 1975); horehound, p. 12 (October 1975); mountain mint, p. 27 (November 1975); willow bark, p. 14 (December 1975); red clover, pp. 26–27 (February 1976); peppermint, pp. 28–29 (March 1976); calamint, p. 10 (April 1976); bloodroot, pp. 30–31 (May 1976); yarrow, p. 13 (June 1976); plantain, pp. 10–11 (July 1976); elderberry, pp. 10–11 (August 1976); bergamont, pp. 34–35 (September 1976); horsemint, p. 8 (October 1976); fennel, p. 12 (November 1976); witch hazel, pp. 8–9 (December 1976).

737. ———. "Don't Underestimate Mustard." *The Ozarks Mountaineer* 28:2–3 (April 1980): 46.

Good discussion of genus *Brassica*, its medicinal uses as a rubefacient and its use in cooking as a condiment.

738. ———. "From an Ozarks Herbal." *The Ozarks Mountaineer* 25:1 (February 1977) through 26:3 (April 1978).

This is a continuation of the series "A Country Doctor's Wife Takes a Look at . . . ." It appeared as follows: dandelion, p. 33 (February 1977); violet, p. 7 (March 1977); trillium lily, p. 34 (April 1977); passion flower, p. 25 (August 1977); another article, incorrectly titled "Dandelion," is actually about tansy, p. 34 (October 1977); johnny-jump-up, p. 35 (April 1978).

739. Taylor, Opal Lee Arnold. *Medicine Time in the Hills of Home*. Silver Hill, Ark.: Published by the author, 1963. 15p.

The first seven pages are devoted to herb remedies—the author is a nurse, and doesn't hold with magic. The rest of the book is brief memories of Christmas dinners, soapmaking, wash day, country school, and the like. An honest book, with no hokum. I knew the author years ago. A friend of Marge Lyon and Otto Rayburn, she used to "beat the strings" of a fiddle. She lives in St. Joe, Arkansas. A second edition was printed in 1973.

740. Thompson, Lawrence S. "*Cannabis sativa* and Traditions Associated with It." *Kentucky Folklore Record* 18:1 (January-March 1972): 1–4.

Hemp as a feed for chickens, a remedy for colds, a poultice to stop bleeding, an aphrodisiac. Thompson is writing about Kentucky, but much of the material applies to Missouri and Arkansas as well.

741. Tidgwell, Flo Montgomery. "Forecasts in Rhyme." *The Ozarks Mountaineer* 30:10–11 (December 1982): 58–59.

Twelve folk beliefs told in rhyme. The author grew up near Stockton in Cedar County, Missouri.

742. Wallace, Jenell. "Folkways Survive." *Springfield Daily News*, 25 May 1982.

Amateur folklorist Mary Scott Hair of Hurley, Missouri, talks about interpreting signs of nature to foretell weather. Under the pen name "Samanthy," she has for years written columns about Ozark folkways for regional publications.

743. Weaver, Mary D. "Witchcraft in the Ozarks." *The Ozarker* 6:7 (August 1969): 5.

Brief anecdote about witchcraft, apparently from Shannon County, Missouri. The author lives at Winona, Missouri.

744. White, Kathleen Kelly. *Ozark Superstitions and Other Tales*. Clinton, Mo.: The Printery, n.d. 12p.

A list of common folk beliefs, no special connection with the Ozarks. But see p. 12 for one short paragraph about the "Angel Crown" of feathers in a dead man's pillow.

745. Wolf, John Quincy [Sr.]. *Life in the Leatherwoods*. Memphis: Memphis State University Press, 1974. 159p.

The chapter entitled "Medical Science in the Leatherwoods" (pp. 87–99) is full of valuable information on folk medicine, herbs and remedies (he names over fifty "yarbs" and many of the remedies concocted from them), ailments, and early backwoods doctors. He says diseases were scarce in the Leatherwoods in those days because as yet nobody had a name for most of them.

746. Wolf, John Quincy [Jr.]. "Two Folk Scientists in Action." *Tennessee Folklore Society Bulletin* 35:1 (March 1969): 6–10.

A water witch at work near Pfeiffer, Arkansas, and a wart-taker at Locust Grove, Arkansas.

747. Wood, Larry E. "The Hornet Spook Light." *Missouri Life* 5:4 (September-October 1977): 23–25.

Another account of the mysterious light seen on a country road near Devil's Elbow, Oklahoma, just across the state line from Hornet, Missouri. Wood lists several local legends, and prints three photographs of the ghost lights that were taken by Marta Poynor.

748. Worthen, Mary Fletcher, compiler. *Matters and Things in General.* Little Rock: Arkansas Territorial Restoration Foundation, 1974. 59p.

The chapter entitled "Remedies," pp. 37–51, is worth reading. This book is comprised of articles published in Arkansas newspapers during the state's territorial period, 1819–1836.

8. Treasure

749. Allen, Chick. *Autobiography of Chick Allen and Folklore of the Early Ozarks.* Cassville, Mo.: Litho Press, 1974. 32p.

A lot of good lost-treasure stories. Also tales of the Bald Knobbers, Belle Starr, the Barrows, and Wild Bill. Allen ran a "museum" close to Silver Dollar City, and as the tourist trade grew, so did his stories. He died in 1980.

750. "Arkansas Diamonds." *Ark/Ozark* 1:4 (Summer 1969): 12–15.

The author claims there are only three diamond mines in the world and one is located at Murfreesboro, Arkansas. Discovered by a farmer in 1906, the land was purchased and mined by various companies until 1925. Now, for a nominal fee, tourists can spend the day playing diamond miner. I was always advised to go on a moonlit night, especially following an afternoon rain. Most of this article is based upon information supplied by Arlin Coger of Huntsville, Arkansas, who possessed "the largest rock crystal collection in this country." *Ark/Ozark* is a slick-paper quarterly.

751. Ayres, Artie. *Traces of Silver.* Reeds Spring, Mo.: The Ozark Mountain Country Historical Preservation Society, 1982. 148p.

The title refers to a lost silver mine said to be located in Stone County, Missouri. A pioneer family named Yocum supposedly minted their own silver coinage known as "Yocum Dollars" from this mine. Besides recounting the Yocum Dollar tales, this is also an informal history of early days in the southwest Missouri Ozarks. The author is a native of the area, and his father was a treasure hunter whose primary quest was the discovery of the Yocum Mine. Ayres is now president of a family business called the Yocum Silver Mine Corporation and has opened a theme park called the Lost Silver Mine Farm to dramatize the Yocum legend.

752. Black, J. Dickson. *History of Benton County 1836–1936.* Little Rock: International Graphics, 1975. 496p.

Benton County (Arkansas) has had its share of treasure lore. The chapter "Minerals and Mining" is full of fascinating information: see pp. 69–70 about a big picnic at War Eagle where "every man there had a piece of rock that had gold, silver, lead, zinc or some other minerals too rare to talk about." On pages 71–74 is the wonderful story of the Kruse gold mine under a wild apple tree in Rogers. Black is a professional photographer who used to run a "photo studio" in Bentonville. A native of Chicago, he never saw Arkansas until 1952. He has no historical training and is not a skilled writer, but he collected a vast amount of material about Benton County, much of it apparently based on interviews with old settlers, although he does not identify his informants.

753. Boren, Kerry Ross. "Dow High's Ozarks Cache." *Carroll County Historical Society Quarterly* 20:1 (May 1975): 20–22.

The High family was among the earliest to settle Carroll County in northwest Arkansas. The village they founded near Berryville bore their name. This article is mostly about the Civil War in that region and the suffering at the hands of the "border raiders." Dow High had made a fortune taking cattle to the gold fields in California, and when the hostilities between the North and the South began, he buried it on his property. But he took his secret with him when murdered by the raiders. The author of this article is a relative of the Highs and lives in Colorado. Some of his facts are a bit confused, but the descriptions of life in the Ozarks during the war are real enough. There is a good photo of Fred High, nephew of Dow, who was one of the last residents of High. (There are numerous references to Fred's writings in volume 1 of this bibliography.)

754. Boyd, Don. *Treasure Hunting in the Ozarks*. Springfield, Mo.: Published by the author, 1975. 120p.

Most of the very early treasure legends are mentioned, as are those of the Civil War era and of the more recent years. All this is accompanied by reproductions of old maps and photographs. There is a good index and a thorough bibliography. In my opinion, Boyd's book is a beautiful job; he has covered a vast amount of material with as much detail as could possibly be presented in so slender a volume.

755. Braswell, O. Klute. "The True and Legendary Story of Yocum . . . Carroll County, Arkansas." *Carroll County Historical Society Quarterly* 14:4, 15:1 (two volumes printed as one) (December 1969, March 1970): 12–25.

This village was named for the Yocum family, who settled the area in the 1830s. There is a brief discussion (pp. 13–14) of the famed Yocum dollars that were privately minted and supposedly contained more silver than their counterparts issued by the U.S. Treasury. There is a photograph of two of these elusive dollars but no explanation of when or where it was taken. Also Braswell is not clear as to which Yocum he thinks made them.

756. Chiles, James R. "Springfield Underground: A Bottomless Pit or a Fortune in Gold?" *Springfield Magazine* 1:11 (April 1980): 42–46.

About the many treasure legends that abound in this southwest Missouri city. One concerns Spanish gold that would be worth one hundred million dollars today if found.

757. Clayton, Joe. "Yocum Coins as Scarce as Unchallenged Tales." *Springfield Daily News*, 23 November 1981.

More about the elusive Yocum family silver mine. This all occurred in the early nineteenth century but it is still one of the most persistent of the lost treasure legends in the Ozarks.

758. Dobie, J. Frank. *Coronado's Children: Lost Mines and Buried Treasures of the Southwest.* New York: Grosset & Dunlap, 1930. 367p.

See "The James Boys' Loot" (pp. 299–301) about the two million dollars Jesse and Frank buried in the Wichitas somewhere around Ft. Sill, Oklahoma. According to this account Frank returned in later years but was never able to locate the spot.

759. "Evidence of Silver Boom Still Remains." *Arkansas Democrat*, Little Rock, 23 April 1950.

The Kellogg Mine located at the now-deserted settlement of Argenta, just a few miles northwest of North Little Rock, has been mined for its lead and silver since the 1840s. So far it has never yielded enough of either to keep the various owners from abandoning it. But the legend persists (as they always do) that a fabulous lode of silver is waiting to be discovered. A nearby resident still acts as caretaker and guards the mine's entrance even though he hasn't been paid for years.

760. Findley, J. W. *Experiences of a Walking Preacher.* Springfield, Mo.: Roberts & Sutter, 1980. 156p.

Reminiscences by a Church of God preacher of his life and ministry in southwest Missouri. Pages 9–12 tell of using a Spanish dip needle to locate gold. More treasure stories on pp. 70–71.

761. ———. *A Voice from the Ozark Hills.* Springfield, Mo.: Roberts & Sutter, 1982. 221p.

Mother Murray's Mine, or Mother Mary's as it is sometimes called, is located southwest of Ava, Missouri, along what is now the Glade Top Trail in the Mark Twain National Forest. At the turn of the century a preacher/revivalist called Mother Murray was holding a revival atop a mountain called the Pinnacle when she had a vision that gold was to be found on that spot. See pp. 196–97 for the author's account of the treasure hunt.

762. Ford, Edsel. "Treasure Hunting in Arkansas." *Arkansas Democrat*, Sunday Magazine, Little Rock, 29 May 1960.

A couple of treasure stories from Benton County, Arkansas—the "Lost Mexican" at Eden's Bluff near Monte Ne, and the Kruse Gold Mine in Rogers. Ford was a resident of the area and a poet of national acclaim.

763. Freeman, Dale. "Hunt Fortune in Gold." In *Ozark Guide Yearbook*, p. 86. Reeds Spring, Mo.: Gerald Pipes, 1961.

Another Spanish treasure story, this one located in what is now downtown Springfield, Missouri. The treasure hunter "witched" for the spot with a peach tree limb that had a piece of gold on the end of it.

764. Goolsby, Elwin L. *The Teeth on the Bradley-Rushing Building and Other Stories*. Sheridan, Ark.: Grant County Museum, 1978. 73p.

Brief treasure tales on pp. 1, 7, 10, 21, an 27.

765. Hudgins, Mary D. "Gold and Silver Boom Town of Bear Through a Decade." *Arkansas Gazette*, 24 January 1971.

The great Arkansas Gold Rush started in the middle 1880s. Miners came from many countries, all mad for gold and silver. Big mining camps like Bear and Silver City appeared near Hot Springs. Bear claimed a population of about five thousand, but the true figure was probably about twelve hundred. Quite a town anyhow, with hotels, brothels, jails, and other modern conveniences. But there was no gold, as state geologist Branner told them the whole time.

766. Ihrig, B. B. *History of Hickory County, Missouri, 1970*. Warsaw, Mo.: The Printery, 1970. 419p.

On pp. 296–97 is the story of a vein of silver known as the Brookshire Silver Mine. Though the legend has persisted, its exact location has been lost since before the Civil War and has little chance of being rediscovered for some time. The alleged location now is beneath the waters of a manmade impoundment.

767. Ingenthron, Elmo. *The Land of Taney, A History of an Ozark Commonwealth*. Point Lookout, Mo.: School of the Ozarks Press, 1974. 523p.

Chapter 12, "The Search for Mineral Wealth," gives another accounting of the Yocum Dollar (pp. 201–3), the "trade coin" allegedly used as a medium of exchange along the White River in Taney County in the 1850s.

768. Johns, Paul W. *Unto These Hills: True Tales from the Ozarks*. Ozark, Mo.: Bilyeu-Johns Enterprises, 1980. 104p.

In 1930, bank robber Jake Fleagle hid out south of Hollister, Missouri. He was apprehended and killed but his estimated $59,000 in loot has never been found. See pp. 43–45.

769. Junas, Lil. *Cadron Creek: A Photographic Narrative*. Little Rock: The Ozark Society Foundation, 1979. 96p.

See p. 26 for the story of gold kept in an eel skin that was hidden in a bluff along the Cadron and was never recovered.

770. Kennedy, Steele T. "Is There Gold Near Cass?" *Arkansas Democrat Magazine*, Little Rock, 20 July 1958.

Cass is a ghost town in Franklin County, Arkansas. This legend has Spanish prospectors hiding their fortune in gold bars and a huge gold cross from bushwhackers during the Civil War. Strange marks on a bluff nearby were said to show the location, and a fellow called "Mexican Charlie" was imported from the Southwest who said he could decipher them. He was later run out of the country. Next a fellow came in and "witched" for it with a peach tree limb. Then another group sold mining stock. Things were looking good until it was discovered that they were salting the diggings with ore being brought down from Joplin. The mine now stands forsaken, waiting for another "Mexican Charlie" to come along.

771. Kennicutt, Wally. *Ozark Nature Gallery*. Paragould, Ark.: White Printing Co., 1979. 114p.

Stories about Spanish and Indian gold in the Arkansas Ozarks. The author says that as late as 1950 a duck was killed near Batesville with a gold nugget in its crop. Kennicutt, a native of Branson, Missouri, is a freelance writer and lives at Cherokee Village, Arkansas.

772. "The Legends of Bread Tray Mountain." *Ozark Highways* (Winter 1973): 6.

About the Yocum Dollar, Spanish silver, and haunted caves. Speaking of former residents on the mountain, a local informant says, "Those old people then didn't believe it half as much as we do now."

773. Madden, Kevin. "Petroglyph: Man Deciphers Rocks in Search of Treasure." *Springfield News-Leader*, 7 March 1982.

While coon hunting in 1963, Ken McGowan of Mountain Grove, Missouri, took shelter in a cave to escape a rain shower. He discovered a large rock covered with letters and numbers chiseled into it. There is a photo of the rock accompanying this article, and though these symbols may appear to be the usual cave graffiti of initials and dates, McGowan maintains that these are a secret cryptogram giving information about a hidden treasure nearby. He is offering half of the treasure to anyone who can decipher the message. Treasure hunters are a fascinating lot.

774. Mahnkey, Douglas. *1863—Civil War Bushwhacker Alf Bolin*. Forsyth, Mo.: Published by the author, 1982. 11p.

This pamphlet was republished from Mahnkey's *Hill and Holler Stories* (see entry 483) and was sold during the celebration of "Alf Bolin Days" in Forsyth, Missouri. See pp. 10–11 entitled "The Buried Treasure of Alf Bolin." Not in the 1975 publication are two maps included here (pp. 8–9) showing the location of Murder Rocks and of Bolin's gravesite. For more on Bolin see pp. 285–89 in Elmo Ingenthron's *Borderland Rebellion* (entry 673).

775. Messick, Mary Ann. *History of Baxter County 1873–1973*. Little Rock: Mountain Home Chamber of Commerce, 1973. 506p.

Page 291 tells of a local hunter who possessed a seemingly inexhaustible supply of silver bullets. Just as he was about to reveal his secret source to his family, he died.

776. Millar, Howard A. *Finders-Keepers at America's Only Diamond Mine*. New York: Carlton Press, 1976. 175p.

A detailed account of the crater of diamonds in Pike County, Arkansas. A fascinating book. It is a pity there are no pictures.

777. Mitchell, Dorothy. "The Rogers Gold Mine." *The Ozarks Mountaineer* 19:4 (May 1971): 18–19.

In the early 1900s a Minneapolis businessman, William H. Kruse, was alleged to possess extrasensory perception. He had been reared in Rogers, Arkansas, and he began sending telegrams to relatives and friends there telling of gold he visioned would be found under an apple tree. An apple tree was located, buildings were constructed, and a shaft sunk. Traces of gold were allegedly found but nothing ever came of it. A tornado blew the building down, and many of those involved went broke. Rogers, Arkansas, has been the subject of many precious-metal and treasure stories.

778. "Old Diaries, Maps, Indicate Table Rock Silver Mine." *Stone County Republican*, Galena, Mo., 8 December 1960.

According to these maps and journals, now in possession of a Mrs. Ola Farwell of Eureka Springs, Arkansas, there existed a fabulous silver mine somewhere in the vicinity of Easley Ford on the White River in Barry County, Missouri. All of this data was found in 1830 by a St. Louis resident in the barrel of a gun. The authors of the material were two men, Pu Deville and Pierre, who had located the mine and had smelted silver bars from the ore. But before they could get away Pierre was killed by Indians and Pu Deville was driven away sans his treasure. Numerous attempts have been made over the succeeding years to find the mine again but to no avail. As with many other treasure legends in the region, the site of the treasure has supposedly been inundated by a manmade lake.

779. O'Neal, Rev. W. B. "Searching for Buried Treasure." *Independence County Chronicle* 3:2 (January 1962): 39–42.

A Civil War veteran returns, many years later, to the site of a skirmish where his troop hid a fortune in gold to avoid its capture. Just as he is about to reveal its exact location, he dies. Many people in Independence County can still show you "just about" where it is.

780. Pipes, Gerald H. "Table Rock Covers Outlaw Loot." *Sunday News-Leader*, Springfield, 13 July 1958.

Concerns sixty-two thousand dollars in stolen gold coins hidden in a cave near the Maberry Ferry on the White River in the 1860s. This site is now one hundred fifty feet under the surface of Table Rock Lake.

781. Rascoe, Jesse. *Oklahoma Treasures: Lost and Found*. Fort Davis, Tex.: Frontier Book Company, 1974. 96p.

More than seventy-five treasure stories. Fifteen or so of these are located in the Ozarks of eastern Oklahoma. See pp. 13–22.

782. Rayburn, Otto Ernest. "Legends of Breadtray Mountain." *Rayburn's Ozark Guide* 6:1 (Summer 1948): 36–38.

Breadtray Mountain is located in Stone County, Missouri, at the junction of the James with the White River. Rayburn tells four treasure tales from there. He doesn't mention that many treasure hunters believe that this place was also the source of the silver used in the legendary Yocum dollars.

783. Schell, Joe C. *Big Sugar Creek Country*. Goodman, Mo.: McDonald County Historical Society, 1969. 95p.

This is about the very southwest corner of Missouri, the part of the Ozarks Vance Randolph first visited as a youth (Noel) and later lived for a number of years (Pineville). An area bounded by Arkansas and Oklahoma, of crystal-clear streams, beautiful hills and hollers, and fascinating inhabitants. See pp. 51–52 and 72 for treasure tales.

784. Skinner, Charles Montgomery. *Myths and Legends of Our Own Land*. Vol. 2. Philadelphia: J. B. Lippincott Company, 1896. 335p.

See pp. 290–91 for a story of a "Spanish silver mine" about eighteen miles southwest of Galena, Missouri. All about the ghosts who hang around the place, too.

785. Steele, Phillip. *Lost Treasures of the Ozarks*. Springdale, Ark.: Published by the author, 1974. 12p.

Fifteen brief treasure tales, most of them well known. The "Callahan Mountain" story (pp. 3–4) is new to me, and the tale of the Huntsville Counterfeiters (p. 7) is different than the version I know.

786. ———. "The Yokum Dollar." *The Ozarks Mountaineer* 27:6–7 (July-August 1979): 16–17.

About this famous "lost mine" of the Missouri Ozarks. (The correct spelling is *Yocum.*) The author lives in Springdale, Arkansas, and is a regular contributor to the magazine.

787. "Stories of Stone County." Mimeographed, Mountain View, Ark., 1972. 30p.

A collection of stories written by grades nine to twelve of the Mountain View, Arkansas, High School. Most are genealogy but some rattle the family skeletons. Page 8 tells of great-great-grandpa who somehow had a government mold and made counterfeit silver dollars, using silver obtained from a secret mine, the location of which he never disclosed.

788. Tatham, Robert L. *Ozark Treasure Tales.* Raytown, Mo.: R. L. Tatham Co., 1979. 31p.

Eight lost-treasure tales, all located in the southern Missouri Ozarks. The author gives detailed information about their circumstances and possible locations and even includes sections of U.S. Geological Survey topographical maps of each general area. I am very familiar with most of these tales, especially that of the Yocum dollar. A descendant, Tom Yocum, was one of the best river guides on the White River, and when not running the river spent his time in search of this elusive silver mine. The author has written a companion book, *Treasure Hunting Tips and Metal Detector Facts* (1979).

789. Tebbetts, Diane, compiler. "Legend Texts of Jesse James." *Mid-America Folklore* 8 : 1–2 (Spring-Fall 1980): 53–85.

Texts of interviews collected by the folklore departments of six different universities. See pp. 61–64 for those under the heading "Jesse's Buried Treasure."

790. Townsend, Will. "Search Continues for More Rare Yocum Dollars." *Treasure Search* 3 : 1 (February 1975): 68–71, 73.

More about the mystery of the Yocum dollars. Townsend (Townsend Godsey) knew about Tom Yocum and his quest as well as anybody, and this account is as close to what's known about it all as the reader will find.

791. Turner, George. *Secrets of Jesse James.* Amarillo, Tex.: Baxter Lane Co., 1975. 64p.

A concise narrative on the lives and times of Jesse and Frank and those individuals who were a part of their story. Concerning the tales of hidden loot buried and never recovered by the James gang, the author states that many adventurers have exhausted themselves "searching for this bonanza without taking into consideration that the various members of the James gang died in poverty." This realization never seems to enter the realm of the treasure hunter's reasoning.

792. Van Buskirk, Kathleen. "An Ozark Dream: Einstein's Silver Mine." *The Ozarks Mountaineer* 30:6–7 (August 1982): 40–43.

What canoeists now thrill to as a run down the St. Francis narrows and a shoot through the breech in the Silvermine Dam were once part of a man's dream of riches. In 1879 William Einstein began operations to extract silver from within the rich veins of lead he had discovered in the bluffs along the St. Francis River in Madison County, Missouri. After investments in machinery and manpower and the construction of a dam for turbine power, the operation was in full swing by 1880. The population of the new town of Silvermine reached close to nine hundred, complete with church, school, and post office. But three thousand ounces of silver from fifty tons of lead was not enough to support the venture, and in less than two years the whole enterprise collapsed.

793. Vickery, Margaret Ray. *Ozark Stories of the Upper Current River*. Salem, Mo.: The Salem News, n.d. 97p.

Good story of a lost silver mine on pp. 71–76.

794. Weaver, H. Dwight, and Paul A. Johnson. *Missouri the Cave State*. Jefferson City, Mo.: Discovery Enterprises, 1980. 336p.

For some good lost-treasure stories see pp. 84, 102, 189, and 194.

795. Wilson, Steve. *Oklahoma Treasure and Treasure Tales*. Norman: University of Oklahoma Press, 1976. 325p.

Eighteen treasure stories, some that have been discovered, some that are legendary. Told by archaeologists and by "pot hunters." This is a valuable work, with many photographs and maps.

9. Foodways

796. Abner, Vannie. *Heir to These Hills: A Story of a Magnificent Land and Its People*. Hicksville, N.Y.: Exposition Press, 1978. 95p.

"Ecrevisse Acadiene" was a gourmet's delight in St. Louis restaurants during the early part of the twentieth century. Consequently fresh fish and mussel shells weren't the only commercial ventures on Ozark streams. See p. 48 for a photo of crawfish shipping-crates on the Niangua River near Hahatonka, Missouri.

797. Allen, Chick. *How They Lived in the Ozarks*. Cassville, Mo.: Litho Press, 1974. 32p.

Some good information on early Ozark preparation and preservation of food, and old recipes. All one needs to know about preparing sow belly, pig hocks, poke greens, sweet tater pudding, and the like. The author was raised in Stone County, Missouri, and knew what he was talking about.

798. Anderson, Clay. "Treasures of the Ozarks Wilderness." *The Ozarks Mountaineer* 24:8 (September 1976): 21–25.

An excellent article by the owner/editor of *The Ozarks Mountaineer* about the gathering of ginseng and wild honey in the wildest parts of Stone County, Arkansas. Clay was in the company of three of the most knowledgeable mountain men of that region, and his graphic description of their methods and their concern for conservation is well worth reading. Also accompanying the group was Billy Jo Tatum of Melbourne, Arkansas, a nationally known wild-foods expert. Many photographs.

799. Auckley, Jim. "Missouri's Outdoor Almanac." *Missouri Conservationist* 36:10 (October 1975): 20.

A fine recipe for venison sausage:
50 pounds venison
50 pounds lean pork
2 ounces whole mustard seed
2 pounds medium salt [whatever that is]
8 ounces pepper
1 ounce saltpeter
1 clove garlic
a set and a half of beef casing (artificial casing not recommended)

Auckley concludes with a cryptic statement: "Used as an hors d'oeuvre, *it will make guests forget about dinner!*" A hundred and fifty pounds of salami seems a good deal, but this article will please many housewives who are appalled once a year by a sudden oversupply of fresh meat. It is surprising how many women say that they cannot eat venison. But most people can eat this sausage.

800. Barleycorn, Michael. *Moonshiner's Manual.* Willits, Calif.: Oliver Press, 1975. 150p.

This soft-covered book has no specific setting, but men who should know tell me that the author must be intimately acquainted in the Cookson Hill area of the western Ozarks. Anyhow, he answers all the questions you would ask about the manufacture of moonshine liquor. As Townsend Godsey says, "You can make whiskey for fifty cents a gallon, the rest of it is *risk* and packaging." Well, as they say, "there's no law against knowing how." This is a good book. See Godsey's review in *The Ozarks Mountaineer* 23:11 (December 1975): 27.

801. Boswell, George W. "Southern Folk Recipes." *Mid-South Folklore* 3:1 (Spring 1975): 13–20.

Boswell collected this material from his folklore classes at the University of Mississippi. See p. 16 for a note on stewed squirrel—it's best to cook squirrel without cutting off the head. This bit of wisdom is well known in the Ozarks, too. At least one squirrel in a stew is left with the head on—better crack the skull so that the brain is exposed. Boswell is a professor of English at the University of Mississippi and also executive secretary of the Mississippi Folklore Society.

802. Brumley, Albert E. *All-Day Singin' and Dinner on the Ground.* Camdenton, Mo.: Albert E. Brumley and Sons, 1972. 64p.

See pp. 35–61, "Pot, Pan and Kettle: Old-Time Cooking Recipes." Over one hundred regional recipes, some I've never seen in print before. Brumley lived in Powell, Missouri, and was a successful songwriter.

803. Buckner, Sue, and H. C. Lendle. "The Delectable Fungus." *Missouri Life* 3:1–2 (March-June 1975): 16–20.

Good color photos of Missouri mushrooms, including corals (both purple and golden). Many country folk gather corals by the bushel every fall. There are also pictures of the morel, the spotted boletus, and the oyster mushroom. Naturally there is a photo of the deadly amanita, one of the very few dangerous mushrooms in Missouri.

804. "Christmas Goose." *Bittersweet* 3:2 (Winter 1975): 28–32.

The old-time Ozarkers often had a few geese, but they kept them for feathers rather than food. However, this is the best piece about cooking a goose that I have ever read. Fine pictures, too.

805. Circle, Homer. "I've Never Met a Fish I Didn't Like." *Sports Afield* 181:6 (June 1979): 12–14.

How to catch and cook "trash fish": carp, bowfin, buffalo, sucker, gar, catfish.

806. Cotanch, Cherine. "The Fine Art of Picking Greens." *The Ozarks Mountaineer* 22:2 (March 1974): 21.

A full-page article about poke, wild lettuce, lamb's quarters, mouse's ear, plantin (*sic*), dandelion, deer tongue, horse sorrel, sheep sorrel, big shawnee, little shawnee, and watercress. Some remarks on cooking wild greens. I have yet to see an article really showing how to identify all these. Above all, I'd like to see a paper with the botanical names, as the vernacular names vary so widely in different localities, perhaps only a few miles apart. I'd like to see colored pictures, such as bird-watchers carry. The lovers of wild flowers have fairly good books—we need something like that for the pickers of wild greens. The author is a young girl who lives in Rogers, Arkansas, but attends a junior college at Claremore, Oklahoma. This is a good article, but we should have better ones, longer, and with colored pictures.

807. Cruise, Gilbert. "Molasses Making Time." *The Webster County Historical Society Journal* 3 (August 1976): 19–20.

Talks about recipes calling for so many "gulps" of molasses, this being the unit of measure used when pouring from a jug. Mr. Cruise isn't a very good writer, but he knows a lot about making molasses.

808. Deane, Ernie. "Meet the Sassafras King of the Ozarks." *Ozark Digest* (May 1975): 12.

The "king" is Frank Richmond of Cotter, Arkansas. He talks about "rossed" bark that sold for eighty cents a pound. There's a shortage now; since incomes are up in the Ozarks, "folks just don't dig up the roots the way they used to." *Ozark Digest* was published monthly by the Ozark Access Center in Eureka Springs, Arkansas, and was edited by Edd Jeffords.

809. ———. *Ozarks Country*. Branson, Mo.: The Ozarks Mountaineer, 1975. 191p.

See p. 36 on "How to Cook Possum." In the Depression days they were called "Hoover Hogs."

810. Deethardt, Dorothy. *Crafty Carp Cookery*. Brookings: South Dakota State University, [1976?]. 33p.

This bulletin tells about methods of cooking, pickling, drying, and smoking carp.

811. ———. *Paddlefish*. Brookings: South Dakota State University, [1977?]. 18p.

This paperback bulletin contains detailed directions for preparing and cooking paddlefish, which have suddenly become abundant in the Missouri River. This is *Polydon spathula*, which the Ozarker calls spoonbill, or sometimes spoonbill catfish. It is not a catfish, but is related to the sturgeon family. It is not uncommon in the White River. Miss Deethardt is a food specialist at South Dakota State University.

812. Densmore, Frances. *How Indians Use Wild Plants for Food, Medicine and Crafts*. New York: Dover Publications, 1974. 397p.

Densmore collected mostly from the Chippewa, but many of the items were common with the Osage, Cherokee, and other tribes well known in the Ozarks, and a check of the plants listed shows many common in Missouri and Arkansas. This is a scholarly work, like a Ph.D. dissertation. There is much material here that I have never seen in print before, but some of it was published in 1926–1927 by the Bureau of American Ethnology.

813. Denton, Ivan. "Making Maple Syrup at Canyon Creek Ranch." *The Ozarks Mountaineer* 25:3 (April 1977): 23, 27.

The best account of this matter that I have seen. Most such papers deal with maple-syrup making as a commercial enterprise. Denton writes for the man who wants to make a few quarts in his back yard, tapping perhaps only ten trees. He shows just how to make elderberry spouts, how to drill the holes in the trees, how to attach the sap buckets made of tin cans. One must tap trees at just the right time— cold nights and warm days. "If it's warm all night the sap won't flow next day, and if it's freezing all day and all night it can't flow." There are only a few good syrup days in the year. You must wait until things are just right, and in three or four days you will get all the sap you need. Each tree will give perhaps ten gallons of sap, which boils down to a quart of good thick syrup. All this and more is described in detail. This brief paper tells you everything you need to know about backyard syrupmaking. It is illustrated with Denton's drawings showing exactly how to do the job.

814. Dunn, Emma Comfort. "Potato Grabblin' Time." *The Ozarks Mountaineer* 25:5 (June 1977): 15.

The practice of reaching under a potato plant to pull out a marble-sized potato, without disturbing the rest of the crop, is called "grabbling." "New potatoes grabbled from the patch are available only to the homesteader. You can't buy anything like them in the market." A grabbled potato must be small, about the size of a grape. If it's as big as a golf ball, throw it away. Some people serve them creamed with French peas or little green beans. I like them boiled, seasoned with salt and butter. Add some parsley if you like.

815. Fitzhugh, Jewell Kirby. "Home Cooking." *The Ozarks Mountaineer* 22:7 (August 1974): 14–15.

All about poor-do, vinegar pie, sheep sorrel pie, soggam custard, thickened gravy, top dozy, cush, and cambric tea. The Ozarker did pretty well through the Great Depression, and Mrs. Fitzhugh is a very good writer. In Stone County we called it *soggrums* instead of *soggam*, and said *them* rather than *it*, but we meant molasses just the same. Jewell Kirby Fitzhugh will do to ride the river with, as Pancho Dobie used to say. What she calls *top dozy* is the thickened gravy that we call *sop* in Arkansas; the light-colored oily part is *top sop*, the thick opaque layer is *bottom sop*.

816. ———. "Sausage, Souse and Pickled Pig's Feet." *The Ozarks Mountaineer* 25:10 (November 1977): 18, 27.

Fine account of a hog-killin', with detailed directions about the preparation and cooking of ribs, backbone, broiled melt, sausage, souse, and pig's feet. She admits that some people ate chitlings and blutwurst and kidney pie, but there is no detail about these delicacies since her family did not care for them.

817. Fitzhugh, Jewell Kirby, compiler. *Old Time Recipes for Modern Day Cooks.* Branson, Mo.: The Ozarks Mountaineer, 1976. 49p.

Practically all of these are recipes that have been handed down from Fitzhugh's mother and grandmother, and good ones they are. She adds personal comments to many and cites her sources for most. This is a valuable work and is indexed. The author lives in Mablevale, Arkansas.

818. Flowers, Paul. "Muscadine Leather." *The Ozarks Mountaineer* 23:9 (October 1975): 21.

This article gives a recipe for this rare confection, known only to some old-time cooks in the Ozarks. "Everybody knows about peach leather," an old woman in McDonald County, Missouri, told me, "but strawberry leather ain't so common." That's true, and still more secret is muscadine leather, because muscadines (rhymes with *wine*, not *green*) are not as common as they used to be. Paul Flowers thinks that muscadine leather was invented by George Washington Carver, who once lived near Diamond, Missouri.

819. Foreman, Diana. "Making Maple Syrup." *Bittersweet* 4:2 (Winter 1976): 23–27.

The sugar season is in January and February, when the temperature is below freezing at night, rising to the forties or fifties in the daytime. Ella Dunn of Walnut Shade, Missouri, shows just how to bore a hole in the tree and drive in an elderberry spout. It takes about forty gallons of sap to make one gallon of syrup. Good photographs.

820. Gibson, Kyra. "Hominy Made with Ashes." *Bittersweet* 4:2 (Winter 1976): 32–33.

Hominy was to the Ozarker what grits were to the deep southerner. Women were noted for their good hominy, as much as for sausages and pies. There were all sorts of secret "receipts" for making it taste like anything but hominy. A fine article with photographs.

821. Hardaway, B. Touchstone. *These Hills My Home*. Point Lookout, Mo.: School of the Ozarks Press, [1972?]. 95p.

The "Hills" are in the beautiful Buffalo River country of Newton County, Arkansas. Much of interest about life there in the early 1900s. See pp. 51–52, "'Lasses Makin'."

822. Harral, Rex. "Gritted Bread Season." *The Ozarks Mountaineer* 28:8–9 (October 1980): 26–27.

About gritted corn meal, corn fodder, corn squeezings, corn flour, all the staples made from corn to help sustain an Ozark family. The author says it was "King Corn," not cotton, that was the key for survival of the early hill families.

823. Henderson, Louise. *Just Like Mother Made: Ozark Recipes*. Cassville, Mo.: Litho Printers, 1964. 72p.

Over 150 recipes collected in southwest Missouri. Ms. Henderson identifies most of her contributors, many of whom are from Barry County. A good regional collection.

824. Honssinger, Nancy. "Various Vittles." *Bittersweet* 3:3 (Spring 1976): 59, 62.

Dandelion buds, purslane, poke shoots—how to cook, how to can and freeze wild greens.

825. Honssinger, Nancy, and Kyra Gibson. "Wild Greens, Values of the Roadside." *Bittersweet* 3:3 (Spring 1976): 52–57.

The best "greens" article I ever saw. Drawings of many: chickweed, henbit, watercress, wintercress, curly dock, wild lettuce, violet, dandelions, chicory, wild onion, bluebell, poke, wild mustard, shepherd's purse, purslane, lamb's quarters, garden sorrel, red clover, swiss chard.

826. Jeffery, Wendell. "A Drink From Nature's Cup." *Missouri Conservationist* 42:5 (May 1981): 26–28.

A fine article about the brews and tonics that may be prepared from eight common plants found in the Ozarks.

Sassafras (*Sassafras albidum*): Recently its sale as a tea was banned by the Federal Drug Commission when it was discovered to contain carcinogenic agents. But he tells of a beer that can be made by combining sassafras with molasses and letting it ferment.

Mints (various families): He mentions six varieties.

Rose hips (*Rosa eglanteria*): Three equal the vitamin C in one orange.

Sumac (*Rhus glabra*): Gather this in August.

Chicory (*Cichorium intybus*): Oven dry and roast the roots.

New Jersey tea (*Ceanothus americanus*): So named for its use as a substitute for the real thing during the Revolutionary War. Sometimes known as redroot.

Dandelion (*Taraxacum officinale*): He gives a recipe for dandelion wine.

Stinging Nettle (*Urtica dioica*): Good for dandruff, and when fed to animals improves manure.

The author is a native of Mount Olive, Arkansas.

827. ———. "Outdoor Edibles . . . Violet Wood Sorrel." *Missouri Conservationist* 42:4 (April 1981): 22–23.

Violet wood sorrel (*Oxalis violacea*) contains more vitamin C than the orange. A recipe for wood sorrel pie calls for two cups chopped wood sorrel along with pie crust mix, eggs, sugar, tapioca, pineapple chunks, and pineapple juice. Prepared in this manner, violet wood sorrel tastes much like sweetened pineapple.

828. ———. "Water Cress." *Missouri Conservationist* 40:4 (April 1979): 8–9.

This member of the mustard family (*Nasturtium officinale*) can be gathered year round. The author tells how to prepare watercress omelet, soup, and tea.

829. Johnson, Claude E. "We Make Our Own Sorghum." *The Ozarks Mountaineer* 25:9 (October 1977): 16–17.

A good paper about sorghum in Taney County, Missouri.

830. Josus. *Suggin Cookbook: Found and Illustrated by Josus*. Newport, Ark.: Suggin Productions, 1974. 163p.

The author is Mrs. Josephine Hutson Graham, of Newport and Little Rock, widely known as a painter and teacher. She is founder and president of the Suggin Society. Bill Lewis, a top-flight feature writer, did a review of this book in the Sunday *Arkansas Gazette* (28 July 1974) with a fine photograph, but it was less a book review than a fine story about Mrs. Graham and the Suggin organization. The chapters I like best are those dealing with White River mussels and coarse fish such as buffalo and suckers. It is the best Arkansas cookbook I have seen.

831. Keys, William E. "Corals—Autumn Bounty." *The Ozarks Mountaineer* 21:9 (October 1973): 33.

Short article, with a good photograph, of a mushroom he says is common in oak-and-hickory forests in the fall. "Not only edible but delicious," he says. He recommends frying them in butter. Has photograph in black-and-white, but he refers to "convoluted *amber* growth," so they are probably yellow. I'm pretty timid about mushrooms, and the only fall fungi I'm sure of is the big field puffball, but I think I'll take a chance with this one.

832. Malone, Ruth Moore. *Where to Eat in the Ozarks*. Little Rock: Pioneer Press, 1964. 162p.

Obviously designed for the tourist trade, the first half of this book is a list of hotels and roadside restaurants. Then comes about fifty pages of Ozark recipes, followed by a collection of old remedies, mostly herbals. The subject of Ozark victuals seems pretty well covered.

833. Malone, Ruth Moore, and Bess Malone Lankford. *The Ozark Folk Center Cook Book*. No place of publication or publisher cited, 1975. 61p.

Though many of the more than ninety recipes are associated by title with geographical locations—"Buffalo River Elderberry Pie," "Blanchard Caverns Possum," "Gunner Pool Tomato Salad," etc.—it is regrettable that there is no identification of the contributors nor their place of residence to further substantiate this publication's value as a regional cookbook.

834. Mancell, J., compiler. *Missouri Cookin'*. Amarillo, Tex.: Baxter Lane Company, 1982. 64p.

A few sound authentic enough, like "Ozarks Mountain Roast Squirrels" and "Mississippi River Catfish." But the only claim to regionalism most of the 150 recipes have is that the publisher has prefixed each with the name of a Missouri town or county: "Joplin Cauliflower and Beef Oriental," "St. Louis Lobster Supreme," "North Kansas City Small Chinese Omelets," etc. There is no identification of the source for any of these recipes. For the tourists.

835. Massey, Ellen Gray. *Bittersweet Country*. Garden City, N.Y.: Anchor Press, 1978. 434p.

This book contains selections of articles that have appeared in issues of the *Bittersweet* magazine. There is much on recipes and cooking. On pp. 28–39 are thirty recipes for good Ozark favorites such as crackling bread, dumplings, green tomato pie, gooseberry cobbler, five different recipes using persimmons, etc. On pp. 40–45 are instructions for making hominy under the direction of Ella Dunn, who lived on Bear Creek in Taney County, Missouri. I have partaken of Aunt Ella's hominy, and no printed superlatives can do it justice.

836. Massey, Vickie. "The Sweeter the Juice." *Bittersweet* 4:4 (Summer 1977): 20–24.

Except for the German and Italian colonies, not many Ozark people went in for winemaking. Those who still make wine drink it themselves. They don't sell it. An old man named Marble, who lives near Lebanon, Missouri, was reluctant to teach a young girl how to make blackberry wine. Finally persuaded, he explained the whole thing in great detail. She sets it all down here, with photographs and drawings and exact measures. Some modern gadgets make it easier, almost foolproof.

837. Myers, Lowell. "Blowing the Coals of Old Fires to Life Again." *The Ozarks Mountaineer* 25:9 (October 1977): 11, 30–31.

About campfire cookery. Very few old-timers will admit that they ever ate mussels, but Myers records his experience as follows: "Burt said, you reckon them things is good to eat? I said Burt, I never saw an Indian diggins that wasn't full of old mussell shells, and I reckon we can do anything them Indians did. So we gathered a bunch of mussels, cleaned 'em the best we knew how, built a big fire and buried 'em in the coals. . . . I can't say they were too good—kind of rubbery. A few weeks later I related the incident to my Dad. He said, 'Man, you can't eat them things, they're poison.' But we did eat, and survived, none the worse for the experience." I had a similar experience, years ago on the White River. Mussels don't taste very good, but they certainly are not poisonous.

838. Packer, Ann Taylor. "What Is Ozarks Cookery?" *The Ozarks Mountaineer* 30:6–7 (August 1982): 20–21.

A straightforward article. Many of the old staples Ozarkers produced and processed by their own hands have been replaced by supermarkets with their packaged or canned varieties, and Ozark gardens now bring forth delicacies hardly heard of fifty years ago, such as celery and zucchini. She still lauds natural foods and grandma's cooking but admits there are some things she just can't do like grandma did and justifies the cornbread mixes and canned "biscuits." Her contention is that nowadays "if you live in the Ozarks and cook, you are doing Ozark cookery!" The article ends with recipes for fresh blackeyed peas, squash au gratin, and orange candied sweet potatoes.

839. Parks, Richard. Letter to the editor. *The Ozarks Mountaineer* 25:10 (November 1977): 5.

Mr. Parks remembers the old "Clay Process" for making sorghum, which he learned a long time ago in Carroll County, Missouri. Very few people nowadays ever heard of it. You just throw a lot of powdered red clay into the juice. The clay settles to the bottom, taking with it all the "impurities." When the juice is cooked, just siphon it off. It needs very little skimming. The resulting syrup is light in color and much superior to ordinary sorghum. It is a lot of trouble, but it makes the finest long sweetening in the world.

840. Paulson, Loma L. "Greens Gathering Through Generations." *Bittersweet* 3:3 (Spring 1976): 57–58.

Remembrances of hunting the "green sass," as the author's grandmother called it. Lots of good information about wild greens and their preparation. She says that "sticky thistle" was the first cooking green gathered in the spring.

841. Pennington, Eunice. *History of Carter County* [Missouri]. Fremont, Mo.: Published by the author, 1969. 70p.

Beginning on p. 39, much is said about pioneer foods, including "yawhappen meal," made from the ground seeds of lily pods (this is the American lotus or yoncopin [*Nelumbo lutea*]). Page 42 tells about wild honey and its uses—a successful bee hunter was called a "honey smeller." See p. 45 for an account of the methods of making moonshine.

842. Phillips, Jan. *Wild Edibles of Missouri*. Jefferson City, Mo.: Missouri Department of Conservation, 1979. 248p.

A wonderful book. Over 150 different wild plants, most of which grow in the Ozarks. A complete presentation of each, giving all the particulars: popular and generic names, physical description, habitat, etc. Also thorough instructions for their preparation is given, many with more than one recipe. If one might be harmful or dangerous, the reader is referred to a separate chapter devoted to these species. Along with line drawings of each, there are excellent color renderings by Cindy Bruner, staff artist for the Conservation Department. The author spent three years preparing this material for publication. She is presently teaching at Webster Groves College in St. Louis County, Missouri.

843. Price, Mary Sue. "Woodland Culture Replaces Symphony for Ozark Woman." *Springfield News-Leader*, 3 February 1980.

About wild-foods expert Billy Joe Tatum of Melbourne, Arkansas. Recipes are given for Jerusalem artichoke biscuits, dandelion flower fritters, Spanish cattail bud pie, papaw custard, stuffed morels baked in cream, and candied violets.

844. Rayburn, Otto Ernest. "Moonshine in Arkansas." *Arkansas Historical Quarterly* 16:2 (Summer 1957): 169–73.

About the making of illegal liquor, with some detailed description.

845. Reed, Teresa. "Sometimes I Let It Age Ten or Fifteen Minutes." *Bittersweet* 3:1 (Fall 1975): 55–64.

All about making corn whiskey. The best account of moonshining I have seen, with magnificent photographs and some humorous anecdotes.

846. Saults, Dan. "Bon Apetit Aux Arcs." *The Ozarks Mountaineer* 25:3 (April 1977): 16.

Labeled "Culinary Report," this is a sane and truthful account of Ozark cookery. Saults knows that the food available to tourists in the Ozarks has always been pretty bad. He says it is getting better, and I believe it is. There are roadside inns and restaurants now where the hungry traveler can get good food, and these places are not as far apart as they used to be.

847. Saults, Helen C. "Catfish and Cornbread." *Missouri Life* 4:6 (January-February 1977): 44–50.

A superior piece covering the whole field of Ozark cookery. One of the few good short articles on the subject. The paragraph about scrapple is a bit strange, but all the rest of it rings true. Of course, we don't have bear meat nowadays, but we've still got turkey and venison, cooked in the old way, and real greens.

848. Seaton, Dorthy. *Ma's Cooking Notes of Pa and the Kids Favorite Vittles.* N.p.: Published by the author, [1975?]. [56p.]

This is a collection of some seventy Ozark recipes, written in longhand, and printed on odd sheets of paper. It has been bound together with a woolen string, and put in a cardboard binder, all to make it look quaint and appealing for the tourists. But the recipes seem very good—some of them better than those in the best-selling cookbooks.

849. Steele, Pauline Davis. *Hill Country Sayin's and Ozark Folklore.* West Fork, Ark.: Hutcheson Press, 1976. [40p.]

This small book contains all sorts of folk materials, not only picturesque sayings and wisecracks, but also place names, play-parties, party games, riddles, folk beliefs, folk medicine, charms, amulets, and superstitions. There are numerous craft references on a variety of subjects, with emphasis upon food and its preparation. She gives instructions for making sauerkraut (p. 18) and seven different ways to fix mushrooms (p. 22). This book is well worth reading.

850. ———. *Hill Country Sayin's and Ozark Folklore: Book Two.* West Fork, Ark.: Hutcheson Press, 1977. [41p.]

More recipes and "how to prepare" hints for vinegar pie, hominy bread, head cheese, salads, etc., and even homemade soap. See pp. 4, 13, 14, 18, 25, 28, 33, 36, 37, and 40.

851. Stratton, Eula Mae. *Ozarks Cookery.* Branson, Mo.: The Ozarks Mountaineer, 1975. 80p.

A good regional cookbook, made up of recipes that the author inherited in longhand from her pioneer grandmother. Ably edited by Clay Anderson. A good book.

852. Tatum, Billy Joe. *Billy Joe Tatum's Wild Foods Cookbook and Field Guide.* New York: Workman Publishing Company, 1976. 268p.

Billy Joe Tatum resides halfway between the hamlets of Allison and Melbourne in north-central Arkansas. Her home, which she calls "Wildflower," sits on top of a mountain in an area of unbounded beauty and isolation. She has lived in this part of the Ozarks most of her life and knows firsthand every mountaintop and holler and the flora thereon for miles around. She is an acknowledged authority on Ozark wild foods and has lectured at universities and club meetings throughout the United States, even having appeared on national television. She is prolific about her subject and has contributed numerous articles to scientific journals as well as popular publications. But this book is her grand opus. The first part (pp. 17–110) is entitled "The Forager's Seasons: A Field Guide to Edible Wild Plants." Each of the four seasons is discussed, and the edible plants to be found at those particular times are given. Next is the guide section with more than seventy species listed alphabetically, from acorn to yucca. These have the usual field guide data but with the added bonus of "How Used" comments describing the edible parts of the plants. Line drawings illustrate each subject. The second part (pp. 115–249), "Cooking the Forager's Harvest: Recipes for Wild Foods," is a significant contribution to the culinary arts with its three-hundred-plus recipes. It must be stated that this book could be called a vegetarian's delight as there are practically no references to meat. This subject is to be covered in a later publication. The recipes are arranged under appropriate categories: soups, vegetables, salads, beverages, etc. I have eaten at B. J.'s "wild suppers" and can attest that she practices what she preaches, serving these dishes in her home as common fare rather than as an occasional experiment. This book is highly recommended, especially to those who wish to escape the doldrums of today's tasteless artificial flavorings, frozen food dinners, and other assorted insults to our epicurean senses. There is a complete index of all items in the final pages. The book was edited by Helen Witty.

853. Thomas, Freeman. "Great Wines for the Making." *Ozark Highways* (Fall 1975): 8–9.

Recipes for making clover blossom wine, blackberry bounce, Thomas dandelion wine, elderberry wine, and grape wine.

854. Trimble, Mary H., compiler. *Aunt Mollie's Shepherd of the Hills Cook Book.* Branson, Mo.: Shepherd of the Hills Farm, 1957. 39p.

Another cookbook for the tourist trade, Aunt Mollie being one of the central characters in Harold Bell Wright's *The Shepherd of the Hills*. Many of the recipes (which total 160, according to the title page) are associated with various figures in the book. There's Uncle Ike's favorite, Wash Gibb's favorite, etc. There is nothing new in these recipes (they appear to be made up of "cut-outs" from previous cookbooks), but the visitor to these hills will come away better off with this cookbook than with most offered in the Ozarks today. Practically all the recipes in it would be common fare on an Ozark table at supper time. Mrs. Trimble and her husband purchased the Matthews homestead (Old Matt and Aunt Mollie in the book) in the 1940s and developed it into the Shepherd of the Hills Farm, one of the most successful tourist attractions in the Midwest.

855. Tucker, Ella Mae. *High on the Hog: Lickin' Good Eatin' Hillbilly Recipes.* Marionville, Mo.: Published by the author, 1966. 48p.

These are recipes for dishes once staples in the Ozarks: squirrel pie, rabbit pie with biscuits, persimmon pudding, huckleberry pie, sourdough bread, hushpuppies, and many others seldom seen in print in today's cookbooks.

856. Wade, Jean, special consultant. *Arkansas Cookin'*. Amarillo, Tex.: Baxter Lane Company, 1975. 64p.

More of the same as *Missouri Cookin'* by Mancell but with Arkansas names. Of no value with regard to Ozark studies. Leave this one for the tourists also.

857. Westermann, Julie. "Sharing a Taste for Turtle." *Springfield News and Leader*, 9 July 1977.

A retired float-fishing guide, who resides on Table Rock Lake in southwest Missouri, says that the loggerhead snapper (*Chelydra serpentina*) is the best eating, far better than the soft-shelled variety (*Trionyx mutica*) normally used. Whereas the soft shell reportedly has seven kinds of tastes, he says the loggerhead has only one. He gives his recipe for preparing it. Some good photographs accompany the article.

858. Wieclaw, Wilma. "Aunt Mary's Year Round Poke Greens." *The Ozarks Mountaineer* 23:5 (June 1975): 30.

How to grow poke in a tub in a warm kitchen. All about the way they do it in southern Europe. Different ways of cooking poke and using the berries.

10. Crafts

859. Anderson, Clay. "In the Mountains." In *The Craftsman in America*, ed. National Geographic Society, pp. 124–49. Washington, D.C.: National Geographic Society, 1975.

Anderson visits the Appalachian area of North Carolina and compares its crafts with those of the Ozarks and makes some interesting observations. He says, "Practically every significant factor in the crafts heritage seems to have a parallel in the Ozarks, with one possible exception . . . ," the establishment years ago of craft schools and guilds to perpetuate these skills. Clay, editor of the *The Ozarks Mountaineer*, emphasizes wood carving above all other traditional Ozark craft skills, perhaps too much. There were many "whittlers" but very few "carvers," in the sense he presents them. The problem in the 1970s is with definition. Are we talking about crafts that are native to the Ozarks, or are the Ozarks becoming a center for all sorts of craftsmen who have moved here recently, motivated by the "back to nature" movement or the lucrative tourist trade?

860. Butler, John R. "Folk Art on the Rural Route." *The Ozarks Mountaineer* 29:1 (February 1981): 36–37.

This is nothing more than photographs of unusual rural mail boxes concocted from unlikely materials like cream separators, old pumps, etc.

861. Call, Cora Pinkley. "Fisherman's Luck." *Ozark Magazine* 2:1 (September 1935): 4–5, 16.

Tale about dynamiting fish. Some thick Ozark dialect. *Ozark Magazine* was printed in Romance, Arkansas, and edited by Claude E. Johnson.

862. Cox, Jim. "North Fork Tapestry: The River and Its People Tell Their Story." *West Plains Gazette* 12 (May-June 1981): 37–50.

A springtime float down the North Fork River in Ozark County, Missouri. The author talks about the river and its many points of interests, the mills, fords, springs, and he tells stories about many of the people who have lived along its banks. On p. 44 is a photograph, taken in the 1920s, of a gigging boat. The boats constructed in this region of the Ozarks differed considerably from those in other parts of the White River watershed. Because of the large pine trees that once grew here, it was possible to construct these, with very few planks, up to lengths of thirty feet and longer. The progenitors of these boats were originally dugouts made from single pine logs, evident in the design of the boat pictured.

863. Cox, Vicki. "The Shingle Maker." *The Ozarks Mountaineer* 29:4–5 (June 1981): 52–53.

Farmer Myers, of near Lebanon, Missouri, uses the "water oak" found along the Osage River. A twenty-inch-diameter tree will produce eight hundred to one thousand shingles, each eighteen by five by one-half inches. A man skilled with his froe and mallet can make around five hundred a day.

864. Cozzens, Arthur B. "The Ozark Gunsmith." *Pioneer America* 4:1 (January 1972): 20–22.

A good account, with photographs, of the author's visits in 1925 with gunsmith Carl Hammar, then eighty-two years of age, in his shop near Steelville in Crawford County, Missouri. The article contains a valuable step-by-step description of this pioneer craftsman's method for re-rifling a gun barrel.

865. Croy, Homer. "Who-ee, Pig-ee." In *America Remembers: Our Best-Loved Customs and Traditions*, ed. Samuel Rapport and Patricia Shartle, pp. 238–40. Garden City, N.Y.: Hanover House, 1956.

A brief treatise on hog calling and hog calling contests (pp. 238–40). Today the objective is "to convince the judges, not the hogs." This is a condensed version of a chapter that originally appeared in Croy's *Corn Country* (see volume 1 of this bibliography, p. 153).

866. Curtis, Maxine. "Fiddles from the Forest." *The Ozarks Mountaineer* 20:11 (December 1972): 18.

Robert Croney of Pottersville, Missouri, begins with the living trees, curing and aging the woods himself. He uses a variety: birch or hard maple for the backs, sides of sassafras, spruce pine tops, black walnut fingerboards, tail pieces from hedge or bow dock (*bois d'arc*). He says it takes fifty-two pieces to make a complete fiddle, twenty-one of which are on the inside.

867. ———. "Nora Flynn: Ozark Midwife." *The Ozarks Mountaineer* 23:5 (June 1975): 28–29.

About "catching babies" in the backwoods in the 1870s. Detailed information.

868. Dablemont, Larry. *The Authentic American Johnboat*. New York: David McKay Co., 1978. 88p.

The bulk of this volume is a fine detailed treatise on "How to Build a Johnboat." But those not passionately interested in boat building should buy the book anyhow, and read chapter 1, also chapters 6 and 7 (pp. 70–85). Dablemont is a very fine writer who knows as much about Ozark streams and float trips as any man alive. He now lives in Harrison, Arkansas.

869. ———. "Hunting Turkeys in Solitude." *Field and Stream* 81:2 (June 1976):
14–20.

Good sensible piece about wild turkeys in the Missouri Ozarks, which he says
is the best turkey country in the Midwest. His use of the word *jake* for young gobbler is strange to me. In Carroll County, Arkansas, we say *tom* sometimes. I have
heard old-timers speak of hen turkeys with beards four or five inches long, but I
never saw one. But Dablemont saw two in one week. He is an Arkansan, but seems
to have done most of his hunting in Missouri.

870. *Daisy Cook Remembers*. Kansas City, Mo.: Mid-America Arts Alliance
Project, 1977. 18p.

Maybe her style was a little "crude and unpolished" as one local art critic
stated, but I found in these paintings a compassionate and knowledgeable presentation of life on an Ozarks farm at the turn of the century. Nowadays we call this style
"primitive," and she has been referred to as the Ozark Grandma Moses (she didn't
start painting until age sixty-one). They carry such titles as "Saturday Night Bath,"
"Cleaning Lamp Chimneys," "The Taffy Pull," "Making Sausage," etc., all depicting scenes from her childhood. Forty of her works appear in this booklet, many in
color. Daisy Cook died in 1977.

871. Dale, Bruce. "An Ozark Family Carves a Living and a Way of Life." *National
Geographic Magazine* 148:1 (July 1975): 124–33.

About woodcarver Ivan Denton and his family, who live near Mountainburg in
northwest Arkansas. Denton came to this rugged part of the Ozarks in the 1950s
after a career as a cowboy. He began raising chickens but was soon making more
income from his intricate carvings of cowboy life and outdoors scenes, and he quit
the chickens altogether. One of his daughters, Terry, became well known on her own
merits for her delicate and detailed miniatures. She observed, "The craftsman uses
hands and head. But the artist uses hands, head, and heart." (Terry died in January
1985.) There are some fine detailed photographs of their works. Dale is a staff photographer for the *Geographic*.

872. Davis, M. E. M. "A Snipe Hunt." *Harper's New Monthly Magazine* 92:549
(February 1896): 352–58.

Color and dialect seem like the Ozarks, but Davis does not say it is set in the
Ozarks or Arkansas. There was, though, a Judge Marcellus Davis in Little Rock
about 1900, who wrote fox-hunting yarns.

873. Deane, Ernie. *Ozarks Country*. Branson, Mo.: The Ozarks Mountaineer,
1975. 191p.

"In Defense of Whittlers" on p. 82 contains Ernie's definition of the difference between "woodcarvers and whittlers," terms the tourist dollars have confused. There are many other references to Ozark crafts. See pp. 44, 51, 80–96, and 169.

874. DeBerry, Willie Davidson. "A 1914 Vacation Trip." *The Ozarks Mountaineer* 22:7 (August 1974): 20–21, 28.

Two rural families, in two covered wagons, traveled from Elkland, in Webster County, Missouri, to a famous recreation area in Camdenton County—the Snyder Castle at Hahatonka. Near the castle they met men who lived by catching crawfish (we called them crawdads), which were put in large metal tubs with wet grass or moss and hauled in wagons to Lebanon, Missouri, then shipped by express to market in Chicago. Many people in the Ozarks eat crawdads, which are much better than shrimp, but they are not sold in local markets, and Mrs. DeBerry's reference to commercial fishermen dealing with them is new to me.

875. Dee, Mae Bilbrey. *Little Acorn Characters.* Coldwater, Mo.: Published by the author, 1970. 30p.

The author was born (1896) and raised in Wayne County, Missouri. This booklet is primarily concerned with instructions and ideas for making dolls out of acorns, but it also has random reminiscences by the author of her early life in the Ozarks.

876. Dickneite, Dan F. "Missouri's Oldest Industry." *Missouri Conservationist* 34:12 (December 1973): 7–9.

Trappers and processors of muskrat and coon skins.

877. Dietering, Blair. *Center Point Road.* Commerce: East Texas State University, 1979. 66p.

Many changes have occurred since the section of the Buffalo River in north Arkansas described by this title was designated a National Scenic Wild River. The land in and around the park is now besieged by tourists and "hippies." Interspersed with the author's narration are the transcriptions of conversations with five long-time natives of the region as they tell "how it was." See pp. 52–53 for a ginseng hunt. Many photographs throughout. The author says that this work, a school project, was divinely inspired.

878. Dunn, Ella Ingenthron. "Dumbull." *Bittersweet* 4:1 (Fall 1976): 58–61.

Describes a toy made of a nail keg and groundhog skin. Good photos and drawings.

879. ———. *The Granny Woman of the Hills.* Walnut Shade, Mo.: Published by the author, 1974. 65p.

A paperback, illustrated by the author. Beginning with the brief story of the Ingenthron family who came from Germany in the late 1840s. After six years in rural Indiana, they came to Missouri. In 1873 they came as homesteaders to Forsyth. All this interested me because I once lived in Taney County and knew many of the Ingenthrons.

Mrs. Dunn's mother was a pioneer granny woman, and when she retired about 1919, "Elly" took over and did the best she could. She describes the whole scene of pioneer life, with chapters on the log cabin, the ash-hopper, the evaporator (for drying fruit), butchering time, maple sugar, cane and sorghum making, brush arbor meetings, fish traps on the White River, childbirth, etc. Plain tales well told. No attempt at fine writing, but Elly just set down the truth as she remembered it. A good job, too.

880. ————. *The Granny Woman of the Hills.* 2d printing. Branson, Mo.: The Ozarks Mountaineer, 1978. 78p.

This second edition appears with some slight changes, "to eliminate typographical errors and improve clarity." The editing was done by Elmo Ingenthron, a nephew, who added a five-page introduction, several photographs, and a concluding chapter entitled "About the Author." This edition is copyrighted by Elmo Ingenthron.

881. Dunn, Emma Comfort. "Trapping Missouri's Furbearers." *Missouri Conservationist* 36:1 (January 1975): 7–9.

Fox, muskrat, etc. Mrs. Dunn lives in Bourbon, Missouri.

882. Fischer, Joseph. "Daisy Cook." *American History Illustrated* 17:8 (December 1982): 22–29.

Daisy didn't begin painting the scenes from her southwest Missouri childhood until she was in her sixties. Between then and her death she produced more than 350 of her memories on canvas. Brief text with eight of her paintings.

883. ————. "She Painted Her Past." *Missouri Life* 5:5 (November-December 1977): 29–36.

Daisy Cook has been called the Grandma Moses of the Ozarks. A teacher in the Branson-Hollister area, she retired about 1960 and took up painting primitives at Silver Dollar City, mostly scenes from her own life on an Ozark farm in the early 1900s. In this article Fischer shows twelve of Daisy's paintings in full color, with a fine colored photograph of the artist. She died in December 1977 at age seventy-five.

884. Fish, Wilma Naugle. *Wilma's Apple Dolls and Romance.* Gainesville, Mo.: Published by the author, 1982. 28p.

About making dolls from dried apples. The Romance in this book is the name of the community in Ozark County, Missouri, where the author was raised.

885. Fleming, Dick. "Water-Witching in the Ozarks." *The Ozarks Mountaineer* 23:3 (April 1975): 20.

A short article about dowsing, with two good photos of a water witch at work.

886. Foreman, Diana. "Fiddlin' Around." *Bittersweet* 5:2 (Winter 1977): 62–69.

Step-by-step instructions on how to make a fiddle by Violet Hensley, the "Whittling Fiddler" from Yellville, Arkansas. She says it takes her about 240 hours from start to the finished product, for which she gets anywhere from $200 to $500. There is an accompanying sound sheet with Violet playing some old favorites on one of her creations.

887. Freyder, Doris. "Antiques, Folk Skills Tell the Story of Ozark Culture." *The Ozarks Mountaineer* 29:2–3 (April 1981): 30–31.

Interviews with four craftspeople who attended the War Eagle (Arkansas) Folklife Fair in 1980. Interviewed were a weaver from Medicine Lodge, Kansas, a collector and restorer of antique guns from Buckeye, Arkansas, a furniture maker from Fayetteville, Arkansas, and a couple from Hindsville, Arkansas, who displayed the contents of a house over one hundred years old that they purchased containing most of the original furnishings.

888. Gerlach, Russel L. "Moonshining in the Ozarks—Past and Present." *The Ozarks Mountaineer* 24:8 (September 1976): 20, 30.

The old-timer was a craftsman who took pride in his craft. The modern moonshiner is an unscrupulous businessman, often a criminal, who goes for high volume and profit from his "liquid corn" with little regard for quality or the safety of his consumers. Gerlach, a geography teacher at Southwest Missouri State University in Springfield, has researched his subject thoroughly. This is a valuable paper, full of authentic detail.

889. Gerstäcker, Friedrich. "Women in the Backwoods." Trans. Ralph Walker. *Early American Life* 13:6 (December 1982): 14–16, 19–23.

This particular article was written for a German magazine in the mid-1840s; in it the author gives an interesting picture of woman's life on the frontier. A good description of her preparation of the family meal is on p. 15. He notes that butter was made by the tiring task of shaking the milk in a jar by hand.

890. Gideon, Gene. " 'Hill Crofters,' the Ozark Craftsmen." *Ozark Highways* (Winter 1972): 25–30.

Mini-sketches of twenty-two of the better known crafts people of the Ozark regions of Missouri and Arkansas.

891. Hardaway, B. Touchstone. *These Hills My Home*. Point Lookout, Mo.: School of the Ozarks Press, [1972?]. 95p.

This is a biography of Frank Villines and his family of Low Gap in Newton County, Arkansas. All about his boyhood, his love affairs and marriages, and his various jobs, all of which seemed very important in Newton County. It is doubtful Ms. Hardaway ever lived in the Ozarks, but from frequent visits over a two-year period she gathered photos and information that she compiled into this family history of the Villines. There is also a lot of information about the Buffalo River and life in the hills in the early 1900s. See pp. 35–39, "The Cedar Harvest," about how they cut the timber and floated it down the Buffalo River.

892. Heck, Terri. "Making Chair Seats from Corn Shucks." *Bittersweet* 9:1 (Fall 1981): 42–47.

A good article about a craft seldom seen nowadays and not often written about. The craftswoman is Irene Haymes, who lives in Laclede County, Missouri. Her step-by-step instructions are accompanied by excellent photographs.

893. Hicks, Bert, and Mildred Hicks. "Pearling on the Black River." *The Ozarks Mountaineer* 28:10–11 (December 1980): 52–53, 66.

In Black Rock, Lawrence County, Arkansas, the harvesting of freshwater mussels for their pearls and shells is still pursued by a very few pearlers just as it was eighty or so years ago.

894. Hough, Stephen. "The Ozark Johnboat." *Bittersweet* 1:2 (Winter 1973): 4–11.

Step-by-step photographs along with diagrams and a parts list trace the construction of a sixteen-foot johnboat, the best vehicle ever conceived for "running" Ozark streams and rivers. The craftsman is one Emmett Massey, a native of Laclede County, Missouri. Following is a companion article, "A Talk with Emmett," pp. 12–14, in which Massey describes the boats further and tells about the Ozarkers' many uses for these square-ended, flat-bottomed boats.

895. Hudgins, Mary D. "The Rise and Fall of Coin Glass." *Arkansas Democrat Magazine*, 18 November 1956.

Pressed-glass dishes and decanters, with the impressions of silver coins set into the glass. Descriptions and two photos of pieces in a museum at Lonsdale, Arkansas. The dollars are dated 1892, and the stuff was somehow connected with Coin Harvey's political campaigns. Only a few thousand pieces were made; then the federal government held that such manufacture was illegal and destroyed twenty thousand dollars worth of molds and other equipment.

896. Hurley, F. Jack. "Logging with a Horse." *Fine Woodworking* 30 (September-
    October 1981): 98–99.

About Rex Harral, of Wilburn, Arkansas, who prefers to log his timber using a
draft horse. The horse, called a timber snaker, drags the cut logs (usually ten foot
long and twenty-two inches wide) out of the timber, and both need a space hardly
more than two feet wide. With this method they can move about without damaging
the young trees. Compare this, he says, with the use of tractors or Caterpillars.

897. Ihrig, B. B. *History of Hickory County, Missouri, 1970*. Warsaw, Mo.: The
    Printery, 1970. 419p.

Most of this book is the usual list of names and dates common to this type of
publication, but this author includes much information about the early crafts. See
pp. 18–19 for log rolling and house raisings; more about log cabins appears on
pp. 37–39. He explains on p. 39 about homemade shoes made of "whang" leather.
On p. 40 he tells of preparing wheat for the mill by using a machine called a wheat
fan that "stirred about as much wind as pulling a turkey backwards." They made
cast iron pots (p. 47), the iron inside "as smooth as the skin on a young negro girl's
forehead." He gives details about making rope beds but says that "many a poor in-
nocent babe . . . was smothered by parents rolling together after the cords sagged
down." Ihrig was county superintendent of schools for many years.

898. Ingenthron, Elmo. "The Pearly Waters." *The Ozarks Mountaineer* 22 : 11 (De-
    cember 1974): 18–21.

Begins with an account of pioneer methods of taking fish, with a fine picture of
a big fishtrap. But most of the article is about pearls and mussel shells. The Indians
ate White River mussels, and the pioneer whites mentioned clam chowder in early
letters, but it appears that mussels were never important in their diet.

899. Jeffords, Edd. "Monument at Buffalo River Is One Man's Gift to Ozarks."
    Ozark Digest (May 1975): 12.

In 1973 a newcomer to the north Arkansas Ozarks, sculptor Robert Bertil Ed
from St. Paul, Minnesota, began work on a statue in honor of the nation's Bicentennial. It was located at Pruitt, close to the Buffalo River, and was to be 60 feet long,
18 feet high, and 13 feet wide, and would weigh 160,000 pounds, no small undertaking. It depicted a father, mother, and child in a canoe and was entitled "Family
Float Trip." Ed was personally financing the project and performing practically all
the labor himself. The entire back page of this issue is an order form showing numerous pen and ink sketches by him for sale to help the cause. But with the sculpture about one-third completed, Ed had exhausted both himself and his resources
and this, combined with his problems with the National Parks Service who super-
vise the Buffalo River, forced him to abandon his monument. He soon left the
Ozarks and his work has since been torn down and cleared away.

900. Jeffries, T. Victor. *Before the Dam Waters: Story and Pictures of Old Linn Creek, Ha Ha Tonka and Camden County.* Springfield, Mo.: Midwest Litho and Publishing Company, 1974. 58p.

Old Linn Creek is now beneath the waters of the Lake of the Ozarks, created in 1930. It was located in central Missouri on the banks of the Osage River, having been an important steamboat port in the early days. Pages 35–37 tell of the tie industry and how the ties were transported down the river.

901. Jennings, Gina. "Making Rugs with Old Toothbrushes." *Bittersweet* 8:3 (Spring 1981): 58–65.

The title refers to the conversion of a toothbrush handle into the needle used in making these rugs. They are neither crocheted nor braided in the strict sense of the word, but done with a combination of both techniques. Along with the text there are step-by-step photographs and diagrams showing the procedure.

902. Johns, Paul W. *Unto These Hills: True Tales from the Ozarks.* Ozark, Mo.: Bilyeu-Johns Enterprises, 1980. 104p.

Many early crafts are described throughout. For a good description of an 1838 tanyard see p. 15. Aunt Cindy Bolin was a nature doctor and many of her herb medicines are listed (pp. 16–17). See pp. 47–62 for detailed accounts of the various mills that have served this region. On pp. 77–79 Johns tells about the early blacksmiths and farriers.

903. Junas, Lil. *Cadron Creek: A Photographic Narrative.* Little Rock: The Ozark Society Foundation, 1979. 96p.

See pp. 24–25 about a "felly" mill that operated on its banks. A felly is the exterior wooden piece (the rim) of a wagon wheel that is supported by the spokes. More about mills on pp. 35–36.

904. Keithley, William. "In the Old Days." *The Ozarker* 5:4 (July 1968): 3.

Brief but detailed account of harvesting wheat. The bundles were beaten with hickory sticks called "wheat frailes" until the grain was "shelled out" and the chaff was "fanned out with turkey wings." Then they hauled the stuff to a clean level place called the "tromper yard" and led horses over the bundles—more tromping. It all seems pretty complicated. Keithley lived on Bull Creek at Walnut Shade, Missouri.

905. Ksara, Kirsten, and Vickie Hooper. "Toys Homemade by R. L. Elgin." *Bittersweet* 10:1 (Fall 1982): 55–70.

Instructions with photographs for constructing twenty-five toys from the simplest of materials, all readily available around the farmyard or household. These were all familiar items to youngsters fifty or more years ago and no batteries were needed. Elgin was raised in Platte County, Missouri.

906. Lamb, Nancy. "Pine Needle Artistry." *The Ozarks Mountaineer* 29:10–11 (December 1981): 44–45.

Twelve-inch to eighteen-inch pine needles are woven into baskets, hot dish mats, and decorative wall hangings by a couple from Versailles in the north-central Missouri Ozarks. They say they learned the art from a "little old lady in Alabama" and claim the craft is European in origin and was brought to America by early settlers who in turn taught the Indians. Five photographs.

907. Lamp, Ann Louise. "Kitchen Utensils of Long Ago." *The Ozarks Mountaineer* 21:2 (March 1973): 14–15.

Brief paper, but well worth reading. All about rolling pins and springerle and marzipan molds.

908. Lee, Robert. "The Slow Tom." *Shannon County Historical Review* 5:1 (April 1968): 2.

Brief description of the little gristmill used to grind the old-timer's corn, sometimes called a Lazy Tom.

909. "Life Goes Fishing." *Life* 10:25 (23 June 1941): 86–89.

There are over a dozen photos in this article. Some are a little posed, but they pretty well describe a typical float on an Ozarks river when this pastime was at its best. Pictured are Jim Owen, whose float-fishing business was nationally known, and three of the greatest guides who ever ran the rivers: Charlie Barnes, 72 at the time, who, along with his brother John, is credited by many as being the creator of the johnboat; Tom Yocum, who spent a lifetime searching for the elusive Yocum Silver Mine; and Jemmie "Little Hoss" Jennings. Those were the days.

910. Lincoln, Robert Page. *Black Bass Fishing.* Harrisburg, Penn.: Stackpole Co., 1952. 376p.

The best book about the theory and practice of bass fishing, with full treatment of smallmouth, Kentucky or spotted bass, largemouth, stripers, and white bass. Lincoln is primarily a bait caster, but he discusses fly-fishing as well, and gives a detailed description of boats, rods, reels, lines, flies, and plugs. Chapter 23 (pp. 342–54) is "An Ozark Float," with mention of Charlie Barnes, Jim Owens, and a brief history of the float-trip business in Missouri and Arkansas. Lincoln credits Charlie with the invention of the Ozark johnboat.

911. Long, Kathy. "Riving Shingles the Old Time Way with Art Corn." *Bittersweet* 9:1 (Fall 1981): 20–26.

Excellent photographs and drawings. Much detail given about the woods and the tools used. Wood splits best when it's green and frozen.

912. Low, Jana, Gina Hilton, and Jenny Kelso. "Visiting Daisy Cook." *Bittersweet* 1:4 (Summer 1974): 38–47.

A visit with this popular Ozark painter at her home in Republic, Missouri. Thirteen black-and-white photos of her canvasses are shown.

913. Ludwig, Stephen. "Trapping Coyotes." *Bittersweet* 4:2 (Winter 1976): 70.

Comer Owen of Greene County, Missouri, traps coyotes as well as hunting them with hounds. He is among the last of the hunter-trappers once an important part of the Ozark culture. But he has lived too long. Town people have invaded his territory with subdivisions; their dogs get in his traps or maul his catches. Their fences injure his hounds and their highways kill them. Those who believe in Walt Disney and Bambi think him cruel and sadistic. I have hunted with Comer and he is neither of those, but is more in harmony with nature than we are with our pesticides and bulldozers. (See related articles in this same issue: "Coyotes Are Like People" by Comer Owen, pp. 60–64, and "The Big Run Around" by Doug Sharp, pp. 65–69.)

914. McRaven, Charles. *Building the Hewn Log House.* Hollister, Mo.: Mountain Publishing Services, 1978. 208p.

This book is the first volume of the Arkansas College Folklore Monograph Series, initially edited by Prof. Richard S. Tallman of Batesville. It is superbly edited and fully illustrated with drawings and photographs showing the step-by-step procedures to follow with each phase of the construction. Though it appears to be complete in its instructions, it will be interesting to hear from one who has actually used it as a guide.

915. ———. "Turnback Mill Restoration." *Old Mill News* 6:3 (July 1978): 3–5.

Restoration of an 1857 mill near Halltown in southwest Missouri. The mill, with an undershot wheel, operated until 1943 when the machinery was sold for scrap during World War II. Director of the restoration was an eighty-year-old Irishman, Bill Cameron, who had called on the mill as early as 1925 as a salesman of leather belting. Cameron has served as consultant on a number of mill restoration projects in the Ozark region. *Old Mill News* is a quarterly publication of the Society for the Preservation of Old Mills, headquartered in Wiscasset, Maine.

916. Massey, Ellen Gray. *Bittersweet Country*. Garden City, N.Y.: Anchor Press, 1978. 434p.

All these articles have previously appeared in issues of the *Bittersweet* magazine. For crafts, see blacksmithing in Pulaski County (pp. 161–75); moonshining (pp. 195–205); constructing an Ozark johnboat (pp. 286–98); weaving (pp. 299–325); and quilting (pp. 326–56).

917. Matthews, Linda. "Coon Creek of Cleburne County." *Independence County Chronicle* 19:1 (October 1977): 56.

The author knows some good stories about her county, with lots of information about the early crafts. Pages 13–25 cover tanning hides, bear and bee hunting, and sorghum making.

918. Merryman, Alice. *Shuckery and Corn Artistry*. N.p.: Published by the author, [1967?]. [10p.]

This item, illustrated with drawings, is a machine copy from the Rare Book Room of the Springfield, Missouri, Public Library. All about dolls made of corn husks and cobs, corn shuck brooms and chair seats, lye soap and hominy, baked corn, grit bread, and Indian corn foods.

919. Messick, Mary Ann. *History of Baxter County, 1873–1973*. Little Rock: Mountain Home Chamber of Commerce, 1973. 506p.

In her introduction Messick says that in north Arkansas it was corn, not cotton, that was the staple of the hill families. She talks at length about the self-sufficiency of their farming and household practices. On p. 95 is an interesting photo of a broom factory run by three members of the Rorie family, all of whom were blind. Chapter 14 (pp. 116–35) has some wonderful stories about the hill doctors and midwives.

920. Morgan, Gordon D. *Black Hillbillies of the Arkansas Ozarks: A Report of the Department of Sociology, University of Arkansas*. Fayetteville: University of Arkansas, 1973. 165p.

According to the author, the crafts of the mountain blacks and whites do not differ. Though there was little intercourse between the two groups, their isolation from changing technologies resulted in the continued use of traditional folk methods of colonial times. Of special interest is the discussion of Ozark frontier architecture, pp. 82–83.

921. Oliver, M. E. *Old Mills of the Ozarks*. Point Lookout, Mo.: School of the Ozarks Press, 1969. [26p.]

A fine picture-book. Twenty full-page sketches, comparable to his silk-screen book *Strange Scenes in the Ozarks* (see volume 1 of this bibliography, p. 337) except that these are black-and-white pictures. The page opposite the drawings carries a paragraph about the history of the mill—when and where it was built, and by whom and under what circumstances. All fascinating. Oliver was born on Drake's Creek in Madison County, Arkansas. He died there in 1973.

922. ———. *Old Mills of the Ozarks*. Point Lookout, Mo.: School of the Ozarks Press, 1971. [61p.]

This is an enlarged edition of the 1969 printing with ten additional mills and their histories included.

923. Payton, Leland, and Crystal Payton. "Quilts." *Missouri Life* 2:5 (November-December 1974): 4–11.

A good article with fine color pictures. Some women nowadays have regular "quilt factories"—they make quilts wholesale, and sell them to gift shops all over the country.

924. Rader, Caryn. "All Gussied Up." *Bittersweet* 5:4 (Summer 1978): 37–42.

A splendid descriptive story about "beauty hints" and cosmetics in rural Missouri around the turn of the century. Miss Rader has collected the material from old-timers around Lebanon, Missouri, and she did a beautiful job with it.

925. Rafferty, Milton D., and Virginia Raskin. *Ozark House Types*. Springfield, Mo.: Aux-Arc Book Company, [1972]. 32p.

Some twenty-five drawings by Raskin, each with a paragraph of descriptive matter by Rafferty. Pleasant reading, because it avoids the technical language of architects. The drawings show all the common types, and the names attached are in the vernacular. A treatment of the double-pen cabin with "dog-run" would have been useful, and a discussion of the "two front doors" question. The last residence pictured is Bonniebrook, the home of Rose O'Neill, on Bear Creek, north of Branson, Missouri. This house had seventeen rooms and is described as a "mansion" and the "show-place of the whole area"; it burned in 1947. This interested me because I lived in that house for more than a year, in the early 1940s, and the "show-place" was pretty primitive.

926. Raup, H. F. "The Fence in the Cultural Landscape." *Western Folklore* 6:1 (January 1947): 1–12.

Good paper with drawings and photos, some from Missouri and Arkansas. Cf. Mamie Merideth's paper in *Southern Folklore Quarterly* 15 (June 1951): 109–51.

927. Rayburn, Otto Ernest. "Ozark Customs." *Arkansas Historical Quarterly* 18:2
(Summer 1959): 73–77.

Some interesting stories about harvesting grain, how fire was kept, a description of a slow tom mill, and the building of a chimney.

928. Reuter, Frank. "John Arnold's Link Chains: A Study in Folk Art." *Mid-South
Folklore* 5:2 (Summer 1977): 41–52.

John Arnold of Monticello, Arkansas, is a whittler who makes wooden chains.
It takes about fifty-five hours to produce a chain that sells for twenty dollars. This
article describes the process in great detail, with large photographs of the whittler
and his work. The author lectures on folk art at North Arkansas Community College. He lives in Berryville.

929. Richardson, Elizabeth E. "The Art of Patchwork." *Tennessee Folklore Society
Bulletin* 16:3 (September 1950): 54–61.

Regarding "the traditional Bride's Quilt," on p. 55 she says, "invitations to a
quilting where the heart design was employed was (*sic*) tantamount to an engagement announcement. Hearts were the insignia for a bride, and up to 1840 such a
design used in any other quilt than that of the bride was considered most unlucky."

930. Roberts, Carla. "A Diamond in the Rough." *Bittersweet* 4:3 (Spring 1977):
4–10.

A fine story about Ella Dunn, old-time midwife of Walnut Shade, Missouri,
with four good photos by Doug Sharp. For "Aunt" Ella's own story, see *The Granny
Woman of the Hills* (entry 879).

931. Robinett, Paul M., and Howard V. Canan. *Black Bass and Ozark Float Fishing*. Point Lookout, Mo.: School of the Ozarks Press, 1974. 119p.

Floating the Gasconade, Current, Eleven Point, and other Missouri streams.
These fellows appreciate the superiority of the smallmouth bass, in cold streams,
over any other fish that swims. Many old-time guides they remember too, and call
them by name. Robinett, an enthusiastic Ozarker from Mountain Grove, Missouri,
who attained the rank of brigadier general in the army and in World War II led a tank
battalion successfully against Rommel in North Africa, always maintained that there
never should have been a south Missouri nor a north Arkansas, but a separate state
of the Ozarks. He died in 1975.

932. Sale, Charles "Chic." *The Specialist*. St. Louis: Specialist Publications,
1929. 29p.

By a professional privy builder. Fine detail, with all arguments pro and con. A beautiful job. It is a mistake to let it go out of print. Machine copies are bringing high prices to the scarce-book *mumserim* in New York.

933. Sampson, Frank. "Missouri's Fur Harvest." *Missouri Conservationist* 38:1 (January 1977): 12–15.

If you're going to understand the Ozark hillman, some knowledge of fur hunting and trapping is important. Far from being an anachronism of the frontier days, it is still an important part of his recreation and a supplement to his income. Besides statistics and dollar values of the Missouri fur harvest, Sampson gives interesting theories on the ebb and flow of various species.

934. Saults, Dan. "Float Fishing." *The Ozarks Mountaineer* 26:3 (April 1978): 21–23, 33.

Nostalgic tales of float trips on the James, White, Niangua, Gasconade, Big Piney, and Buffalo. All written in Saults's best style, which is very, very good. Page 23 mistakenly says the article is continued on "page 29."

935. Schmalstig, Mary. "Ode to the Commode." *Bittersweet* 7:3 (Spring 1980): 42–49.

This is the most candid and informative article I've ever seen in print about outhouses and chamber pots. It's all here, covering the subject from the most primitive structures up through the days of the WPA. Government regulations for grade A milk barns moved them indoors, according to one informant. This is a sensible article, not the joking around that usually accompanies this subject. Much about the social proprieties that existed. Good photographs and drawings. Included is James Whitcomb Riley's *Passing of the Backhouse*.

936. Scott, Donna. "Washboard Washing." *Bittersweet* 3:2 (Winter 1975): 63–66.

Details about washing clothes, the old way, and the use of blueing, starch, and so on. She quotes her informant, ninety-four-year-old Mary Moore of Laclede County, Missouri, as saying, "You take a hot day and this was a hot job!" Good photographs.

937. Seay, Sarah. "Modernizing a Mountain Art." *Bittersweet* 1:2 (Winter 1973): 36–41.

One of the very few authentic old-time dulcimer players in the Ozarks today, Bill Graves of Richland, Missouri, describes how after the Civil War his grandfather made what Graves thinks was the first dulcimer. Quite a contrast to the description in the second part of this article of Lynn McSpadden's modern-day dulcimer shop in Mountain View, Arkansas.

938. Seitz, Dick. "Missouri Wolf Chase." *Hunting Dog Magazine* 7:12 (December 1972): 22–23, 35, 44.

Good account of hunting coyotes (*Canis latrans*) in the southwest Missouri Ozarks. This particular chase takes place in Polk County. There's a note of respect for the quarry as one hunter says, "There are lots of provisions to take care of people when they get old and partly disabled: social security, pensions, nursing homes, etc., but the coyote has to make his own living up to the last day he's on this earth."

939. Sharp, Doug. "The Big Run-Around." *Bittersweet* 4:2 (Winter 1976): 65–69.

Good account of a coyote hunt with Comer Owen and his dogs. Good photographs. Comer has made his living for the past sixty-five years by hunting, trapping, and fishing. He pursues his vocation with a zeal inherited from his forefathers and doesn't let much stand in his way. (It is told that an airliner once had to delay its takeoff while Comer and his Walker hounds chased a coyote down the main runway of the Springfield, Missouri, airport.)

940. ———. "Ozark Turkey Talk." *Bittersweet* 5:3 (Spring 1978): 34–43.

All about wild turkeys in Missouri. Methods of hunting, photographs, types of calls, etc. Description and picture of the latest "diaphragm call" so highly praised by many hunters. According to Sharp, only one hen out of a hundred has a beard, and hen's beards are short and inconspicuous.

941. ———. "Skinning the Coyote." *Bittersweet* 4:2 (Winter 1976): 71–75.

This paper, illustrated with drawings and photographs, shows exactly how to "case" coyote pelts. The average skin is worth about fifteen dollars.

942. Sharp, Doug, and Steve Ludwig. "White Oak Baskets: Baskets the Lyn Marble Way." *Bittersweet* 3:2 (Winter 1975): 46–55.

A visit with a veteran basketmaker of Falcon, Missouri, telling how to make the splits, how to weave the baskets, etc. Fine photographs show everything in detail.

943. Shields, Wayne F. "The Chariton River Fish Trap." *Missouri Historical Review* 61:4 (July 1967): 489–96.

Big fish traps were once community projects for the towns along the major rivers of the Ozarks. Many, such as the subject of this article, were well constructed and lasted for years. One of the best known in the Missouri Ozarks was the Cedar Point trap located on the White River just above Forsyth (see p. 300 in Ingenthron's *Land of Taney* [entry 455]). State regulations on limits of fish ended what traps were still in use. It is rumored, though, that illegal trapping may still exist, but in a more mobile form using gill and trammel nets.

944. Soric, Peggy. "Woman Brings Special Craft to the Ozarks." *Springfield News-Leader*, 13 September 1981.

Cheri Russell of Ozark, Missouri, is thought to be one of only twelve persons in the United States practicing the craft of restoring wicker furniture. Though a native Ozarker, she learned this trade while living away from the Ozarks. She tells how to distinguish manmade paper wicker from the wood wicker.

945. Stewart, Melinda. "Tie Making." *Bittersweet* 5:3 (Spring 1978): 75–78.

Much detail, good photographs of a once-common trade in the Ozarks.

946. Stewart, Melinda, and Linda Lee. "Stalking the Wild Bee: Finding and Cutting Wild Bee Trees." *Bittersweet* 8:2 (Winter 1980): 26–37.

This is a very detailed narrative of bee coursing, cutting the tree, and getting the honey. It goes on to give instructions on capturing the queen, she being the key to saving the hive. All this is demonstrated by an abundance of step-by-step photographs.

947. Tebbetts, Diane. "Earl Ott: Fishing on the Arkansas." *Mid-South Folklore* 5:3 (Winter 1977): 101–13.

A fine detailed story of the tribe of commercial fishermen of the 1920s and 1930s. Earl Ott was one of the old houseboat clan, and Diane Tebbetts is his daughter. She knows her subject and sets down the old stories and traditional lore without pulling any punches. An excellent account of commercial fishing on the White and the Arkansas.

948. Townsend, Will. "A Lost Valley Derelict." *The Ozarks Mountaineer* 24:6 (July 1976): 23.

Photo of a very old log cabin, showing the "chamfer and notch" method of joining the logs at the corners. Much better than the common "saddle notch" joint, but rare nowadays. It requires a very skillful craftsman.

949. Van Horn, Donald. *Carved in Wood: Folk Sculpture in the Arkansas Ozarks*. Batesville: Arkansas College Folklore Archive Publications, 1979. 149p.

About woodcarving in the north-central Arkansas Ozarks. The author concentrates upon four carvers that he calls "folk sculptors." Biographical sketches of each, along with critical comments about their carvings and motivations. Much of the text is based upon hours of personal interviews with each subject. One of the most ballyhooed of Ozark crafts is woodcarving. Van Horn makes some good observations throughout about all this, what is indigenous and what has been inspired by the tourist dollar.

The author is a sculptor and teaches at Texas Eastern University in Tyler, Texas.

950. Vance, Joel M. "It's Sucker Grabbing Time." *Missouri Conservationist* 36:4 (April 1975): 16–19.

About the shoaling of the redhorse (*Moxostoma carinatum*) and the yellow sucker (*Moxostoma erythrurum*) in Ozarks streams and the big fish fry at Nixa, Missouri. Sucker Day is the big day at Nixa.

951. "The Village Smithy." *Ark/Ozark* 1:1 (Fall 1968): 34–36.

Blacksmith Isaac Doss of Berryville, Arkansas, still practices the almost forgotten art of hammer welding.

952. Wallis, Michael. "Smoking Ozark Style: Corncob Pipes, an American Tradition." *American West* 19:3 (May-June 1982): 20–24.

About the "Missouri Meerschaum." First produced in Washington, Missouri, in 1868 by a Dutch immigrant named Tibbe, the original factory is still in operation in the same location today.

953. M. [Matt Flournoy Ward]. "A Day's Sport in Arkansas." *New York Spirit of the Times* 18:16 (10 June 1848): 189.

Harpooning fish at Willowby, Arkansas. Some frontier atmosphere.

954. Waterman, Todd. "Noodling: The Old Art of Catching Fish with the Hands." *Bittersweet* 8:1 (Fall 1980): 56–59.

This is the best and most complete account I've seen about this subject, the practice of which is now outlawed in the Ozarks. "Noodling" is the practice of reaching, with bare hands, into submerged hollow logs or underneath rocks and ledges along the river banks and feeling for the large catfish that nest there. When one is located, the noodler puts his hand or a large hook into its mouth and catches it. This was (and clandestinely still is) a time-honored method of putting meat on the table, but this article tells of the many dangers that could present themselves to the noodler. I was too much the coward to ever try it, and it still scares the hell out of me to watch 'em do it!

955. ———. "Rail Fences: Their History and Construction." *Bittersweet* 9:1 (Fall 1981): 4–15.

There are two types: the self-supporting or zig-zag, and the straight lined, supported by posts. This is a fine article with photographs and drawings showing each step of the construction of both types, from the splitting of the logs for rails to the finished fence.

956. ———. "Tie Rafting: Floating Railroad Ties on Ozark Rivers." *Bittersweet* 7:2 (Winter 1979): 44–55.

A fine piece about railroad ties and tiemakers. Many good photographs and drawings.

957. Watts, Patsy. "Plumgrannies." *Bittersweet* 7:3 (Spring 1980): 32–33.

This aromatic plant, also known as vegetable peach, was once common, but is apparently unknown to many hillfolk nowadays. Watts quotes many old-timers.

958. Weaver, H. Dwight, and Paul A. Johnson. *Missouri the Cave State.* Jefferson City, Mo.: Discovery Enterprises, 1980. 336p.

One of the earliest crafts practiced in Missouri took place in its caves. Gunpowder was a necessity for the early pioneers, and the saltpeter found in caves was a primary ingredient. For stories of those that were a major source see pp. 115–17, 273. An interesting story also is that of the caves beneath the city of St. Louis that served as breweries and beer gardens. See pp. 278–85.

959. Webb, Joanne. *How to Make Your Own Dried Apple Dolls.* Onia, Ark.: Published by the author, 1976. 6p.

Instructions, illustrations, photographs, and full-size patterns. Enough to get the job done.

960. White, Lydia A. *Grandma Ozark's Company's Coming Cook Book.* Clinton, Mo.: The Printery, [1982]. 32p.

Though there are reproductions of advertisements from the 1920s throughout, there is nothing "old-timey" nor uniquely Ozark about these recipes (the norm for most of these cookbooks put out for the tourist trade—they could be "local" anywhere in the country). The "company" in this cookbook is going to find out that Grandma Ozark has gone cosmopolitan. Over half of these recipes are of an international flavor: crab rangoon, Mexican pie, chicken quiche, etc. But, in many instances so have the Ozarks nowadays. It's not at all unusual to find the noon special in some little crossroads restaurant featuring lasagna or cashew chicken or taco salad. But you can bet it'll still be served with hominy and mashed potatoes and gravy.

961. White, Mahlon N. *Pretty Privies of the Ozarks: Actual Photographs of Vanishing Americana*. Clinton, Mo.: Democrat Publishing Co., [1968?]. 24p.

Has pictures of twenty-two privies, including one splendid brick specimen in perfect condition.

962. Williams, Harry Lee. "Season Comes on Spring River for Challenge to the Fisherman." *Arkansas Gazette Sunday Magazine*, 23 March 1958.

Good article on the redhorse (genus *Moxostoma*) and fishing for them in the Spring River area of north-central Arkansas. How to snag and cook them. Williams says that "female redhorse are quickly returned to the water, as none but the males are brought home by those with a spark of sporting blood."

11. Fiction

963. Alvarez, H. G. *Return to War Eagle*. Little Rock: Pioneer Press, 1963. 229p.

A juvenile novel. Much of the action takes place in northwest Arkansas, but the author shows little knowledge of the region or the people although he lived for a time in Greenwood, Arkansas.

964. Archer, Myrtle. *The Young Boys Gone*. New York: Walker and Company, 1978. 218p.

A juvenile story about the Civil War in the southwest Missouri Ozarks. To escape marauding armies and guerrillas, a family flees to a remote part of the mountains and makes their home in a cave. The story is mostly about their trials and tribulations by being forced to live off the land. There are some references to wild foods, home remedies, and pioneer crafts. The author makes a few errors in describing the Ozarks at that time, but these are minor and it is a good story anyway. The book's jacket says that Archer was raised in the wilds of northern Idaho and now resides in southern California; it does not mention if she ever lived in the Ozarks.

965. Arner, Lloyd William. *Sandy: Biography of a Boy*. New York: Carlton Press, 1964. 281p.

An intelligent, thoughtful man writes a series of essays about his boyhood on a farm in the Missouri Ozarks. He's a pretty good writer, too. But Sandy's young life was dull and uneventful, and so is his book.

966. Baker, Walter I. *Reminiscences*. Point Lookout, Mo.: School of the Ozarks Press, [1964]. 42p.

This little book is in three parts. Part 1 is the tale of a Missouri farm boy who turns schoolteacher and goes to Colorado in 1876. It is apparently fiction, with plenty of gunplay and Wild West adventure. Part 2 is the "true biography" of a young doctor who begins his practice in a small Ozark town about 1900. It is a rather dull story. Part 3 tells of a young couple who settled in the White River country in the late 1890s, where they lived on a farm for fifty years. These people were apparently relatives of the author. Baker is a good writer, but his book has little interest for the general reader. He lives in Springfield and was connected with the Southwest Missouri State University.

967. Bent, Silas. *Buchanan of the Press*. New York: Vanguard Press, 1932. 280p.

Novel about Missouri newspaper folk. It's a good story, but deals mostly with Springfield and St. Louis. Not much of interest to the folklorist.

968. Borland, Hal. *The Amulet*. Philadelphia: J. B. Lippincott Company, 1957.
224p.

About a Missourian who rode with Sterling Price and fought at Wilson's Creek
during the Civil War.

969. Bowden, Alta Goode. *Ann of the Ozarks*. Dallas: Royal Publishing Co.,
[1966]. 177p.

A foolish juvenile story about country folk somewhere in southern Missouri.
A conventional tale, very few regional references.

970. Byrd, Thomas S., Jr. *Pioneer from Missouri*. Philadelphia: Dorrance and Co.,
[1972]. 117p.

Novel about John Thomas Byrd, doubtless an ancestor of the author. John T.
left Jefferson County, Missouri, and went to California in 1849. He came back with
gold enough to buy a good Missouri farm, where he spent the rest of his life, with
time out for service in the Confederate army. Much good material about pioneer
farm life in Jefferson County. The book reads like a straight biography, but the
jacket blurb calls it a novel. Thomas S. Byrd served as a captain in World War II and
spent many years as a school administrator in California.

971. Carleton, Jetta. *The Moonflower Vine*. New York: Simon & Schuster, 1962.
352p.

About Henry County, Missouri, where the author grew up. Her folks lived in
the "Tebo Bottoms." Her father was superintendent of schools at Centerview. Her
descriptions fit the country around Leesville.

972. Carlson, Tom. " 'Foxhound Feud' Stirs Mystery Memories." *Springfield
News-Leader*, 1 August 1976.

In 1931 a feud erupted near the village of Pearl, Missouri, over the killing of a
foxhound. All the details are in this article along with photos of the participants.
Although MacKinlay Kantor always denied it, this incident was undoubtedly the
basis for his popular novel *The Voice of Bugle Ann* (see volume 1 of this bibliography, p. 376). Metro-Goldwyn-Mayer Studios even came to this area in 1936 and
shot footage for a movie by the same name.

973. Carter, Maxine. *The Teething Thirties*. New York: William-Frederick Press,
1968. 114p.

The story of a teenage girl who grew up in bitter poverty in the Ozarks during
the Depression of the 1930s. Her parents ran a ramshackle "tourist camp" that
served vagrants and white trash. The writing is amateurish but strangely effective.
Mrs. Carter lives on a farm near Mountain View, Missouri.

974. Chittum, Ida. *The Hermit Boy*. New York: Delacorte Press, 1972. 164p.

A juvenile novel with all the ingredients typical of an Ozark adventure story. City children visit a relative who lives deep in the wilds of the mountains, where they encounter a wild boy, a ghost town, a mysterious cave, and a lost treasure, which, as always, becomes the key to the happy ending. There are a couple of references to home remedies and hill sayings but not enough to cite as being distinctly Ozarkian. According to the cover blurb, the author was raised in the Missouri Ozarks, but it doesn't say where. She now lives in Finley, Illinois.

975. Clements, William M. "The Red Herring as Folklore." *The Armchair Detective* 12:3 (Summer 1979): 256–59.

The "red herring" in this article is a term pertaining to literary methodology in constructing the plot of mystery novels, in this case *The Camp-Meeting Murders* by Vance Randolph and Nancy Clemens (see volume 1 of this bibliography, p. 392). Clements discusses the authors' use of Ozark folklore to develop the plot of this murder mystery set in the Ozark Mountains.

976. Croy, Homer. *Boone Stop*. New York: Harper, 1918. 320p.

A good story of rural Missouri. Croy lived at Maryville.

977. ———. *Mr. Meek Marches On*. New York: Harper and Brothers, [1941]. 307.

An old-fashioned novel in Croy's best style. All about a farmer near Joplin, Missouri, who moves into town, runs a shoe store, marries a nice girl, and has a pretty daughter. One day he gets mad and refuses to pay his poll-tax. From this point on it's a typical Croy *Saturday Evening Post* formula tale, but well written. The author has been in Joplin, and he knows the Missouri scene. The dialect is sparingly used, but there are no serious mistakes in it.

978. Dorrance, Ward. *A Man About the House: A Novella*. Columbia: University of Missouri Press, 1972. 115p.

This is a realistic piece of fiction. The "house" is a brothel in a small Missouri town in the 1920s. The story includes a hunchback watchmaker and a retired madam, with much frustration and bitterness. It's a good story, well written, but there are few regional references in it and little of interest to the folklorist. Dorrance is a Missourian, but for many years was a professor of English at Georgetown University in Washington, D.C. Dorrance has come a long way since *We're from Missouri* and *Three Ozark Streams* (see volume 1 of this bibliography, pp. 156, 466), though perhaps in the wrong direction, away from regionalism, that is. I still think Dorrance is a very good writer, vastly underestimated by his contemporaries.

979. Dorrance, Ward, and Thomas Mabry. *The White Hound*. Columbia: University of Missouri Press, 1959. 205p.

Four short stories by Dorrance and four by Mabry, bound together with an introduction by Carolyn Gordon, of whom I know nothing except that she lives in Princeton, New Jersey. Dorrance grew up in the part of Missouri that is known as Little Dixie, and he writes about the people who live there.

Mabry was born in Clarksville, Tennessee, but now lives on a big farm near Allensville, Kentucky, where he raises Hereford cattle and grows tobacco. His stories are set in the tobacco country of middle Tennessee. It seems to me the stories have little in common, but they are all very well done, with meticulous attention to detail. Two of Dorrance's tales and three of Mabry's first appeared in the *Sewanee Review*. Dorrance has lived in Europe and New England for some years, but he's still a Missourian.

980. Draper, Cena Christopher. *Ridge Willoughby*. Austin, Tex.: The Steck Company, 1952. 119p.

This is juvenile fiction about a twelve-year-old boy growing up in the northern part of the Missouri Ozarks in the early 1900s. It has the usual plot for these adventure stories, but this author shows a better-than-average knowledge of Ozark ways. Especially see pp. 70–79 for a good account of "noodling" for fish.

981. Duncan, Clark. *Sunnyridge: A Story of the Missouri Hills*. Grand Rapids, Mich.: Wm. B. Eerdmans, 1945. 248p.

A novel about the adventures of an orphaned girl growing up somewhere in the Ozarks, trying to live the Christian life. She is saved in the last pages from marrying an evil man. Pretty uneventful.

982. Durre, Lloyd. *The Clinch Hollow Story*. Branson, Mo.: School of the Ozarks Press, 1970. 165p.

A run-of-the-mill novel, set in the Ozarks region, with some mention of the Bald Knobbers, etc. But there is no dialect and few folklore references. The author, who taught art in the high school at Branson, Missouri, plays the part of the old shepherd in the Shepherd of the Hills extravaganza put on for the tourists.

983. Erdman, Loula Grace. *The Years of the Locust*. New York: Dodd, Mead and Co., 1947. 234p.

A very sensitive and perceptive novel about the prosperous farmers in central Missouri, not too far south of the Missouri River. Miss Erdman knows her subject and tells it like it is. She teaches creative writing at West Texas State College, but she was born and grew up in Missouri.

984. Eustis, Helen. *The Fool Killer*. New York: Pocket Books, 1955. 181p.

First published by Doubleday in 1954. Novel about the legend of the Fool Killer, a monster supposed to chop the heads off people who make fools of themselves. Nameless—not "Jesse Holmes." See pp. 13–15, 22–29, 163–79.

O. Henry wrote a story entitled "Jesse Holmes, the Fool Killer." See Jay B. Hubbell, *The South in American Literature* (1954), p. 662, for information on the Fool Killer.

985. Fountain, Sarah. *Arkansas Voices*. Little Rock: Rose Publishing Co., 1976. 258p.

An anthology of Arkansas literature. Most of the great names are here, and many not so great. Fountain is an assistant professor at the University of Central Arkansas. Missing are Charlie May Simon, Constance Wagner, Joseph Nelson, and Friedrich Gerstäcker.

986. Gallaher, Art, Jr. *Plainville Fifteen Years Later*. New York: Columbia University Press, 1961. 301p.

Plainville USA, by Carl Withers (James West), is a wonderful anthropological study of a small town in the Missouri Ozarks, the record of a year of residence and intensive study (see volume 1 of this bibliography, p. 531). The present work by another anthropologist covers the same town in 1954. Gallaher is not so good a writer as Withers, but has the advantage of newer, more sophisticated methods. Both of these books are required reading for every student of the Ozark scene. The town of Plainville is really Wheatland, in Hickory County, Missouri. Foreword by Carl Withers.

987. Gibson, Arrell M. *Wilderness Bonanza: The Tri-State District of Missouri, Kansas, and Oklahoma*. Norman: University of Oklahoma Press, 1972. 362p.

See p. 250. Gibson doesn't think much of Lillah Davidson's much-quoted *South of Joplin* (1939), especially her treatment of the labor troubles of the 1930s. (See volume 1 of this bibliography, p. 360).

988. Godsey, Townsend. "Ozark Novel." *Arkansas Gazette*, 28 July 1957.

Fine full-page story about Harold Bell Wright's *Shepherd of the Hills* and a discussion of the legends about it, as they are still told by the people around Branson, Missouri.

989. Gwaltney, Francis Irby. *Destiny's Chickens*. Indianapolis: Bobbs-Merrill, 1973. 355p.

Realistic novel about little people in a small college in a small town in central

Arkansas. These characters are more concerned with sex than the hill people I have known. All of the taboo words are here, tallywhackers and gillyclickers everywhere. Gwaltney's lower-class people talk very broad Franklin County dialect. The upper classes speak a nondescript, generalized "southern" English familiar to readers of regional fiction. Gwaltney, a native of Traskwood, Arkansas, was a professor of English at the Arkansas Polytechnic Institute, Russellville. He wrote many novels, but is remembered chiefly as the author of *The Yeller-Headed Summer* (see volume 1 of this bibliography, p. 369). He died in 1981 in Russellville at age fifty-nine.

990. ———. *Idols and Axle Grease*. Indianapolis: Bobbs-Merrill, 1974. 150p.

The story of a boy growing up in a small town in central Arkansas. It is a fascinating tale, a beautiful, gentle account of a lot of nice people.

991. ———. *A Step in the River*. New York: Random House, 1960. 305p.

Novel about politics, blacks, and small towns, with some Arkansas dialect.

992. Hagen, Lyman B., ed. *The Arkansas Stories of Charlie May Simon*. Little Rock: August House, 1981. 84p.

Few authors of children's literature have written about a region with more feeling and familiarity of its land and its people than did Charlie May Simon in her stories about life in Arkansas. She was the daughter of Wayman Hogue and the wife of John Gould Fletcher, both famous Arkansas writers. Hagen has selected six of her stories, long out of print, to reacquaint the present generation with her written words. Two of these stories, "Buttons" (p. 10) and "The Geography Lesson" (p. 38), take place in the Ozarks. Hagen teaches in the department of English at Arkansas State University, Jonesboro, Arkansas.

993. Harington, Donald. *The Architecture of the Arkansas Ozarks*. Boston: Little, Brown and Co., 1975. 376p.

A wildly romantic novel, full of Freudian symbolism, still realistic in part, specific to the point of obscenity. It chronicles six generations of the legendary Ingledew family who settled in the town of Stay More, in Newton County, Arkansas. Long passages of erotic lyricism, mixed with ancient jokes and anecdotes, folk tales, old backwoods sayings, wisecracks, and superstition. Every word rings true; it's all genuine Ozark stuff. I have heard many of these items myself. Some I have published in my own books, but many I once knew but had somehow forgotten until I recognized them in this novel. All lies and fantasy, but true as God's gospel. All the lies you hear about Arkansas are true, more true than any collection of historical facts could ever be. It is by far the best Ozark novel I have ever read. God knows what the literary scholars and critics will make of it, but for my money it is the best regional novel since *Huckleberry Finn*.

Note: McCann says he does not altogether agree with me that this is "the best regional novel since *Huckleberry Finn*," but he does agree with me that Harington knows his early Ozarks. Even though it's fictionalized, Harington presents the pioneers, the Civil War, and the Reconstruction period in our Ozarks as truthfully as any word McCann has seen in print.

994. ———. *The Cherry Pit*. New York: Random House, 1965. 342p.

This is Harington's first book and, as with those that followed, is written as only an Arkansan could tell it. The setting is Little Rock, but through the personage of one of the principal characters, whose roots are in the hills of north Arkansas, there are some references to the Ozarks. Of special note are his comments about Ozark speech on p. 267. He knows his Ozarkers.

995. ———. *Lightning Bug*. New York: Delacorte Press, 1970. 212p.

A novel featuring violent action—dirty fighting, bank robberies, moonshiners, and gunplay. Bloody rapes and unorthodox sex doings all over the place. Obscene clowning seen through the eyes of a five-year-old boy. The best male character almost kills himself busting a crazy woman out of a mental hospital in Little Rock. The heroine meets Jesus Christ in a peach orchard on Ledbetter Mountain.

Despite all this, it's a fascinating story, though much inferior to Harington's later novel *The Architecture of the Arkansas Ozarks*.

996. Harlin, Amos R. *For Here Is My Fortune*. Branson, Mo.: The Ozarks Mountaineer, 1979. 160p.

A reprint of this 1946 novel about life in Gainesville and West Plains in the Missouri Ozarks. (See comments on the original edition in volume 1 of this bibliography.) Well worth reading.

997. Heath, Evelyn. *Hillbilly Homestead*. New York: Exposition Press, 1965. 120p.

An autobiographical novel about rural life in the middle West in the early 1900s. The bulk of the book (pp. 40–92) is concerned with Sims Valley, in Howell County, Missouri. Plenty of hardship and pioneer customs and local history. A good straightforward narrative. Mrs. Heath lives in Cabool, Missouri.

998. Heinlein, Robert Anson. *Starman Jones*. New York: Scribner's, 1953. 305p.

An Ozark farm boy becomes captain of a spaceship. This book is "superior science fiction," according to the *New York Times*. Heinlein is a native of Butler, Missouri.

999. Hill, Weldon. *A Man Could Get Killed That Way*. New York: D. McKay Co., 1967. 277p.

A wild adventure yarn with a lot of Ozark color.

1000. ———. *Onionhead*. New York: D. McKay Co., 1957. 378p.

Novel about the Oklahoma Ozarks. The author's real name is Bill Scott, and he lived on a farm in Oklahoma near Westville.

1001. ———. *Rafe*. New York: David McKay Co., 1966. 342p.

Novel about a backwoods boy in eastern Oklahoma—Indians, moonshiners, Cookson Hills stuff. Good review in the *Northwest Arkansas Times* (Fayetteville), 7 January 1966.

1002. Howard, Guy. *Walkin' Preacher of the Ozarks*. Branson, Mo.: ABC Publishing Service, 1976. 193p.

This is a paperback reprint; the book was first published by Harper and Brothers in 1944 (see volume 1 of this bibliography, p. 374). The reprint carries a valuable introduction by Townsend Godsey, for many years a professor of English at the School of the Ozarks, Point Lookout, Missouri. Dr. Godsey knew the Walkin' Preacher as well as anybody, and he tells me that the story is essentially true.

1003. Hulse, Edgar E. *Light on the Lookout: A Novel of Romance in the Ozarks*. Point Lookout, Mo.: School of the Ozarks Press, 1972. 170p.

Young backwoods boys and girls trying to acquire book-learning enough to get jobs teaching in the country schools. Some schoolboard members are very wicked: they drink whiskey and are addicted to gambling and fornication. But the nice young people who go to Sunday School always beat the scoundrels and get the best jobs. Virtue always triumphs, and you can't defeat education. The author was born in the Ozarks but spent most of his life teaching in rural schools in California. He tells a few old jokes, but the book has no literary merit and is of little value to the serious student. Hulse is now retired and lives in Springfield, Missouri.

1004. ———. *Romance, When and Where You Find It*. Point Lookout, Mo.: School of the Ozarks Press, 1976. 217p.

Also subtitled *A Novel of Romance in the Ozarks*. Pulp fiction. The melodramatic story line is not bad, but the writing is not the best.

1005. Hurst, Vida. *They Called Her "Sin" for Short*. New York: M. S. Mill Co., 1937. 252p.

Vida Hurst wrote many novels. This one is about the Ozarks.

1006. Ingenthron, J. H. *A Fictitious Love Affair and Other Short Stories*. Forsyth, Mo.: Published by the author, 1945. 49p.

The title story and the fourth (about the army camp) may be fiction, but the other tales are well known to me. Everybody in Taney County, Missouri, remembered Uncle Dave and Uncle John, and we all heard about the old sow. I believe that these stories are true in every essential detail. Ingenthron was a lawyer in Forsyth, Missouri. I knew him well.

1007. Inmon, James Bayard. *Orphans of the Ozarks*. Point Lookout, Mo.: School of the Ozarks Press, 1971. 238p.

A factual history of Greene County, Missouri, woven together with the Horatio Alger story of a bound boy, an orphan, who succeeded in getting himself a good farm and a pretty Delaware wife. It is very badly written, incredibly naive. The author lived in Springfield, Missouri. I knew some of his family. They were real hill people.

1008. ———. *A Pioneer from the Ozarks*. Point Lookout, Missouri: School of the Ozarks, 1973. 307p.

Inmon likes to write in the first person about frontier life and events that occurred long before his time. Sometimes he seems to think of himself as a reincarnation of his own grandfather, who served in the Mexican War and went to California in 1849. At other times he appears as the ghost of his grandfather, which makes him about 175 years old!

1009. Jayne, Mitchell F. *The Forest in the Wind*. New York: Bobbs-Merrill Co., 1966. 150p.

At first glance this is just a superior juvenile addressed to teenage boys, rather in the manner of Ernest Seton-Thompson at his best. But it is really a thoughtful, highly sophisticated account of wildlife in the Ozarks—lively tales of fox, deer, wolf, even hawks and owls. The author is a profound student of the relationship of wild creatures to the environment. He could have walked with Thoreau and John Burroughs in the big woods, and he has studied the Ozarks scene when ecology was just a textbook term. (For a number of years he was a member of a nationally acclaimed folk music group, the Dillards.) This book is highly recommended to intelligent readers everywhere.

1010. ———. *Old Fish Hawk*. New York: J. B. Lippincott Co., 1970. 279p.

Fish Hawk was an Osage Indian, who spent his old age with the white settlers in the Missouri Ozarks. Jayne is not a great novelist but he is a good writer, and he knows the Ozarks. He knows about hunters, and Indians, and wild animals. This book is now (1980) being made into a motion picture. Jayne grew up in Kahoka,

Missouri, attended the University of Missouri, taught in Dent County, Missouri, and now lives near Salem, Missouri.

1011. Jones, Douglas C. *The Barefoot Brigade*. New York: Holt, Rinehart and Winston, 1982. 313p.

A Civil War novel about the Third Arkansas Infantry Regiment. The principal characters are from the Buffalo River region in the northwest Arkansas Ozarks; the story begins there but quickly leaves that locale and follows their adventures throughout the war in the eastern campaigns. As in all his works, Jones develops his characters superbly and makes use of folklore and customs throughout. Perhaps my preferences have become too provincial, but in my estimation his other Civil War epic, *Elkhorn Tavern* (1980), is a far better story and definitely of more value to those interested in what life was like in the mid-nineteenth-century Ozarks. Jones was born in Winslow, Arkansas, near Fayetteville, and also lived for a time in Fort Smith. He now lives in Fayetteville.

1012. ———. *Elkhorn Tavern*. New York: Holt, Rinehart and Winston, 1980. 311p.

A novel based upon the Battle of Pea Ridge (Confederate name, Elkhorn Tavern) in northwest Arkansas. This was the largest engagement of the Civil War fought in the Ozarks. The author's grandparents lived in this area, and the stories they related to him of life in the nineteenth century there inspired this work. It is an excellent account of the perils faced each day by the inhabitants of the Arkansas-Missouri border during the war. The *New York Times Book Review* correctly stated that Jones has convinced the reader that this is how life must have been in that place at that time. *Elkhorn Tavern* won the 1981 award for the best novel of the year from the Friends of American Writers.

1013. ———. *Weedy Rough*. New York: Holt, Rinehart and Winston, 1981. 345p.

Jones brings his Pay family into the twentieth century, to a small town called Weedy Rough, located between Ft. Smith and Fayetteville in western Arkansas. The central character is Deny Gene Pay, grandson of Eben, the young lawyer in *Winding Stair* (Holt, Rinehart and Winston, 1979). This is life in the Ozarks just before and during the Great Depression. There is a good account of a fox "race" on pp. 97–104. Jones's portrayals of life in the Ozarks during the periods he writes about are vivid and authentic and well worth reading.

1014. ———. *Winding Stair*. New York: Holt, Rinehart and Winston, 1979. 277p.

The title refers to a section of the Ozark Mountains in Indian Territory not far from Fort Smith, Arkansas, that was under the jurisdiction of Judge Isaac Parker and his federal court. In 1890 a number of murders were committed by a band of border ruffians. This is the story of their apprehension, the trial in Judge Parker's court, and their subsequent hanging. "Hanging" Judge Parker was a harsh magistrate but so was this borderland he presided over, and Jones (through the words of his principal character, Eben Pay) says that he doesn't deserve the "misunderstanding and apathy" perpetrated by the newspapers of his day (p. 51). There is little for the folklorist in this book, but it is good reading and an enlightening look at life in the Arkansas–Indian Territory region in those days of lawlessness.

1015. King, Hester. "Paradise Bent." *University Review* 4:2 (Winter 1937): 120–21.

This is a wonderful piece of Missouri writing. I do not wish to forget it. The author lived at Old Linn Creek, now inundated by the Lake of the Ozarks. The *University Review* was published in Kansas City, Missouri.

1016. Kroll, Harry Harrison. *Fury in the Earth.* Indianapolis: Bobbs-Merrill Co., 1945. 264p.

A realistic novel of the New Madrid earthquake and the heart-breaking hardships that followed. A vivid picture of the sordid and violent life in the river towns.

1017. Lane, Rose Wilder. *Old Home Town.* New York: Longmans, Green and Co., 1935. 309p.

This novel gives a very acute picture of small-town life. But there are few Ozark references. The little town might be anywhere. Mrs. Lane lived for many years on a farm near Mansfield, Missouri. I knew her. She was a tremendous personality and a very fine writer. Her mother, Laura Ingalls Wilder, who lived with her at Mansfield, was a writer, too—she is remembered for a series of juveniles beginning with *The Little House on the Prairie.*

1018. Leach, Peter. "Strawberries." *The Human Crowd: New Fiction from the Minnesota Review* (new series) 16 (Spring 1981): 69–78.

A brief bit of fiction about strawberry pickers in southwest Missouri during World War I.

1019. Legman, Gershon. *Mark Twain's Mammoth Cod.* Milwaukee: Maledicta Press, 1976. 25p.

Mark Twain's bawdy *1601: A Tudor Fireside Conversation* was first published in 1880; it was written in 1876. Legman has dug up another "unprintable" piece, which Twain wrote over sixty years ago, here published for the first time.

Legman thinks that Mark Twain may be the author of "Change the Name of Arkansas." What he says about this, with many local references, is especially interesting to Ozark readers. Also printed here is Twain's famous "Some Remarks on the

Science of Onanism," written in 1879, hitherto circulated only in typescript and mimeograph copies.

1020. McArthur, Perry. *Table Top Mountain, A Story of the Ozarks*. New York: Exposition Press, 1966. 117p.

A childish novel about a Pentecostal preacher's travels and preaching in the southern Ozarks. The author was born in Ardmore, Oklahoma, and now lives near Bull Shoals Lake in Missouri, but spent much of his life in Arizona and points west. He shows no knowledge of the hill people, their speech, or their way of life. The book is of no value to the folklorist or the student of local history.

1021. McCall, Edith. *Butternut Bill*. Chicago: Benefic Press, 1965. 48p.

This is one of a series of juvenile books, written principally for grade-school level, about a young boy and his donkey, Lazy Daisy, and their everyday adventures in the Ozarks. Other titles attest to McCall's Ozark theme: *Butternut Bill and the Big Catfish* (limblining for fish), *Butternut Bill and the Bee Tree* (coursing bees and wild honey). The author, a retired schoolteacher, moved to the Ozarks in the late 1950s and wrote her first Butternut Bill book in 1960. Illustrated by Darrell Wisket of Harrison, Arkansas.

1022. Matthews, Norval M. *The Promise Land*. Point Lookout, Mo.: School of the Ozarks Press, 1974. 174p.

An historical narrative of the Ozarks and its early history, competently written. There is no attempt at dialect and not much folklore. But it is pleasant reading.

1023. Maurer, Bill. "Literature Unfair to Ozarks' Image." *Springfield News-Leader*, 19 November 1978.

Report of an address by writer Lida Wilson Pyles (see entry 1043) of Carthage, Missouri. She decries the stereotyped image of the ignorant hillbilly created by such books as Thomas W. Jackson's *On A Slow Train Through Arkansas* (1903) and *Through Missouri on a Mule* (1904) (see volume 1 of this bibliography, p. 170). Maurer is a staff writer for the *News-Leader*.

1024. Milburn, George. "Honey Boy." *Collier's* 93:10 (10 March 1934): 24.

This is Milburn's well-known short story of mistaken identity. It is reprinted in Randolph's *Ozark Anthology* (Caxton Printery, 1940), pp. 17–22.

1025. Miller, Helen Topping. *A Man Ten Feet Tall*. Indianapolis: Bobbs-Merrill Company, 1957. 327p.

A good formula novel about a boy from the Arkansas Ozarks who struggles through college and medical school and returns to practice in the backwoods. Realistic picture of the Arkansas scene. Miller lives in east Tennessee and "has written forty novels since 1910."

1026. Mitchell, Marie. *The Night the Coyotes Sang*. New York: David McKay Co., 1966. 151p.

Juvenile tale of a delinquent big-city boy, changed by a vacation in the Missouri Ozarks. The author lives in Kansas City, Missouri.

1027. Morgan, Speer. *Belle Starr: A Novel*. Boston: Little, Brown and Company, 1979. 311p.

A beautifully written novel, but a dismal and depressing tale. I have interviewed many old-timers who knew Belle Starr well, and they told a very different story. As Mogan says (p. 311), his purpose was not to present the historic Belle Starr, but "to re-create her character, using both facts of history and imagination." The author is a professor of English at the University of Missouri–Columbia.

1028. Oldham, Demma Ray. "Liza Turns the Tide." *Pictorial Review* 32:7 (April 1931): 12–13, 27, 30.

Oldham was born in DeQueen, Arkansas, and spent fifteen years in Idabel, Oklahoma. He now lives in Oklahoma City and writes humorous stories about country women in Arkansas. See Marable and Boylan, *Oklahoma Writers* (1939), pp. 24–25.

1029. Oskison, John Milton. *Black Jack Davy*. New York: D. Appleton & Co., 1926. 311p.

Novel about the Indian Territory, outlaws, moonshine, gunfighters, etc. The author, a Cherokee, was born at Tahlequah in 1874. He also wrote *Wild Harvest: A Novel of Transition Days in Oklahoma* (New York: Appleton, 1925) and *Brothers Three* (New York: Macmillan Co., 1935).

1030. Parker, Faye. "Crepe Paper Roses." *Ozark Review* 3 (Winter 1980): 38–45.

A poignant story of the relationship between a young girl and her grandmother during a summer visit to the farm. The grandmother makes crepe paper roses to be sold for Decoration Day. Some attempt at dialect.

1031. Parkhurst, Liz Smith. *The Arkansas Traveler*. Little Rock: August House, 1982. 44p.

Parkhurst has rewritten this famous tale for juvenile readers, and she's done an excellent job. All the essential elements of the story have been preserved. Her introduction, though, is of interest to adult readers, for she discusses different studies that have been made of this work.

1032. Patrick, Michael. "The Razorback as a Legendary Creature in the Novels of Mitchell Jayne and Donald Harington." *Missouri Folklore Society Journal* 1:1 (1979): 33–43.

Talks about the symbolism of the razorback hog as used in two novels about the Ozarks: Jayne's *Old Fish Hawk* (entry 1010) and Harington's *The Architecture of the Arkansas Ozarks* (entry 993). Some mention of the legends surrounding the razorback's existence in the Ozarks. Patrick is an English teacher at the University of Missouri–Rolla. This mature and thoughtful piece was originally read to the Missouri Folklore Society at Columbia, Missouri, in November 1978.

1033. Pennington, Albert Joe. *Big Boy, the Story of a Dog*. Fremont, Mo.: Published by the author, 1970. 100p.

No folklore references. The author is a farmer and dog breeder who lives near Fremont, Missouri.

1034. Pennington, Eunice. *Black Boy, the Story of a Pup*. Fremont, Mo.: Published by the author, 1977. 31p.

A juvenile pamphlet.

1035. ———. *Master of the Mountain*. Fremont, Mo.: Pennington Trading Post, 1971. 134p.

This is fiction—a first novel. Based on a Civil War legend, she says. A sensational novel of Missouri in the 1860s. Not much folklore; some light on pioneer customs and local history. Mrs. Pennington is a librarian and a writer of feature stories for several Missouri newspapers.

1036. ———. *Perry the Pet Pig*. Point Lookout, Mo.: School of the Ozarks Press, 1972. 80p.

Paperback juvenile about two children and a pig on an Ozark farm.

1037. Pilkington, Sam Clay. *The Romance of Wilson Creek*. Philadelphia: Dorrance & Company, 1961. 112p.

A love story set against the background of the Civil War and the Battle of Wilson's Creek, fought just south of Springfield in southwest Missouri. Little folklore content.

1038. Ponder, Hazel K. *Deep in the Hills*. Philadelphia: Dorrance, 1970. 94p.

Juvenile story of a little girl named Honey, growing up in the Ozark back-woods, alone except for her aged grandmother. A slow-moving, uneventful tale, but well written. Much detail about primitive household tasks. The author spent her girlhood in Ripley County, Missouri.

1039. Portis, Charles. *Norwood*. New York: Simon and Schuster, 1966. 190p.

This is Portis's first book, a humorous study of contemporary life in Arkansas. Portis was born in Hamburg, Arkansas, and now lives near Little Rock.

1040. ———. *True Grit*. New York: Simon & Schuster, 1968. 224p.

This is the story of a 14-year-old Arkansas girl searching for her father's mur-derer in the Indian Territory shortly after the Civil War. Seems genuine and authen-tic enough. The author is a newspaper man who had worked in Fayetteville and Little Rock. It first appeared serialized in the *Saturday Evening Post* (18 May, 1 June, and 15 June 1968). In 1969 it was made into a movie starring John Wayne.

1041. Pride, John F. *Bald Knobbers and Other Humorous Tales of the Ozark Moun-tain Hillbilly*. N.p.: Published by the author, 1926. 113p.

Four short stories in thick dialect. The author can't write, but he has been in the Ozarks. See p. 108 for a mention of *Hookrum* as a place name. I have heard that Pride lived in southern Missouri, but now in his old age he lives in North Little Rock. On the title page he says he is "author of *Three Years in the Arkansas Ozarks*" but I haven't been able to trace that one. *Bald Knobbers* is a cheap red paperback, but I paid ten dollars for it at a bookshop near Branson.

1042. Pruett, Marybelle. *Smokey Waters of the Ozarks*. Point Lookout, Mo.: School of the Ozarks Press, [1974?]. 104p.

A juvenile novel about a girl who thinks herself an orphan, raised by her mater-nal grandmother in the hills near Table Rock, Missouri. The old lady, the real central character, defends the old ways. The writing seems very good to me, especially in the matter of dialect. A threadbare plot, but nevertheless a good book. Her use of *air* for *are* is all right, but she uses the same respelling to mean *our*. This is disturb-ing, but I can pick no other flaws in the dialect. I know nothing of the author except that she lives in Kirbyville, Missouri, and sells her books by mail from her home.

1043. Pyles, Lida Wilson. *Stranger at the Gate*. Cassville, Mo.: Litho Printers, 1976. 122p.

A sensational novel about a drunken woman in a tiny settlement, somewhere in southern Missouri. The author, a native of Eagle Rock, Missouri, has always lived in the Ozarks. When I knew her in the 1940s she was in Eureka Springs, Arkansas, but her present residence is Carthage, Missouri. She writes well and has done many good features for regional papers. She knows the Ozark country, but makes little use of dialect or local color. *Stranger at the Gate* was reportedly to be made into a movie by a Hollywood production company, with part of the film to be shot on location in Eureka Springs, Arkansas.

1044. Roberts, Carla, and Diana Foreman. "From Hills to Hotels." *Bittersweet* 4:4 (Summer 1977): 46–62.

All about Harold Bell Wright and his best-selling novel, with details and photographs of the "tourist attractions" in the Shepherd of the Hills country around Branson and Hollister. Some facts about Wright that I had never heard.

1045. Robertson, Mary Elsie. *Jordan's Stormy Banks and Other Stories*. New York: Atheneum, 1961. 241p.

Twelve stories, earthy yet fantastic, mostly about religious fanatics in the hill country. Some, but not all, of these stories are about Arkansas. The author grew up on a farm near Charleston, in western Arkansas. She was educated at the University of Arkansas and did graduate work at the University of Iowa. Francis Gwaltney praised this book to the skies, and Gwaltney must be taken seriously. He says her rural dialect is good.

1046. Saults, Dan. "No Misery of Creativity." *The Ozarks Mountaineer* 25:5 (June 1977): 30–31.

Saults observes that "millions of words have been written about the Ozarks since Henry Schoolcraft began scrawling in his journal in 1818" but that the region has never produced any really important literature. "Ozarkians have been brooding and introspective, they set down local history and tales, family legends, the stuff of folklore rather than epics." We have Otto Rayburns and Vance Randolphs and Roscoe Stewarts, but no literary giants—no Thomas Wolfe, no Bernard DeVoto.

So far as I understand him, the Ozark writers are too limited to be important; most of us are not really regional—we are local, even parochial.

Also, we are too contented, too satisfied. Great literature grows from unhappiness, strife, and rebellion. In the Ozarks, he says, "the splendid misery of creativity is replaced by kindly recording of little tales that soothe the soul." So mote it be.

Nevertheless, Saults's brief paper is the best survey of the whole field of Ozark writing that I have seen.

1047. Severs, Vesta-Nadine. *Lucinda*. St. Louis: Concordia Publishing House, 1978. 128p.

A juvenile novel set in the 1860s in southwest Missouri. The Civil War as seen through the eyes of a sixteen-year-old girl. The dialect is overdone, and there is a good deal of religious propaganda. There are some references to pioneer customs.

1048. Shaw, Naomi. *Let the Hallelujahs Roll*. Harrison, Ark.: New Leaf Press, 1977. 174p.

Mostly about Protestant evangelists in the Ozarks—old-time camp meetings and the like. Pretty dull. The author came from Iowa and married an Ozarker. They now live "on the Missouri-Arkansas line."

1049. Shelby, Kermit. "Fritter-Minded." *Collier's Magazine* 108 : 12 (20 September 1941): 18, 69–72.

A lighthearted short story about romance in the southwest Missouri Ozarks. Some local color. The title is good dialect. I met this fellow years ago at Marvel Cave.

1050. ———. "Legend of the Lonesome Valley: Did Lonesome Johnny Conjure Dock Blackwood's Pretty Wife?" In *Ozark Guide Yearbook*, pp. 14–16, 79–82. Reeds Spring, Mo.: Gerald Pipes, 1962.

This short piece of fiction is the sad tale of a lad born with a caul or "the veil" covering his face and therefore predestined to a life of misfortune and tragedy. He becomes a wandering fiddler and the story becomes almost Arthurian: a damsel in distress, a cruel and jealous husband (he even chains her to the cabin), a daring rescue by the hero, untimely death, roaming spirits, etc. Of course, the plot is almost as old as storytelling, but Shelby weaves it into an Ozark setting and does show a familiarity with Ozark life and customs. Though I don't quite agree with the *Ozarks Guide* editor that "it is one of the very best Ozarks stories ever written," it is worth reading. (It won the author a $2,500 prize from the Writer's Guild of America!)

1051. Shelton, Jess. *Hangman's Song*. Philadelphia: Chilton Publishing Co., 1960. 314p.

A strong, savage novel, set in the hills of Missouri and Arkansas. Much of the later action takes place in the Choctaw country in what is now Oklahoma. The title comes from a traditional ballad (Child no. 95) still sung in the Ozarks. The backwoods atmosphere is good, but the dialect is not very convincing. Shelton is a native of central Missouri. He is the author of another novel, *Brood of Fury* (Chilton Publishing Company, 1959), about the Civil War in Missouri.

1052. Shepard, Fern. *Ozark Nurse*. New York: Macfadden-Bartell Books, 1967. 127p.

The only thing Ozarkian about this piece of pulp fiction is the mention of the word *Ozarks* on p. 9.

1053. Simon, Charlie May. *Razorbacks Are Really Hogs*. Champaign, Ill.: Garrard Publishing Co., 1972. 48p.

A pleasantly written juvenile tale about the young farmer who tried to keep the wild hogs out of his truck garden. He finally built a hog-tight fence, but the razorbacks swung in on grapevines!

1054. Smith, Jewell Ellen. *Great Jehoshaphat and Gully Dirt!* Winston-Salem, N.C.: John F. Blair, 1975. 226p.

A badly written but strangely effective story. Violent crime in rural Arkansas, seen through the eyes of a little girl.

1055. Stanley, Caroline Abbot. *Order No. 11: A Tale of the Border.* New York: The Century Company, 1904. 420p.

A romantic novel about the Missouri-Kansas border in the early 1860s. See chapter 21, "Oh, Sister Phoebe," pp. 192–99, for a fine description of a Jackson County, Missouri, play-party. A little too sentimental for modern taste, but a fine story nevertheless. This was reprinted in 1969 (Clinton, Mo.: Democrat Publishing Company).

1056. Starr, Fred. *Of What Was, Nothing Is Left: A Suspense-Packed Tale of Arkansas.* North Quincy, Mass.: Christopher Publishing House, 1972. 140p.

Fred Starr knows the Ozarks all right, but this fantastic novel is different from his other books. It has no great value for the folklorist, but is well written. I have heard that Irene Carlisle, a poet who lived in Fayetteville for many years but is now in California, was somehow involved with Starr in the writing of this book.

1057. ———. *To Keep a Promise.* North Quincy, Mass.: Christopher Publishing House, 1969. 173p.

A juvenile about a boy who lived in rural Arkansas in the 1920s. Alan Gilbert (*Arkansas Gazette*, 12 October 1969) says it is a good job.

1058. Steele, Paul. *The Branded Oak.* West Fork, Ark.: Hutcheson Press, n.d. [24p.]

A paperback adventure story for teenagers, set on Beaver Lake, located in northwest Arkansas. The author's real name is Paulene Davis Steele. Formerly a teacher in Fayetteville, Arkansas, she died in 1979.

1059. Stevens, D. W. *Jesse James, the Midnight Horseman, or, The Silent Rider of the Ozarks.* New York: Frank Tousey, [c. 1894]. 65p.

This is no. 522 of the *New York Detective Library* series of dime novels. William A. Settle, Jr. (see entry 1630) thinks this was written by John R. Musick, who often used the name "Stevens." Musick (1849–1901) was born in St. Louis and lived in north Missouri during the 1870s.

1060. Stokes, Manning Lee. *The Dying Room.* New York: Phoenix Press, 1947. 256p.

A mystery novel, set in Mena, Arkansas. The author's wife, Goldie Ratliff Stokes, once lived in Mena. In January 1949, she was in Mena and said she was collecting material for another novel. Stokes sometimes used "Ford Worth" as a pen name.

1061. Stong, Phil. *Hiram, the Hillbilly.* New York: Dodd, Mead and Company, 1951. 104p.

Hiram was a gray mule "with large, sad eyes the shape and color of Long Island oysters," but he lived in the Ozarks. Stong had been in the hills, all right. I met him years ago in Eureka Springs, Arkansas. He was familiar with backwoods life and country folk generally, but he was not particularly interested in folklore, and little of it appears in this amusing juvenile. According to the jacket blurb, it is "good Americana," and so it is, but there are not many specific Ozark references. But chapter 3, entitled "Fox Hunt" (pp. 37–61), is well worth reading, as is chapter 5, "Square Dance" (pp. 68–87).

1062. ———. *Missouri Canary.* New York: Dodd, Mead & Co., 1943. 77p.

A fantastic juvenile, about farm boys and troop maneuvers during World War II. Well written and amusing, but not important. "Missouri Canary" is an old term for a mule.

1063. Stuart, Florence. *Mountain Sweetheart.* New York: Arcadia House, 1960. 223p.

A juvenile novel, set in an Ozark town that must be Eureka Springs, Arkansas. Many local references—the annual festival, Lake Leatherwood, Mud Street, etc.

1064. Tucker, Nathaniel Beverly. *George Balcombe: A Novel.* New York: Harper & Brothers, 1836. Vol. 1: 282p.; Vol. 2: 319p.

A novel of mystery and adventure, set in Virginia and Missouri. The author came to Missouri in 1815 and lived here fifteen years. Contains some colorful information about frontier life in eastern Missouri. The first edition was published anonymously according to the Library of Congress catalog. It is said that Tucker was a half-brother to John Randolph of Roanoke, famous Virginia politician.

1065. Wallace, Edward Tatum. *The Moon Is Our Lantern.* Garden City, N.Y.: Doubleday & Co., 1953. 315p.

About Oklahoma in the 1920s. Rayburn (*Ozark Guide* [Spring 1953]: 40) reviews it as "a novel of love and passion," "too rich for my blood, too highly spiced to get our stamp of approval."

Wallace is remembered for his novel *Barington* (see volume 1 of this bibliography, p. 407), a splendid story about his hometown of Greenwood, Arkansas.

1066. Walston, Marie. *To See the Wind*. Valley Forge, Penn.: Judson Press, 1974. 127p.

A novel about an Ozarker marrying schoolmarm from city, adopting a blind boy abandoned by his parents, etc. Of no great value.

1067. Walton, Bryce. *Cave of Danger*. New York: Thomas Y. Crowell Co., 1967. 264p.

A novel for young people about spelunking in the Ozarks. Interesting stuff about caves but no folklore. The author was born in Blythedale, Missouri, and explored many caves in his youth.

1068. Whitman, Virginia. *Ozark Obie*. Nashville, Tenn.: Broadman Press, 1961. 160p.

A good juvenile about a country boy somewhere in the Missouri Ozarks who becomes a guide for visiting fishermen. Whitman lives near Barnumton, Missouri, on the Lake of the Ozarks. She has done several books for adults, but this was her first juvenile book. She has written a sequel to this story, *Secret of the Hidden Ranch* (Zondervan, 1964).

1069. Williams, Miller, ed. *Ozark, Ozark: A Hillside Reader*. Columbia: University of Missouri Press, 1981. 193p.

An anthology of prose and poetry by thirty-four Ozark writers. These selections are presented in chronological order determined by the birth date of each author. Half of these selections are prose, equally divided between fiction and nonfiction. The authors are Charles J. Finger, Wayman Hogue, Thomas Hart Benton, Otto Ernest Rayburn, Vance Randolph, Fred Starr, Leonard Hall, Robert L. Morris, Ward Allison Dorrance, Don West, Francis Irby Gwaltney, Roy Reed, Miller Williams, William Harrison, Harry Minetree, Donald Harington, Speer Morgan, and Frank Sanford. The editor is a member of the English Department at the University of Arkansas–Fayetteville.

1070. Wilson, Charles Morrow. *Stars Is God's Lanterns: An Offering of Ozark Tellin' Stories*. Norman: University of Oklahoma Press, 1969. 213p.

These fifteen stories about the Ozarks contain some very good material. The author was born and raised in Fayetteville, Arkansas, and he is knowledgeable. I doubt if many of these tales had much oral circulation, but they are good stories anyhow. See Joe Huddleston's review in the *Arkansas Gazette*, 25 June 1970.

12. Plays

1071. Bruton, J. J.; J. P. Lee; J. S. Rafferty; W. G. Holland; George Preston; J. B. Melton; John Hedgepeth; Joseph Kyle; J. W. Bruton; J. F. Eddleman; R. H. Vaughn; and T. J. Stotle. *Bald Knob Tragedy of Taney and Christian Counties, Missouri in Eight Acts*. Sparta, Mo.: Privately printed, 1887. 25p.

This play "was wrote freely and set in type" by the twelve "composers and proprietors" listed on the title page. It isn't much of a play, from a drama critic's point of view, but every episode represents an actual happening in the Bald Knob "troubles." The *Tragedy* was presented only once, in the spring of 1889, for a carefully selected audience, on the stage at the Sparta High School. The audience, as well as the cast and all the theater staff, were violently prejudiced—many were kinfolk or connection of Bald Knobbers or the Bald Knobbers' victims. My copy of the play is a reproduction from Gordon McCann, who told me (10 April 1975), "They held an all night meeting and it was decided that since proper names were used freely and unchanged in the play and many of the persons were present in the theater, that all copies of the play, both in print and manuscript, a dozen or more in all, must be destroyed at once. But somehow one printed copy was not destroyed that night—it turned up recently in the estate of an old resident who died a few years ago. It was under the lining of a lady's trunk—it may be the old lady did not know of the script's existence." McCann says he believes that this photocopy and the printed text from which it was made are the only two copies in existence. Probably this is not true (although quite possibly McCann believes it), but there are certainly not *many* copies. McCann told me, "I am bound by the most solemn oaths not to publish this material or to reveal it to anyone. Therefore, it is not practicable for me to describe the fortuitous strategy by which it came into my possession."

1072. Cantwell, Jean. "The Loves of Rose." Unpublished manuscript, Branson, Mo., 1981.

This musical covers a nineteen-year period of Rose O'Neill's life, with scenes alternating between her Ozarks home at Bonniebrook and her career in New York. To date it's only been performed near Hollister, Missouri, at a summer theater located across the highway from the School of the Ozarks, whence came the cast. Cantwell, a teacher and oboe player from Branson, wrote it with the assistance of composer Lloyd Norlin, a music-store owner from Deerfield, Illinois. Cantwell is also active in the Kewpiesta Festival held each year for the International Rose O'Neill Club. The only copy of this manuscript is in the author's possession.

1073. Harkins, Peter. "Things Are Not Always What They Seem To Be." *Arkansas Gazette*, 24 April 1955.

Preparations to film a million-dollar Republic picture, *Come Next Spring*, an

Arkansas movie by an Arkansas author. The movie people traveled over Arkansas but had difficulty finding places that *looked* like Arkansas, so most of the shooting was done in California.

1074. King, Johnny. *Johnny the Country Boy*. Springfield, Mo.: Roberts & Sutter, 1973. 140p.

This book is full of interesting material. The piece called "Stock Company Shows" (pp. 37–40) has some ancient dialogue.

1075. McNeil, W. K. "A Preliminary Jesse James Filmography." *Mid-America Folklore* 8:1–2 (Spring-Fall 1980): 86–92.

A very complete list of films dealing with Jesse James, thirty-one in all. In defense of the movie industry's inaccuracy in depicting the facts of Jesse's life and exploits, McNeil says it must be remembered that these films were not designed for anything other than entertainment. He says that *The Great Northfield Minnesota Raid* (1972) is the most accurate to date.

1076. Messick, Mary Ann. *History of Baxter County—1873–1973*. Little Rock: Mountain Home Chamber of Commerce, 1973. 506p.

In 1927 the Graphic Photography Company of Hollywood came to Mountain Home, Arkansas, and made a Civil War drama titled *Souls Aflame* (see p. 62). Local extras received $1.50 per day.

1077. Morris, Robert L. "The Success of *Kit, the Arkansas Traveler*." *Arkansas Historical Quarterly* 22:4 (Winter 1963): 338–50.

Play by Edward Spencer, who sold it to F. S. Chanfrau in 1868. There is considerable information about this drama in Masterson, *Tall Tales of Arkansas* (see volume 1 of this bibliography, p. 176), pp. 241, 443.

1078. Poindexter, C. A., and Bracken Fitzpatrick. *The Historical Background, Setting and Synopsis of "Jesse James" Filmed at Pineville, Missouri*. Pineville, Mo.: Democrat Press, 1938. 31p.

A souvenir booklet, sold to the tourists for twenty-five cents. Badly written and full of errors, but good photographs of local scenes and people. For a more reliable account see Frank Condon, "Local Ghost Makes Good" (*Colliers*, 26 November 1938, pp. 14, 44–46).

1079. Walker, Don. *Fun and Games with "Jesse James"*. Pineville, Mo.: McDonald County News-Gazette Printing Co., 1976. 74p.

This pamphlet has nothing to do with the historical Jesse James, but is about a movie called *Jesse James* that 20th Century-Fox filmed in 1938. Many of the scenes were made in Pineville, Missouri, and this booklet is concerned with the actors who appeared there—Tyrone Power, Henry Fonda, John Carradine, Nancy Kelly, and others. The book has no great value, but sells pretty well to the tourists. The author was a police reporter on the *Joplin Globe*. Retired now, he runs a motel near Pineville.

1080. Wilson, Lanford. *The Fifth of July*. Toronto: McGraw-Hill, Ryerson, 1978. 129p.

Supposedly this play is representative of a wealthy family living in Lebanon, Missouri. The author lived there until he was five years old and returned for visits until age thirteen. But, other than the use of a few regional names, there is little in the characters and situations that designate this play as being set in the Ozarks.

1081. ———. *Talley's Folly*. New York: Hill & Wang, 1979. 60p.

This is Wilson's second play about the Talley family of Lebanon, Missouri, the first being *The Fifth of July* in 1978. This is a much better work and won a Pulitzer Prize in 1980. The entire play takes place on a folly or boathouse and there are only two characters, the daughter of a wealthy Lebanon family and a Jew from St. Louis who has come to woo her. The dialogue and social content of this play are more identifiably Ozarkian than were those of *The Fifth of July* and reveal to a greater degree Wilson's familiarity with these people.

1082. Wooten, Denham Lee. *Annals of the Stage in Little Rock, Arkansas, 1834–1890*. M. A. thesis, Columbia University, 1935. 159p.

Some of this material was used in "The History of the Theatre in Arkansas," *Arkansas Gazette Sunday Magazine*, 18 November through 22 December 1935.

13. Verse

1083. Allen, Allie Belle. *Sorghum Time in the Ozarks*. Branson, Mo.: The Ozarks Mountaineer, 1977. 29p.

A retired schoolteacher tells, in bad verse, how her father makes molasses at Cherokee City, Arkansas. The booklet contains several good photographs. Miss Allen is a native of Rogers, Arkansas.

1084. Atwill, Mattie. *Ode to the Ozarks*. New York: Carlton Press, 1966. 86p.

There is little verse in this book, no order and few references to the Ozarks. It is a collection of reflective essays, with a strong religious cast. The pleasant thoughts of a pleasant lady, a retired businesswoman who has spent most of her life somewhere between St. Louis and Springfield, Missouri. Little to interest the folklorist or student of local history. The title is a bit misleading.

1085. Aubrey, Jane Jones. "Conservation in the Ozarks." *The Ozarks Mountaineer* 23:9 (October 1975): 26.

An unforgettable bit of verse. I know nothing of the writer except that she lives in Mission, Kansas.

1086. Ballard, George. *Ozark Ballards*. Fayetteville, Ark.: Democrat Publishing and Printing Company, 1928. 62p.

Paperback edited by Lessie Stringfellow Read. The author was a young black who "once worked in a barber shop, now he repairs Buicks." His verse is not bad, some of it in black dialect. One of his best pieces is "On the Death of Woodrow Wilson." Lessie Read describes him as a "jazz singer." He was born in Cincinnati, Arkansas.

1087. Bartholomew, Rev. Noyles O. *The Picturesque Ozarks of Missouri*. Eldon, Mo.: Eldon Chamber of Commerce and others, 1931. [16p.]

An early chamber of commerce–type publication extolling the beauties of the then newly formed Lake of the Ozarks in the north-central Ozarks. This is practically all done in a form of light verse known as "acrostics."

1088. Bogan, Jim. "Missouri Litany." In *Ozark, Ozark: A Hillside Reader*, edited by Miller Williams, pp. 154–55. Columbia: University of Missouri Press, 1981.

Some light verse composed entirely of Missouri place names.

1089. Boggs, Tom. *Lyric Moderns in Brief*. Prairie City, Ill.: James A. Decker, 1940. 83p.

A collection of mixed verse, among them three poems, "from manuscript," by Mary Elizabeth Mahnkey: "Priority," p. 24; "Befooled," p. 32; and "The Proud Bride," p. 34. Boggs lived for a time in Forsyth, Missouri, and was a neighbor to Mary Elizabeth.

1090. Bolinger, Arthur Joel. *Mine Eyes Unto the Hills*. New York: Vantage Press, 1966. 143p.

Subtitled "An Ozark Anthology," this is a book of mediocre "poems," but the Ozark color is there and it is true and genuine and authentic. My literary friends tell me I have very low taste in verse, but I enjoyed reading this book.

1091. Bosworth, Marcellus. *"Sit a Spell": Poems of the Ozarks*. Lake Ozark, Mo.: Lake Printing Co., 1974. 60p.

A paperback of mediocre verse, eighty-one poems in all. About half of these do, or could, pertain to the Lake of the Ozarks region in central Missouri. The author, a retired postal employee, is from East St. Louis, Illinois. He calls himself "The Bard of Osage Beach."

1092. Bourland, Dr. Richard D. "Lanark's Poet of the World. . . ." *The Carroll County Historical Society Quarterly* 24:2 (Summer 1979): 9–14.

Winner of numerous awards and tributes in the field of poetry, Glen Ward Dresbach lived his final years in Eureka Springs, Arkansas. See the poem "Mountain Air—The Ozarks" (p. 13). Other Ozark references are found in his work *Collected Poems, 1914–1948* (see volume 1 of this bibliography, p. 431).

1093. Capehart, Rachel Friend. *For Hearts Grown Cold*. Neosho, Mo.: Privately printed, 1972. 48p.

A little book of pretty good verse, but few local references, and very little folklore.

1094. Chalfant, Thelma King. *Love Thy Neighbor*. New York: Vantage Press, 1969. 47p.

Autobiography in verse, wandering through the Middle West. See "Our New Home in Arkansas" (pp. 20–23) and "Our Home in Missouri" (pp. 29–33).

1095. Cohen, Gerald Leonard, ed. *Interesting Missouri Place Names*. Rolla, Mo.: Published by the editor, 1982. 76p.

See pp. 18–19 for a poem entitled "A Small Excursion" that uses fifty-six unusual Missouri place names as its theme. It was written by a St. Louis poet, Mona Van Duyn, and first appeared in *Merciful Disguises: Published and Unpublished Poems* (Atheneum Press, 1973).

1096. Creech, Omer E. *Living Altars of the Ozarks*. Cassville, Mo.: Litho Printers, 1973. 112p.

For more than thirty years Creech served as principal and teacher in the public schools—not in the Ozark backwoods, but in Vermillion County, Illinois. During this time he served also as a volunteer "interim and supply minister for a number of churches in that area." His writing is not very good. His "living altars" are high peaks and ridges, or "crests of the mountains." He visited many, and while on these high places he was moved to write "Poems and reflections"—the verses seem very bad to me, and the reflections senseless.

Some of the material in this book is reprinted from a previous publication, *Soul Talk of the Ozark Hills*, copyrighted 1972. Creech once lived near Branson, Missouri, but the people I interviewed in Branson do not remember him.

1097. ———. *Missouri Clay*. Cassville, Mo.: Litho Printers, 1975. 107p.

Very bad verse, with some brief sermons, also very poor. If you like the author's *Living Altars of the Ozarks*, you'll enjoy this one too. There are a few scraps of local history but no folklore worth considering. The kind of people who think Harold Bell Wright is a great novelist will think highly of Omer E. Creech.

1098. Crump, Bonnie Lela. *Round Robin of Unique Eureka*. Eureka Springs, Ark.: Times-Echo Press, 1956. 102p.

A paperback for the tourist trade, with photos and letters from the village notables, bad verse, and worse prose fillers.

1099. Dickey, R. P. *Concise Dictionary of Lead River, Missouri*. Taos, N.M.: Black Bear Press, 1972. 86p.

Shapeless verse of uneven merit, but it's all authentic small-town stuff, based on Dickey's boyhood in Flat River and St. Francois County, Missouri. Somewhat reminiscent of *Spoon River*, but in the modern fashion of four-letter words as well as situational obscenity. But it is much better than most verse of this sort. The author teaches contemporary poetry and creative writing at Southern Colorado State College at Pueblo.

1100. Dresbach, Beverly. "Edsel Ford: In Memoriam." *Ark/Ozark* 2:3 (Spring 1970): 13–16.

A tribute to the memory of the "Poet Laureate of the Ozarks," who died in

1970. The author is the widow of another famous poet, Glen Ward Dresbach, of Eureka Springs, Arkansas.

1101. DuBois, Harold J. "The Memphis Express." *The Little Balkans Review* 1:2 (Winter 1980–1981): 21–25.

Memories, set to verse, of the Frisco Railroad's run from Springfield, Missouri, to Memphis, Tennessee. This passed through the Missouri-Arkansas Ozarks and the author's hometown, Cabool, Missouri.

1102. Fancher, Burr. *Selected Verse by an Ozark Maverick.* Albany, Oreg.: Published by the author, 1977. 118p.

A collection of very poor verses mostly about the author's family. The section called "Ozarkia" (pp. 1–16) carries a few local place names. The Fanchers were from Carroll County, Arkansas.

1103. Ford, Edsel. *Looking for Shiloh.* Columbia: University of Missouri Press, 1968. 64p.

A book of verse, and much of it is very good verse, it seems to me. But excepting "White River Float" (p. 19) and "Night Drowning" (pp. 20–23) there are very few Ozark references. This is odd, because Ford spent much of his life in north Arkansas and graduated from the University of Arkansas at Fayetteville in 1952. He was familiar with many of the old ballads and tales.

1104. ———. *Raspberries Run Deep.* Hindsville, Ark.: Ozark Arts and Crafts Fair Association, 1975. 100p.

This book, published after Ford's death, is a collection of verses from his early writings, selected by Blanche Elliot and Hank Spruce. Ford lived near Avoca, Benton County, Arkansas. He was a very intelligent fellow, sensitive and perceptive. He was thoroughly familiar with the Ozark scene and wrote a lot of good verse.

1105. Fountain, Sarah. *Arkansas Voices: An Anthology of Arkansas Literature.* Little Rock: Rose Publishing Company, 1976. 258p.

Chapter 5 (pp. 175–247) is devoted to the Arkansas poets—Fred Allsopp, Maya Angelou, Besmilr Brigham, Jack Butler, Glen Ward Dresbach, John Gould Fletcher, Edsel Ford, Fay Hempstead, Richard Hudson, Booker T. Jackson, Rosa Zagnoni Marinoni, Lily Peter, Albert Pike, James Whitehead, and Miller Williams. A pretty good selection. Fountain is assistant professor of English at the University of Central Arkansas.

1106. Garrison, Theodore. "The Folk Singer." *The Ozarks Mountaineer* 23:2 (March 1975): 25.

A sonnet, by the Dr. Garrison who took his M.A. at the University of Arkansas in 1944 with a collection of forty-five Searcy County folksongs for a thesis. This is the only poem of his that I have seen. A pretty good one, I think.

1107. Githens, Beverley. *No Splendore Perishes*. La Porte, Ind.: Dierkes Press, 1946. 50p.

Good verse by a poet who lived in the Ozarks, but it contains very few regional references.

1108. Hair, Mary Scott. *Rhymes from Spring Creek Valley*. Birmingham, Ala.: Published by the author, 1972. 20p.

Pleasant Valley and Hurley, primitive settlements in the wilds of Stone County, Missouri, where the author lives, are the setting for these verses. This is a pleasant little book, with many local references. I like some of these verses very much.

1109. Hennessey, George Vest. *Sparks from the Ozarks*. Springfield, Mo.: A & J Printing, 1977. 122p.

This paperback is a collection of artless, unpretentious newspaper verse. Many local references, mostly to Springfield and Greene County. See "Shootout on the Square" and "Wild Bill's Last Stand."

1110. Hickman, Ruth Hughes. *Days of Song*. Greenfield, Mo.: Vedette Press, 1971. 185p.

This has been advertised as an Ozark book, and the author lives in Greenfield, Missouri, but there is very little regional material. See pp. 41–43 for "The Ozark Hills in June" and pp. 71–72 for "Ozark Autumn." The rest of the book is largely concerned with religious matters, and might have been written anywhere.

1111. Hinton, Ted. *Ambush: The Real Story of Bonnie and Clyde*. Austin, Tex.: Shoal Creek Publishers, 1979. 211p.

Page xv begins a sixteen-stanza poem, "The Story of Bonnie and Clyde," allegedly composed by Bonnie Parker in April 1933 just before the Barrow Gang escaped from police in a fusillade of gunfire in Joplin, Missouri. The first stanza reads as follows:

You've read the story of Jesse James—
Of how he lived and died;
If you're still in the need
Of something to read,
Here's the story of Bonnie and Clyde.

They were both finally gunned down by law officers in Louisiana in May 1934. But between April 1932 and their deaths, they were credited with the murders of twelve persons.

1112. Hite, Otis. *Book of Songs*. Eureka Springs, Ark.: Ozark Guide Press, 1950. 32p.

Pleasant, unpretentious, and undistinguished verse. A few Ozark place names and local references. Hite was a native of Washington County, Arkansas. He was a hunter, trapper, root digger, and fisherman who knew a lot of backwoods lore, but his books are of small value to the folklorist.

1113. Hunnicutt, William H. *Ozark Humor*. Holdenville, Okla.: McIntyre-Hunnicutt Publishing Co., 1953. 24p.

A pamphlet of very bad verse. There is very little mention of the Ozarks in it, and no humor at all so far as I can see.

1114. Ike, Carl B., and Hazel Dagley Heavin. *Memory's Autograph*. Lowell, Mass.: Alentour House, 1939. [26p.]

The first half of this small booklet consists of verse by Ike, while the second half contains the efforts of Heavin. For the most part average poems, some of them in a style akin to that of Edgar Guest, that might have been written anywhere. One item by Heavin, "Hillbilly," is relevant to this bibliography.

1115. Kastendieck, Augusta M. *The Power of Life*. Boston: Christopher Publishing House, 1957. 62p.

Sentimental and religious verse. Few local references, although the author is often called an "Ozark poet."

1116. Kent, Walter J. *Symphony of the Ozarks*. Springfield, Mo.: Published by the author, 1961. 104p.

Newspaper verse, much of which first appeared in a Springfield daily. Very few local references.

1117. King, Johnny. *Johnny the Country Boy*. Springfield, Mo.: Roberts & Sutter, 1973. 140p.

Much of the material in this book is not very different from other nostalgic chronicles, but it does contain a fine collection of "Autograph Album" verses (pp. 41–44).

1118. King, Sterling Price. *On Wings of Rhyme*. Edgerton, Mo.: Edgerton Journal Printing Company, n.d. [26p.]

Commonplace verse. The author had evidently lived in the Ozarks, but there is no dialect and few local references.

1119. Kirk, E. R. *Introduction to Happiness*. Norwood, Mo.: Published by the author, 1945. 18p.

A book of verse. Though Kirk sometimes signs his stuff "Ozark Pete," there is nothing about the Ozarks in this little book.

1120. Krone, May. *Ozark Trail of Poetry*. Osage Beach, Mo.: Distributed by Herman Krone, 1971. 48p.

Although the preface calls the author the "Ozark Poet," there are only a few verses in this book that pertain to the Ozarks. The rest are religious in nature and do not represent any particular region.

1121. ———. *Poetry from the Ozarks*. Osage Beach, Mo.: Distributed by Herman Krone, 1966. 48p.

Mostly religious verse. A few extol nature in the Ozarks. See "Springtime in the Ozarks" (p. 6), "Painted Hills" (p. 14), "Ozark Hills" (p. 23), "Autumn in the Ozarks" (p. 44).

1122. Lair, Jim. "The Poet Laureate of the Ozark Mountains." *Carroll County Tribune*, Berryville, Arkansas, 30 September 1981.

An excellent biographical sketch about Mary Elizabeth Mahnkey of Oasis, Missouri. Her works achieved national recognition during the 1930s, and she was praised by the great literary minds of the day. Lair covers all the pertinent facts of her life in this brief article. He did his homework.

1123. Lisher, Mary L. *From an Ozark Rocking Chair*. Branson, Mo.: The Ozarks Mountaineer, 1975. 32p.

Preface by Clay Anderson, good photographs by Charles and Linda McRaven. The verse is not too bad, though there is little attempt at dialect or local color. The author lived at Joplin, Missouri.

1124. Ludwig, Oswald C., ed. *Arkansas Poems*. Conway, Ark.: Log Cabin Book and Job Print Co., 1893. 106p.

Verse by all sorts of writers, from Albert Pike to Charles S. Blackburn.

1125. Lyon, Marguerite. "Lady of the Hills." Unpublished manuscript, Forsyth, Mo., 1948. 234p.

This is about poet/writer Mary Elizabeth Mahnkey of Forsyth, Missouri. It contains three of her poems that were never published, pp. 69, 169, and 199.

1126. Mahnkey, Douglas. "Vance Randolph: An Appreciation." *Missouri Folklore Society Journal* 4 (1982): 35–36.

Mahnkey tells of Randolph's visits to his parent's store and mill at the old settlement of Oasis in Taney County, Missouri (now inundated by Table Rock Lake). Mahnkey's mother, Mary Elizabeth Mahnkey, was a renowned Ozarks poet, and reprinted here is one of her poems, "Priority," that was a favorite of Randolph's. He knew this poem by heart and recited it frequently.

1127. Marinoni, Rosa, and Hala Jean Hammond. *Arkansas and Oklahoma Poets.* New York: Henry Harrison, 1935. 96p.

See Margaret Richter's "An Ozark Plowman," p. 40, and "Ozark Autumn," p. 41.

1128. Mason, Perry J. *Human Interest in Poetry and Prose.* Springfield, Mo.: Artcraft Printing Co., 1937. 31p.

A paperback pamphlet containing brief bits of sentimental meditation. The author was a schoolteacher who lived at Bois D'Arc, Missouri. He knew a lot of good Ozark stories, but there are few local references in this book.

1129. ———. *Through the Years.* Aurora, Mo.: MWM Color Press, 1950. [96p.]

This book of verse has some good stuff in it, with many Ozark references. I thought it much better than his previous works. The foreword was written by Guy Howard, the "Walkin' Preacher of the Ozarks." Mason and Howard taught in neighboring schools in Hickory County, Missouri, at one time.

1130. Meadows, Chris. *Old Matt's Memories in Poems.* Cassville, Mo.: Litho Printers, 1979. 72p.

Meadows isn't much of a poet, but he has some nice memories. A native of the Ozarks, he has performed the part of Old Matt in the Shepherd of the Hills Pageant near Branson, Missouri, for many years.

1131. ———. *Short Stories and Poems of the Ozark Hills.* Point Lookout, Mo.; School of the Ozarks Press, 1971. 88p.

There are no short stories in this book—just a series of brief factual articles. There is nothing that can fairly be called a poem, either, although the last part of the book (pp. 72–88) is devoted to bad verse. Some of the articles are pretty good. See

"The Ozark Hillbilly" (pp. 13–16), "White River Shelling" (pp. 20–23), and "Fishing" (pp. 46–56).

1132. Nicholson, William F. "Looks Menacing, But He's Peaceful." *Springfield Leader-Press*, 21 October 1969.

This article has a good photograph of Louis "Moondog" Hardin, who roamed New York City dressed in a Viking outfit complete with spear. Hardin, who is blind, lived for some time in Hurley, Stone County, Missouri. He says he took the name "Moondog" in honor of a dog he had that howled at the Ozarks moon. He is a poet and a musical composer of some note. He now lives in Germany.

1133. O'Neill, Paul. "Letter to/from a Famous Lady." *The Ozarks Mountaineer* 23:7 (August 1975): 18.

In 1939 well-known Ozark poet Mary Elizabeth Mahnkey wrote a letter to an equally famous Ozarker, Rose O'Neill. She included a poem titled "Lee O'Neill," written some years before about Rose's sister, Mary Ileana. The poem tells how "Lee" shocked her mountain neighbors by riding astride instead of side-saddle, which was generally considered the proper method.

1134. Peter, Lily. *The Green Linen of Summer and Other Poems*. Nashville, Tenn.: R. M. Allen, 1964. 114p.

People whose opinion I respect say that some of these verses are very good indeed, but they are way over my head. I have been told that Miss Peter is the only authentic poet in Arkansas since John Gould Fletcher, and feel that her book is somehow important, but I can make nothing of it and can't find any regional references at all. The book has gone into several printings and has been widely quoted.

1135. Peters, Ida. *Poems and Articles by the Little Lady of the Ozarks*. Licking, Mo.: Derrickson Publishing Company, [c. 1959]. 75p.

1136. ———. *Poems by the Little Lady of the Ozarks*. Licking, Mo.: Derrickson Publishing Company, 1963. 51p.

1137. ———. *Echoes of the Hills by the Little Lady of the Ozarks*. Licking, Mo.: Derrickson Publishing Company, 1965. 45p.

Mrs. Peters seems to have been just a nice small-town lady who wrote down her thoughts in verse, no matter the subject, a kind of amateur Mary Elizabeth Mahnkey. These three editions contain over 350 of these little meditations on a wide range of subjects: "Back to Central Standard Time," "Goldwater for President," "Gossipers Holding the Line," etc.

1138. Rees, George Nicholas. *Oh, Lovely Ozarkland*. Tucson, Ariz.: V. Carter Service, 1957. 24p.

A book of sentimental verse with some Ozark references, mostly about the area around Springfield, Missouri. The title poem won him the "Poet Laureate of Ozarkland" award in a contest sponsored by local radio stations. I met this fellow once. He was a florist up around Nixa, Missouri, as I recall, a farmer and a gardener. He has published others, one a book of bad verse called *The Gold Lark* (Springfield, Missouri, 1937). See volume 1 of this bibliography, p. 443.

1139. Roddy, Florence Howery. *Faces of Nature Fashioned by God*. Ardmore, Penn.: Dorrance and Company, 1980. 83p.

Mostly religious and sentimental verse. Four of the poems specifically mention the Ozarks: "Beautiful Ozark Mountains" (p. 8), "Christmas in the Ozarks" (p. 10), "Homesick" (p. 27), and "Song of the Ozarks" (p. 49). The author lived for a time in the Ozarks near Anderson in the southwest corner of Missouri.

1140. Russell, Beth. *Mountainburg Philosophy in Song and Verse*. Little Rock: Parkhurst-Eaton, 1980. 59p.

Sentimental poetry about mother, sunsets, rainbows, etc., and religious verse. Few references to the Ozarks and little for the folklorist. But her foreword interests me. She describes her upbringing in Arkansas, where she waltzed and two-stepped and didn't cavort with "the rougher element of the community who went to square dances where there was often drinking." And her thoughts on writing: she says she does not use four-letter words "that stink" and has not found it necessary to confine her thoughts to the reproductive organs nor a graphic description of their functions. She speaks of a "VR" and his research and says that she doubts it included her section of the Ozarks as her relatives and neighbors "were sacred and incest was a hanging offence." I mention these statements only to make a point. Ms. Russell's opinions on these matters are not necessarily prudish and certainly aren't uncommon in the Ozarks. There always has been, is, and undoubtedly always will be a school of thought here that considers some music (mainly that of the fiddle), square dancing (or any kind of dancing for that matter), and the public discussion of loose morals or the publication of bawdy material as something close to mortal sin. For a good article about one aspect of this, see Galbraith's "The Devil's Own Instrument" (entry 92).

1141. Steele, Pauline Davis. *Hill Country Sayin's and Ozark Folklore: Book Two*. West Fork, Ark.: Hutcheson Press, 1977. [41p.]

Sentimental verse about nature and memories of family and school days. See pp. 25, 27, 28, 29, 32, and 34.

1142. Taylor, Diane. *Creek Music: Ozark Mountain Ballads*. Little Rock: August House, 1981. 62p.

Forty poems, easily read and understood, with the word *Ozark* used liberally throughout. But I found nothing distinctively Ozarkian about any of them, their stories being of a general nature that could be applied to most rural areas in the country.

1143. Wiley, Dorothy B. "Mt. Sherman Bookman." *The Ozarks Mountaineer* 30:1 (February 1982): 55.

A patronizing piece of verse about Ted Richmond, who in the 1940s ran a lending library located on Mt. Sherman in the wilds of Newton County, Arkansas. He got a lot of publicity for his efforts (see *Saturday Evening Post*, 8 November 1952). After FDR's death, Eleanor Roosevelt even contributed a large number of books from her husband's library. For more on "Twilight Ted" see Townsend Godsey's *These Were the Last* (entry 1377), pp. 82–85.

1144. Williams, Miller, ed. *Ozark, Ozark: A Hillside Reader*. Columbia: University of Missouri Press, 1981. 193p.

This anthology includes poems by seventeen twentieth-century resident Ozark poets, but few of the poems themselves are about the Ozarks. James Bogan's "Missouri Litany" is composed entirely of Missouri place names. Williams is a poet himself and a member of the English Department of the University of Arkansas–Fayetteville.

1145. Wilson, Harry. *The Young Brothers' Massacre. Springfield News-Leader*, 3 January 1982.

A narrative poem that appears with an article titled "50 Years Later, Memory of Massacre Lives On" by staff writer Renee Turner. It commemorates the anniversary of this tragedy in which six Springfield lawmen were gunned down by desperadoes Harry and Jennings Young. Mr. Wilson, now eighty-three and still living in Springfield, composed this poem at the time of the incident.

14. Miscellaneous

1146. Abbott, John S. C. *The Civil War in America*. Vol. 2. New York: Ledyard Hill Publications, 1866. 629p.

Describing the Battle of Pea Ridge, Abbott writes, ". . . the notorious Ben McCulloch, one of the most coarse and brutal of the ruffians on the border, received his mortal wound from a minnie ball piercing his breast. As he was borne from the field to die, with horrid oaths he declared that he would not die; that he was not born to be killed by a Yankee. In this state of mind he lingered for a few hours, and at eleven o'clock at night, from the sulphurous gloom of the battlefield, his stormy spirit ascended to the tribunal of God. A few moments before his death, the surgeon told him that he could not possibly recover, and had but a few moments more to live. Fixing an incredulous look upon the surgeon, his only reply was, in contemptuous tones, 'Oh, Hell!' These were his last words on earth. Who can imagine what was his next utterance when he stood in the presence of his Maker!" (p. 237). Abbott was a preacher from New Haven, Connecticut.

1147. Abbott, Lawrence F. "Arkansas Traveler." *Outlook* 146:5 (1 June 1927): 146–48.

Chatty letter about an editor's visit to Arkansas. He has high praise for the Missouri Pacific Railroad, the *Arkansas Gazette*, and the College of the Ozarks at Clarksville.

1148. Albin, Edgar A. "Collecting Folklore in the Ozarks." *Ozarks Highways* (Fall 1972): 6–10.

This is a fine slick-paper quarterly magazine published by the Ozark Highways Travel Association in Kimberling City, Missouri. Albin was a professor in the Art Department at the University of Arkansas with the late Dave Durst. He became head of the Art Department at Southwest Missouri State University until his retirement in 1974. His story is a good job, with fine large photographs of me and Mary Celestia Parler and Max Hunter. Several anecdotes, including the old one about "I think they're gaining on us—"; he makes it "damn fools" instead of "sons of bitches."

1149. Alexander, T. H. "The Return of the Troubadours." *Reader's Digest* 34:205 (May 1939): 39–41.

In 1934 the first National Folk Festival was held in St. Louis. It was the creation of a young lady from Kentucky, Sarah Gertrude Knott. She had come into the Ozarks six months earlier and held eighteen mini-festivals to discover those artists who represented the "Anglo-Saxon" culture. Out of four hundred or so who participated, she selected sixty-five to go to St. Louis. This first festival was a huge success, and it became an annual affair staged in a different city each year. This article is about the sixth festival, held in Washington, D.C.

1150. Aley, Tom. "The Sinkhole Dump and the Spring." *Missouri Conservationist* 33:2 (February 1972): 16–17.

One of the most picturesque and tranquil scenes in the Missouri Ozarks is the Hodgson Mill, located in Ozark County. It has appeared in practically every photo essay published about the Ozarks and on calendars, book covers, and postcards, and has been the subject of generations of tourists' snapshots. It is usually depicted in the same perspective, the mill in the background with the small mill pond in the fore. At one side of the pond dam there projects a pipe with a cup hanging next to it. Many a thirsty traveler, myself included, has refreshed himself with the clear, cool spring water issuing from the pipe. Fifteen miles to the north is located the Dora Sink. The Ozarks are what geologists term a karst region, full of caves, underground streams, innumerable springs, and countless sinkholes. For years the Dora Sink has been a catch-all for community trash, everything from dead animals to septic tank sludge. In 1971 Tom Aley, a hydrologist with the U.S. Forest Service, dumped tracer dye into this sinkhole. One axiom applicable to karst terrain is that what goes down is gonna' come up somewhere; well, no one drinks from the Hodgson Mill spring anymore. Our changing Ozarks. See Vineyard's *Springs of Missouri* (entry 318), pp. 168–169, and the National Geographic Society's *America's Hidden Corners* (1983). The dustcover of that book has an excellent photo of the mill, which is also pictured on p. 148.

1151. Ashmore, Harry S. *Arkansas: A Bicentennial History.* New York: W. W. Norton Co., 1978. 202p.

This is one of a series administered by the American Association for State and Local History under a grant from the National Endowment for the Humanities. It is comparable to John Gould Fletcher's *Arkansas*, but less impressionistic. The emphasis throughout is upon economic, political, and racial matters. All of the great names are here, and many lesser ones. I was delighted to find a favorable mention of my latest opus (pp. 192–93). Ashmore was for twelve years editor of the *Arkansas Gazette*, where he was awarded the Pulitzer Prize.

1152. Babcock, Bernie. *Yesterday and Today in Arkansas.* Little Rock: Jordan and Foster, 1917. 104p.

Subtitled "a Folio of rare and interesting pictures from Mrs. Babcock's collection for Stories and legends of Arkansas." Mostly about Little Rock in the 1880s and 1890s. More than 150 pictures of historic landmarks with early advertisements, not easily found elsewhere.

1153. Bentley, Max. "Smackover, and Seekers of Oil." *Harper's Magazine* 148 (December 1923): 73–84.

Fine article about the oil boom towns in Arkansas.

1154. Benton, Thomas Hart. *Benton Drawings*. Columbia: University of Missouri Press, 1968. 135p.

A collection of Benton's best sketches, reproduced in black and white. Most of them are of Missouri and the Ozarks. I knew Benton and saw some of these drawings years ago, but many are new to me.

1155. ———. "The Missouri Murals." *Missouri Life* 1:1 (March-April 1973): 25–35.

Benton tells about the pictures and how he painted them at the Missouri Capitol Building, Lincoln University, the River Club (Kansas City, Missouri), the Truman Library (Independence), and the Joplin City Hall. Splendid colored photographs. A beautiful piece of work.

1156. ———. "Thomas Benton Paints a History of His Own Missouri." *Life* 2:9 (1 March 1937): 32–37.

Splendid pictures, some in color, from Benton's murals in the State House in Jefferson City. Intelligent comment.

1157. Berry, Earl. *History of Marion County*. Little Rock: Marion County, Arkansas, Historical Association, 1977. 523p.

This is a good book, full of folklore material. Instead of documenting it all with footnotes and annotations, Berry has each of his informants write his or her contribution and sign it. This eliminates the necessity for the "scholarly trappings" that offend so many readers, but preserves all the essential data just the same. This seems a good way to write these county histories, avoiding the appearance of professional or academic craftsmanship. It's a way for a historian to keep from losing his amateur standing and still be sound.

1158. Berryhill, Horace. Letter to the editor. *The Ozarks Mountaineer* 30:1 (February 1982): 4–5.

Berryhill reminiscences about his family's encounters with wild hogs. He lives in the village of Violet Hill in Izard County, Arkansas, which had some of the wildest razorbacks in the Ozarks.

1159. Billington, Ray A. "Best Prepared Pioneers in the West." *American Heritage* 7:6 (October 1956): 20–25, 116–17.

This article, about the Mormon settlement of Utah, also appeared as part of a chapter in Billington's *The Far Western Frontier: 1830–1860* (Harper & Bros., 1956). On pp. 116–17 is an account of the Mountain Meadows Massacre in November 1857, when one hundred twenty members of the Fancher wagon train that had departed Harrison, Arkansas, a few weeks earlier were killed by Indians and Mormons. (The story still can be heard around Harrison that the "Indians" were actually Mormons in disguise, hoping to divert responsibility for the killings.) Billington lays the blame for this incident upon the provocations of a group of "Missouri Wildcats" traveling with the train, who "abused Indian converts, turned their cattle into Mormon fields, killed chickens with their bull whips, and shouted profane insults at Mormon women." (Also see *The Mountain Meadows Massacre* by Juanita Brooks [entry 1165], p. 219.)

1160. Black, J. Dickson. "The Need For Continued Study." In *Proceedings of the Conference on Ozark In-Migration*, pp. 111–12. Eureka Springs, Ark., 1976.

A good letter commenting on the Conference on In-Migration, held in Eureka Springs, Arkansas, in May 1976. Black is the author of a good book, *History of Benton County, Arkansas* (entry 1330).

1161. Blount, Roy, Jr. "C'mon, They're Not All Dumber Than Two Dollar Dogs!" *TV Guide* 28:5 (2 February 1980): 4–6, 8.

Talks about television's stereotype of the rural South. The author, who says he's from the South, contends that "no ethnic group associated with California, New York, or any other part of the world has ever been so ill-served by the situation comedy as the Ozark Mountain white by *The Beverly Hillbillies*."

1162. Bowen, Elbert R. "The Circus in Early Rural Missouri." *Missouri Historical Review* 47:1 (October 1952): 1–17.

Taken from Bowen's Ph.D. dissertation, "A Study of Theatrical Entertainments in Rural Missouri Before the Civil War" (University of Missouri, 1950). It has since been published under the same title as University of Missouri Studies Volume 32, University of Missouri Press, 1959, 141p. Bowen is a professor of speech and drama at Central Michigan College.

1163. Bradley, James. *The Confederate Mail Carrier*. Mexico, Mo.: Published by the author, 1894. 275p.

This book describes the battles and hardships of the Confederate soldiers from Missouri, also the adventures of the notorious Captain Grimes and his female accomplices in smuggling mail through the lines. Badly written, but full of unintentional humor. See especially chapter 2 (pp. 9–13) and the rural schoolmaster's farewell speeches to his mother and his sweetheart when he enlisted in 1861.

1164. Bradley, Matt. *Arkansas: Its Land and People*. Little Rock: Museum of Science and History, 1980. 112p.

A large book full of beautiful color photos, many of Ozark scenes. Little text. Bradley, a native of Pine Bluff, presently lives in Little Rock. He has been on numerous assignments for *National Geographic*.

1165. Brooks, Juanita. *The Mountain Meadows Massacre*. Norman: University of Oklahoma Press, 1974. 316p.

This is the standard historical work on the subject. It was first printed in 1950 by Stanford University Press. This edition is the fifth printing by the University of Oklahoma Press since they obtained the new edition, copyrighted 1962. Brooks is a Mormon from Utah, but she pulls no punches.

1166. Campbell, William S. *One Hundred Years of Fayetteville, 1828–1928*. Fayetteville, Ark.: Privately printed, 1928. 120p.

This book is written in flowery and bombastic English that seems ridiculous today. But it is full of detailed information, and is good reading for anybody who wants the facts about the history of this town. Full of good photographs of old-timers, and the houses they built. W. S. Campbell was secretary of the Fayetteville Chamber of Commerce and is remembered by many of the old-timers. The book has been reprinted (1977) by the Washington County Historical Society.

1167. Carpenter, Allen. *Arkansas from Its Glorious Past to the Present*. Chicago: Children's Press, 1967. 95p.

Despite the title, this is not a conventional history, but a hodgepodge of historical episodes, with a great number of brightly colored drawings by Roger Harrington. Beginning with Huddleston's discovery of the diamond mine near Murfreesboro in 1906, we find the prehistoric Bluff Dwellers on p. 18 and De Soto on p. 24. But it is a pretty good book for the tourist trade and has been used in some Arkansas schools.

1168. ———. *Missouri, From Its Glorious Past to the Present*. Chicago: Children's Press, 1966. 95p.

This is a juvenile history with special chapters about celebrated Missourians such as Mark Twain and Harry Truman. Jesse James and Calamity Jane are not forgotten. For Ozark references see pp. 12, 29, 42, 44, 76, and 77. Not important to the folklorist.

1169. Cheatham, Edgar, and Patricia Cheatham. "Autumn in the Ozarks." *Odyssey* 14:5 (September-October 1981): 4–9.

This tourist publication does mention most of the really worthwhile places to see in the north Arkansas Ozarks with special emphasis upon the Ozark Folk Center in Mountain View. *Odyssey* is a travel magazine published by the Gulf Auto Club.

1170. Clarke, Kenneth, and Mary Clarke. *A Folklore Reader*. New York: A. S. Barnes & Co., 1965. 430p.

This book has been criticized for lack of organization, as being thrown together too casually, but I find much of value in it. The two-page introduction contains this: "The study of folklore is not likely to become a science any sooner than is the study of literature or music . . . it still belongs largely to the humanities" (p. 8). I particularly enjoyed the selections from Stith Thompson and MacEdward Leach, also Thelma James on "Problems of Archives." See also pp. 273–77 for "Folk Etymology, or Every Man His Own Lexicographer." There are only two specifically Ozark pieces, both from my own writings. The first is the title story from the *Talking Turtle* (1957) on pp. 209–11. The second is the final chapter from *Ozark Superstitions* (1947) on pp. 254–66.

1171. Coates, Helen R. *The American Festival Guide*. New York: Exposition Press, 1956. 299p.

See pp. 189–91 for the Ozark Folk Festival at Eureka Springs and pp. 191–92 for the Folklore Festival of the Arkansas Folklore Society at the University of Arkansas, Fayetteville. Pages 206–9 carry an account of the first National Folk Festival, staged by Sarah Gertrude Knott at St. Louis in 1934.

1172. Cochran, Robert. "The Man Who Wrote About Pissing." *Center for Southern Folklore Newsletter* 1:1 (Spring 1978): 5.

About my *Pissing in the Snow* and its relation to my earlier Ozark folklore collections. The *Newsletter* is a quarterly, published by the Center for Southern Folklore at Memphis, Tennessee.

1173. Coffin, Tristram P., and Hennig Cohen. *Folklore in America*. Garden City, N.Y.: Doubleday & Co., 1966. 256p.

Despite the distinguished folklorist editors named on the title page, this book is badly edited and badly indexed. The only Ozark items I can find are "Nudity and Planting Customs," pp. 137–39, which is my "Nakedness" paper from *Journal of American Folklore* (1953), "Ozark Mountain Riddles," pp. 165–66, which is a paper by Randolph and Spradley from *Journal of American Folklore* (1934); and a description of a game called "Snap," pp. 186–87, which is a paper by Randolph and Clemens from *Journal of American Folklore* (1936).

1174. Cook, Tom. "Ancient Worlds Under Ozark Mountains." *Bull Shoals Gazette* (September 1950): 11–12.

A good description of Marvel Cave, Old Spanish Cave, Fairy Cave, Meramec Cave, and other Missouri caverns. The *Gazette* looked like a newspaper, but it was a monthly magazine published at Gainesville, Missouri.

1175. Coues, Elliott, ed. *The Journal of Jacob Fowler*. Lincoln: University of Nebraska Press, 1970. 152p.

The expedition was in 1821–1822, but Fowler's journal, *Memorandum of the Voige by Land from Fort Smith to the Rocky Mountains*, was not published until the turn of the century, with introduction and notes by Elliott Coues, the great ornithologist. Dr. Coues's introduction is reprinted here, just as he wrote it in 1898. His splendid notes are all here, but have been corrected and brought up to date by later scholars. Colonel Fowler's journal is printed just about as he wrote it, too, spelling and all. It's a wonderful book.

1176. Croley, Victor A. "Will Rogers' Second Home." *The Ozarks Mountaineer* 25:9 (October 1977): 15.

A brief but important note on the great humorist in Arkansas. Rogers found his bride in the Ozark resort called Monte Ne, where her family lived. Croley prints a photograph of Mr. and Mrs. Rogers, which I had not seen before. Many people think that Rogers, Arkansas, was named for Will Rogers, but the fact is that the town took the name of an early railroad official, long before Will Rogers appeared on the scene.

1177. Crump, Bonnie Lela. *Unique Eureka Springs, Arkansas*. Eureka Springs: N.p., 1967. 113p.

This is a greatly revised version of the 1956 edition with many more pictures and additional data. See p. 27 for an article and photo of Sam Leath, who believed he had found messages carved by Indians in the rocks around Eureka Springs. Also, p. 32 for a photo of author Marge Lyon.

1178. Dailey, Janet. "Hills and Hollows and Folklore Galore." *New York Times*, 5 September 1982, pp. 13, 15.

This is nothing more than a Chamber of Commerce pitch for the tourist industry, a travelogue of the attractions in and around Branson, Missouri, and not all the good ones at that. There is a companion article, "Things to See and Do in the Missouri Ozarks (with an Arkansas Side Trip)." Janet Dailey is a successful writer of pulp novels (more than seventy to date) who recently moved to southern Missouri.

1179. Darling, Frank Fraser. *Pelican in the Wilderness*. New York: Random House, [1956]. 380p.

A British naturalist and conservationist, Dr. Darling spent some time in the Missouri Ozarks, traveling from Columbia through Springfield, Hollister, Ava, and

Willow Springs (pp. 202–8). He doesn't appear to have too high a regard for the Ozark "hill-billie." This book is mostly history, description, travel notes.

1180. Deane, Ernie. "It Could Be Good-by to the Ozarks." *Springfield Daily News*, 26 May 1976.

He points out the perils of "progress" in connection with the "Conference on In-Migration," held at Eureka Springs, Arkansas, in May 1976.

1181. ———. "On Progress: Real and Supposed." *The Ozarks Mountaineer* 22:7 (August 1974): 38.

The Ozark country is a land of small towns, small farms, small industries, incredibly beautiful hills and lakes and streams and forests. We have little crime and plenty of elbow room. We have clean air and clean water, and a peaceful, tranquil way of life. Shall we turn this into something like Coney Island or some California beach resort? If a man wants heavy industry, let him go to Detroit, not try to move Detroit down to Arkansas.

1182. ———. "Ozarks Country."

This is a syndicated column that appeared in more than fifteen newspapers in the Ozark region. It appeared weekly and covered a variety of Ozark subjects. Many were folklore related. A number were combined and published in paperback by Deane using the same title, *Ozarks Country* (Branson, Mo.: The Ozarks Mountaineer, 1975).

1183. ———. " 'Progress' at Any Price: Too Costly, Says Ernie Deane." *The Ozarks Mountaineer* 24:6 (July 1976): 36–37.

Ernie talks about the many problems besetting the Ozarks in these times. He has a good eye and tells it as it is: rapid and excessive growth in many areas, severe damage to the ecology and regional culture, pollution, etc. He says that if we fail to organize and awake the government and the public to these dangers, "We'd better bid goodbye to the tranquility, pure air and water, forested hills and easy going life of the Ozarks as presently known and enjoyed."

1184. Dorson, Richard M. "Whoppers, Jingles, Graffiti." *New York Times*, 7 February 1975, p. 31.

"The folklorist is interested in all forms of what might be called underculture, in contrast with the elite, the uppercrust, the official, the formal culture. He studies folk-literature as compared with art literature, folk-history as against documentary history, folk arts and not the fine arts, folk religion rather than theologies, folk-medicine and belief as against medical science—the list can be extended to all spheres of human activities." That's Dorson at his best, telling it like it is.

1185. Downs, Robert B. *Books That Changed the South*. Chapel Hill: University of North Carolina Press, 1977. 292p.

Robert Downs still believes that printed words influence people. His thesis is that the economic, social, and political behavior of a society is shaped largely by books. Concentrating on the publications of twenty-five authors, from Capt. John Smith in 1624 to C. Vann Woodward in 1951, he recounts the ways in which specific books have influenced cultural development of the southern states. Especially interesting to me is the chapter on Hinton Rowan Helper's *The Impending Crisis* (1857). On p. 123 he says that "Three men in Arkansas were hanged" for the mere possession of copies of Helper's book. But, as yet, I have been unable to verify this assertion.

1186. Driftwood, Jimmy. "Folk Festivals." *International Musician* 64:11 (May 1966): 8–22.

Festivals may preserve folk music for posterity, just as material culture is saved in museums, but otherwise festivals aren't much good.

1187. Ellis, Roy. *Shrine of the Ozarks*. Springfield: Southwest Missouri State College, 1968. 283p.

Despite the romantic title, this is just a history of the State College at Springfield. It's a good job, too. Ellis taught economics there and in February 1926 became president, a position he held until his retirement in 1961. At that time he concluded the longest tenure as a college president in the nation.

1188. Ellsworth, Henry Leavitt. *Washington Irving on the Prairie: A Narrative of a Tour of the Southwest in the Year 1832*. New York: American Book Co., 1937. 152p.

The author was with Irving when they came through eastern Oklahoma. His account is much more realistic than Irving's sugar-coated *Tour on the Prairies*. Ellsworth was a Yankee who graduated from Yale in 1810. He never learned to spell, but his book sounds like the truth. It is certainly more entertaining than Irving's story.

1189. Emrich, Duncan. *Folklore on the American Land*. Boston: Little, Brown and Co., 1972. 707p.

This is an introduction to the whole subject of American folklore. I think it is one of the best. Some of the academic folklorists do not agree; see the savage review by Dorson in *Western Folklore* (1973): 141–43. Emrich devotes the first 189 pages to folk speech, a subject many folklorists are not much interested in. He does not slight such items as autograph albums, epitaphs, nicknames, cattle brands, names of hound dogs and racehorses, quilt patterns, and street cries, which are admittedly on the periphery of folklore. My wife used this good book as a text in her folklore classes at the University of Arkansas.

1190. ———. *The Hodgepodge Book*. New York: Four Winds Press, 1972. 367p.

A vast collection of folk beliefs, superstitions, riddles, nonsense jingles, children's rhymes, game-songs, choosing-up rhymes, jumprope rhymes, ball-bouncing rhymes, proverbs, popular sayings, taunts, childish insults, and juvenile wisecracks generally. The book is addressed primarily to children, and there is little conventional documentation. But the general notes in the back of the book are useful, and the fifty-page bibliography is one of the best I have seen, with many Missouri and Arkansas references. Emrich died in August 1977, at which time he was working on a book concerning the folklore of death.

1191. Fair, James R., Jr. *The North Arkansas Line*. Berkeley, Calif.: Howell-North Books, 1969. 304p.

This railroad was 365 miles long, from Joplin, Missouri, to Helena, Arkansas. Its entire turbulent history is fully documented and profusely illustrated, and a bibliography is provided. The natives always said that M. N. & A. stood for "May Never Arrive." The author has a Ph.D. in chemical engineering and teaches at Washington University; he grew up in Little Rock. This is the kind of book to delight old railroad buffs.

1192. Faubus, Orval Eugene. *Down from the Hills*. Little Rock: Pioneer Press, 1980. 510p.

This large book is a collection of newspaper articles and cartoons covering Faubus's career from 1954 to 1966. It contains a great number of anecdotes and stories, mostly political in nature. The "Hills" in the title are those found in Madison County in the north-central Arkansas Ozarks where he was raised.

1193. Felsen, Henry G. "The Timeless Country." *Redbook Magazine* 109:2 (June 1957): 54, 99–102.

A good travel article about the Ozarks, both Missouri and Arkansas.

1194. Fisher, George. *All Around the Farkleberry Bush*. Little Rock: Published by the author, 1967. [110p.]

Fisher is a political cartoonist. This book is made up of about one hundred of his cartoons, most from the *North Little Rock Times*, dated 1964–1967. The first half of the book mostly concerns Orval Faubus; anything about Faubus and Madison County had a good deal of Ozark folklore in it.

1195. ———. *Fisher*. Little Rock: Rose Publishing Company, 1978. 160p.

More than three hundred of Fisher's best cartoons, with a foreword by James O. Powell, editorial director of the *Arkansas Gazette*. Of Ozark interest are a caricature of Ozark writer and former *Gazette* reporter Ernie Deane (p. 74), a cartoon depicting the troubles being experienced between the newly opened Ozark Folk Center in Mountain View and the local musicians (p. 154), and one referring to the controversial views of evangelist Gerald L. K. Smith, who died in 1976 in Eureka Springs (p. 47). I particularly enjoyed those concerned with then-governor David Pryor's ill-fated simile used to compare benefits to be derived from a proposed tax plan with that of being able to buy a new coon dog, thereafter referred to as Pryor's "Coon-dog" plan (pp. 6–12).

1196. ———. *Fisher's Gallery*. Little Rock: Rose Publishing Co., 1974. 160p.

Another fine collection of Fisher's political cartoons, first published in the *Arkansas Gazette*. Fisher was born near Searcy, Arkansas, and grew up in Beebe. There is a good photo of Fisher with a short biography on the back cover of the *Gallery*. He has always been interested in Arkansas folklore and is active in the Rackensack Folklore Society in Little Rock.

1197. ———. *Fruit of the Farkleberry*. Little Rock: Published by the author, 1969. 138p.

This collection of cartoons covers the period 1968 to 1969 and contains a fine foreword by Ernie Deane. Many refer to Arkansas governors Winthrop Rockefeller or Orval Faubus, but Fisher is a personal friend of Rockefeller, which makes him pull his punches where Rockefeller is concerned. Fisher has been around Little Rock for a long time and has a sharp ear for dialect.

1198. Fleming, John. *The Blanchard Springs Cavern Story*. Little Rock: Gallinule Society Publishing Co., 1973. 56p.

A good journalistic account of this newly developed cavern in Stone County, Arkansas, with photographs by Larry Obsitnik of the *Arkansas Gazette*. See the chapter entitled "The Mystery" (pp. 20–23) for the story of the cane torches and the Indian remains found inside the cavern.

1199. Fountain, Sarah. *Arkansas Voices: An Anthology of Arkansas Literature*. Little Rock: Rose Publishing Co., 1976. 258p.

This is apparently intended as a text for secondary schools. It is expurgated almost to the point of evisceration. I think Fountain leans too heavily on Fred Allsopp. Sometimes she misses the point entirely, as on p. 104; she thinks that Sen. Cassius M. Johnson was involved in "a dispute about the spelling of the name of the state"! An entertaining book, but don't take it too seriously.

1200. Gerstäcker, Margarethe. "Greetings from Margarethe Gerstäcker." *Arkansas Historical Quarterly* 10:3 (Autumn 1951): 305–6.

From the eighty-year-old daughter of the great German adventurer. The letter is not much, really; it is written in German (the article contains an English translation) and speaks pleasantly of the *Quarterly* and of Prof. Clarence Evans of Tahlequah, Oklahoma, who has translated much of her father's writings.

1201. Graham, Josephine Hutson. "*Suggin*: A Part of Newport." *Newport* (Arkansas) *Independent*, Centennial Edition, 11 August 1975.

A long article, nearly a full page, about the Suggin Folklife Society, a widely known organization founded by Graham and other descendants of Arkansas pioneers. A good newspaper story, but lacks the punch of Graham's wonderful paintings.

1202. Griffin, Gordon S. "The Cemetery: Another Place for Outdoor Study." *Missouri Conservationist* 42:10 (October 1981): 10–11.

The author says cemeteries are an available place for discovery and study. Besides being wildlife refuges, they provide study opportunities for the subjects of mathematics, language arts, science, geology, social study, geography, and art. He lists a sort of lesson plan for each subject.

1203. Hall, Leonard. *Ozark Wildflowers*. St. Louis: Sayers Printing Co., 1969. 32p.

A beautiful little book, with photographs in full color of about fifty of the most conspicuous wildflowers in the Ozarks, with a short description by Hall himself, who also took most of the pictures. The author lives on Possum Trot Farm near Caledonia, Missouri, but travels all over the Ozarks. A good writer and a fine fellow. He was studying ecology when it was only a book word to most of us.

1204. ———. "Preserving Missouri's Unique Wilderness." *Midwest Motorist* 48:1 (October 1976): 11–14, 16–18.

The 1970s became a decade of decision for Ozarkers. Should our land-use purposes include the preservation of "wilderness"? The author describes seven areas in the Missouri Ozarks placed under consideration for "wilderness" preserves by the Congress.

1205. Hallum, John. *Biographical and Pictorial History of Arkansas*. Albany, N.Y.: Weed, Parsons & Co., 1887. 581p.

Mostly biography of eminent Arkansas lawyers, soldiers, and politicians. Good reading but not much folklore. The book is marked "Vol. 1," but no second volume was ever published so far as I know.

1206. Hammack, Bob. "Ozark Folk Center." *Center for Southern Folklore Newsletter* (Spring 1978): 1.

A good account of the Ozark Folk Center at Mountain View, Arkansas, opened in 1973, dedicated to the "preservation and sharing of the Ozark Mountain way of life." Under the leadership of Dr. William McNeil, formerly of the Smithsonian Institution, the center has acquired a considerable library, volumes dealing with the customs, music, and crafts of the Ozark region. There is also a great and growing collection of documents, manuscripts, photographs, LP records, and tape recordings of Ozark music. Bob Hammack was at the time the article was written a member of the staff. The *Center for Southern Folklore Newsletter* was published twice yearly in Memphis, Tennessee, but is now defunct.

1207. Hempstead, Fay. *Pictorial History of Arkansas from the Earliest Times to the Year 1890*. St. Louis: N. D. Thompson Publishing Company, 1890. 1,240p.

The author was born in Little Rock in 1847 and died in 1934. He witnessed many of the events he writes about.

1208. Hobson, Dick. "The Grandpappy of All Gushers." *TV Guide* 19:17 (24 April 1971): 16–20.

The "gusher" was a television program started in 1962 called *The Beverly Hillbillies*. It's about a hill family (the locale started in Appalachia but after a few episodes changed to the Ozarks) who become millionaires when they strike oil in their "swamp," as this author puts it. They move to Beverly Hills, California, and for nine years and 274 episodes (a number were actually filmed at a theme park near Branson, Missouri) portray the stereotypical image of the illiterate, naive mountain folks in a cultural collision with the California city slickers. At first criticism reigned supreme throughout Ozark communities. Here was that old hillbilly stuff they'd been trying to live down all these years on national television for all the country to see! But the rest of the country wasn't worried about it at all. In fact, they thought it was downright entertaining, and a lot of them started coming into these hills to see just what it was all about. And when they came they spent lots of money. It didn't take the area's chambers of commerce long to figure this out, and suddenly all sorts of "hillbilly" promotions began cropping up in some of the most unlikely places. One metropolitan area, for decades a vehement opponent of the hillbilly image, discarded the old "Keys to the City" award and began making visiting dignitaries (including some members of the show's cast) "Honorary Hillbillies."

1209. Horton, Roy F. *Inspiration Point and Its Personalities*. St. Louis: Bethany Press, 1961. 96p.

There is a fine high ridge a few miles north of Eureka Springs, Arkansas, that had been called Rock Candy Mountain since the pioneer days, until some German crackpot built a big stone house up there. Then came an itinerant preacher named

Scoville and changed the name of the place to Inspiration Point! Next a Campbellite college from Oklahoma took over, and now it functions as a kind of summer school and part-time art colony, specializing in amateur theatricals. The "personalities" described are mostly evangelists and their womenfolk, and people connected with the art colony, the sort of people who think Inspiration Point is a better name than Rock Candy Mountain!

1210. Huey, Edith Lancaster. *Ozark Wild Flowers*. Little Rock: Woods Brothers Publishers, 1977. 46p.

Only three or four paragraphs of text, but there are eighty of the finest color photographs. Most of the conspicuous Ozark wildflowers are represented, with the botanical and vernacular names of each. Huey is a retired teacher, a native of Stone County, Arkansas. She now lives at Allison, Arkansas, several miles north of Mountain View.

1211. ———. *Ozark Wild Flowers II*. Little Rock: Woods Brothers Publishers, 1978. 62p.

Eighty-eight magnificent color photographs. Fully as good as the author's first collection (see preceding entry). Highly recommended. Huey tells me she has close to twenty-five hundred color slides of Ozark flora and fauna.

1212. Hunt, Robin Larkey. *Ozarkian Philosophy*. Silver City: New Mexico Western College Print Shop, 1957. 60p.

Brief reflections by the author, mostly about understanding education. He says he was raised in the Ozarks but doesn't say where.

1213. Hunter, Max Francis. "Miscellaneous in the Ozarks." Unpublished manuscript, Springfield–Greene County, Missouri, Public Library.

In his introduction to this collection Max explains about the material. "I don't want to throw these tapes away and I would like to get them, kindly all together so, that's what I'm starting is just a miscellaneous collection." And that's just what it is, a potpourri. Most of it is musical, songs taped off commercial recordings, many of them old 78's, or from tapes people have given him. There is a little bit of everything: Xavier Cugat's orchestra playing South American music, Perry Como singing pop music, the country music of the Carter Family, the ballads of Almeda Riddle. If Max was listening to the radio or watching TV and a particular song, or sermon, or play came on that he liked, he taped it. All this is contained in an index volume and ten volumes with tapes. The index lists the person doing the performing and what they're doing (singing, fiddling, talking, etc.) and where the recording is located in the collection. The ten volumes, each with their own tape, give the same information, but with comments about the performer and the material and its source—

records, radio, etc. It should all be fascinating listening to future generations, a kind of time capsule.

1214. Ingenthron, J. H. *Uncle Dave's Theory on How to Get Rich.* Forsyth, Mo.: Published by the author, 1945. 14p.

This little story is about a miserly, penny-pinching fellow who lived near Forsyth, Missouri. Despite the fictitious name and the author's declaration that "any similarity to persons living or dead is purely coincidental," all of us familiar with Taney County in those days recognize "Uncle Dave," and he was every bit as much a character as Ingenthron portrays him. A story is still told in those parts that when the government bought up land for Bull Shoals Lake in the 1950s many owners felt they hadn't received a fair price. When the question was asked if anyone had gotten what they wanted, someone said "Uncle Dave" was satisfied, to which one of those present declared, "My God, you don't think old Uncle Sam is any match for Dave, do you?" J. H. Ingenthron was a lawyer in Forsyth and a brother of Ozarks historian/writer Elmo Ingenthron.

1215. Jeffords, Edd, ed. *Proceedings of the Conference on Ozark In-Migration.* Eureka Springs: Arkansas Humanities Committee, 1976. 124p.

See papers by Ernie Deane (pp. 1–2), "Effects of In-Migration on Folklore" (pp. 35–36) by Dr. William Clements of Arkansas State University, and "The Ozark Mountain Blacks" (pp. 66–69) by Gordon D. Morgan of the University of Arkansas.

1216. Johnson, Claude E. *"The Ozark Magazine—A Brief History." The Ozarks Mountaineer* 25:6 (July 1977): 32–33.

In 1934 Johnson, encouraged by Otto Ernest Rayburn, began to publish his little magazine at Romance, Arkansas. The first issue (August 1934) was hand set and printed on a slide-lever hand press in a cow barn. Later Johnson got a bigger press that would print two pages at a time, run by a gasoline motor from a washing machine. Rayburn brought Johnson to see me at Galena, Missouri, in 1942, and I understood that the *Ozark Magazine* was still being published at that time. I don't remember when it ceased publication, but Johnson says in this story that he "chickened out of the publishing business the year before Pearl Harbor." This "Brief History" is a pretty good story, better than most of the articles in the *Ozark Magazine*. Johnson knew many of the old-timers—Cora Call, Sam Leath, May Kennedy McCord, Royal Rosamond, Thomas Elmore Lucy, and others. His writings were of no great importance, but he was a part of the "Ozark writers movement" of the time, which had considerable influence on Rayburn and other serious writers who were to follow him.

1217. Jordan, Philip D. "History and Folklore." *Missouri Historical Review* 44:2 (January 1950): 119–29.

A shorter version was printed in the *Arkansas Historical Quarterly* 9 (Summer 1950): 110–15. Jordan was professor of history at the University of Minnesota.

1218. Kearney, John W. *Eureka Springs the Resort of the Ozarks*. Buffalo, N.Y.: Matthews-Northrup Works, [189?]. 55p.

Fancy wooden cover, with "Souvenir of Eureka, MDCCCCVII" burned on the outside. A folding map of the Frisco Railroad system in back. List of twenty-nine hotels, with rates, etc. Much material about the waters and diseases cured by their use. Photographs of hotels, street scenes, six-horse stage, mule-drawn street cars, Sanitarium Lake, and scenic spots in surrounding country. The only copy I have seen is owned by Mrs. Olive Ellis, Eureka Springs, Arkansas. Kearney also wrote another work with the same publisher titled *The Summit of the Ozarks—Eureka Springs* (1903, 63p.), which I have never been able to locate.

1219. Kemper, L. P. *Arkansas: Personal Reminiscences*. Siloam Springs, Ark.: Published by the author, 1925. 12p.

Very little that is personal or reminiscent. It's just the story of a tour of the state, with a good measure of chamber of commerce boasting.

1220. Lankford, George. "The Arkansas Traveller: The Making of an Icon." *Mid-America Folklore* 10:1 (Spring 1982): 16–23.

This is the story of Edward Washburn and his famous painting that became the unofficial symbol of the state of Arkansas. Many Arkansans still consider the painting and the story it portrays a perpetuation of the derogatory hillbilly stereotype and a source of embarrassment.

1221. Leath, Sam A. "Historical Events of Yesteryear—Recorded by Indians." *Carroll County Historical Quarterly* 2:1 (January 1957): 1–5.

About the "pictographs" at Blue Springs, which Leath claims to have translated into bad English. He says they recorded events as early as 1541 and as late as 1839.

1222. Lee, Robert. "The Arcadian Magazine." *Shannon County Historical Review* 3:1 (Spring 1966): 6.

Reflections on Otto Rayburn and the magazine he edited at Eminence, Missouri.

1223. ———. "Myths About the Ozarks." *Shannon County Historical Review* 5:1 (April 1968): 2.

A brief editorial discussing some of the misconceived stereotypes of the Ozarks. Dr. Lee is editor of the *Historical Review*, published monthly at Eminence, Missouri. The name was changed to *The Ozarker* in May 1968.

1224. Leuzzi, Marlene, and Robert Kershner. *Kewpies in Action.* Englewood, Colo.: Published by the authors, 1971. 121p.

A collection of photographs of Rose O'Neill's Kewpies from various private collections. Ranging from dolls made of celluloid to bisque, paper cut-outs, etc., with some narrations of interest to collectors. Of no real value to folklorists.

1225. Levy, Natalie. "Kewpie Doll Revival." *Missouri Life* 7:5 (November-December 1979): 32–37.

Mostly about the Kewpiesta held annually since 1967 in Branson, Missouri, commemorating the memory of Rose O'Neill and her creations. Branson is ten miles south of Bonniebrook, Rose's home in the Ozarks and her burial site.

1226. Lisenby, Foy. "Talking Arkansas Up: The Wonder State in the Twentieth Century." *Mid-South Folklore* 6:3 (Winter 1978): 85–91.

Discusses recent attempts to overcome the bad press that emphasized the state's backwardness and poverty, especially Mencken's talk of "primitive theology and backwoods morality." Our image is a little better now. Even New Yorkers realize that we are not all dimwitted hillbillies. Our professional boosters are not so bad as formerly, tourism is big business, and even in-migration has its advantages.

1227. Lyle, Wes, and John Hall. *Missouri Faces and Places.* Lawrence, Kans.: Regent's Press of Kansas, 1977. No pagination.

This is one of those "pictorial essays" as they're called. Not much text. About thirty of the more than one hundred photographs are of Ozark people and scenes. No folklore.

1228. McCanse, Keith. *Where to Go in the Ozarks.* Springfield, Mo.: Chamber of Commerce, 1932. 96p.

A tourist-oriented publication, mostly advertising for motels, hotels, and resorts. But it does present a very thorough list with brief descriptions of most of the rivers and streams, out-of-the-way fishing and camping spots, springs, caves, roads, and numerous other points of interest in the Ozarks. This is an informative little publication to acquaint students of the Ozarks with the infant tourist industry in the thirties. At this time Jesse James had not as yet hidden in every cave and sinkhole in south Missouri.

1229. McGrade, Margaret C., and Viola M. Barrett. *Eureka Springs: Today and Yesterday.* Eureka Springs, Ark.: Ark-Ozark Books, 1973. 98p.

A paperback for the tourist trade, with descriptions of local scenery and brief biographies of the village notables. Most of these have appeared previously in the *Ark/Ozark Magazine*, a quarterly published in Eureka Springs. The story of Irene

Castle is pretty well done, and so is the piece about Otto Rayburn, but some of the others are pretty bad.

1230. McKay, A. F. "Eureka Springs, The Gem of the Ozark Mountains." *Daily Times-Echo*, Eureka Springs, Ark., September 1894.

Fine full-page article, apparently reprinted from *American Climates and Resorts*, published by the American Health Resort Association. Compares Eureka with Hot Springs, with which "it is so often confounded in the minds of physicians and others." The author was a physician who had lived in Eureka Springs.

American Climates and Health Resorts, in which this article appeared in 1893, was a journal published in Chicago. It was edited by Dr. McKay, who visited health resorts all over America.

This same article was reprinted in the Eureka Springs *Weekly Flashlight*, 16 June 1901.

1231. McKnight, Olin Eli, and Boyd W. Johnson. *The Arkansas Story*. Oklahoma City: Harlow Publishing Company, 1955. 419p.

A history for high schools. The first two chapters (pp. 1–36) are worth reading, and there are some fine photographs. McKnight teaches in a college at Arkadelphia. Johnson is superintendent of schools at Green Forest. The best high school text of Arkansas history now available (1956), but that doesn't mean too much!

1232. Marsh, Susan Louise, and Charles Garrett Vannest. *Missouri Anthology*. Boston: Christopher Publishing House, 1932. 128p.

Several reviewers have mentioned this book as involved with folklore, but most of it is just sentimental prose collections for school children. On pp. 80–84 are references to the Ozark region.

1233. Martin, Blunt Hervy. *Early Ozark Martins*. Point Lookout, Mo.: School of the Ozarks Press, 1973. 194p.

This is a paperback, which the author describes as "a hodgepodge of genealogy, memoirs, personal opinions, and philosophical views," and that's just what it is. It was recommended to me by friends whose opinions I respect, but I can find no significant merit in it. It is just the autobiography of a successful smalltime businessman, nothing more.

1234. Martin, Ronald. *Official Guide to Marvel Cave*. Springfield, Mo.: Ozark Mountain Publishers, 1974. 55p.

This paperback is the "only authentic history of Marvel Cave ever published," according to the blurb on the jacket. The author guided visitors through the place for several years, and he did a good job with this book. I visited the place many times, and was acquainted with the Lynch sisters and with Fred Prince, who made the map of the explored parts of the cavern. In the 1930s I thought I knew as much about Marvel Cave as anybody, but Martin recorded many things that I did not know and published photographs that I had never seen.

1235. Masterson, James R. *Arkansas Folklore*. Little Rock: Rose Publishing Co., 1974. 443p.

The first edition of this book appeared with the title *Tall Tales of Arkansaw* (see volume 1 of this bibliography, p. 56). It was published in 1943 by Chapman and Grimes of Boston. This facsimile reprint meets a great need. Nothing has been changed but the title page. It is a fine scholarly job, with rich documentation.

1236. *Mid-South Folklore*. 1973–1978. A folklore journal published at Arkansas State University, Jonesboro.

Three issues a year. Founded in spring 1973. Edited by Prof. William Clements. A fine scholarly job, with footnotes, documentation, bibliographies, etc. Modeled after *Indiana Folklore*, using material from Missouri, Arkansas, Kentucky, Louisiana, Oklahoma, Tennessee, and Texas. A good deal of local history, but much about crafts and traditional industry. Beginning with the spring 1979 issue, the name was changed to *Mid-America Folklore*.

1237. Milburn, George. "The Menace." *American Mercury* 25:99 (March 1932): 324–34.

Good account of an anti-Catholic monthly called *The Menace*, published from 1911 to 1931 at Aurora, Missouri. Fascinating detail, some regional background information.

1238. Miller, Giles E. *The Arkansaw Travelers*. Eureka Springs, Ark., 6 June 1907. 64p.

This is an illustrated souvenir edition of the *Daily Times-Echo*, issued when the Arkansaw Traveler's Association (traveling salesmen) met for their fourth annual session. Full of revealing bits of local history. See p. 12 for an account of the police department, where Miller says that Eureka Springs is not full of the "go as you please" element common in other resort towns. Some of our visitors, he says, "require just enough of the Bohemian life to elicit some criticism from those who have not travelled enough to know the ways of the world, but there's no really bad deportment here."

1239. ———. *Daily Times-Echo*. Eureka Springs, Ark., 24 April 1905. 31p.

This is a special edition, with many fine photographs, marking the twenty-fifth anniversary of the incorporation of the town. Some good bits of old lore and local history. See the painting of Dr. Messick and his donkey (p. 5). Note the comparison with Hot Springs (p. 14). In the latter part of the booklet (pp. 25–31) are interesting accounts about other towns nearby, such as Berryville, Marshall, and Leslie.

1240. Miller, Ron. "A Fraority for Hillbillies." *The Ozarks Mountaineer* 21:6 (July 1973): 26.

Account of a tongue-in-cheek organization, secret and coeducational, founded at the University of Missouri in 1951. The membership consisted entirely of students from Taney County. It was known far and wide as Alpha Gamma Taney. The author names many of the charter members. He says very little about their activities, but there are still people in Columbia who remember some good stories.

1241. Miller, Terry E. "Voices from the Past: The Singing and Preaching at Otter Creek Church." *Journal of American Folklore* 88:349 (July-September 1975): 266–82.

This article interested me because of the reference (p. 268) to an obscure Baptist cult known as Two-Seeds-in-the-Spirit, a doctrine expounded by Daniel Parker (1782–1844) in the 1820s that caused many old-timers to separate from the Primitive Baptist Church. Most Parkerite churches were farther south, but Otter Creek Church is still flourishing in Putnam County, Indiana. See the "Two-Seeds-in-the-Spirit" story in my *Who Blowed Up the Church House?*, pp. 140–42.

1242. *Missouri, Heart of the Nation.* New York: American Artists Group, Inc., 1947. 62p.

Pictures, some in color, by fourteen contemporary painters, with a five-page introduction by Charles van Ravenswaay. See Ozark pictures by George Schreiber, a Belgian (pp. 15, 16, 22, 25, 29, 52), Ernest Fiene, a German (pp. 13, 20, 26, 48), and Howard Baer, of Pennsylvania (pp. 25, 41, 42, 45, 49, 51). They all lack the authentic detail found in George Caleb Bingham and Thomas Hart Benton, who are not represented in this collection. Some paperback copies are marked "The Scruggs-Vandervort-Barney Collection" and sold for fifty cents a copy in St. Louis.

1243. Mohr, Charles E., and Howard N. Sloans, eds. *Celebrated American Caves.* New Brunswick, N.J.: Rutgers University Press, 1955. 339p.

Twenty-four brief papers by a mixed bag of speliologists and spelunkers. But the chapter "Ozark Cave Life" (pp. 269–89) was written by Mohr himself. It is a very good chapter, with the best description of Marvel Cave that I have seen.

1244. Moon, Christine Cooper. *Dear Christy . . . Memories of My Fifty Years.* New York: Exposition Press, 1955. 127p.

Memories of childhood in a rural community in central Missouri in the early 1900s. Many folklore references. A pleasant story.

1245. "Mysterious Blue Spring—One of Arkansas' Most Scenic Attractions."
      Ozark Highways (Fall 1975): 11–13.

The water from this spring has its origin "from a glacier somewhere in the Pacific Northwest." Nearby is Hieroglyphic Rock, which Sam Leath claimed to have
deciphered (see volume 1 of this bibliography, page 489).

1246. Nall, Don A. "Eyewitness to a Hanging." *Independence County Chronicle*,
      22:3 (April 1981): 3–8.

Along with the written sources the author researched for this article, he obtained a firsthand account from ninety-three-year-old Sherman Rutherford, who witnessed the event in 1904. The culprit had killed the local sheriff in a gun battle on
the main street of Batesville, Arkansas. Just prior to his execution he attempted
suicide and consequently was too weak to stand on the gallows so he could be hung
properly. According to Rutherford, "they had to strap a board to him in order to hold
him straight so they could drop him."

1247. Nightingale, Alice Allen. "Frost Flowers or Rabbit Ice." *The Ozarks Moun-
      taineer* 24:10 (November 1976): 17.

A very fine account of this peculiar phenomenon, by the professor emeritus of
botany at the School of the Ozarks, with a fine photograph by Townsend Godsey.

1248. Noble, G. Kingsley. "Creatures of the Perpetual Night: An Account of an Ex-
      pedition to the Ozarks in Search of the Blind Salamander." *Scientific American*
      139:5 (November 1928): 430–32.

The author found blind salamanders (*Typhlotriton spelaeus*), called "gray
ghosts," in Marvel Cave, near Notch, Missouri. This article has good photographs
and some general information about Ozark caverns. This cave is now just another
attraction of a tourist theme park. Noble was a curator of amphibians and reptiles at
the American Museum of National History.

1249. Omans, Art. *Ozark Portraits: A Jug Of Laughs*. Springfield, Mo.: McCann
      Printing, 1982. 64p.

The author calls himself the "Ozark Cartoonist," and his portraits are nothing
more than a bunch of outlandish and ridiculous hillbilly cartoons, just what the tourists love to buy. This is designated book no. 2. I have not seen no. 1 but I'm sure it's
more of the same.

1250. Parler, Mary Celestia. "Ozark/Arkansas Folklore." Fayetteville, Ark.: Ozark/
      Arkansas Folklore Society, 1974. No regular pagination.

The Ozark (later the Arkansas) Folklore Society was founded by John Gould
Fletcher, who became its first president, in 1949. Fletcher died in 1950, but Pro-

fessor Parler, the permanent secretary, carried on for ten years, built the membership up to more than three hundred, and published fourteen issues of a mimeographed *Bulletin* (1950 to 1958). In 1974 Miss Parler and I, not wishing to see the
society's brief history sunk without a trace, gathered up the fourteen issues of the
Bulletin and bound them together. I wrote a three-page history of the Arkansas
Folklore Society by way of a preface. Because the numbers and dates of the various
issues of the *Bulletin* are somewhat confused, it may appear that the file is not complete, but it is. We published only fourteen issues, and they're all here. There are two
copies of this book in the University of Arkansas Library; one in the possession of
Dr. Herbert Halpert, now at St. John's Newfoundland, Memorial University of Newfoundland; one at Arkansas College at Batesville; another at the Ozark Folk Center,
Mountain View, Arkansas; and I have one copy. Thus there are only six copies of
this book in existence.

The Arkansas Folklore Society was reactivated in 1977 and merged with the
Ozark States Folklore Society in 1981, but publication of the *Bulletin* was not
resumed.

1251. [Patrick, Michael D.] "Preserving Ozark Folklore for Posterity." *The Ozarks
    Mountaineer* 29:1 (February 1981): 48–49.

About the work the author and his students at the University of Missouri–Rolla
are doing to document the folklore of their region. Too brief to be of much value.

1252. ———. *The Role of Folklore in the Study of Gerontology.* Rolla: University
    of Missouri at Rolla, [1978]. 32p.

A mimeograph booklet about students who were sent out to interview elderly
and retired folk in south-central Missouri. They collected tall tales and oral history
from old-timers.

1253. Penick, James Lal, Jr. *The New Madrid Earthquakes of 1811–1812.* Colum-
    bia: University of Missouri Press, 1976. 181p.

This is not an accounting of scientific facts such as Fuller's 1912 publication,
but rather the use of contemporary sources to reconstruct and describe the effects of
this disaster upon the people as well as the topography. He examines many of the
earthquake legends and the apparent facts they are based upon. Aside from the direct effect the quakes produced upon the eastern edge of the Ozarks in the St. Francis
and lower White River region, they also had a profound influence on the in-migration and the religious fervor of the area, says Penick. The Methodist Church in-
creased its membership in the area by 50 percent between 1811 and 1812, while its
increase nationwide was less than 1 percent.

1254. Pennington, Eunice. *History of the Ozarks.* Point Lookout, Mo.: School of
    the Ozarks Press, 1971. 98p.

Covers a wide range of subject matter, with such chapter headings as "Plant Life," "Indians," "Explorers," "Traders and Trappers," "Hunters," "Churches," "Events Following the Civil War," "Interesting Places," "Famous Ozark People," "Literature," "Forests," "Agriculture," various industries, and so on. Naturally such a book contains some interesting material, but this one has little of value to the serious student of folklore. The author was a librarian in Van Buren, Missouri.

1255. Pflieger, William L. *The Fishes of Missouri.* Jefferson City: Missouri Department of Conservation, 1975. 343p.

Treats about two hundred species that have been taken in Missouri. More than one-third of these are from the Ozarks region. This book will be of interest to ichthyologists and may settle some arguments between fishermen. It's a mighty fine book.

1256. Powell, Hazel Rowena. *Adventures Underground in the Caves of Missouri.* New York: Pageant Press, 1953. 63p.

Despite the title, there are no adventures in this opus. It is just a guidebook to fifteen caverns that are "open to the public," government inspected for your safety, and electrically lighted (p. 32). The author is a granddaughter of old Truman Powell, who developed Fairy Cave, near Reeds Spring, Missouri.

1257. Randolph, Vance. "The Pineville Mastodon." *The Ozarks Mountaineer* 25 : 10 (November 1977): 22–23.

Story of a carving on a deer bone, dug up in Jacobs Cavern near Pineville, Missouri, in 1921. Most archaeologists thought it was a fraud. Dr. Vernon C. Allison always believed that the carving was really the work of a prehistoric Bluff Dweller, dated about 12,000 B.C. See his paper "The Antiquity of the Deposits in Jacobs Cavern," *Anthropological Papers of the American Museum of Natural History* 19 (1926).

1258. Rayburn, Otto Ernest. "Fisherman's Luck." *Rayburn's Ozark Guide* 6 : 1 (Summer 1948): 55–59.

This article originally appeared in his *Ozarks Country* (1941). See p. 59 for a photo of Robert Page Lincoln on a float trip down the James River.

1259. ———. "Kingston-in-the-Ozarks." *Mountain Life and Work* 5 : 1 (April 1929): 7–9.

The story of the Rev. E. H. Bouher and his social and educational work at Kingston, Arkansas, "thirty miles from the whistle of the locomotive."

1260. Richmond, W. Edson. "A Scientific Discussion of Origin and Meaning of the Word 'FOLKLORE.'" *The Ozarks Mountaineer* 6 : 1 (November 1957): 14.

A full-page article of excerpts from an address entitled "Folklore: An Exercise in Definition," which Professor Richmond delivered at the ninth annual meeting of the Arkansas Folklore Society, at Fayetteville, 28 June 1957.

1261. Rogers, Sherman. "A Defense of Arkansas." *The Outlook* 129:8 (26 October 1921): 294–98.

An answer to an article in the *New York Times* alleging that Arkansas is almost bankrupt, largely because of road-building graft. Rogers is happy because there are so few foreigners in the state, where "even a foreign accent" is seldom heard. He quotes with approval a farmer who remarked that an Industrial Workers of the World agitator showed up, "but between sundown and sunup he just naturally disappeared, and he's never been heard tell of since. You can draw your conclusions about what happened to him" (p. 298).

1262. Rorty, James. *Where Life Is Better, an Unsentimental American Journey.* New York: Reynal and Hitchcock, 1936. 383p.

Story of the author's wandering through the United States. On p. 338 is a misunderstood wisecrack from John Gould Fletcher; a whole chapter (pp. 357–64) deals with labor trouble in Marked Tree, Arkansas. Rorty shows some understanding of the Ozark people.

1263. Ruth, Kent. *How to Enjoy Your Western Vacations.* Norman: University of Oklahoma Press, 1956. 422p.

An illustrated guidebook, with some definite and detailed information about routes, side trips, reading, hotels, camps, rates, and so on. Pages 2–30 are devoted to the Ozarks of Missouri, Arkansas, and Oklahoma. In the back of the book there is some information about the Colorado Rockies, the Black Hills, the Pacific Northwest, New Mexico, Texas, Arizona, Utah, and even California. But the first thirty pages are good!

1264. Saults, Dan. "Changes Coming to the Ozarks." *The Ozarks Mountaineer* 27:8–9 (September-October 1979): 26–27, 60–61.

A fine article about tourism, with emphasis where it belongs. Saults is a trained journalist and was for many years a public-relations man with the Missouri Department of Conservation. Also, he is a civilized fellow who can write English, an ability not too common in these parts.

1265. ———. "Changes on the Timeless River." *Missouri Life* 2:2 (May-June 1974): 46–52, 55.

Fine story about the White River, with a discussion of the dams, especially the first one, which made Lake Taneycomo. Splendid color photographs. There is a sequel to this in the July-August 1974 issue of *Missouri Life*, pp. 58–62.

1266. ———. "Man's Increasing Loneliness." *The Ozarks Mountaineer* 25:2 (March 1977): 17, 38.

A brief but thought-provoking article. As Bertrand Russell said long ago, modern man is "master of a mainly lifeless and subservient material environment." One of the major (though often subconscious) factors in the back-to-the-land business is the desire to find creatures that are *not* too subservient, not too law-abiding. Some very good people used to have a secret admiration for outlaws and gunfighters like Frank and Jesse James. Now many of us are fascinated by wildlife—"things that fly or run," as witness "our manifold bird-feeders, our glee at having seen a deer, the traffic jam when a flock of Canada geese set down to feed last fall at a powersite on Lake Taneycomo . . . all these are manifestations of human loneliness as increasingly only our own kind is left on the globe." Saults discusses our new in-migrants too; they come to enjoy the simple life, but once settled in, they begin to demand more power lines, better highways, better schools, more industry—all parts of the complex civilization they left behind.

1267. ———. "A Question for the Ozarks: How Do We Want to Be?" *The Ozarks Mountaineer* 29:1 (February 1981): 52–53.

Saults is a good writer and this brief article is one of his best. Randolph considered him the best contemporary writer in the Ozarks. We may not all agree with what he has to say, but even when what he says may be wrong it's well worth reading.

1268. ———. "Words for Wary Immigrants." *The Ozarks Mountaineer* 26:5 (June 1978): 14–15.

Good advice for city folk who come seeking a Garden of Eden in the backwoods. Saults knows the Ozarks as well as anybody, and he writes better than most of us.

1269. Saults, Dan, ed. *Rivers of Missouri*. Columbia, Mo.: M. F. A. Publishing Co., [1949]. 100p.

Stories about twelve of Missouri's principal rivers, each written by a member of the Conservation Commission who knew them best. All about the damage man has done and continues to do to the watersheds: clear cutting, overcultivation, channelization, needless dams, etc. Lots about the people and the rivers. These fellows knew what they were talking about, forecasting an ecology movement that the public now (in the 1970s) is beginning to heed.

This book is a publication of the Missouri Department of Conservation.

1270. Schary, Dore. "Dore Schary Remembers MGM." *American Film* 5:1 (October 1979): 53–54.

A brief excerpt from Schary's book *Heyday* (Little, Brown and Co., 1979). He describes his collaboration with Vance Randolph on an Ozark script for Marie Dressler and Wallace Beery in the 1930s. (Schary makes the unfortunate mistake of stating that Randolph died in the late 1960s!) Schary, a screenwriter, later became head of production at MGM, the world's largest studio. He died in July 1980.

1271. ———. *Heyday: An Autobiography.* Boston: Little, Brown & Company, 1979. 389p.

In 1933 the author's first assignment for Metro-Goldwyn-Mayer Studios was to write a script for a movie that was to have its setting in the Ozarks. It was to star two very popular actors of that era, Wallace Beery and Marie Dressler. MGM even hired an authority on the Ozarks to collaborate on the script. The fellow's name was Vance Randolph, and the pay was to be five hundred dollars per week. In later years Vance told that in those days he found it hard to believe that anyone would be paid that kind of money to write, especially about the Ozarks. After weeks of writing and putting the thing together, they presented it to the producer for his approval. More weeks of waiting, and finally they were called into his office. His comments: "It stinks! . . . not authentic enough!" Vance's immediate verbal and then physical reaction to these remarks resulted in both he and Schary being fired on the spot! See pp. 77–79.

1272. Schiska, Alan. "The Connor Hotel's Faded Elegance." *The Ozarks Mountaineer* 25:6 (July 1977): 26–27.

The Connor was the finest hotel in Joplin, perhaps in Missouri. One book is quoted as saying it was the best hotel west of the Mississippi. Another historian makes it read "west of the Hudson." The early writers were not given to understatement. It was a solid, conservative place for the best people in Joplin. It had much in common with the Coates House in Kansas City, or the old Planters' in Saint Louis. Elegant is the word for it, not gaudy or garish or swank or smart. And Schiska tells the story well, with all the dates and everything. It's a pity that the old Connor has fallen into ruin, and that the progressive citizens are about to tear it down to make room for a library, or a supermarket, or something. But to my generation, and my friends, the Connor was just the big hotel across the street from the House of Lords.

1273. Sherman, Jory. "In the Winter Woods." *Oz-Com* 4:1 (Winter 1979): 19, 34.

A pleasant bit of prose about winter in the Ozarks. *Oz-Com* (Ozark Communications) is published quarterly for the modern "homesteaders."

1274. ———. *My Heart Is in the Ozarks.* Harrison, Ark.: The First Ozark Press, 1982. 168p.

Thoreauvian prose by the author, an urbanite, telling his impressions of the Ozarks after five years residence in the hills of northwest Arkansas and southwest Missouri. Some parts of this have appeared previously in other Ozark publications.

This large paperback is nicely illustrated by Sherry Pettey. Pleasant reading but no folklore.

1275. Skinner, Glenn "Boone." *The Big Niangua River*. Cassville, Mo.: Litho Printers, 1979. 200p.

The Niangua River begins just north of the town of Charity in Dallas County, Missouri, and eighty twisting miles later flows into the Lake of the Ozarks near Hahatonka State Park. The author gives practically a mile by mile description of the river and of points of interest along the way. Interesting are the number of snapshots taken from the front of a johnboat, a setting familiar to those of us who used to "run" the rivers.

1276. Smith, Gerald L. K. *The Miracles on the Mountains*. Eureka Springs, Ark.: Elna M. Smith Foundation, 1979. 75p.

Sub-titled "The Story of the Giant Statue of Christ of the Ozarks and Associated Sacred Projects," this is just a revised version of the 1967 edition.

1277. ————. "The Story of the Statue: The Christ of the Ozarks." Eureka Springs, Ark.: Elna M. Smith Foundation, 1967. 70p.

The author was an old-time evangelist who used to go about the country lecturing and selling tracts about antisemitism and the Red Peril. In recent years he lived in Eureka Springs. Just outside the town he set up a gigantic concrete statue (they say it is as high as a seven-story building) representing a bearded man with outstretched arms (see George Fisher's cartoon in the *Arkansas Gazette*, 23 June 1966). This can be seen from everyplace in town. It is offensive to many of the citizens, but there is no denying that tourists come in great numbers to see it, and the people who operate tourist camps and motels have come to regard Smith and his statue as a great tourist attraction. This paperback booklet tells all about Smith and his "sacred project" and is well illustrated with many photographs. Smith died in 1976.

1278. Smith, Kenneth L. *Illinois River*. Little Rock: Ozark Society Foundation, 1977. 71p.

A fine book about the Illinois and its tributaries, from its source southwest of Fayetteville, Arkansas, to its juncture with the Arkansas River near Gore, Oklahoma. Boating, float-fishing, swimming, picnics—all these features are emphasized in magnificent photographs by the author. After ten years with the National Park Service, Smith now lives in Fayetteville, Arkansas.

1279. *Smithson's Lost Gift, Why the Original Bequest Never Reached the Institute, Was Gobbled by Arkansas*. Washington, D.C., 1895. 8p.

Apparently reprinted from the *Washington Post* (8 September 1895). Subtitle printed on the cover of this pamphlet: "Strange Story of the unexpected bequest of the eccentric English scientist and Uncle Sam's qualms at accepting it—Finally invested in state bonds, and by a sharp manipulation of the Swamp Land Act it was absorbed by Arkansas." The U.S. government "in a spirit of shame" built the Smithsonian Institution from other funds, but the author says that every dollar of the original bequest was stolen by Arkansas. The anonymous author gives detailed information, with names and dates. An odd bit of Arkansas history. Cf. note about Smithson in "Editor's Study," *Harper's Monthly* 96:575 (April 1898): 805–6.

1280. Stoltz, Diane T. "Torrid Sixties Influence ASU Professor." *Jonesboro Sun*, 17 December 1978.

Brief interview with Dr. William M. Clements, professor of English at Arkansas State. The popular interest in American folklore began with the back-to-simple-things, ecology, and communal-living notions that enthralled young people in the 1960s. Clements was editor of *Mid-South Folklore* from 1973 to 1979.

1281. Symmes, John Cleves. *The Symmes Theory of Concentric Spheres Demonstrating that the Earth Is Hollow, Habitable Within and Widely Open About the Poles*. Compiled by Americas Symmes from the writing of his father, Capt. John Cleves Symmes. Louisville, Ky.: Bradley & Gilbert, 1878. 69p.

The elder Symmes lived in Missouri, and his original work, a pamphlet titled *To All the World: I Declare the Earth Is Hollow and Habitable Within!*, was published in St. Louis in 1818. There were men still living in Rolla, Missouri, and Columbia, Missouri, as late as 1900 who were inclined to take the "Symmes Theory" quite seriously, and it was still remembered and discussed by literate Missourians in McDonald County down to the beginning of World War I. I have never seen either of these pamphlets, but have met men who remembered them and considered them as among Missouri's contributions to scientific knowledge.

1282. Tallman, Richard S., and A. Laurna Tallman. *Country Folks*. Batesville: Arkansas College Folklore Archive Publications, 1978. 134p.

A handbook for student folklore collectors. It is a very good one, too. Experienced teachers tell me that it is better than Goldstein's *Guide for Field Workers in Folklore*, widely accepted as the standard handbook. Intended for undergraduates, but a lot of people with Ph.D. degrees would do well to study this book. See especially the section entitled "To the Teacher" (pp. 107–25), and the Appendix (pp. 128–30), which deals with archives. Many of the procedures here described have been used successfully at the University of Arkansas since 1948. The Tallmans were teachers at Arkansas College in Batesville, and the material is addressed primarily to Arkansas students. I think highly of this handbook. Every serious student of Arkansas folklore and folklife should read it.

1283. Tebbetts, Diane O. *Resident and Tourist Perceptions of the Ozark Folk Center*. Fayetteville, Ark.: Division of Agriculture, Special Report no. 24, 1976. 33p.

An attempt by the questionnaire method to find out what people think of the Ozark Folk Center at Mountain View, Arkansas. The analysis of the resulting body of data is presented simply and plainly. This is a valuable paper. The author is a former teacher at Arkansas College.

1284. Thrailkill, John W. *Eureka Springs, Arkansas, as a Curative Resort for Invalids*. St. Louis: Tedford and Harnett, n.d. 17p.

There is internal evidence that this pamphlet was published about 1880; some of the material is quoted by Kalklosch (*The Healing Fountain: Eureka Springs, Arkansas* [1881], pp. 112–19). Interesting glimpses of medical practice in a backwoods resort. The author was a physician, a professor in the American Medical College of St. Louis. It seems to be a rare item: I have seen only one copy, in the Carnegie Library at Eureka Springs.

1285. Todd, Linda. "The Castle at Hahatonka." *The Ozarks Mountaineer* 26:10–11 (November-December 1978): 42–43.

The best paper on Snyder's Folly that I have seen. A historical sketch, with names and dates. A good photograph of the building as it was in the 1930s.

1286. Wade, Ruth Gier. *Arkansas Wildflowers*. Paragould, Ark.: White Publishing Company, 1977. 92p.

Brief description of 250 flowering plants, each illustrated by a drawing by Laura F. Miller. But these drawings are not in color so they add little to a book on wildflowers. There are occasional references to their medicinal uses and as food. Mrs. Wade lives at Cherokee Village, in Sharp County, Arkansas.

1287. Watkins, Paul, Jr. "Painters Three." *Missouri Life* 3:1–2 (March-June 1975): 26–37.

Three young Missouri painters who paint Missouri birds, with some of their work. David Plank of Salem, David Besenger of Flat River, and Gary Lucy of New Haven. They're all good, but I like Lucy's pictures best. Some labels are confused, so that Plank's white crowned sparrow is marked Carolina chickadee, and fine chickadees are marked English sparrows. And Besenger's nuthatch is called a white-breasted nut-*bath*.

1288. Weaver, H. Dwight, and Paul A. Johnson. *Meramec Caverns: Legendary Hideout of Jesse James*. Jefferson City, Mo.: Discovery Enterprises, 1977. 126p.

Lester B. Dill owned and operated the caverns from 1933 until his death in 1980. He conducted his business much in the same manner as did P. T. Barnum his circus. Dill contended that his attraction was like a moving picture show with only one picture. After a while you have to have something extra to draw people. Missouri's readily available legends of Jesse James provided Dill with the needed gimmicks. Not content with promoting Jesse's use of the cave as a hideout, Dill and his son-in-law, Rudy Turilli (see Turilli's *I Knew Jesse James*, entry 565), found in 1949 a centenarian living in Lawton, Oklahoma, who claimed to be Jesse James. They lost no time producing documents, sworn affidavits, and "ex-members" of Jesse's gang to substantiate his authenticity. Dill promptly moved him "home" to Meramec Caverns and proceeded to petition the courts to change the pretender's name (J. Frank Dalton) back to Jesse James. The petition was denied, and Dill lost the court case. But he gained a fortune in free publicity and a lot of tourists.

1289. Whitman, Alan. *Christian Occasions: A Photographic Study of Unusual Styles of Religion in American Life*. Garden City, N.Y.: Dolphin Books, 1978. 144p.

The cover of this mostly pictorial book shows the collosal "Christ of the Ozarks." Pages 14–31 are about this biblical theme park established by Gerald L. K. Smith, located at Eureka Springs, Arkansas. Also on display are models of a full-scale Holy Land he planned to reconstruct in Arkansas. He estimated the cost of this project to be around twenty million dollars. Smith died in 1976.

1290. Whitman, Virginia. *Gifts from the Land*. Philadelphia: Muhlenberg Press, 1960. 164p.

A series of very brief essays, with some twenty fine photographs borrowed from the Missouri Department of Conservation. The photographs are the work of Don Wooldridge and Gerald R. Massie. Each essay begins with a paragraph about the beauties of nature in the Ozarks, but the rest is so heavily loaded with irrelevant meditations about the supernatural, with many quotations from religious books, that it is pretty rough going. It is of small interest to a serious student of the Ozark scene. The author is a native of Colorado, but now lives on the shore of the Lake of the Ozarks.

1291. [Wilcoxin, Reba.] "University of Arkansas Department of English Research in Folklore." *Arkansas Alumnus* 12:2 (November 1958): 4–8.

Splendid photographs of Prof. Mary Celestia Parler and some of her informants—Fred High, Mary Brisco, Fred Smith (the sweet-smelling barber of Bentonville). I have not seen the November *Alumnus* but only a slick-paper offprint distributed by the department. This article is unsigned, but it was written by Reba Wilcoxin, secretary of the University of Arkansas Alumnae Association.

1292. Wiley, Ray, and Doris Wiley. "Where the Hills Are High but Not Too Mighty." *Household* (Topeka, Kans.) 56:4 (April 1956): 26–27, 34, 36, 54–55, 92–93.

Story of an eleven-day trip through the Ozarks, from the Lake of the Ozarks in Missouri to Hot Springs, Arkansas, a guide for tourists. The story ends with a bit of doggerel:

The people are the friendliest
The scenery is the prettiest
The food is the yummiest
The fishing is the . . .

The last word of the rhyme is missing but I gather that the Wileys did not catch too many fish.

1293. Woodbury, Charlie. "The White River, 1907." *White River Valley Historical Quarterly* 6:12 (Summer 1979): 6–8.

Excerpts from a journal kept during an eight-day float taken in August 1907. The author, seventeen at the time, wrote down his experiences and what he observed along the way. Note the mention of the whiskey boat and of pearl hunting (p. 8). The section of the White River they floated no longer exists, having been inundated by dams in the 1950s.

1294. Worthen, Mary Fletcher. *Matters and Things in General*. Little Rock: Arkansas Territorial Restoration Foundation, 1974. 59p.

A "Desultory of Miscellaneous Wisdom gleaned from Newspapers published in Arkansas during its Territorial years . . . guides to conduct, long-lost recipes and practical hints for young and old, a veritable compendium of life as it was lived 150 years ago." A fascinating book. Each item appears just as it was printed—no editing or correcting. The author lives in Little Rock; I'm told she is a cousin of the late John Gould Fletcher. A good job, well written, well printed, and well bound.

1295. Wylie, John E. "Frost Flowers II." *Missouri Conservationist* 40:1 (January 1979): 27–29.

Eight fine color photographs—the finest rabbit-ice pictures I have ever seen. Wylie refers to a previous article (*Missouri Conservationist* [November 1977]: 16–17), which describes and explains these strange formations in detail.

15. Bibliographies

1296. Clark, Thomas D. *Travels in the Old South: A Bibliography*. Norman: University of Oklahoma Press, 1956. 3 vols.

Contains some Arkansas material. Every entry "accompanied by a critical comment by a specialist." Reviewed by Ted Worley in the *Arkansas Gazette*, 17 June 1956.

1297. Cochran, Robert, and Michael Luster. *For Love and for Money: The Writings of Vance Randolph*. Batesville: Arkansas College Folklore Archive Publications, 1979. 115p.

This is an annotated bibliography, and the annotations are very good indeed. Scholarly but not pedantic. The list is remarkably complete, more than 250 titles, and the authors have studied every item. Cochran is an associate professor of English in the University of Arkansas at Fayetteville and Luster is a graduate assistant. Both men knew Randolph personally and had access to much material not available to the public. Any reader who likes Randolph's Ozark stories should read Cochran and Luster's *For Love and for Money*.

1298. Deane, Ernie. *Ozarks Country*. Branson, Mo.: The Ozarks Mountaineer, 1975. 191p.

Pages 121–22 tell of Otto Ernest Rayburn, who collected and wrote about the Ozarks for over forty years. This great wealth of information, which he entitled "Ozark Folk Encyclopedia," now resides in the Special Collections department of the University of Arkansas Library. "Welcome to *Bittersweet*," p. 173, is about Ellen Massey and her high school students in Lebanon, Missouri. They publish a *Foxfire*-type of quarterly devoted entirely to the Ozarks.

1299. Dundes, Alan. *Folklore Theses and Dissertations in the United States*. Austin: University of Texas Press, 1976. 610p.

This is one of the Bibliographic Series sponsored by the American Folklore Society. It's all listed chronologically, from 1896 to 1968, but is not too well organized and the indices are difficult. Despite that, it contains a lot of material not available elsewhere. An important work but there are some odd omissions; e.g., as W. K. McNeil points out in his review in *Western Folklore* (July 1977, pp. 265–67), Dundes doesn't mention the chaps who got their degrees at Cooperstown. George E. Lankford, of the Arkansas College at Batesville, also reviews this book (*Journal of American Folklore*, January-March 1979, pp. 102–3).

1300. Fitzgerald, Alice Irene. *Missouri's Literary Heritage for Children and Youth.* Columbia: University of Missouri Press, 1981. 255p.

This is an annotated bibliography of 301 juvenile and young-adult books about Missouri. About forty of these pertain to the Ozarks, most having been published in the twentieth century. The annotations are summaries rather than critical discussions. Fitzgerald is a professor emeritus of education at the University of Missouri–Columbia.

1301. Flanagan, Cathleen C., and John T. Flanagan. *American Folklore: A Bibliography, 1950–1974.* Metuchen, N.J.: Scarecrow Press, 1977. 406p.

This work excludes "material folklore" altogether—no folk architecture, no folk arts and crafts, no folk games, no folk dance. The Flanagans give all their attention to verbal lore, ballads and songs, tales, anecdotes, myths and legends, and literary treatments. There are 3,639 numbered entries. Most of them are annotated. The comments are very brief but always forthright and sensible. No nonsense, no cryptic wisecracks. A good book.

1302. Flanagan, John T. "Folklore." In *American Literary Scholarship 1972*, ed. J. Albert Robbins, pp. 372–400. Durham, N.C.: Duke University Press, 1974.

See p. 400 for a good brief review of Duncan Emrich's *Folklore on the American Land*, which is required reading, and pp. 373–74 for a flattering notice of volume 1 of this bibliography. *American Literary Scholarship* is an annual.

1303. Gutowski, John. "An Inventory of Sources Pertinent to the Folklore of Jesse James." *Mid-America Folklore* 8:1–2 (Spring-Fall 1980): 8–37.

A list of 209 items pertinent to the folklore of Jesse James. These items are divided into eight categories: "Bibliographies and General Works on the Western Hero"; "Popular Biographies of Jesse James"; "Articles Dealing Specifically with Jesse James"; "Miscellaneous Popular History"; "Autobiographies and Memoirs"; "Collections of Tales, Legends and Anecdotes"; "Collections of the Ballad"; and "Jesse James in Literature." The bibliographer gives brief critical analysis of most of them. He considers *Jesse James Was His Name* by William A. Settle, Jr. (entry 1630) the most outstanding from the historian's viewpoint. A few that he cites as of value to the folklorist are George Huntington's *Robber and Hero* (Christian Way Company, 1895), Robertus Love's *The Rise and Fall of Jesse James* (G. P. Putnam's Sons, 1926), and Homer Croy's *Jesse James Was My Neighbor* (Duell, Sloan & Pearce, 1949). Gutowski is currently dean of St. Mary's College in Orchard Lake, Michigan.

1304. Hunter, Max Francis. "The Max F. Hunter Collection." Springfield–Greene County, Mo., Libraries. 75 vols., 1956–1980.

This astounding collection of Ozarkiana was compiled by Springfieldian Max Hunter over a period of twenty-four years. It is contained in seventy-five volumes (notebooks), each with an accompanying reel-to-reel tape, and is divided into six categories: folksongs, 44 vols. (see entry 44); fiddle tunes, 1 vol. (see entry 97); jokes, 7 vols. (see entry 452); miscellaneous, 11 vols. (see entry 1213); sayings, 6 vols. (see entry 205); visits, 6 vols. (see entry 1402). In volume 1 Hunter says, "All of Side One on Tape One has an introduction to my collection that was recorded over several periods. Things I have read about, some of my thoughts and some of the things that happened to me over the years." This collection is a valuable contribution to the study of balladry and to the study of folk cultures. Hunter has given a legacy to the Ozarks that present and future generations will treasure. There is a duplicate of the song collection in the Folksong Archives of the Library of Congress, as well as in the Joint Collection, Western Historical Manuscript Collection–Columbia and State Historical Society of Missouri Manuscripts. The latter also has photocopies of the written material.

1305. Kraus, Joe W. "Missouri in Fiction: A Review and a Bibliography." *Missouri Historical Review* 42:3–4 (April-July 1948): 209–25, 310–24.

Contrary to comments made by various literary critics that Missouri has had no real "literary renaissance, no mid-western revolt, etc.," Kraus presents numerous works (all fiction) that he maintains have proven to be of enduring value. His very complete bibliography of 207 titles, with brief comments about each, lists most of those worth mentioning that were Ozarks oriented. For a present-day comment on this same subject, see an article by Dan Saults in *The Ozarks Mountaineer*, June 1977.

This is a two-part article. Only the second part is concerned with the Ozarks.

1306. Meyer, Duane. "The Ozarks in Missouri History." *Missouri Historical Review* 73:2 (January 1979): 143–49.

The Ozarks have been neglected by Missouri historians. Meyer admits culpability in his own work, *The Heritage of Missouri* (1963). But times are changing. He discusses the important contributions to social and ethnic history by Southwest Missouri State University's Ozark Studies Department, by Russell Gerlach in his *Immigrants in the Ozarks* (entry 1369), and he especially gives tribute to Ellen Massey and the Lebanon High School for their publication *Bittersweet*.

Meyer, a native of Iowa, was president of Southwest Missouri State University in Springfield, Missouri, and a history professor himself.

1307. Miller, E. Joan Wilson. "Review of Vance Randolph, *Ozark Folklore, a Bibliography.*" *Journal of American Folklore* 86:342 (October-December 1973): 410.

This is a very flattering review. "This bibliography is a major research tool, clearly printed, adequately indexed. Here is a compiler who reads footnotes carefully, takes a personal interest in authors, knows their pseudonyms, occupations and places of residence. If he knows of an item but has not read it, he says so. If the dialect is not authentic, he says that, too. . . . Documentation, cross references, and his own opinions are all here. We also know where Randolph has deposited unprintable materials in manuscript and on microfilm . . . what a precedent Randolph has set for more regional bibliographies!"

This reviewer is an Englishwoman, a geographer turned folklorist.

1308. "Missouri Field Recordings in the Archive of Folk Culture". *Missouri Folklore Society Journal* 4 (1982): 105–10.

This article is published as being a complete listing of the Missouri field recordings to be found in the Archives of Folk Culture at the Library of Congress. These discs and tapes cover a period from 1936 to 1976. They comprise not only songs and ballads, but instrumental music—mostly fiddle—and tales, reminiscences, and oral histories. Each collection is identified by an Archive of Folk Song (AFS) number and a brief description of its contents. This collection contains material collected by such notables as Vance Randolph, Mary Parler, Alan Lomax, Sidney Robertson, and Max Hunter. Copies may be purchased from the Library of Congress. (See p. 94 of Godsey's *These Were the Last* [entry 1377] for a photo of Randolph using a cumbersome, battery-operated disc recorder he had borrowed from the Library of Congress in the 1940s. He is recording fiddler Deacon Hembree of Reeds Spring, Missouri.)

1309. Mott, Frank Luther. *Missouri Reader*. Columbia: University of Missouri Press, 1964. 383p.

Brief excerpts from books about Missouri. He lists seventy-odd Missouri writers, with a thumbnail biography of each. All of the great names are here, and a great many lesser talents, all the way from Mark Twain down to Commodore Rollingpin and Harold Bell Wright. It's fascinating reading. Mott was for many years a professor of journalism at the University of Missouri.

1310. O'Leary, Theodore M. "Hobby Huddle." *Profitable Hobbies* 12:5 (May 1956): 1–7.

Interview with Otto Ernest Rayburn, with an account of his "Ozark Folk Encyclopedia," "which will contain from twenty-five to thirty volumes." This material is now at the University of Arkansas.

1311. Randolph, Vance. "Chronological Bibliography." Typescript, Fayetteville, Ark., 1975. 72p.

I did this list of all that I have written or collaborated on, from a verse in the old *Masses* (February 1915) to my "Foreword" in Ernie Deane's *Ozark Country* (1975). It is a complete list of all my published works, on many subjects. About 85 hardbound books, 90 pamphlets and paperbacks, and 150 magazine and newspaper pieces. Roughly 300 or more items altogether. This is everything I have published, pseudonyms and all, except for a few ghosted books, which must be kept confidential to protect the customers who paid cash for secrecy. The only copy I have is a photocopy made for me by the boys at the Library of Congress from their carbon. It is bound up, optimistically, with half-a-dozen blank pages at the end; if I should live long enough to write any more, I can add the titles in longhand. The original has been lost. Another copy is in the library at the University of Arkansas–Fayetteville. (See entry 1297 for an annotated bibliography of Randolph's work.)

1312. Schroeder, Walter A. *Bibliography of Missouri Geography: A Guide to Written Material on Places and Regions of Missouri*. Columbia: University of Missouri–Columbia Extension Division, 1977. 260p.

See especially the section on "Speech and Literature" (pp. 135–37) and the list of place-name titles (pp. 138–42). The final chapter, "The Geography of Recreation," is valuable, too.

1313. Wolz, Lyn A. "Anglo-American Folk Music in Missouri: An Annotated Bibliography." *Missouri Folklore Society Journal* 4 (1982): 51–104.

This article, originally written for a Master's degree in library science at the University of Missouri in 1975, is presented in three parts: Part I, "The Preface" (pp. 51–52), defines the objectives and organization of the work; Part II, "Reviews of Folk Music Activity in Missouri" (pp. 52–70), is a discussion of the prominent scholars and collectors of traditional Missouri music, principally those connected with ballads and songs, and their contributions, and a good synopsis of the interest in folk music this activity brought about in Missouri and the Ozarks; Part III, "The Bibliography" (pp. 70–104), consists of two hundred twenty items covering the period 1903 to 1982 with annotations, some in great detail. She has also included a few commercial recordings and video productions. This bibliography shows much research and has a good balance in the chronology of the items reviewed, without an overproportion of easy-to-acquire recent materials. Thus it presents a proper survey of the resources on this subject.

16. Folklife

1314. Abner, Vannie. *Heir to These Hills: A Story of a Magnificent Land and Its People*. Hicksville, N.Y.: Exposition Press, 1978. 95p.

The setting is Hahatonka, now a state park in the Missouri Ozarks, northwest of Lebanon. But at the time the author lived there it was a small community near a popular spring and trout lake. On a bluff above the lake stood the castlelike home of a wealthy Kansas Citian. (Its burned-out shell still stands as a well-known Missouri landmark). For five years, until the location was inundated by the Lake of the Ozarks in 1931, her parents ran the general store and post office. Her story is about the local natives, the wild city folks who summered there, and the evil tree cutters who invaded the area to clear timber for the new lake. It's all a pleasant but uneventful bit of fiction. Her use of Ozark dialect is not the best, and there is little else to interest the folklorist.

1315. Adams, Emmett. *The Plime Blank Truth, Ozarkian Style*. Point Lookout, Mo.: School of the Ozarks Press, 1972. 452p.

The author is a fox-hunting man, and his book is made up of selections from his writing in the fox-hunter's journals such as *The Red Ranger*, *The Hunter's Horn*, *Hound Dog*, and the like. It is written in the fox-hunter's jargon—all about fox-chases (races, he calls them), field trials, bench shows, and fox-hunters' conventions. The dialect is not easy for those of us who are not fox-hunters, but I'm sure it is authentic and that Adams knows his subject. He was born in Taney County and still lives in Forsyth but is known to fox-hunters all through the Midwest. There are scattered bits of folklore all through the book.

1316. ———. "Wild Hoggin' in the Ozarks." *The Ozarks Mountaineer* 29:2–3 (April 1981): 44–46.

Exciting accounts of wild hog hunting by two early hog raisers in the days of open range. These were "domestic hogs gone wild . . . not to be confused with the Virginia or European Boars." They were referred to as "hazel splitters" and were as dangerous as any creature in the wild.

1317. Aid, Toney. "The Old-Timers Club." *The West Plains Gazette* 1:1 (Spring-Summer 1978): 5–8.

See p. 8 for a paragraph about the notorious "Post," a secret order that flourished in Howell County, Missouri, in the early days but is seldom mentioned in print. Cf. p. 10 in Randolph's *We Always Lie to Strangers* (1951) for a brief description of this organization. *The West Plains Gazette* is a new slick quarterly of West Plains, Howell County, Missouri.

1318. Aley, Thomas. "People of the Hills and Hollows." Typescript, 1975. 35p.

Prepared for the Little Rock Corps of Engineers, "A research report for an interpretive program at the Table Rock Visitor Center." This is a sort of cultural geography rather than straight history, showing the pioneers in southwest Missouri in relation to the land. First the hunters and trappers of 1800–1830, nomads who cultivated no land, built no homes, no fences. Then the homesteaders, 1830–1860. Next the Civil War period, 1860–1865, and the Repopulation era, 1865–1890. In 1890–1920 the population reached its highest peak. By 1900 things were much as they are today. This is a very good paper with an adequate two-page bibliography. It is now used as dialogue for a slide program at the visitor center at Table Rock Dam in southwest Missouri.

1319. Allen, Chick. *Ozark Indian History*. Cassville, Mo.: Litho Printers, [1974]. 32p.

All about the Indians who lived in the Ozarks: Osage, Delaware, Cherokee. This is the sort of approach that makes the history professors grit their teeth in dismay, but it interests the folklorist.

1320. Allen, Eric. *God Walks the Dark Hills: The Dramatic Story of the Reverend Harold Boyd*. Bella Vista, Ark.: The Bella Vista Press, 1966. 99p.

Paperback about the boyhood of a high school dropout from the Cookson Hills of eastern Oklahoma, set in the depression of the 1930s. Boyd's people were moonshiners and bootleggers. His childhood was spent in honkytonks and dance halls, but he joined the church and turned evangelist. Both Boyd and Allen live in Fort Smith, Arkansas. See pp. 84–85 for an account of a Cherokee ceremony, the burning of a white chicken; I don't know if it is authentic or not.

1321. Anderson, Clay. "The Ozarks: 'I've Been on This Place 84 Year.'" In *American Mountain People*, ed. National Geographic Society, pp. 100–129. Washington, D.C.: National Geographic Society, 1973.

The author is the editor of the *The Ozarks Mountaineer*, a monthly magazine published at Branson, Missouri. He is interested in seeking out unusual characters, especially craftsmen such as woodcarvers, and is generally interested in religion, social life, folk music, and folklore, in particular Jimmy Driftwood and the Ozark Folk Center at Mountain View. Jim Owen's float trips were known to fishermen all over America, and tourism generally brings money into the Ozarks; Anderson is involved in all these things, realizing that the days of regional isolation are over. He is progressive to a degree, but "not too *damned* progressive," as one of his fellow townsmen told me. A native of southeast Missouri, he has lived in Branson since 1965.

1322. Bell, Clare. *Legacy of Courage*. Point Lookout, Mo.: School of the Ozarks Press, 1972. 261p.

This is a biography of the author's father, Charles Christian Bell, who told stories about the Bell family. He came from Scotland by way of Germany after the revolution of 1848 and settled in Boonville, Missouri. This well-written book sees them through the Gold Rush, the Civil War, some Indian troubles, and various business enterprises on the western and Texas frontier. In the early chapters there is some good information about pioneer life in the Little Dixie area of Missouri.

1323. Bentley, Max. "Smackover, and Seekers of Oil." *Harper's Magazine* 148 (December 1923): 73–84.

Fine article about the oil boom towns in Arkansas.

1324. Benton, Thomas Hart. "The Ozarks." *Travel and Leisure* 3:3 (June-July 1973): 30–33.

This article, with three of Benton's pictures, one in full color, is by all odds the best float-trip story I have ever read.

1325. ———. "Thomas Hart Benton Paints the History of His Own Missouri." *Life* 2:9 (1 March 1937): 32–37.

About the Benton murals in the State House in Jefferson City. There were complaints that they presented a bad image of Missouri, what with those scenes showing Jesse James, slaves, a hanging, etc. "True or not," they said, "it wasn't a fitting way for a son of Missouri to tell the story of his state."

1326. Beveridge, Nancy L., ed. *Possum Haw*. Rolla, Mo.: Triad Printing Co., 1974. 85p.

In 1972, impressed by the success of the *Foxfire* book, the students at the Rolla, Missouri, High School began to interview old residents in their area and put all the interviews together into a book. The result is something like the *Bittersweet* material collected by the high school students at Lebanon, Missouri, and it is mighty good. The informants' names and addresses are given throughout. In many cases all was recorded on tape, and transcribed exactly as the old-timers spoke. The collectors were students in Beveridge's "Word Study" classes and their primary interest was in dialect, but they soon became engrossed in folk-belief, music, dance, and other folkloristic stuff and recorded memories, old customs, and bits of local history and legend. There are many drawings and photographs, and very good ones they are. But this was the only issue ever published.

1327. Beveridge, Thomas R. "A Look at the Ozarks." *Interface* 3:2 (January 1972): 2–9.

Dr. Beveridge taught geology and engineering for many years at the state college in Rolla, Missouri, but this is a popular article about the Ozark culture. He became a dedicated regionalist like the rest of us. "Often a convert is the most devout member of his faith," he writes (p. 9). "As a north Illinoisian, I find that I am now an Ozark fanatic. Flat land, cities and people who won't take time for the rural social amenities worry me." *Interface* is a University of Missouri–Rolla publication.

1328. ———. *Tom Beveridge's Ozarks.* Pacific Grove, Calif.: The Boxwood Press, 1979. 85p.

When Beveridge died in 1978, he left a collection of short papers, popular lectures, and a series of articles that had originally appeared in the *Rolla Daily News* under the heading "Hardscrabble Village." His widow gathered up twenty-two of these and published this little book, and a very good book it is. Beginning with "the name 'Ozarks,'" many papers deal with geological matters, natural caves and tunnels, bridges, sinkholes, and so on. But he writes also of the pioneer settler, place names, ethnic origins, religion, dialect, and general culture. All good reading, with many fine photographs by George E. Miller. He had been Missouri state geologist and at the time of his death was an instructor at the University of Missouri–Rolla. His writings reflect some in-depth studies of the people and their culture. Brief bibliography.

1329. BeVier, Thomas. "Where the Hippies Came to Die." *Mid-South*, the Sunday Magazine section of *The Commercial Appeal*, Memphis, Tenn., 6 June 1976, pp. 6–8, 10.

A feature story about the land-loving settlers from the cities who invaded northwest Arkansas in the 1960s and 1970s. Photographs by Charles Nicholas.

1330. Black, J. Dickson. *History of Benton County 1836–1936.* Little Rock: International Graphics, 1975. 496p.

This account of a northwest Arkansas county is pretty good for a county history. The story of Coin Harvey and the Liberty Party (pp. 140–53) is well worth reading; so is the "Small Talk" chapter, a collection of brief clips from unidentified Benton County newspapers. Chapter 27 (pp. 349–453) offers two hundred fine old photographs. See p. 429 for a rare portrait of Clyde "Pea Ridge" Day, the hog-calling pitcher who helped the Kansas City Blues win the American Association pennant in 1929. The final chapter consists of photocopies of advertisements from the files of Ozark newspapers.

1331. Bourke-White, Margaret. "The South of Erskine Caldwell Is Photographed by Margaret Bourke-White." *Life* 3 : 21 (22 November 1937): 48–52.

Photographs from *You Have Seen Their Faces* (Modern Age Books, 1937) by Miss White and Erskine Caldwell, including several from Arkansas.

1332. Bowen, Iris O'Neal. *Hully-Gully, How Many?* Mablevale, Ark.: Foreman-Payne Publishers, 1971. 56p.

Bowen's book is full of vivid pictures of rural life and rural customs in Arkansas in the early 1900s. I like the stories about her college life—I know that it is all true (pp. 52–54).

1333. Brandt, Terry. "Getting Hitched." *Bittersweet* 3:4 (Summer 1976): 12–20.

Interviews with old-timers about marriage.

1334. Brown, Miriam Keast. *The Story of Pierce City, Missouri.* Cassville, Mo.: Litho Printers, 1970. 128p.

A concise history of the communities of Pierce City, Wentworth, Pulaskifield, and Freistatt in southwest Lawrence County, Missouri. Originally the predominant settlers were the Scotch-English, but the coming of the railroad and availability of cheap land brought settlement by large contingents of Polish, Swedish, German, and Irish immigrants. Today a polyglot of surnames abound: O'Dwyer, Gasser, Wrobleski, Kuklenski, Smith, etc.

1335. Brown, Omer E. *Son of Pioneers.* Point Lookout, Mo.: School of the Ozarks Press, 1973. 184p.

Memoirs of an Ozark lawyer. Born near Lutie, Ozark County, Missouri, in 1894, Brown died in Sedalia in 1971. He had written the book over a term of years, and it was published by his family after his death. The best part of the book is about his boyhood in the country. His adult life is that of a typical country lawyer.

1336. Brownlow, Louis. *A Passion for Politics: The Autobiography of Louis Brownlow.* Chicago: University of Chicago Press, 1955. 606p.

This is volume 1, or the "First Half" as the author designates it, and concludes in January 1915. Brownlow was a member of a well-known pioneer Missouri family in Buffalo, near Springfield, Missouri. Born in 1879, he had no formal education, but learned the printer's trade. A great reader, a very good writer, the champion name-dropper of all time, his passion for politics drove him a long way from Buffalo. The whole book is fascinating reading, but the first 165 pages, entitled "Buffalo, Missouri," deal with his boyhood in the Ozarks and contain much of interest to the student of folklore and local history. I have not seen a copy of the "Second Half."

1337. Butts, Opal Stewart. *Tales of Old Hickory County.* Dallas, Tex.: Royal Publishing Co., 1966. 83p.

Fact and fiction about Hickory County in south-central Missouri—the place where anthropologist Carl Withers wrote *Plainville, U. S. A.*, under the name "James West." Butts is a very good writer, and this is a good book.

1338. Caldwell, Erskine. *Afternoons in Mid-America*. New York: Dodd, Mead, and Co., 1976. 276p.

As a boy in west Tennessee, Caldwell heard the old story that "shadows were always longer West of the River"—the Mississippi, that is. Years later he made a tour of the Middle West, to see about this. The book, he says, records his random observations and reflections. His impressions of Marked Tree and Evening Shade, Arkansas, and New Madrid, Missouri, are worth reading. Caldwell is a well-known novelist, author of *Tobacco Road, God's Little Acre*, and other bestsellers.

1339. Case, Perry. "The Long Drive." *American Heritage* 11:3 (April 1960): 64–80.

In 1866 a young Indiana farmer, Perry Case, was hired to take part in a cattle drive that was to begin near Waco, Texas. This was to be no ordinary drive, herding the cattle to the railheads in western Missouri, but rather was to drive them directly to the stockyards in Chicago. The drive began in May. They reached Fort Smith, Arkansas, in July and proceeded into the Ozarks. They crossed the White River near Fayetteville, went on to Yellville, and on 23 August into Missouri. They proceeded to Jackson (near Cape Girardeau) and ferried across the Mississippi River at Jonesboro, Illinois, finally reaching Chicago on 3 November, six months and nearly fifteen hundred miles from their start. In their travels through the Ozarks (pp. 76–80) Case gives a heartrending account of the terrible conditions and hardships being suffered by the Ozarkers in the year following the Civil War. In his old age he dictated his story to a relative, Nancy Gay Case Hughes, and died a few weeks later in 1926. This is a fascinating story!

1340. Clanton, Blanch Pogue, et al. *The Story of Stella*. Noel, Mo.: Pogue Printing Co., 1976. 136p.

Stella is an old town in Newton County, Missouri. Mrs. Clanton and a few friends formed the "Stella Book Committee" that collected the material, but the actual writing was done by a large number of citizens. Stella did not become an incorporated town until 1930, but the first settlers came in the early 1820s. The book tells the whole story, and I enjoyed reading it because I know some of the people involved.

1341. Cochran, Hamilton. *Noted American Duels and Hostile Encounters*. Philadelphia: Chilton Publishing Co., 1963. 319p.

Not much folklore, but worth reading for the vivid picture of army posts, frontier towns, and pioneer life generally. Many Missouri and Arkansas references. Cochran is the author of several books about pirates and other adventurers.

1342. Coffin, Tristram, and Hennig Cohen. *Folklore from the Working Folk of America*. Garden City, N.Y. : Anchor Press, 1973. 464p.

Many items from Arkansas and Missouri. See pp. 5–6, 37–38, 163, 419, 424, 433, and 435.

1343. Cook, Warren. "The Pine Log War." *Neosho* (Missouri) *Daily News*, 2 September 1977.

Brief account of a dispute over the pineries located in McDonald County in southwest Missouri. Residents of adjoining Newton County were helping themselves to the pine logs, and the "war" between the two counties over possession of the timber reached such proportions that federal marshals from Washington, D.C., were sent to restore order. All this occurred in antebellum days, but the animosities created endured until long after the Civil War.

1344. Cowan, J. E. *Life in the Powell-Cyclone Community of McDonald County, Missouri*. Noel, Mo.: McDonald County Press, 1973. 160p.

A well-written book about an isolated community on the banks of Big Sugar Creek east of Pineville, Missouri. Not an ordinary local history, but rather in the manner of what is called rural sociology. It includes many photographs of prominent citizens—not studio portraits like the Goodspeed books, but more outdoor candid-camera stuff, and amateur snapshots. This is another book that fascinated me because I know so many people up that way.

1345. Crump, Bonnie Lela. *Yesterday in the Ozarks*. Eureka Springs, Ark.: Times-Echo Press, n.d. No pagination.

This is a paperback scrapbook, mostly clippings from newspapers, with comment in longhand by Dr. Crump. Badly written and badly printed. The clippings are not identified or dated, but the book was probably published around 1968. The author died in 1976.

1346. Cushing, Charles Phelps. "Floating Through the Ozarks." *Outing Magazine* 58:5 (August 1911): 537–46.

Cushing floated from the old clubhouse on James River just above Galena, Missouri, to Branson, Missouri. It was a four-day trip, and the guide estimated the distance as two hundred miles—Cushing figured it at less than half of that. (He was correct—it's about seventy-five miles.) He identified the guide only as Jim, but the photographs look pretty much like Charlie Barnes—surprising how youthful Charley looked in 1910! It took them four days to float from Galena to Branson, but it is only twenty miles by railroad. Cushing was not a fisherman. He just took a few photographs, smoked his pipe, and enjoyed himself.

1347. Dablemont, Larry. "The Thanksgiving Coon Hunt." *Missouri Life* 3:4 (September-October 1975): 44–47.

A well-written and humorous account of a coon hunt staged in the wilds of Texas County, Missouri, in 1963. Dablemont has lived all his life in the Ozarks and knows what he's talking about. Also by this author: *The Authentic American Johnboat* (entry 868).

1348. Darby, Ada Claire. *"Show Me" Missouri*. Kansas City, Mo.: Burton Publishing Co., 1938. 157p.

A guidebook to the entire state, well written. The emphasis is on regional and local history throughout, but the author says little about crimes and criminals and avoids the boasting and vulgarity of the chamber-of-commerce crowd. This is, in my opinion, a much better job than the official guidebook compiled by the WPA Writers Project of the 1930s. See the chapter on the Ozarks (pp. 50–58), also the story of the "boot-heel" (p. 49), which differs from the popular newspaper tale. The author has done several juveniles, mostly romantic fiction.

1349. Dark, Harris E. "Summer Lingers Long in the Ozarks." *Better Homes and Gardens* 35:9 (September 1957): 65, 150–51.

A good summer-tourists' account of the region. All about routes, scenic spots, hotels, and so on. A few remedies and references to old customs.

1350. Davis, Pauline Ayre. *My Hundred Years*. Point Lookout, Mo.: School of the Ozarks Print Shop, 1973. 130p.

The story of a country woman who saw hard times in Nebraska and Kansas. But she came to Arkansas (p. 90), and the rest of the book is worth reading for occasional insights into the rural life of the early 1900s. The author now lives in Hollister, Missouri.

1351. Deane, Ernie. *Ozarks Country*. Branson, Mo.: The Ozarks Mountaineer, 1975. 191p.

"April Is Sassafras Tea Time," p. 50, tells of this time-honored tradition. I've known folks who couldn't "get goin'" about their springtime chores without liberal amounts to thin the blood. "The Old Stuff Has Charms," p. 74, tells of the first annual folk festival and its participants, held in 1963 in Mountain View, Arkansas. There are other references to folklife throughout this book. Much of this material first appeared in Ernie's "Ozarks Country" column in the Springdale, Arkansas, *Daily News* and later as a weekly feature in more than a dozen regional newspapers. He was also a professor at the University of Arkansas, but he still writes like a newspaperman.

1352. DeArmond, Fred. *Enraptured Amateur*. Springfield, Mo.: Mycroft Press, 1973. 136p.

In this little paperback, the author ranges far and wide, dealing unpleasantly with many aspects of life and literature. He is against most everything that seems good to me, and for much that I think is bad. But he's a skilled journalist, and he knows the Ozarks as well as anybody. His brief chapter titled "Ozark Utopia" (pp. 61–70) is well worth reading.

1353. Dietering, Blair. *Center Point Road*. Commerce: East Texas State University, 1979. 66p.

The author visited Newton County, Arkansas, and studied the hillfolk around Lost Valley and Hemmed-in Holler. He wrote detailed accounts of their way of living and made many photographs. Dietering is a skilled photographer, with a sharp eye for detail. As a writer he is not so good. But I enjoyed this slick-paper booklet, anyhow.

1354. Duden, Gottfried. *Gottfried Duden's 'Report,' 1824–1827*. Columbia, Mo.: The State Historical Society of Missouri, 1919. 135p.

This is the famous *Bericht über eine Reise nach den westlichen Staaten Nordamerikas*, published in 1829, translated by William G. Bek in 1919. Duden came to the United States in 1824 and settled a farm near Washington, Missouri. During his three-year stay, he spent his idle hours writing his observations of the Missouri frontier. After returning to Germany, he published his "Report." This came at a time of unrest and economic depression in Europe, especially in Germany. His description of the Trans-Mississippi region was a straw for the German immigrants to grasp, and they came by the thousands to this "Utopia." But, being predominantly blue-collar workers and professional people, many were ill-equipped for the rigors of frontier life and returned defeated to Germany, forever vilifying Duden for having misled them. But Duden's report was, for the most part, straightforward and factual, and he did not deserve this. It is excellent reading, of much interest to the folklorist with its many references to life-styles, place names, and folk arts and crafts. This is a book I enjoyed reading.

1355. ———. *Report on a Journey to the Western States of North America and a Stay of Several Years Along the Missouri (During the years 1824, '25, '26, and 1827) by Gottfried Duden*. James W. Goodrich, general editor. Columbia: The State Historical Society of Missouri and the University of Missouri Press, 1980. 372p.

This is a much more complete treatment of Duden's work than was William Bek's *Gottfried Duden's "Report"* (see preceding entry). It is a new translation with extensive footnotes, a bibliography, an appendix, and an index. But the folklore references remain essentially the same as in Bek's version. Of added value though is the editor's "Appendix II," which, along with the explanatory notes, cites supplementary sources of information for much of the physiological and folklife material contained in Duden's narratives of life in early nineteenth-century Missouri.

1356. Duncan, Robert S. *History of the Baptist in Missouri*. St. Louis: Scammell & Company, 1882. 937p.

The author writes that this is the complete history of the Baptists from their earliest times in Missouri to 1880, and that, other than the Catholics who came with the Spanish and French, these early Baptists were the first Christians to set foot in the state (p. 35). The first part of this voluminous work is a general history of these missionaries and their troubles with Indians and Catholics. In the second part are the histories of the establishment of the many church districts throughout Missouri and their activities. There is practically no mention of the Civil War, a wise move for any publication that was to be sold in a postwar border state. There is a wealth of material to be gleaned from this large work, especially for those interested in the folklife and religious customs of these early Ozark settlers.

1357. Dunn, Emma Comfort. "Life in a Tourist Camp." *The Ozarks Mountaineer* 25:5 (June 1977): 18.

In the old days, before the federal highway systems came to the Ozarks, tourists came on the trains and stayed in hotels in town. But when people began to travel in motor cars, tourist camps sprang up along the highways. The first tourist camps were pretty primitive—just a row of one-room shacks, no indoor plumbing, just a big water bucket and a wash basin. One outside privy served several cabins; one well or one big hydrant furnished water for the whole place. But a single cabin cost only $1.00 a night. Two people could get a cabin with a double bed for $1.50. Later came heated cabins with a shower and indoor toilet—these were not called camps, but tourist courts. Finally came much better places, with a closed shelter for one's car, and a pretty good restaurant in the center of a group of cabins. This was called a motel. Some motels had a bar as well as a lunch counter, even a sort of beer garden, with tables under the trees. The best motels cost as much as the hotels in town. Dunn knows all about tourist camps, as her parents operated a good one on Highway 66 during the Depression.

1358. Edmonds, Charles K. "Big Sugar Country." *Missouri Life* 1:2 (May-June 1973): 28–36.

A little romanticized perhaps, but this is required reading. Bill Nunn made the splendid photographs and helped Edmonds write the story. I lived in Pineville for ten years, and this story is as true as God's own Gospel.

1359. *Eureka Springs, Arkansas*. St. Louis: Woodward and Tiernan Printing Co., 1892. 47p.

Advertising the "Interstate Summer Normal and Educational Assembly." The booklet is mostly "historical and descriptive of the Springs and the surrounding country," plus nineteen pages of advertising. It is worth reading for the occasional references to backwoods life and customs.

1360. *The Eureka Springs of Arkansas*. Buffalo, N.Y.: Matthews, Northrup and Company, 1886. 32p.

A paperback pamphlet, illustrated with drawings, with much space devoted to the Crescent Hotel and the "upwards of forty springs . . . within the corporate limits." A few references to old customs and local history.

1361. Findley, J. W. *Experiences of a Walking Preacher*. Springfield, Mo.: Roberts & Sutter, 1980. 156p.

Reverend Findley might be termed a social chronicler for his neck of the woods. Having spent his lifetime living and preaching in a six-county area of southern Missouri, he sets down a multitude of happenings and events in the lives of the people he knew. Though his style is a bit erratic and may lack the polish of the professional, his writings have a straightforwardness along with a sense of humor that gives the reader a fleeting look at life in those parts, the good and the bad. Besides the souls saved by his preaching and the good-neighborliness of the people, he tells of souls lost, of fights, drunks, wife-beaters, etc. One interesting story is that of the participation of two black preachers and their quartet in a two-week revival held in Ozark County. These were the first blacks many of the people had ever seen. Also see pp. 15, 25, and 42 for some practical jokes, a favorite pastime for Ozarkers.

1362. ———. *A Voice from the Ozark Hills*. Springfield, Mo.: Roberts & Sutter, 1982. 221p.

More of Reverend Findley's "telling it like it was." He says much about the everyday business of living in the Ozarks during the first part of this century. On the Fourth of July you touched off black powder under an anvil and threw cotton-rock onto a bonfire for your noisemaking. For tooth powder, mix charcoal and salt and chew the end of a red willow twig for the brush. Make baby powder from burnt clay. On a cold morning, to warm bare feet drive cattle off where they've been lying and stand there a few minutes. He thinks the *Age of Reason* an infidel book and the Equal Rights Amendment a trick of the Devil. In the chapter entitled "The Things That Be" (pp. 124–43) he gives his theories on the Creation, the Garden of Eden, evolution, the evils of man, and how man got his Adam's apple. Findley's writings hold a strange fascination for me.

1363. Fink, Oliver F. "Missouri's Old French Pocket." *St. Louis Post-Dispatch*, 20 February 1955.

Fine article with fifteen photographs, all about the "Old Mines French" who live in the Ozark foothills some sixty miles south of St. Louis. About six hundred families have preserved much of the colonial way of life for nearly two hundred years. These are the so-called "Missouri Creoles" whose folklore has been studied by Carrière and Dorrance.

1364. Fish, Wilma Naugle. *Wilma's Apple Dolls and Romance*. Gainesville, Mo.: Published by the author, 1982. 28p.

Only the first five pages concern themselves with making dolls from dried apples. The rest are reminiscences, set down in a very heavy, hard-to-decipher dialect, of the author's youth in the old settlement of Romance in southern Missouri.

1365. Fleming, John. *The White River of the Ozarks: From Sabertooth Tigers to Fighting Rainbows*. Conway, Ark.: Gallinule Society Publishing Co., 1973. 56p.

Beginning with brief accounts of the geology and archaeology of the White River region, Fleming summarizes the pioneer culture and the steamboat and railroad eras and ends with a fine account of sports and recreation. A good competent job it is, too. Fleming had a deep enthusiasm for the White River area, and when he died his ashes were scattered over the stream near Mountain View, Arkansas.

1366. French, William A. "At Home in Missouri." *The Ozarker* 16:9 (January-February 1980): 15–16.

French, a well-known writer of novels and poetry about the Ozarks, moved with his family to Shannon County, Missouri, in 1907. He was fourteen at the time and began keeping a day-by-day diary. It is mostly accounts of hunting and life on an Ozark farm and is to be presented unedited and in serial form, beginning with this issue. French died in 1980 at age 88.

1367. Geer, Gene. "The Meadows-Bilyeu Feud." Typescript, Ozark, Mo., 1958. 12p.

These twelve pages were intended for the book *Christian County—Its First Hundred Years*, but as many persons emotionally connected to the incident were still living at that time (1958), it was decided not to include it in the book. I received a typescript copy from Gordon McCann in 1975. (Another copy is in the Christian County Library, Ozark, Missouri.) The incident was the killing in 1898 of three Bilyeu men by one John S. "Bud" Meadows in a quarrel over a rail fence. Geer was clerk of the probate and magistrate courts of Christian County, Missouri. Both the Meadows and Bilyeu families are still well known in the Ozarks. I knew many of them in the 1940s when I was collecting songs and folktales in the backwoods.

1368. Gentry, W. Messick. "One Man's Reminiscences of Wayland Arbor School and Religious Meetings." *Izard County Historian* 6:1 (January 1975): 14–16.

Excerpts from the writings of W. Messick Gentry, a north Izard County resident, covering a period from 1883 to 1914. All about revivals, preachers, and protracted meetings. This is a brief but informative article. I would like to have seen more of Gentry's reminiscences.

1369. Gerlach, Russel L. *Immigrants in the Ozarks: A Study in Ethnic Geography.* Columbia: University of Missouri Press, 1976. 206p.

This is the best treatment of the historical-cultural geography of the Missouri Ozarks that I have seen. Based solidly upon Gerlach's personal fieldwork, the emphasis throughout is upon the profound influence of the German and Swiss settlers. I was particularly impressed by his discussion of the Amish and Mennonite communities—their religion, architecture, and agricultural practices as related to those of the old-stock Americans from the Appalachians.

1370. ———. "Origins of Early Ozark Settlers." *Bittersweet* 4:3 (Spring 1977): 12–18.

Good paper about the French, Germans, Italians, and other Europeans who came into the Ozarks and their influence on the old-stock Americans from the Appalachians. Read what he says about the modern immigrants, the Amish and Mennonite colonies, and also the retired people and the young city folks who want to find a better life-style by a "return to nature" and have established little communes in the Missouri Ozarks.

1371. Gerstäcker, Friedrich. *Wild Sports in the Far West.* Durham, N.C.: Duke University Press, 1968. 409p.

Gerstäcker was a young German adventurer who spent the years 1837–1843 traveling about in the frontier regions of Arkansas and northeast Texas. Shortly after his return to Germany he published a narrative of his wanderings, *Streifund Jagdzüge durch die Vereinigte Staaten Nordamerikas* (1844). An English translation appeared in 1854 under this somewhat misnamed title of *Wild Sports in the Far West.* Gerstäcker was an excellent observer, and his accounts of the backwoods people of the Arkansas Ozarks are among the best to be found. This is a reprint of the 1854 edition with introduction and notes by Edna L. Steeves and Harrison R. Steeves. Ted Worley checked this work for authenticity and found Gerstäcker to be essentially accurate in all his accounts. There is a review of an 1859 edition in volume 1 of this bibliography, pp. 106–7. Gerstäcker also wrote some fictional accounts based upon his experiences, but to my knowledge they have never been translated into English.

1372. Gibson, Arrell M. *Wilderness Bonanza: The Tri-State District of Missouri, Kansas, and Oklahoma*. Norman: University of Oklahoma Press, 1972. 362p.

An interesting look at the era of the great lead and zinc mining between the 1870s and 1930s. It was wild times for a while around places like Joplin, Webb City ("the town jack built"), and Granby in Missouri, and at the last great strike at Picher, Oklahoma. Though this is primarily a historical account of those times, there are some interesting glimpses of life in the camps. In 1875 Joplin had seventy-five saloons and, as one local miner put it, "Suez was still east of us and there were no Ten Commandments."

1373. Gilmore, Robert Karl. "Theatrical Elements in Folk Entertainment in the Missouri Ozarks, 1885–1910." Ph.D. dissertation, University of Minnesota, June 1961. 290p. (Copy in Southwest Missouri State University Library, Springfield.)

Gilmore says that, as outside professional entertainment was not available, the rural communities of the Ozarks developed their own, and he discusses a great number of these activities at length. His chapter entitled "Literaries" (pp. 33–67) tells of debates, kangaroo courts, spelling bees, ciphering matches, and declamatory and dramatic productions. Other chapters cover closing school programs (p. 68), protracted meetings (p. 96), baptizings (p. 113), pie and box suppers (p. 131), Fourth of July picnics (p. 143), Decoration Day exercises (p. 156), old settlers and old soldiers reunions (p. 158), baseball (p. 176), band concerts (p. 180), court week (p. 188), and hangings (p. 192), to name a few. But he excludes activities such as square dances and play-parties, saying that he considers these "self-entertainment" (pp. 10–11). For his study he selected a twelve-county area in south-central Missouri. His information is based upon personal interviews with thirty-seven informants and upon newspaper accounts, all documented. The appendix (pp. 238–90) contains transcriptions of twenty-three of these interviews. His title is a bit misleading, for his "theatrical elements" are actually excellent descriptions of many pastimes enjoyed by Ozarkers at the turn of the century. It is a far better treatment of this subject than most comparable works recently published. Gilmore is presently dean of faculty at Southwest Missouri State University in Springfield, Missouri.

1374. Gingery, Lewis Francis. *Memory Trail*. Point Lookout, Mo.: School of the Ozarks Press, 1970. 178p.

The memoirs of a fox-hunting man. Gingery was the editor and publisher of *Red Ranger*, a nationally known monthly issued at Rushville, Missouri. A strange character, he had most of the manly virtues traditional on the frontier. But he had no formal education and was given to episodic outbursts of what his detractors called "irrational and turbulent" conduct. He hated vivisection, and steel traps, and Harry Truman, and game hogs and vaccination. He firmly believed rabies was a myth. No man ever had rabies, he said, but many people have been killed by Pasteur's vaccine.

Both his parents were born in Germany, so he said that both world wars were tragic mistakes, and so on. He defended these opinions publicly and privately everywhere. Eccentric almost to the point of lunacy, he had many sterling personal qualities that endeared him to the common man! Emmett Adams of Forsyth is not given to extravagant speech, but he wrote an enthusiastic preface for Gingery's book. And old Jim Owen of Branson waxed almost lyrical in his praise. Gingery died in 1976 at age 97.

1375. Gish, Anthony. "Yes, I'm a Hillbilly." *Esquire* 7:4 (April 1937): 95, 128, 130.

The finest defense of the old-timers that I have seen. The author is Fern Shumate, Springfield, Missouri, who did many Ozark books and articles under the name "Nancy Clemens." She was a native of Cedar County, but worked as a newspaper reporter in Springfield for many years. This paper is reprinted in Randolph's *An Ozark Anthology* (1940, pp. 128–46).

1376. Glasgow, Mary. "Character Sketch." *Ozark Review* 1:1 (Spring 1978): 14–15.

A fine brief study of houseboat people on the Black River near Pocahontas, Arkansas. *Ozark Review* is announced as a "literary regional" magazine, to be published twice a year at Piedmont, Missouri. The editor is Steve Wiegenstein, a native of Madison County, Missouri. This first issue is devoted to short poems and occasional brief prose pieces. I know nothing of Mary Glasgow, and the editor says only that she lives at Crystal City, Missouri.

1377. Godsey, Townsend. *These Were the Last.* Branson, Mo.: The Ozarks Mountaineer, 1977. 127p.

This is a collection of more than 140 splendid photographs of old-time Ozark hillfolk—fox-hunters, fishermen, ferrymen, granny women, bee hunters, weavers, basketmakers, country storekeepers, coffinmakers, berry pickers, blacksmiths—all the plain people who have left their indelible marks on the Ozarks scene. Most of these photographs were made in the 1930s and 1940s. Many of them are pictures of men and women I knew personally. This is beyond all question the finest picture book ever put together in this region. Godsey made these photographs himself. He has lived among hillfolk for a long time and he knows his subject. I wrote three paragraphs by way of a preface for this book, but the publisher set it in caps on the dust jacket. It is a pretty good blurb at that.

1378. ———. "Time Makes Friends in the Ozarks." *The Ozarks Mountaineer* 25:2 (March 1977): 18–19.

Godsey describes the backwoods mentality at length, with effective examples and illustrations. He thinks immigrants and the old-time hillfolk are gradually coming to understand each other.

1379. Gravley, Ernestine. *Hang Onto the Willows*. Shawnee, Okla.: Bison Press, 1957. 192p.

Life in northwest Oklahoma in the early 1900s. This is a biography of Dr. Oscar C. Newman (1876–1953), who began his practice in the old town of Grand when it was still in Oklahoma Territory. Lots about cowboys, Indians, and gunfighters. Very interesting reading. The title is good dialect. The author, who also writes juvenile books, formerly lived in Arkansas and now lives in Shawnee, Oklahoma.

1380. Griffith, Cecil R. *The Missouri River: The River Rat's Guide to Missouri River History and Folklore*. Leawood, Kans.: Canfield and Sutton, 1974. 96p.

The material in this book was assembled by C. R. Griffith, a river pilot who was born in Kansas and spent his entire life on the Missouri. After his death in 1970, the book was edited by Kenneth R. Canfield and Richard L. Sutton, Jr. They also wrote a brief biography of Griffith (pp. 87–93). The book traces the whole course of the Missouri from Three Fork, Montana, to its juncture with the Mississippi eighteen miles above St. Louis. Griffith lists every river town by name, tells how the name was acquired, and records any legends or anecdotes that came to his attention. "Old Griff" was a great man. He will long be remembered by all who love the river.

1381. Grose, George R. *The Man from Missouri*. Los Angeles: Times-Mirror Press, 1943. 156p.

Dreary story of a successful businessman, James E. MacMurray, as told to Grose. MacMurray was born near Hannibal, Missouri, in the 1860s. The first twenty-six pages contain some description of pioneer life in rural Missouri.

1382. Gusewelle, C. W. "A Continuity of Place and Blood." *American Heritage* 29:1 (December 1977): 96–108.

The author lived in the Ozarks around Osceola, Missouri, for a while, and he tells his observations and thoughts, in an almost poetic prose at times, about the land and his neighbors. What he says about timber and "burning off" the land is worth reading. This entire article is thought provoking and enjoyable reading but there is little folklore.

1383. ———. "Moonrise to Mourning: Echoes of the Race." *Audience* 2:3 (May-June 1972): 73–78.

Fox-hunting in the wilds of Douglas County, Missouri. Good narration about Walker hounds and the thrill of the race. (He says its never called a "chase.") *Audience* was a hardback bimonthly that ceased publication in 1973.

1384. Gustorf, Frederick. *The Uncorrupted Heart: Journal and Letters of Frederick Julius Gustorf, 1800–1845*. Columbia: University of Missouri Press, 1969. 182p.

Gustorf was born in what is now the state of Hesse, West Germany. He came to America in 1834, spent four years in the north Atlantic states, mostly in Massachusetts and Connecticut, where he made his living tutoring college students in German. He met Harriet Martineau, "English political writer," in Philadelphia, and came west to visit the German colonies in Missouri and Illinois. His diary and correspondence give a vivid picture of social conditions in the American Midwest in the first half of the nineteenth century. Not much folklore, but a good discussion about pioneer customs and the like. Gustorf married an Englishwoman, raised an American family, and died in Peoria, Illinois. His widow and children could not read his German script, but they kept his manuscript. It was translated and edited in the 1950s by Fred Gustorf of San Francisco, great-grandson of the diarist.

1385. Hagen, Harry M., ed. *Misselhorn's Pencil Sketches of Missouri*. St. Louis: Riverside Press, 1974. 158p.

Seventy-seven fine drawings of rural scenes and historic places in Missouri. Roscoe Misselhorn has traveled about the state for many years, sketching whatever caught his eye. There is an old-fashioned charm in these drawings that is lacking in the photographic picture-books. Many of the best pictures are from the Ozarks.

1386. Hair, Mary Scott. *O Happy Day*. North Newton, Kans.: The Mennonite Press, 1966. 64p.

This is presented as "a history of the Methodist Church at Hurley, Missouri," but it is much more than that. To me it is a beautifully written study of an isolated hamlet in the Missouri Ozarks, from about 1900 to 1965. It contains a lot of information about village life and customs.

1387. Haldeman-Julius, Marcet. "Is Arkansas Civilized?" *The Debunker* 9:1 (December 1928): 3–16.

About Charles Smith of Little Rock, imprisoned in 1928 for putting a sign in his office window: "Evolution is true. The Bible is a lie. God is a Ghost." *The Debunker* was a monthly edited and published by E. Haldeman-Julius at Girard, Kansas. The issue discussed here is still very much alive in the 1980s, as is shown by the recent controversy in Arkansas over the creation-science bill.

1388. Hall, Leonard. *A Journal of the Seasons on an Ozark Farm*. Columbia: University of Missouri Press, 1980. 208p.

This is a reprint of the 1956 edition, originally published under the title *Coun-*

try Year (see volume 1 of this bibliography, p. 479). Hall, born 1899, has written a new preface for this edition. Illustrations by George Conrey.

1389. ———. "Life Visits the Ozarks." *Life* 20:21 (27 May 1946): 138–41.

Leonard Hall, of Possum Trot Farm, is a well-known writer who for years did a weekly column about rural life in the Missouri Ozarks for the *St. Louis Post-Dispatch*. The photographs and text are about the people and places he writes about. There is an especially fine one of the Powder Mill Ferry, a typical scene, with the ferryman's home located just up the road from the river's edge. The full-cover photo for this issue is of Tom Moss, a river guide who lived above the Log Yard Hole on the Current River.

1390. Hancock, Angela, and Nancy Honssinger, eds. "We Hardly Talk Italian Any-
     more." *Bittersweet* 7:1 (Fall 1979): 4–13.

An entire community came to the United States from Italy in 1898 and settled in Sunnyside, Arkansas. But, because of the maladies of the delta country and the broken promises of their American sponsors, most left for the highlands of the Ozark Mountains. Of one group who settled in what became Tontitown in northwest Arkansas, much has been written. But another large group settled in the Missouri Ozarks and founded the little settlement of Rosati in Phelps County. Joe and Sophie Piazza reminisce about their lives and the little-known story of the early days of Rosati and its now-famous vineyards.

1391. Hardaway, Billie Touchstone. *These Hills My Home: A Buffalo River Story.*
     Republic, Mo.: Western Printing Company, 1980. 179p.

This is a "Revised and Expanded Edition," nearly twice as large as the 1972 publication. More about Frank Villines (1885–1979), the Buffalo River and its environs, and Newton County, Arkansas. The author lives in Louisiana and, according to the back cover, is presently writing a novel about the Civil War in the Ozarks.

1392. Harty, John. *Licklog Holler*. New York: Vantage Press, 1971. 106p.

Good general book about life in the "eastern Missouri Ozarks" about 1900. Chapters on the Ozark farm, the rural school, the crossroads store, the country church, health problems, courtship, and marriage. A pleasant little book, full of intimate first-person narrative, with much accurate detail and no sentimental hokum. Harty was a native of Bollinger County, received a Ph.D. from the University of Missouri, taught at Northeast Missouri State College, and was later a professor of physics at the University of New Mexico. He died in 1967.

1393. Haswell, A. M. "The Story of an Ozark Feud." *Missouri Historical Review*
     20:1 (October 1925): 105–9.

A laconic account of the Alsup-Fleetwood "trouble" that demoralized Ozark and Douglas counties in Missouri prior to the Civil War. Haswell was associated with the Alsup clan in 1873 and could hardly be called an impartial witness. The Alsups were Unionists, while most of the Fleetwoods cast their lot with the Confederacy.

1394. Haworth, John J. "Taney County Baldknobbers." Unpublished typescript, ca. 1937. 11p.

This is a graphic picture of the post–Civil War days in Taney County, Missouri. All about a vigilante group called the Baldknobbers and their counterparts, the Anti-Baldknobbers. Whippings, shootings, and hangings all over the place, no law and order at all. Times were rough, and it got so bad that the governor threatened to send down the state militia to put an end to it all. My copy carries the notation that this was to appear in the 1937 centennial issue of the Taney County newspaper, but it was never published. It is unclear to me how I came by this typescript, and I know little about the author except that he was an "Anti-Knobber" and in later years a judge in Taney County. But it is interesting from the Anti-Baldknobber point of view, what professional writers call "prime source material."

1395. Holliday, Don R. "Autobiography of an American Family." Ph.D. dissertation, University of Minnesota, 1974. 254p.

I have seen only a machine copy that seems to be part of a Ph.D. dissertation. The ribbon copy is in Dr. Holliday's possession at Springfield, where the author teaches at Southwest Missouri State University. It gives a vivid, detailed picture of rural life in Taney County, Missouri, from about 1880 to the 1970s. The emphasis throughout is upon economic and sociological matters.

1396. Hoten, Margaret Gerten. "Life in the Ozarks—Then and Now." *White River Historical Quarterly* 2:9 (Fall 1966): 13–19.

The author settled on a farm near Chadwick, Missouri, in 1897. This is the first of three articles she wrote about her experiences. All three are well written, straight-forward accounts of pioneer life, with no sentimental hokum. Her people were from Germany.

1397. Hough, Danny. "Keeping Company." *Bittersweet* 3:4 (Summer 1976): 4–11.

Courtship in the backwoods. Interviews with old-timers.

1398. Hubert, Renee, ed. *Ozark Country Sunshine—History of the Blue Eye School District.* Blue Eye, Mo.: Blue Eye High School, 1976. 32p.

Done in the style of *Foxfire* and *Bittersweet* by the students of the Blue Eye High School. Besides the facts and dates pertaining to the school and towns comprising the school district, other chapters briefly cover the subjects of recipes, cures and remedies, sayings and colloquialisms, and legends and folktales. The small town is divided by the Missouri-Arkansas line so both states can claim a "Blue-Eye," named in honor of its first postmaster. This town once gained national headlines when its schools were closed due to an epidemic of *pinkeye*.

1399. Hulse, Edgar. *Life and Love in the Ozarks*. Springfield, Mo.: Midwest Litho Co., 1973. 229p.

Hulse describes this book as an autobiography. He was born and reared in the wilds of southwest Missouri—one of the most delightful spots in America, full of the most interesting people. But he chooses to write about the dismal little towns along the railroads, and the dreadful people who live there. I am familiar with these centers of culture, where if a girl is too clumsy to be a waitress, they send her to a "Teacher's College," and if a boy is too slow to be a farmer, he goes to a "Bible College" and becomes an evangelist. What Hulse says about all this is true enough, but it is a sordid and depressing story and has little to interest the folklorist.

1400. Hulston, John K. *An Ozarks Boy's Story 1915–1945*. Point Lookout, Mo.: School of the Ozarks Press, 1971. 248p.

Begins with a splendid preface (in dialect) by Dale Freeman, a Springfield newspaperman who was the author's friend. See pp. 6–7 for his grandfather's tale of the slow mill: A man says, "I can eat that meal as fast as your burrs grind it out." How long? "Until I starve to death, I reckon." Hulston's people were all millers, mostly in Dade County, Missouri. Memoirs are as good a way as any to present local history. A good deal about Drury College and Washington University. The author is a lawyer in Springfield.

1401. ———. *An Ozarks Lawyer's Story 1947–1976*. Republic, Mo.: Western Printing Company, 1976. 527p.

This is a continuation of Hulston's first work (see preceding entry) and concerns itself mostly with his life and career in Springfield, Missouri. No folklore.

1402. Hunter, Max Francis. "Visits from the Ozarks." Unpublished collection, Springfield–Greene County, Missouri, Library. 6 vols.

The index volume for this collection lists the thirty-six persons interviewed. They are in alphabetical order by name only, the only additional information being their location in the other five volumes containing the material. In these volumes, each with its own tape, Max names the informants, where they live, date of the interview, and the setting (on the front porch, in the kitchen, etc.), and gives a brief resumé of the conversation and its location on the accompanying tape. These "visits" are interviews and conversations with a variety of persons on a mixed bag of subjects.

1403. James, Bill. *Anklin' Around Our Mountain*. Colby, Kans.: Prairie Printers, 1973. 56p.

Paperback pamphlet, random recollections of a boy who lived at Schaberg, Arkansas, for five years in the 1920s. He went to school there, and Isabel France was his teacher. Includes a good photograph of Mrs. France, here published for the first time.

1404. Jeffries, T. Victor. *Before the Dam Waters: Story and Pictures of Old Linn Creek, Ha Ha Tonka and Camden County*. Springfield, Mo.: Midwest Litho and Publishing Company, 1974. 58p.

Old Linn Creek, in the north-central Missouri Ozarks, was destroyed in 1930 to make way for an impoundment that became the Lake of the Ozarks. This story about the old town and its destruction is written almost apologetically by a native son who was hired as a lawyer to represent the electrical company constructing the lake.

1405. Johns, Paul. "A Town Gone Fishin': Nixa's Sucker Day." *Springfield Magazine* 2:12 (May 1981): 29–31.

Practically the entire population of this Christian County, Missouri, town heads for the rivers to "grab" suckers (*Catostomus commersoni*). This fish fry has become an annual spring celebration and has grown to such proportions that the regional sucker population can hardly satisfy the demand. Also, the numbers being caught were exceeding the state game regulations. Though not publicized, it is reported (Springfield *Daily News*, 30 April 1981, p. 5B) that a sizable shipment of ocean perch now helps the cause.

1406. Jones, Stratford C. "School, Club, Congregation: 'The Fellowship of Kindred Minds.'" In *Life in Rural America*, ed. National Geographic Society, pp. 152–73, 192–95. Washington, D.C.: National Geographic Society, 1974.

This section is about religion in rural America. There are some good pictures of a baptism in the Buffalo River near St. Joe, Arkansas, and a church meeting in Omaha, Arkansas (pp. 156–59). Jones travels with a Southern Baptist preacher in the area around Harrison, Arkansas (pp. 171–72). The author is a Yale graduate and a professional writer.

1407. Keathley, Charles E. "Boyhood Recollections of Cattle Hunting." *The Ozarks Mountaineer* 22:9 (October 1974): 22–23.

Good story of southeast Missouri. Tells the plain truth about free-range cattle, ticks, and chiggers.

1408. Keefe, James F. "Missouri Rifles: The Living Tradition." *Missouri Conservationist* 40:11 (November 1979): 10–13.

He says that in Missouri "shooting and hunting with muzzle loading firearms never did entirely die out . . . ." He is correct. I well remember seeing an occasional muzzle-loading rifle or damascus-wrapped shotgun still being used by grandsons or great-grandsons of the original owner. Although he speaks with some truth that this was due to old traditions, many of these "atavistic souls" would have dumped grandpa's old gun had they had the price of a new one. There are good color photographs and a list of five Missouri craftsmen currently making muzzle-loading firearms.

1409. King, Edward. "The Great South." *Scribner's Monthly Magazine* 8:6 (October 1874): 658–64.

A fine firsthand description of social and economic conditions in Arkansas. This is listed in some bibliographies as "Travels in Arkansas."

1410. King, Johnny. *Johnny the Country Boy.* Springfield, Mo.: Roberts & Sutter, 1973. 140p.

The author gives a vivid description of life in an Ozark community just after the turn of the century. I especially like the section about the old burying ground (pp. 45–48). Also see the chapter titled "Sounds and Smells" (pp. 105–8).

1411. Kuyper, Mary Youngblood. *From Rags to Riches.* Hollister, Mo.: The Village Printery, 1977. 22p.

This pamphlet deals with the Wilson Creek schoolhouse, a one-room log building near Reeds Spring, Stone County, Missouri. Recently it was moved to the tourist attraction at Silver Dollar City. Kuyper tells of her childhood at this school, before it became a tourist attraction. She writes very well.

1412. Lane, Rose Wilder. "Reynard Runs: A Fox Hunt Is Still a Fox Hunt in the Ozarks." *North American Review* 230:3 (September 1930): 354–60.

A good account. Her description of this event is correct, as are her fox-hunting terms. This is just as Lane must have seen it happen around her childhood home near Mansfield, Missouri.

1413. Lankford, George E. "The Cherokee Sojourn in North Arkansas." *Independence County Chronicle* 18:2 (January 1977): 2–19.

The Cherokee lived in Arkansas from 1795 to 1828, but there is little documented history of this period. The Cherokee traditions are obscure. Lankford's brief paper is the best treatment of the subject that I have seen fully documented, with an adequate bibliography. Lankford is a professor at Arkansas College, Batesville. The *Chronicle* is published quarterly in Batesville by the Independence County Historical Society.

1414. Lappin, Samuel Strahl. *Where the Long Trail Begins*. Cincinnati, Ohio: Standard Publishing Company, 1913. 65p.

See information about Polk County, Missouri, in the 1870s, with occasional mention of the Springfield area. Not too important.

1415. Laune, Seigniora (Russell). *Sand in My Eyes*. Philadelphia: J. B. Lippincott Co., 1956. 256p.

Mostly about Woodward, Oklahoma, at the turn of the century. Author was a native of Little Rock, where she died shortly before this book was published. Fascinating glimpses of frontier culture. Illustrated by Paul Laune.

1416. Lawson, V. L. *The Lead Belt Mining Riot of 1917*. No publishing data given; copyrighted by Susan D. Lawson, 1976. 106p.

The locale is the old mining area of Flat River and Bonne Terre, Missouri. Local labor felt threatened by foreign laborers who had been imported in ever-increasing numbers to work the mines. Rumors circulated that the aliens were waiting for the Americans to be drafted into World War I so that they could take over their jobs and women. An interesting account of a little-known incident, but it has little folklore material.

1417. Lemke, W. J., ed. *The Hermanns of Old Hermannsburg*. Fayetteville, Ark.: Washington County Historical Society, 1965. 67p.

A fine book about the founders of the fine Ozark town of Hermannsburg, which most of us know as Dutch Mills. It is all straight history, fully documented by letters and diaries—the pioneer Hermanns were not illiterate. Lemke was a professor of journalism at the University of Arkansas, but his primary interest was local history. I knew him well, and he was quite a fellow.

1418. ———. *The Story of Tontitown, Arkansas*. Fayetteville, Ark.: Washington County Historical Society, 1963. 34p.

All about Father Bandini and the forty Italian families who settled this northwest Arkansas community in the 1880s. The good father was quite a man. He looked after his flock, led them through the hard times of settling the seven hundred acres they had purchased and planting the vineyards that were to become so famous, and, at his death in 1917, saw them firmly established as a part of the Ozarks scene.

1419. Lenox, David F. *Memoirs of a Missouri Confederate Soldier*. Texarkana, Tex.: Published by the author, 1906. 58p.

Lenox was a native of Phelps County, Missouri, and for the major part of the Civil War was engaged in scouting and recruiting behind the Northern lines in southern Missouri. This is one of the finest chronicles of this genre I've read, but other than a few references to folk medicine and some dialect (e.g., the use of "cow-brute," p. 13), there is little folklore.

1420. Lewis, David. *The Current River and Tributaries*. Eminence, Mo.: Ozark Custom Printing Co., 1978. 46p.

The words "Montauk to Lower Big Creek . . . Historical and Geographical" are printed on the cover, and that pretty well describes the book. With many good maps and photographs, it presents a detailed picture of the Upper Current region. It is a damn good book, full of splendid material, much of it collected from real old-timers, and is superbly written in plain language with no academic gobbledygook.

According to the foreword Lewis grew up on the banks of the Current, where his family has lived for 150 years.

1421. Lincoln, Robert Page. "Float Trip in the Ozarks." *Arkansas Gazette*, Sunday Magazine, 15 June 1941, pp. 3, 10.

Lots of good facts about the boats used to float Ozark rivers and streams. They're called johnboats, and there's nothing quite like them anywhere else in the United States.

1422. "Living in the Ozarks." *Lion*, January 1976. 17p.

Lion is a monthly newsletter, edited and published in Pettigrew, Arkansas, by Joel and Sherri Davidson. Thirty-six issues appeared from 1973 to 1976. It seems to be a semiofficial organ of the loosely organized "new homesteaders"—mostly young folk from the cities who have fled the evils of the "establishment," which represents industrial urban culture. They buy small farms and try to wrest a living from the land. They are experimenting with co-ops, new types of primitive architecture, solar heating, hydraulic rams, and organic gardening. The natives call them "hippies," and there is a good deal of long hair, wild-looking costumes, and unconventional life-styles among them. It is interesting to watch them trying to mix with the old-timers. This newsletter, now in its third year, is filled with letters from the new colonists, all about their difficulties. These back-to-the-land enthusiasts are always interesting to me. I think it is a mistake to ignore their influence upon our culture. They talk a little wildly about Thoreau and how they have "seceded" from modern civilization. There are some fanatics and crackpots, of course, but it won't do to brush them off too hastily. Let's wait and see.

1423. Lynch, Virgil E. *Thrilling Adventures*. Portland, Maine: Southworth Press, 1928. 174p.

Lynch was a hunter and trapper raised in the Missouri Ozarks, on the Current, Jacks Fork, and Big Piney rivers. His first five chapters (pp. 3–75) deal with the Ozarks in the late 1890s, with lots about backwoods life, much killing of deer, timber wolves, wildcats, otter, mink, coon, and turkeys.

Rayburn told me that a second edition was issued by the *Forest and Stream* Publishing Company in 1932. I have not seen this second edition.

1424. McAdoo, Julia. "Where the Poor Are Rich." *American Mercury* 81:380 (September 1955): 86–89.

Fine penetrating article by a city woman who moved to the Ozark hills in Arkansas. Her neighbors have everything they want, because they are content with little. A good discussion of the better class of hill people.

1425. McBride, Mary Margaret. *How Dear to My Heart.* New York: Macmillan, 1940. 196p.

About rural Missouri, but much of it is about the prairie regions of the state rather than the hill country. The author is a native of Paris, Missouri, and was educated at the University of Missouri.

1426. McCurdy, Frances Lea. *Stump, Bar, and Pulpit: Speechmaking on the Missouri Frontier.* Columbia: University of Missouri Press, 1969. 218p.

This is a revised version of McCurdy's Ph.D. dissertation (University of Missouri, 1957), and it is a good job. I very much enjoyed the chapter "Onward Christian Soldiers" (pp. 149–77). McCurdy is a professor of speech at the University of Missouri.

1427. McCutchen, Henry Grady. *History of Scott County Arkansas.* Little Rock: H. G. Pugh and Co., 1922. 74p.

A pretty good county history. See pp. 44–50 for a detailed account of the "Scott County War" of 1874–1879.

1428. McDonough, Nancy. *Garden Sass—A Catalog of Arkansas Folkways.* New York: Coward, McCann, and Geoghegan, 1975. 319p.

House-raising, old-time games, honey-gathering, musicmaking, water witching, food preserving, quilting, hog butchering, and general making-do in Arkansas—with practical advice on keeping traditional ways. This is a damn good book, recommended to every serious student of matters Ozarkian. This author has given a general survey of the whole region. Just what I *tried* to do in my *The Ozarks* (1931) and *Ozark Mountain Folks* (1932), both published by the Vanguard Press, and both long out of print. People who like the best-selling *Foxfire* books will enjoy *Garden Sass.* The writing is better than the *Foxfire* books, and the photographs are just as good.

1429. McGinnis, A. C., ed. "History of Independence County, Arkansas." *Independence County Historical Society* 17:3 (April 1976): 119.

Mostly historical accounts, names, and dates. Some items of interest to folk-lorists: on pp. 12–29, information about very early settlements (1800–1830) along the White River; pp. 64–66, account of Brooks-Baxter War and a discussion of Powell Clayton, carpetbag governor of Arkansas who later settled in Eureka Springs, built the Crescent Hotel, and was prominent in the beginnings of the Missouri–North Arkansas Railroad.

1430. McKinley, Dan, and Phil Howell. "Missouri's Wildlife Trail, Part I (1700–1936), Part II (1937–1976)." *Missouri Conservationist* 37:7 (July 1976): 1–61.

This issue is a wonderful job, the whole story of fish and game in Missouri from 1700 to 1976. All kinds of interesting bits of information chronologically arranged. In 1843 turkeys were selling for twenty-five cents each, dried venison hams for fifteen cents each. In 1852 bottom prairie grass (*Spartina cynosuroides*) reached above the shoulders of riders on horseback. In 1885 German carp were stocked in Missouri waters. By 1889 practically all of Missouri had been invaded by the house sparrow. Many more facts, along with numerous sketches by famous wildlife artist Charles Schwartz. This is the best single issue of the *Missouri Conservationist* I've ever seen.

1431. Mapes, Ruth B. *Old Fort Smith: Cultural Center on the Southwestern Frontier*. Little Rock; Pioneer Press, 1965. 160p.

This book is a simple story from the building of the fort and army life in pioneer days down to the present. There is very little sensational stuff; only one short chapter is devoted to "Judge Parker and the Outlaws." The emphasis throughout is upon business and social life, school and church, with carefully edited quotes from early newspapers. A pleasant and revealing book. I was interested in the pages about Thyra Samter Winslow.

1432. Martin, Donnis, and Gladys Martin. *Ozark Idyll: Life at the Turn of the Century in the Missouri Ozarks*. Point Lookout, Mo.: School of the Ozarks Press, 1972. 141p.

The Martin twins tell the story of their childhood in El Dorado Springs, Missouri. School affairs, childish pranks, family outings and camping trips, a few anecdotes and sketches of small-town life. Not much for the folklorist. There is a kind of clean folly, a fresh quality for me at least, in these books, but no real importance.

1433. Massey, Ellen Gray, ed. *Bittersweet Country*. Garden City, N.Y.: Anchor Press/Doubleday, 1978. 434p.

Selection of articles from the quarterly magazine *Bittersweet*, written and published by high school students of Lebanon, Missouri, directed and sponsored by

Massey, a teacher in the Lebanon High School. It is a magnificent job. Interviews with old-time Ozarkers, illustrated with photographs, also by students. One of the best Ozark books, fully as good as the famous *Foxfire* series from Rabun Gap, Georgia. Massey is an extraordinary teacher, and her students are inspired by something near genius. See a good review by Dan Saults in the weekly *Taney County Republican* (Forsyth, Missouri, 16 November 1978). Highly recommended.

1434. ———. "Ozark Studies in Lebanon School." *The Ozarks Mountaineer* 19:11 (December 1971): 16–17.

A new course was offered in the Lebanon, Missouri, high school curriculum entitled "Ozarkia." It was taught by Massey, and what a teacher she proved to be. Very shortly thereafter it evolved into the nationally acclaimed publication *Bittersweet*.

1435. Mathews, Hubert C. *Hubert: Here, There and Yonder*. Springfield, Mo.: Published by the author, 1976. 185p.

A paperback autobiography of a farm boy from the Missouri backwoods who attended William Jewell College, Liberty, Missouri, and became a successful Baptist preacher. A man of limited intelligence and mediocre education, he had other qualities that made for success in his profession—tremendous energy, boundless enthusiasm, an unfailing sense of humor, a genuine love for the church and his denomination. He pastored churches in Missouri, Nebraska, California, and Massachusetts. After more than fifty years of active service, he retired to Springfield, Missouri. This book is well written, and I enjoyed reading it. What little he says about the Ozark country is true, with no chamber of commerce hokum, no punches pulled. Hubert died in 1981 at age eighty-seven.

1436. Mathews, John L. "Tontitown." *Everybody's Magazine* 20:1 (January 1909): 3–13.

Fine story about this Italian settlement in Washington County, Arkansas. Much information about Father Bandini and his early troubles with the Ozark backwoodsmen.

1437. Matthews, Linda. "Coon Creek of Cleburne County." *Independence County Chronicle* 19:1 (October 1977): 56.

Cleburne County is in north-central Arkansas. The author is a graduate of Arkansas College and is now an executive secretary in Washington, D.C. There are a lot of good stories and facts about the early history and folklife of the county in this little chronicle. She writes in a not-too-academic style that seems to be a good way to tell these stories. Especially see pp. 44–56 for biographies of Charles Noland (Pete Whetstone), and Frederick Gerstäcker, whose writings she thinks helped contribute to the stereotype that gave Arkansas a "bad reputation."

1438. Matthews, Norval M. *An Amazing City*. Webb City, Mo.: Sentinel Printing Company, 1976. 40p.

Just an accounting of names, dates, and happenings about the southwest Missouri community of Webb City. This town had a rip-snortin' reputation during the height of the mining boom, but little mention is made of these incidents.

1439. Mays, Armon T. "Early Life Along the Buffalo River." *Ozark Society Bulletin* 12:1 (Spring 1978): 9.

An old-timer writes about Grinder's Ferry, Duff, and Gilbert, settlements along the Buffalo River in Searcy County, Arkansas. A good photograph of Grinder's Ferry in 1916. This quarterly is published by the Ozark Society, a nonprofit organization founded in the 1960s, dedicated to preserving the ecology and natural wonders of Ozark wilderness regions.

1440. Mesnard, Alma Woods. *Girl from Arkansas*. Fayetteville, Ark.: Rubert Publications, 1966. 126p.

Autobiography of a woman in northwest Arkansas. Not much folklore, but many fine glimpses of country life. She graduated from the Pea Ridge, Arkansas, High School in 1912. Good account of her childhood around Bentonville and Pea Ridge.

1441. Miller, Giles E. "Then and Now." *Points* 1:1 (January-March 1900): 1–2.

Points was a slick-back monthly edited by Miller, and he starts off the first issue with this editorial. Tells how he first came to Eureka Springs in 1879. In the summer of 1881, he says, "it was estimated that fully 22,000 people resided within the corporate limits of the city of Eureka Springs" (p. 2). "It was pretty tough, as the cowboy, the dude and the sporting man were here in all their glory," and the author used to dig bullets out of the frame of his house with a jackknife in the mornings, after some of the boys "had had a good time" the night before. The place is very different now, says Miller, so he had returned from Chicago to edit and publish this little magazine. *Points* was well printed with many good photographs, always boosting the village and its healing waters and its progressive citizens. Jeanette Bullock, of one of the pioneer families, showed me many copies dating from 1900 to 1903. There is no complete file in existence, so far as I know.

1442. Minick, Bob, and Roger Minick. *The Hills of Home: The Rural Ozarks of Arkansas*. Photographs by Roger Minick, Stories by Bob Minick. San Francisco: Scrimshaw Press, 1975. 155p.

This father-son team visited us in 1974. Son Roger showed us about a dozen splendid pictures, but we did not see any of Bob's writing.

Roger's photos are wonderful, Bob's writing is clear and adequate. But they have put in a lot of "drawings and etchings" by Leonard Sussman which are appalling, no less. It seems that Sussman worked from the Minicks' talk, and never even saw the Ozarks. Some of his drawings, as a student at the University of Arkansas said, are like "a retarded Grandma Moses."

1443. Mink, Charles R. "The Ozark Hillbilly: A Vanishing American." *Missouri Folklore Society Journal* 3 (1981): 31–46.

This is a discussion of the stereotypes of the Ozark mountain people and their origins. The author cites numerous nineteenth- and twentieth-century writers and entertainers he feels have perpetuated the image of the ignorant, lazy Ozarker. He says the term *hillbilly* has not been found in print earlier than 1900. Mink teaches history and folklore at Lincoln University in Jefferson City, Missouri.

1444. Misselhorn, Roscoe. *Ozark Sketch Book Number One*. Point Lookout, Mo.: School of the Ozarks Press, [1970]. [17p.]

All Ozark scenes, a good job. Misselhorn has a later work, *Sketches of Missouri* (1974), with more of the same but covering the whole state.

1445. Moffatt, Walter. "Steamboat Coming 'Round the Bend, 1822." *Arkansas Gazette*, 15 January 1950.

Full-page story about early steamboating on the Arkansas River. The author is a professor at Hendrix College, Conway, Arkansas. All about cultural and social conditions in pioneer Arkansas.

1446. Moon, Christine Cooper. *Dear Christy: Memories of My Fifty Years*. New York: Exposition Press, 1955. 127p.

Memories of childhood in a rural community of central Missouri, in the early 1900s. A pleasant story with many folklore references.

1447. Morgan, Gordon D. *Black Hillbillies of the Arkansas Ozarks: A Report of the Department of Sociology, University of Arkansas*. Fayetteville: University of Arkansas, 1973. 165p.

This is an enlightening and objectively written account of blacks in the Ozark Mountains. There never were many, and today, with the exception of a few scattered settlements, their presence is practically negligible. Most were apparently freed slaves and lived in dire poverty, a condition they shared with many of their white hill neighbors. Due to their isolation, they failed to develop much of a distinctive culture, unlike their brethren in the larger black settlements of the lowlands. The majority finally moved to town where work, no matter how menial, was available and at least made life more tolerable. The author was assisted by Dina Cagle and Linda Harned.

1448. Morgan, Jeanette. *How It Was on Miller's Mountain*. Rogers, Ark.: Timber-wolf Press, 1980. 46p.

The author transcribed accounts of her visits with three Benton County, Arkansas, residents. There is much about life in the Ozarks during the depression years of the 1930s. Times were rough. They talk of the tedious task of peeling the bark of the black haw bush, which was sold at twelve cents a pound for medicine (pp. 5–6).

1449. Moseley, Jean Bell. "Possum Holler." *Ozark Guide* 6:2 (Autumn 1948): 25–28.

About life along the St. Francis River in the eastern Missouri Ozarks. She later wrote a book, *The Mockingbird Piano* (see volume 1 of this bibliography, p. 336), about this region. There is a good full-page photo of Moseley.

1450. Mottaz, Mable Manes. *Lest We Forget—A History of Pulaski County, Missouri, and Fort Leonard Wood*. Springfield, Mo.: Cain Printing, 1960. 81p.

Much discussion about customs and folkways of the early settlers. Any allusion to the passing of the "old ways" are definitely true when applied to this county. It now is the location of the largest army training post in the United States.

1451. Myers, Dena, ed. "It Takes Experiences All Added Up to Make a Life." *Bittersweet* 9:4 (Summer 1982): 44–51.

Pleasant reminiscences by Mary Scott Hair of her life in the Ozark hamlet of Hurley, Missouri. Since 1948, using the pen name Samanthy, she has written for area newspapers recording the lives and folklore of her family and neighbors. Although she is most knowledgeable about Ozark folkways, this article is more a history of the community and has no folklore references.

1452. Nance, Mary Huff. "Road of Promise." *The Ozarks Mountaineer* 22:5 (June 1974): 13.

Nance tells how her grandfather brought his family from Ohio in a covered wagon. They intended to settle on the Kansas prairies, but when they got to Cedar County, Missouri, everything looked so fine that they went no further. Nance was a great personality, an authority on the history of Cedar County. I knew her years ago in Springfield, where she and her family were running a greenhouse and florist shop.

1453. "The 1941 Mountain View Festival." *The Ozarks Mountaineer* 19:3 (April 1971): 18.

Held just four months before Pearl Harbor, this Stone County Folkways Festival became the forerunner for the Ozark folk festivals that gained national prominence in the 1960s and 1970s. Interesting photos by John Quincy Wolf, Jr.

1454. Noe, Fay. *Our Home in the Ozarks*. Chicago: Adams Press, [c. 1968]. 63p.

This pamphlet is described on the title page as a "Companion Book" to Noe's *All in a Lifetime* (see entry 500). It is a collection of brief reminiscences and pointless household anecdotes—like the bright sayings of children, of no interest except to the immediate family. The author was a long-time resident of Houston, Missouri, where she died in 1973.

1455. Norman, Frona. "The Joplin I Knew." *Missouri Life* 1:1 (March-April 1973): 19–24.

Norman, according to her pictures a John Held–type flapper of twenty-six, took over the old Worth Hotel, next door to the House of Lords, in 1924. Joplin was a live-wide-open town in those days. Prohibition hardly slowed us down. The Worth was the hotel for "drummers" and theatrical people. She knew Percy Wenrich, who wrote "Put on Your Old Gray Bonnet" and other pop songs, and who told how he used to finagle his way into the House of Lords to hear Scott Joplin play. She recalls Titanic Slim Thompson (she says he was born at Rogers, Arkansas), Hickory McCullough, Verne Wilder, and many other gamblers. She tells the old stories about Titanic—the pumpkin on the Connor roof, how he weighed the rocks along the roads around Joplin, and all that. Frona did some painting, too, murals in clubs and gambling dens. Some nudes, and one showing a dog behind a bush, for Hick McCullough to bet on, in his hotel at Claremore, Oklahoma. She tells about Col. Jimmy Worth, and the electric lights in his *shoes*. She's a sprightly old lady now, and runs a rooming house on Joplin Street, just a few blocks from Fourth and Main. I knew her about fifty years ago; she is *still* beautiful! Cf. Dolph Shaner's *Story of Joplin* (see volume 1 of this bibliography, p. 206).

1456. Nuttall, Thomas. *Journal of Travels into the Arkansas Territory, 1819*. Philadelphia: Thomas H. Palmer, 1921. 296p.

Nuttall was an English botanist and zoologist, professor of natural history at Harvard, who traveled from the mouth of the Arkansas River to Fort Smith. He was honest and sharp-eyed. Good stuff about wildlife, Indians, frontier customs, etc.
Cf. Richard G. Beidleman, *The 1818–20 Arkansas Journey of Thomas Nuttall* (*Arkansas Historical Quarterly* 15:3 [Autumn 1956]: 240–59).

1457. Ogden, George W. *Sooner Land*. New York: Dodd, Mead & Co., 1929. 329p.

Early days in Oklahoma. The author, born in 1871, has written several Western novels.

1458. "The Old Stomping Barn." *Shannon County Historical Review* 5:1 (April 1968): 7.

Describes a building in which wheat was separated from the straw by cattle or horses "tromping it out." Stomping barns are scarce now, but there is at least one still standing in Madison County, Arkansas. This article is unsigned, but I believe it was written by Dr. Robert Lee.

1459. Owen, Comer. "Coyotes Are Like People." *Bittersweet* 4:2 (Winter 1976): 60–64.

An old hunter sets down his observations. I know Comer and he believes in his way of life. Though he lacks the formal credentials of a professional conservationist or ecologist, he may know more about nature's ways than the whole pack of them put together, and it would behoove us to listen to what he says. There are three companion articles in this issue: "The Big Run Around" (pp. 65–69); "Trapping Coyotes" (p. 70); and "Skinning the Coyote" (pp. 71–75).

1460. Owen, Lyle. *Memories of an Ozarks Mother*. Branson, Mo.: The Ozarks Mountaineer, 1978. 96p.

Stella Owen, the author's mother, a native of Nebraska, has lived in Taney County, Missouri, since 1921. At the age of ninety she wrote her "remembrances" in longhand, a manuscript of some 160,000 words. Lyle Owen has written a good brief biography of his mother, but Stella is a remarkable woman, and it is to be hoped that her own book will be published eventually, just as she wrote it.

1461. Parker, Julia. *Out of the Past*. Springfield, Mo.: Empire Printing Co., 1968. 130p.

A history of Texas County, Missouri. Well written. One of the most entertaining county histories I have seen, with many folktales and anecdotes. The author wrote features for various newspapers. She lived in Houston, Missouri, where she died in 1973 at age ninety-two.

1462. Pennington, Eunice. *History of Carter County* (Missouri). Fremont, Mo.: Published by the author, 1969. 70p.

This book is hardback but has poorly mimeographed pages, hardly legible in places. For the most part it is names, dates, and historical facts, but the last half is worth reading. Page 23 tells of a Negro settlement made up of freed slaves that existed for some time in the area. Page 35 is about the wild hogs (razorbacks?) that roamed the hills, thought to be descendants of those that came with De Soto.

1463. ———. "Ozark Folklore." *The Ozarker*.

Although the title says "folklore," this column, which appears regularly, is primarily a narrative of the history of this south-central region of Missouri. Only occasionally are there references to folklore. *The Ozarker* was published ten times a year in Eminence, Missouri.

1464. ———. *Ozark Folkways: Book 1*. Piedmont, Mo.: Piedmont Printers, 1978. 56p.

This book begins with an "Introduction to Folklore" (pp. 3–6), but the author knows nothing about folklore as the term is used by the professional folklorists. Her book is full of fake "legends" about Indians, undocumented local history, foolish discussion of Nashville country music, and poorly written verse. However, it is still worth reading for a few revealing items like "The Legend of Carry Nation" (p. 24) and the priceless "Glossary of Ozark Terms and Expressions" (p. 51). Pennington is the author of several successful juveniles. She lives on a farm in Carter County, Missouri.

1465. Pennington, Eunice, ed. *Midwestern Fun, Facts and Folkways* 1:1 (Summer 1977): 4.

This is a mixed bag: a brief discussion of her thoughts on folklore, a short story titled "Johnie and the Rattler" with an "explanation" of its relation to folklore, a square-dance call, and a couple of poems called "historical poetry." This was to be a quarterly publication but Pennington wrote me (December 1978) that issue number 2 was so large that she just published it in book form as *Ozark Folkways: Book 1*.

1466. "Pioneer Identity Retained by Kingston." *Carroll County Historical Society Quarterly* 21:3 (Autumn 1976): 1–15.

A fine article about this little Ozark community located in Madison County in northwest Arkansas. The oldest store is approaching the century mark and is still operated by the same family. Shortly after it was built it leaned to one side. Rather than straighten it, a smaller building was erected on that side to keep it from collapsing, so today it remains "catawampus." In 1953 the bank was held up; when captured with his small take, the robber exclaimed, "It's a helluva bank that doesn't have any more money than that!"

1467. Poague, Haysler Allen. *As I Remember*. Clinton, Mo.: Democrat Publishing Co., 1968. 155p.

Everything that anybody wants to know about the town of Clinton and Henry County, Missouri—and Judge Poague has a good memory. Descended from a pioneer family, he knows as much about Clinton as anybody, and he has set it all down here, with a great number of good photographs. This is no ordinary county history.

1468. Primm, Alex. "Protecting Our River Heritage." *West Plains Gazette* 12 (May-June 1981): 24–29, 58–60.

This is about floating and fishing on the Niangua and other major rivers in the Missouri Ozarks. There is some discussion of "noodling" for catfish (p. 26). It is said that the Ozark variety grows big enough to chomp a man's arm off. A fine photo

(p. 27) by Townsend Godsey of Uncle Wylse Yandell, who operated Moore's Ferry on the White River just below Forsyth, Missouri.

1469. Pyles, Lida Wilson. "It Happened in the Ozarks." Unpublished manuscript, Carthage, Mo., 1982. 197p.

In her introduction, "Meet An Ozarkian," the author says that one Archibald Billy and his clan came to the New World from the British Isles and settled in the Mississippi Delta country, where they were called "Low Land Billys." Another branch of the family settled in the Ozarks and became the "Hill Billys." The experts may not wholly agree with Lida's etymological conclusion, but she has observed these "Hill Billys" and their mountains for a lifetime and knows them as well as anyone. This manuscript covers a variety of subjects, with chapter headings such as "Moonshiners and Bootleggers," "Hawg Killin' Time in the Ozarks," "Ozarks Cooking," "Telephones Come to the Ozarks," and so on. Students of Ozark folklife will find this interesting reading. The only copy of this manuscript is in the author's possession.

1470. Rafferty, Milton D. *The Ozarks: Land and Life*. Norman: University of Oklahoma Press, 1980. 282p.

Though this was written to serve as a textbook for Ozark studies, it is a reference that anyone who writes about the Ozarks, even fiction, should have at his elbow. There's nothing really new in it, but for the first time it's all compiled into one volume with texts complemented by a wealth of maps, charts, photographs, and excellent bibliographies at the end of each chapter. Subject matter progresses from the first settlers to the present-day tourism, with the author having acquired much of his information on contemporary subjects firsthand. This is a splendid job.

1471. Rhodes, Richard. *The Ozarks*. New York: Time-Life, 1974. 184p.

This is one of the Time-Life Series called *The American Wilderness*. Rhodes is a professional writer who lives in Kansas City; his chief interests are nature study and biology, with the emphasis on ecology. He has much in common with Leonard Hall, author of *Possum Trot Farm*, who lives on a farm in Iron County, Missouri, and wrote a column on ecology and rural life for the *St. Louis Post-Dispatch*. Rhodes's book is full of magnificent Time-Life photographs, many in full color. One of the most enjoyable Ozark books I have ever read. The first chapter, titled "Another Kind of Wilderness," is a fine introduction to the whole subject of the Ozarks. The chapter titled "A Natural Refuge for Migrants" (pp. 128–41), with its fascinating treatment of the paddlefish and other mysterious and little-known creatures of the Ozark streams, is an unforgettable piece of writing. Every serious student of the regional literature should own this book. I have read it many times, and never tire of the magnificent writing or the splendid photographs.

1472. ———. "Home to the Ozarks." *Reader's Digest* 119:715 (November 1981): 153–57.

The author speaks of cabins lit by kerosene lanterns, without telephones, and of young people doomed to a life of bare survival if they remain. This may have been the case in some parts of the Ozarks years ago, but is certainly not in 1981. Rhodes authored *The Ozarks* (see preceding entry), a wonderful book, but this article does not do him justice.

1473. Rice, Patricia. "The Missouri French." *St. Louis Post-Dispatch*, 6 April 1981.

Through the encouragement of scholars and folklore organizations, an effort is being made to preserve and perpetuate the music, language, and folkways of this last bastion of the eighteenth-century settlements in "La Vielle Mine" (Old Mines) region of the Ozarks.

1474. Roselli, Bruno. "An Arkansas Epic." *Century Magazine* 99:3 (January 1920): 377–86.

An Italian army officer was sent, in uniform, to the United States during World War I for some propaganda purpose. He came to Fayetteville, where an Italian professor at the University of Arkansas told him of an Italian settlement nearby. In this fine article he describes his visit to Tontitown. It is a good piece of writing. Cf. a full-page story about Tontitown by John H. Francis Pozza (*The Ozarks Mountaineer* [May 1953]: 5).

1475. Russell, Theodore Pease. "Old Times." Newspaper column, *Iron County Register*, 1884—1899.

Russell, a Connecticut Yankee, came to Missouri's Arcadia Valley in the eastern Ozarks in 1838. After a productive life as a farmer, subsistence and commercial hunter, community leader in church, school, and politics, father of a large family, and eminent village elder and philosopher, he wrote, under the pen name "T. P. R.," a fifteen-year-long reminiscence for the *Iron County Register*. Presented with clarity, insight, and occasional humor, Russell's writings, much like those of Silas Turnbo a few counties to the west (see volume 1 of this bibliography, p. 211, and also entry 568 in this volume), are an important source for the history and folklore of a part of the Ozarks that has had no Vance Randolph or Otto Ernest Rayburn. For introductions to Russell, see Dan Saults, "19th Century Hunting Tales," *Missouri Conservationist* (July 1983): 22–27; Elizabeth Holloman, "TPR and the Trail of Tears," *Ozarks Panorama* (publication of the Ozarks Writers League) (1984): 16–17; and Elizabeth Holloman, ed., "A Trip from Connecticut to Missouri, by TPR," *The Ozarks Mountaineer*, in two parts: December 1981, pp. 52–54, and February 1982, pp. 44–45. A selected edition of Russell's columns is forthcoming from the University of Missouri Press.

1476. Saultmore, D. C. "The Irish Wilderness." *The Ozarks Mountaineer* 25:6 (July 1977): 17–19.

This is by Dan Saults, wonderfully done in an allegorical style, full of learned allusion and literary fantasy, comparing an excursion to the Irish Wilderness with an adventure of Cervantes's Don Quixote. The Wilderness is a wild, heavily forested area located mostly in Oregon County in south-central Missouri. In the 1850s a priest, Father John Hogan, led his flock of Irish immigrants away from the railroad labor camps south of St. Louis to settle this region. But the harshness of the terrain and then the Civil War doomed the venture and it was abandoned.

1477. Saults, Dan. "Lo the Pore Native." *The Ozarks Mountaineer* 26:1 (February 1978): 26–27.

Saults comments on the notion that the old-stock Ozarker is an endangered species, pushed into oblivion by the more progressive "furriners" who have invaded the Ozark country in recent years.

1478. Scully, Julia, and Peter Miller. *Disfarmer—the Heber Springs Portraits, 1939–1946*. Danbury, N.H.: Addison House, 1976. 135p.

Mike Disfarmer (real name Meyer) was an eccentric photographer who lived in Heber Springs, Arkansas, and photographed the citizens. He died in 1959, and Miller collected his pictures, while Scully wrote a splendid fourteen-page introduction. The result is a magnificent portrait of a small town in Arkansas. It is an invaluable record of the period.

1479. Sechler, E. T. *Leaves from an Ozark Journal: 1927–1970*. Springfield, Mo.: Westport Press. 3 volumes: vol. 1, 1927–1936, 109p.; vol. 2, 1937–1946, 142p.; vol. 3, 1947–1970, 234p.

Condensed and abridged by Sarah F. Greer, this is the diary of a "Christian" (Campbellite) minister, of southwest Missouri. The Reverend Sechler, or perhaps an editor, has cut out a good deal of the text, and I have been told that much colorful detail of folklore and local history was lost. I wish that I could have seen the original manuscript. Even as it is, I certainly enjoyed reading the Reverend Sechler's adventures.

1480. ———. *Our Religious Heritage. Church History of the Ozarks (1806–1906)*. Springfield, Mo.: Westport Press, 1961. 123p.

This paperback has nothing much to do with religion per se, but it does give a series of concise accounts of the different denominations and the men who established the various churches in the Ozarks. Sechler is a little vague about the Catholic missions that came in with the Spanish and French, but very strong on the later Protestant churches. The book is dedicated to the "pioneer missionaries." Sechler was a minister—or at least a lay reader and evangelist—in the Campbellite Church, and the author of several books about his ministry. A graduate of Drury College, he lives in Springfield. Retired now, he still "serves his denomination *with zest* as an *ad interim* pastor."

1481. Seitz, Dick. "Missouri Wolf Chase." *Hunting Dog Magazine* 7:12 (December 1972): 22–23, 35, 44.

Most Ozarkers who follow this sport refer to the coyote (*Canis latrans*) as a "gray wolf" and talk about going wolf hunting, their wolf hounds, wolf traps, wolf signs, etc. But though the red wolf (*Canis niger*) and the coyote are similar in color and characteristics, biologists tell us that the range of the red wolf, though once abundant in the Ozarks, is now thought to be only a small area in the south of Arkansas. But I'm not about to try telling this to my "wolf" hunting friends.

1482. Shamel, H. Harold. *Seeds of Time, A Story of the Ozarks*. No publication data given. 278p.

I do not know where or when this book was published, but it is a substantial job, well written, well printed on good paper, well bound. The only copy I have seen is in the Springfield, Missouri, Public Library.

The Shamel family were farmers near Ellsworth, Kansas, in the early 1890s. Because of drought, populists, and hard times, the Shamels loaded their stuff in a covered wagon and moved to the Ozarks. That was in 1892, and the author of this book was a small boy—seven years old.

Their neighbors were good people, but not progressive like the folks in Kansas. They still lived in a "hand made culture" (p. 95), wove cloth, and all that. The author describes this handmade culture in some detail, and has many thoughtful comments about dialect and backwoods customs.

The story of the G. A. R. reunion at Cassville, Missouri, is well worth reading. The horse-powered merry-go-round is still with us. I saw two of them in Stone County, Missouri, in the late 1930s.

In 1897 the Shamels became disgusted with the rocky farm, the hillbilly neighbors, the bitter poverty. They sold everything that they had, climbed into the old mover's wagon, and went back to Kansas. "Our sojourn in the Ozarks was over," and thus ends his chronicle.

1483. Shiras, Ginger. "Snowball: Finding Elbow Room in the Ozarks." *Arkansas Gazette*, 22 August 1976.

A fine story of the hippies who have settled on farms around Snowball, Arkansas, and their pleasant relations with the old-timers. Reprinted in *Proceedings of the Conference on Ozark In-Migration*, Eureka Springs, Arkansas, 1976 (in the appendix, unpaginated).

1484. Simon, Howard. *Cabin on a Ridge*. Chicago: Follett Publishing Co., 1970. 159p.

Howard Simon was an artist—a painter and illustrator in New York. In 1930 he came to the Arkansas Ozarks and homesteaded a hillside farm near a place called Cove Valley. He built a log cabin and lived there five years. His experiences and contacts with his backwoods neighbors are well worth reading about.

1485. Smith, Kenneth L. *The Buffalo River Country*. Fayetteville, Ark.: The Ozark Society, 1967. 176p.

A fine book, well written and full of very fine large photographs and maps. Float trips, fishing, cave exploring, archaeology, fossils, wild flowers, log cabins, old mills, local history. Lots of place-name references throughout. See pp. 88–91 about the visit by the National Geographic in 1945.

The Ozark Society was a determining factor in the Buffalo being designated a National Wild River by the government in 1972 thereby keeping the river as it was, prohibiting the construction of dams to inundate it. There are fine descriptions and pictures of Lost Valley and Hemmed-In Holler. Everything Smith says about the river is true. I have seen nearly all of the Buffalo myself. It is not the best fishing water in Arkansas, but it is the most beautiful scenic stream in the whole Ozark region. Smith's photographs are the very best, many of them in color.

1486. Smith, Maggie Aldridge. *Hico. A Heritage—Siloam Springs History*. Cassville, Mo.: Willard Burton, 1976. 447p.

A vast collection of brief accounts written by prominent citizens, mostly about small-town merchants, preachers, schoolteachers, and the like, of great interest to the descendants of pioneer families. Many fine old photographs of village schools and churches, baseball teams, bands, fraternal orders, and social doings. See pp. 195–202 for the story of John E. Brown College, which is well worth reading. This was a Benton County, Arkansas, Bicentennial publication.

1487. Spence, Hartzell. "Modern Shepherd of the Hills." *Saturday Evening Post* 225:19 (8 November 1952): 26–27, 130–31, 133.

This article caused a furor in the Ozarks when it appeared. Along with his story of Ted Richmond and his Wilderness Library located on Mount Sherman in Newton County, Arkansas, Spence devoted equal space to the backwardness of Newton Countians, whom he described as barely literate, living a marginal subsistence, supplementing their meager income by selling their votes, serving on bought juries, cutting government timber, and bootlegging. But, according to Spence, after Richmond arrived and began distributing his books, times got better. He credits the inhabitants' belief that Richmond possessed "prescience" as being a large part of his "success" in winning their confidence. Newton Countians were so infuriated they held a protest meeting. See the front-page story in the *Springfield News and Leader*, 9 November 1952. As one protestor put it, Spence was just another writer "who spends eighteen hours here and thinks they know all about us!" I have been told that this furor had much to do with Richmond's hasty departure from the area soon after; he abandoned his library and never returned.

1488. Spring, Naomi Rosalyn Wrinkle. *Memories of the Lower Ozark Bear Creek Territory*. N.p.: Published by the author, [c. 1973]. 2 vols: vol. 1, pp. 1–96; vol. 2, pp. 97–192.

It is not even clearly stated who is the author, but Spring's name is printed on the outside of the heavy paper binding. There is no title page. It is very difficult to find out anything about this book. It is printed on fine paper, with many good photographs. It seems to be a badly written account of several large families who intermarried and populated whole school districts. Very nice, successful people. But all the interesting facts about pioneer life in Missouri must have been carefully edited out. This book must be fascinating reading for descendants and neighbors and "connection," but it is pretty dull for the rest of us.

1489. Stewart, John. "Little Italy of the Ozarks." *Missouri Life* 3:3 (July-August 1975): 40–45.

This is the story of the families brought from Bologna, Italy, to a plantation at Sunnyside, Arkansas (across the Mississippi River from Greenville, Mississippi), in the 1890s. They were to work in the cotton fields, but because of broken promises and malaria many left. One group settled Tontitown in the northwest Arkansas Ozarks (the article erroneously says "six miles away"—it's over three hundred). The subjects of this story founded Rosati, in the Missouri Ozarks southwest of St. Louis. Just as in Tontitown, the grapes and good wines have been the mainstay of livelihood.

1490. Stewart, Melinda, and Kathy Long. "What Would the Neighbors Think?" *Bittersweet* 7:4 (Summer 1980): 42–52.

An open and frank discussion by nine elderly informants about the moral codes of their youth. Everything from family, church, and school to divorce, pregnancy, and "girls gone wrong." Essential reading for the serious researcher.

1491. Stone County 4-H Council, ed. *The Faces of Rackensack*. Mountain View, Ark.: Stone County Leader, 1972. [80p.]

Biographies with photographs of most of the members of the Stone County organization formed in the 1960s to preserve the "old ways." In 1973 the federal government built a permanent folk arts facility in Mountain View that is now operated by the state of Arkansas and has become not only a major tourist attraction, but also an important depository of Ozark folk material.

1492. Stottle, Burr S. *The Unexpurgated Observations, Versifications, and Reminiscences of Burr S. Stottle.* N.p.: Published by the author, 1981. 79p.

Some reminiscences of the author's upbringing in Bradleyville, Missouri. But it is mostly personal observations and opinions on a variety of subjects, along with some attempts at poetry and a wealth of maxims, adages, and sayings. There is very little to interest the folklorist.

1493. Sutton, Leslie Parr, and Maribeth Lynes. *Visits with Ozark Country Women.* Little Rock: August House, 1979. [48p.]

Photographs of twenty-one women, a few newcomers, but mostly women who have lived their lives in the hills. They call this a photo-essay. Sutton took the pictures and Lynes wrote the text. There is very little dialogue and no folklore.

1494. Swank, Roy. *Trail to Marked Tree.* San Antonio: The Naylor Company, 1968. 165p.

Reminiscences of frontier life in eastern Arkansas, Crittenden County mostly. Some good materials on old customs, jokes, songs, and stories. The adventures of two boys in the Arkansas lowlands.

1495. Taylor, Orville W. *Negro Slavery in Arkansas.* Durham, N.C.: Duke University Press, 1958. 282p.

This is a careful, well-documented study. The problems of slavery in Arkansas are treated in detail, but do not differ greatly from those encountered elsewhere in the upper South. A few towns in the Ozarks had significant populations. Fayetteville in Washington County, for example, showed 967 in the 1860 census. For an excellent account of today's blacks in the Ozarks see Gordon Morgan's *Black Hillbillies of the Arkansas Ozarks* (entry 1447).

1496. Taylor, W. O. *The Old Timers Did It This Way: As I Remember.* Melbourne, Ark.: Published by the author, 1976. 107p.

This paperback contains the memoirs of an old man who spent his life in south Arkansas as a schoolmaster and Baptist preacher. Taylor, in his retirement, lives near Melbourne, Arkansas, and is the father of Billy Joe Tatum.

1497. Terry, Dickson. *There's a Town in Missouri . . . .* St. Louis: New Sunrise Publishing Co., 1979. 136p.

Brief articles (originally published in *The Midwest Motorist*, a publication of the Automobile Club of Missour) about the following Missouri towns: Springfield, Sedalia, Cape Girardeau, Hermann, Lamar, and Joplin, all located in the Ozarks, and Fulton, Independence, Hannibal, St. Louis, Lexington, and St. Joseph. All well written and accurate. I like especially the story of Lamar (pp. 63–69) because of the account of my old friend Arthur Aull, editor of the *Lamar Democrat*. Terry was for many years a reporter on the *St. Louis Post-Dispatch*. He died in 1978.

1498. Thanet, Octave. "The Farmer in the South." *Scribner's Magazine* 25:4 (April 1894): 399–409.

Brief mention of conditions in Missouri and Arkansas. Alice French (1850–1934) wrote many novels under the name Octave Thanet. She lived at Clover Bend, Arkansas.

1499. Thomas, Rosemary Hyde. *It's Good to Tell You: French Folktales from Missouri*. Columbia: University of Missouri Press, 1981. 246p.

The first part of this book (pp. 2–206) contains the transcriptions in "Old Mines" French and in English of twenty-one stories collected by the author in the 1970s. The last part (pp. 208–42) concerns itself with the Old Mines region, its people and their culture. Their present-day characteristics are compared with the observations of some of the earliest nineteenth-century accounts, principally those by Christian Schultz, Jr. (*Travels on an Inland Voyage*, 1810), Henry M. Brackenridge (*Views of Louisiana, Together with a Journal of a Voyage up the Mississippi River in 1811*, 1814), and John Bradbury (*Travels in the Interior of America in the Years 1809, 1810, and 1811*, 1819), and with two twentieth-century writers, Joseph Médard Carrière (*Tales from the French Folklore of Missouri*, 1937) and Ward A. Dorrance (*The Survival of French in the Old District of Ste. Genevieve*, 1935). According to Thomas the most drastic change in the folklife of the French communities occurred in the 1940s with the mechanization of mining in the area. But in spite of this, the results of these comparisons showed that the inhabitants still retained their basic French traits first observed over one hundred sixty years before.

1500. Tichy, Stella. "Czechs in the Ozarks." *The Svornost* (Chicago), 17 August 1941.

About Karlin, a Bohemian settlement twenty-three miles north of Springfield, Missouri. *The Svornost* was a Czech-language daily, with a few feature stories in English. I knew this author when she lived near Branson. The story is interesting for comparison with other foreign settlements in the Ozarks, such as Tontitown, Arkansas.

1501. *Tiff City, Missouri*. Tiff City, Mo.: Tiff City Bicentennial Committee, 1976. 103p.

This paperback was assembled and produced by the citizens of Tiff City "to celebrate the 200th birthday of our country." It is not well written or well printed, but the essential facts are there, and some of the photographs are pretty good. Tiff

City, we are told, "was once a thriving town of 200 people, but now it is a quiet little place with a population of sixty-six." But most of them are very *nice* people, including one extraordinarily pretty little girl who says she is a full-blood Potawotami (pp. 43–44).

1502. Trollope, Anthony. *North America.* New York: Harper & Brothers, 1862. 623p.

See pp. 379–96 for a description of pioneer Missouri, with discussion of manners and customs. Trollope made his way from St. Louis to Rolla at the beginning of the Civil War.

1503. Tyler, Virginia. *Around Town: An Anthology of People, Places and Things in Picturesque Eureka Springs, Arkansas: 1967–1972.* Eureka Springs, Ark.: Eureka Springs Times-Echo Press, 1973. 31p.

This is comprised of clips from the author's weekly column in the village newspaper. Pleasant little pieces about residents old and new. I have read the column for many years, and learned a great deal about Eureka Springs that I would not have known otherwise.

1504. Van Buskirk, Kathleen. "When Road Work Paid the Poll Tax." *The Ozarks Mountaineer* 25:7 (August 1977): 22–23.

All about road-building in the early days. Every able-bodied man between the ages of twenty-one and sixty-five worked four days every year. If he brought his team, he worked only two days. Of course, he could avoid the whole business by paying cash, but eight dollars was a lot of money in those days. Also, everybody realized that the roads were good for everybody in the country. A man's pride was involved. Most of them did their four days on the road.

1505. Van Cleef, A. "The Hot Springs of Arkansas." *Harper's New Monthly Magazine* 56 (January 1878): 193–210.

A fine article, with pictures of the Garland County jail, a log building into which the prisoner descends by a ladder which is then pulled up (p. 198). See p. 200 for a drawing of the "corn hole," a pool in which people soak their feet. Hot Springs was still primitive in those days, with ox teams and covered wagons all over the place, and hunters killing deer and bear close by.

1506. Vance, Joel M. . "Bugle in the Hills." *Missouri Conservationist* 43:5 (May 1982): 24–27.

The author has written extensively for this monthly publication of the Missouri Conservation Commission, and this is one of his most informative contributions. All about the one thing dear to many Ozarkers' hearts, their hounds, whether they be black and tans, Walkers, redbones, or blueticks. I know many of these fellows personally, and what Vance says about them is gospel. He cites examples of this fervor from throughout history and ends the article with George Vest's famous 1870 eulogy to Old Drum.

1507. Vandeventer, W. L. "Justice in the Rough." Typescript, Springfield, Mo., 1952. (Copy in Christian County Library, Ozark, Mo.) 197p.

W. L. Vandeventer (1889–1953) was for many years an attorney and judge in Springfield, but he was born at Garrison, Missouri, in 1889. His father and other relatives were Bald Knobbers. Vandeventer had long been assembling material for a Bald Knobber book. This manuscript was written in the late 1940s, but is not precisely dated. He showed it to me once, in the early 1950s, at his Springfield office. I actually held the neatly bound typescript in my hands for a moment, but had no chance to read it. He gave it, for reading and correction of spelling, grammar, and the like, to his good friend Lucille Adams Anderson, long-time librarian at Ozark, Missouri. She returned it to him at Springfield, but it somehow disappeared after his sudden death. I tried for many years to locate it, without success until May 1975, when Gordon McCann suddenly appeared with a fine copy. He was not too explicit about where he got it, but hinted that Lucille Anderson had something to do with it. Lucille Morris, author of *Bald Knobbers* (see volume 1 of this bibliography, p. 499), wrote me in May 1975 that she had never seen the Vandeventer manuscript.

The author tried to make it read like fiction, but it is really history, with real names and dates. It is strongly pro–Bald Knobber stuff, with no punches pulled. For about three years ending in March 1887, parts of Taney, Christian, and Douglas counties, Missouri, were Bald Knobber country, and this is what Vandeventer writes about. His manuscript is a simple straightforward historical account, very well and carefully written. It is a pity that it was never printed. I think he knew more about the Bald Knobbers than any of the others, although his bias cannot be denied.

1508. Vaught, Elsa, ed. *The Diary of an Unknown Soldier*. Van Buren, Ark.: Press-Argus Printing Company, 1959. 45p.

This pamphlet-diary was found on the battlefield at Prairie Grove in Washington County, Arkansas. It covers a period from September to December 1862. The writer was a member of the 19th Iowa and kept this account of his travels through southern Missouri and northern Arkansas. There are some good descriptions of the Ozark countryside during the Civil War.

1509. Velikonja, Joseph. *The Italian Contribution to the Geographic Character of Tontitown, Arkansas and Rosati, Missouri*. Florence, Italy: Universita di Firenze, 1969. 28p.

A careful study of these two Italian villages in the Ozarks. Both of these communities were settled by Italians brought to the United States in 1895 to a plantation called Sunnyside on the Mississippi River in southeast Arkansas. Dissatisfied with broken promises and living conditions in the Mississippi River bottoms, many left. Tontitown and Rosati were founded by two groups of these dissenters. What he says about Tontitown is true enough; I know little about Rosati. This paper was translated by Don Fischer of Southwest Missouri State University in Springfield, Missouri.

1510. Verser, Garnett Houston. *Ozark Jewel*. New York: Vantage Press, 1977. 112p.

Verser says she is a descendant of Sam Houston, and this is the story of her family, who settled near the Osage River at Tuscumbia in Miller County, Missouri. There are scattered references to early folkways and pioneer life throughout, but it's not much different from most family histories of this type.

1511. Wakeley, Maudine. *Aunt Marg, "Little Mother of the Hills."* San Antonio: The Naylor Co., 1954. 73p.

This author, whose real name is Maude Huffman, lived for many years at Idabel, Oklahoma. This book is all about her pioneer mother, who spent her life in the Arkansas hills. It has much about backwoods customs and rural life generally.

1512. Walker, Rhea Harris. "Pioneer Drummers and Peddlers." *Izard County Historian* 9:4 (October 1978): 32–35.

Drummers called on the merchants, and peddlers took their wares directly to the customer. Reminiscences of these frontier salesmen.

1513. Wayland, Paul T. "With a Circuit Rider in 1841–1842: Old Diary Recalls Meetings and Preachings." *Arkansas Gazette*, 27 May 1956.

Half-page article, with quotes from the diary of the Rev. Robert Ridgway, who traveled through Arkansas in pioneer days. A Methodist preacher, he visited and described many frontier towns. See the *Gazette* issue of 3 June 1956 for a continuation of this paper, with more quotes from the Ridgway diary.

1514. Weaver, Linda. "From a Schoolteacher's Notebook." *American Mercury* 63:274 (October 1946): 418–25.

Good account of common school in an Ozark village.

1515. Webber, Everett, and Olga Webber. "In Them Hills." *Holiday* 1:7 (September 1946): 27–29.

About Eureka Springs, Arkansas, and the surrounding area. Good photographs and the text contains some dialect. The authors lived in Eureka Springs and make some interesting comments about Ozarkers.

1516. West, Anne. "Maifest." *Ford Times* 49:5 (May 1957): 55–59.

The annual spring festival at Hermann, Missouri, an old German town "tucked in the blue-hazed foothills of the Ozarks." All about *Maiwein* and other nice things.

1517. White, Kathleen. *An Ozark Grandma "Remembers."* Clinton, Mo.: The Printery, 1975. 24p.

A collection of newspaper articles excerpted from the *Clinton Eye* in the 1930s. Reminiscent items under the headings "Remember way back when . . . ."

1518. Whitty, Walter Irwine. *Through the Valley.* Chicago: Clarke McElroy Publishing Company, 1931. 325p.

The naive autobiography of a befuddled lawyer who lived in Fayetteville, Arkansas. Small-town gossip about fraternal orders, local politics, and the like. There are many references to well-known Arkansans, the names thinly disguised. A few funny stories about Fayetteville.

1519. Wihebrink, Ronald. *History of the Whites Creek and the Irish Wilderness.* Springfield, Mo.: U.S. Department of Agriculture–Mark Twain National Forest, [1970]. 59p.

This author calls himself a "forest historian" and is an employee of the Mark Twain National Forest. This seems to be a very thorough study of this area, a region of which I have no personal knowledge. Father Hogan founded an Irish settlement here in 1858 or 1859 to get his Irish laborers out of the city slums—they were mostly railway workers in St. Louis. Wihebrink gives very detailed accounts of the Civil War period, with long reports by officers of both armies.

1520. Wilder, Laura Ingalls. *On the Way Home.* New York: Harper and Row, 1962. 101p.

The diary of a trip from South Dakota to a new home near Mansfield, Missouri, in 1894. Wilder did a series of popular juveniles—*Little House on the Prairie, Little House in the Big Woods,* etc. I remember visiting her place at Mansfield to see her daughter, Rose Wilder Lane, who wrote several good Ozark novels in the 1930s.

1521. Wilson, Ira M. "White River Canoe Trip." *The Ozarks Mountaineer* 28:4–5 (June 1980): 56–57.

An account of a ten-day float trip in 1917 from Branson, Missouri, to Cotter, Arkansas, ten days on the river. It's a good look at the river and the people who lived along it in those days. Wilson relates some interesting encounters with a few of these Ozarkers. Some of the dialogue is reminiscent of that in *The Arkansas Traveler*.

1522. Wilson, Joe. "Old Mines: The Enduring Village." *Tradition* 7:4 (Fall 1977):
   1, 3.

Founded in 1723 by French lead miners, the Old Mines region of Washington County, Missouri, still retained a vestige of its French language and culture when "discovered" anew in 1975 by members of the Missouri Friends of the Folk Arts. See also the photograph and text in the previous issue of *Tradition* (7:3, Summer 1977) about Old Mines fiddler Joe Politte, who appeared in the 39th National Folk Festival in 1977. *Tradition* is a now-defunct magazine that was published by the National Council for the Traditional Arts.

1523. Wilson, Maria Allis. *Marshfield and Her Cyclone; or Rachel Weeping for Her Children*. St. Louis: Christian Publishing Company, 1881. 236p.

A compilation of personal reminiscences by survivors of the cyclone that struck Marshfield, Missouri, 18 April 1880. The author was a crippled girl from Baltimore, who could walk only with crutches or a heavy cane; she came to teach the Marshfield School in 1876; after the cyclone she persuaded some forty survivors to write down accounts of their experiences, which she published with very little editing beyond correcting errors in spelling. She supplied titles for each item, as "Sallie Blankenship's History," "W. J. Moore's History," "Sarah Smith's History." These brief narratives are incredibly naive and startlingly effective. For a long moment the Marshfield disaster seems somewhere between the fall of Troy and the Crucifixion. Sallie Blankenship makes this Missouri tornado comparable to Captain Ahab's Moby Dick, the personification of evil in the Great White Whale. There is really no folkloristic value in this book, but it gives so vivid and moving a view of a Missouri village in the frontier period that I cannot persuade myself to omit it from this book.

1524. Withers, Robert Steele. "The Story of John." *Liberty* (Missouri) *Tribune*, 27 September 1951.

A long story about Negro slaves in Missouri, with a few good references to customs of the white pioneers.

1525. Wolf, John Quincy [Sr.]. *Life in the Leatherwoods*. Memphis: Memphis State University Press, 1974. 159p.

The author died in 1949; this book was edited by his son, John Quincy Wolf, Jr., who certainly made a beautiful job of it. The book begins with a superb introduction by F. Jack Hurley, a frequent visitor to the region discussed in the book. The Leatherwoods are the foothills of the eastern Ozarks—along White River north of

Calico Rock. The elder Wolf was born during the Civil War and flourished in the 1870s and 1880s. He had a sharp eye, an attentive ear, and a wide range of interests, and contributed brief items to many newspapers. He had little formal education, but his son, who gathered up his papers, was a trained scholar, with a Ph.D. in English literature from Johns Hopkins—one of the few real scholars to become interested in Ozark folklore; most of us are enthusiastic amateurs. I cannot praise this opus too highly. It has been many years since a book has given me so much pleasure. Note especially the editor's afterword.

1526. ———. "My Fifty Years in Batesville, Arkansas." Edited by Nancy Britton and Nana Farris. *The Independence County Chronicle* Two parts: part 1: 23:1–2 (October 1981-January 1982): 1–49; part 2: 23:3–4 (April-July 1982): 50–104.

This is a good account of life and thought in a turn-of-the-century Ozarks town (the fifty years are 1887–1937). See pp. 66–68 for the visit of the Ringling Circus in 1899 and pp. 90–92 for the Armistice celebration in 1918.

1527. Yingling, Sarah. *The Heritage*. Point Lookout, Mo.: School of the Ozarks Press, 1973. 75p.

The "heritage" was simply a cabin that the author and her family built on their ancestral acres on the Current River in Missouri. They moved into it and lived, in a measure, as she remembered her parents' way of life. It was only make-believe, she realized: they have electricity, modern plumbing, etc.

The first three chapters tell how they built the cabin, with fine descriptions of "Country Living" and "Parental Care"—all good reminiscent stuff about the author's childhood in the backwoods. The last two chapters, "Christian Faith" and "The Sunset of Life," are just long-winded, reflective essays—not much better than sermons, and very poor sermons at that. But the early part of the book, especially chapter 2 (pp. 9–35), is well worth reading.

1528. Zahorsky, John. *From the Hills*. St. Louis: C. V. Mosby Co., 1949. 388p.

The memoirs of a pediatrician, a series of autobiographical essays. Born in Hungary in 1871, he came to America as an infant, grew up on a farm near Steelville, Missouri, graduated as an M.D. from the Missouri Medical College, St. Louis, in 1895. The book deals mostly with details of his practice in St. Louis. He retired to the old farm in 1947. He uses the word *Ozarks* all through the book, but seems to know little about the Ozark culture. In his old age he became an amateur botanist, and the chapter on "Weeds" (pp. 372–87) has a lot of good material. Zahorsky was quite a fellow.

17. Biographies

1529. Abernathy, Barbara Trimble, and Mary H. Trimble. *Cordially Yours—Rose O'Neill*. Branson, Mo.: Published by the authors, 1968. [34p.]

A slick-back booklet for the tourist trade. The text is nothing to write home about, but there are many splendid photographs, and some full-page illustrations of Rose's drawings and jingles from the *Ladies Home Journal*, the *Delineator*, and other popular magazines. The emphasis throughout is upon the Kewpies, with little attention to the artist's more serious work. The authors are connected with the Shepherd of the Hills tourist attraction outside Branson, not far from the site of O'Neill's home, Bonniebrook. I do not believe either of them ever knew her.

1530. Allsopp, Fred W. *The Life Story of Albert Pike*. Little Rock: Harper News Service, 1920. 130p.

Pike is almost forgotten now, but he was a great man in Arkansas once. Editor, lawyer, politician, and Masonic scholar, he was a brigadier general in the Confederate army and led a motley force of Indians into battle at Pea Ridge. They fought well at first, but all ran away when the Yank artillery opened up—they had never heard cannon fire before. Allsopp was an Englishman who served many years as an editor of the *Arkansas Gazette*. He says Pike was a poet and philosopher, but Allsopp's opinions about literature and philosophy are those of a not-too-bright schoolboy. This book is well organized, however, and lists all the important facts of Pike's career.

1531. Andrews, James G. "A Suggin Who Needs Suggins." *Mid-South* (the Sunday Magazine section of *The Commercial Appeal*, Memphis), 17 August 1975, pp. 14–15, 18, 20.

Good information, with photographs by James Shearin, about Josephine Hutson Graham of Newport and Little Rock, who is a painter and feature writer and head of the Suggin Folklife Society.

1532. Anoe, Pearl. "Polly House, Eureka Springs Newspaper Woman." *Arkansas Gazette Magazine*, 15 June 1941. p. 8.

Good story about Polly House, with a photograph of her and some citizens who helped fight the bank robbers. I knew House and have heard her tell about the bank robbers. We knew her as Annie House, but when she was young she must have been quite a girl, and they called her Polly all over the state.

1533. Arnold, Margaret. *Profiles: Real Arkansas Characters*. Little Rock: August House, 1980. 47p.

These are brief character studies of a variety of Arkansans. Of interest is the interview titled "Billy Joe Tatum: Arkansas Wildflower" (pp. 21–27). Billy Joe lives on a mountain close to Melbourne and is an acknowledged authority on wild foods.

1534. Asbury, Herbert. *Carry Nation.* New York: Alfred A. Knopf, 1929. 307p.

This is a good book, and I enjoyed every word of it. But only in the last few pages are there any Ozark references. We all know that Carry lived in Eureka Springs, Arkansas, in her later years. Her last public speech was delivered in the street outside the Basin Park Hotel, where she suffered the stroke that caused her death.

1535. Aten, Ruth Black. *She Kept Men Standing.* Chicago: Adams Press, 1967. 375p.

The biography of Sadie McCoy Crank, a fire-ball evangelist. Born in rural Illinois during the Civil War, she attended country school wearing one boot and one shoe. She taught school, then became a Sunday School evangelist and finally a Campbellite preacher—the second woman to be ordained in that sect. She married another Campbellite preacher and spent most of her life preaching against sin and saloons in the Ozarks—at Liberal and Mindenmines in Missouri and Paragould in Arkansas. She was the author's great-aunt. Ruth Black was born in western Illinois and grew up in one of the churches founded by Sadie McCoy. She writes well, and her book is a vivid and moving tale.

1536. Ball, Larry D. "Murrell in Arkansas: An Outlaw Gang in History and Tradition." *Mid-South Folklore* 6:3 (Winter 1978): 65–75.

A fine documented account of the famous scourge of the Arkansas Territory, who still lives in oral tradition. Ball is associate professor of history at Arkansas State University, Jonesboro.

1537. Banes, Marian Tebbetts. *The Journal of Marian Tebbetts Banes.* Fayetteville, Ark.: The Washington County Historical Society, 1977. 159p.

Marian Tebbetts Banes was born in Fayetteville in 1850. Her father was Judge Jonas M. Tebbetts, a prominent lawyer and politician who had settled there in the 1840s. This journal, which she apparently wrote in the 1930s, is a biography of Judge Tebbetts, but it is liberally interspersed with her memories of growing up in Fayetteville. She writes from the perspective of a proper young lady of the South, but her descriptions of the everyday business of living there are a vivid and enlightened look at northwest Arkansas in the 1850s and 1860s. There is much of value to folklorists in this work. It is published as a dual volume with the reprint of William S. Campbell, *One Hundred Years of Fayetteville, 1828–1928* (see entry 1166), her journal being the second half of the book.

1538. Barrett, Viola M. "Monte Ne." *Ark/Ozark* 2 : 1 (Fall 1969): 2−5.

A condensed version of the life of W. H. (Coin) Harvey and his "monument to a dying civilization" near Rogers, Arkansas. The author says, "Coin Harvey may have been born ahead of his time," or, according to his detractors, "Maybe he shouldn't have been born at all." See Snelling's *Coin Harvey, Prophet of Monte Ne* (entry 1635).

1539. ⸺. "Who Was Rayburn?" *Ark/Ozark* 2 : 3 (Spring 1970): 2−7.

Folklorist, teacher, writer, publisher, Rayburn spent forty years recording a way of life that was fast disappearing in the Ozarks. His library and his large manuscript collection are now at the University of Arkansas, Fayetteville.

1540. Breihan, Carl W. *Younger Brothers*. San Antonio: Naylor Co., 1961. 260p.

Breihan's account of the Hot Springs stage holdup in January 1874 is brief and factual, much less detailed than the "legends" related by Sam Leath and other Arkansas storytellers. It appears that Cole Younger was not present at this robbery.

1541. Breihan, Carl W., and Charles A. Rosamond. *The Bandit Belle*. Seattle, Wash.: Hangman Press, 1970. 144p.

Nothing about Belle Starr that I had not seen before, but there are several incidents and anecdotes about other Oklahoma outlaws and some good photographs. Breihan reprints Henry Starr's little book, not easily available.

1542. Brisco, Mary S. "The Story of My Life." Handwritten manuscript, High, Ark., 1954. Unnumbered. (Copy in Parler Collection at the University of Arkansas Library, Special Collections, Fayetteville.)

This old woman has done her autobiography in pencil in an old-fashioned "Jumbo" tablet used in the country schools. She had only a fourth-grade education. She had no idea of printing it, but wanted to leave an account to each of her grandchildren. She knew nothing of any copying machinery, or even carbon paper, but was going to copy the whole thing in pencil. The pages are not numbered, but the tablet of ruled paper looks about three-quarters of an inch thick. Realizing that "there were just too many grandchildren" for her to give each a handwritten copy, she gave up that plan, but presented one complete manuscript to Mary Celestia Parler, a close friend who taught English at the University of Arkansas. About 1974, long after the author's death, Professor Parler got somebody to type the whole thing and to make a machine copy of the longhand original. There was no expurgation, no "editing" of the text. Miss Parler wrote a brief introduction and preserved the typescript, machine copy, and original penciled manuscript in one bound volume, with a fine cabinet photograph of Brisco pasted on the front of it.

I knew Brisco for many years. I am sure that her story is true. There is much of value in it for the student of Ozark life. Portions of this story may be found in *Mid-South Folklore* (Winter 1977).

1543. Clemens, Nancy. "As Always, Vance." *The Ozarks Mountaineer* 29:2–3 (April 1981): 20–21.

In the 1930s, Fern Nance Shumate (pseudonyms Nancy Nance, Nancy Clemens, Anthony Gish) wrote extensively about the Ozarks. During this period she collaborated with Randolph on two articles and three books, the most notable being *The Camp-Meeting Murders* (see volume 1 of this bibliography, p. 392). She writes of their relationship over the years, recounting some humorous incidents that occurred. This article is a good insight into Randolph's character, written by one of those few privileged to have a close friendship with him. Reproduced is part of a letter, in his handwriting, written in January 1979.

1544. Clements, William M. " 'Collecting Birdskins': A Role for the Nonfiction Regionalist." *The Southern Quarterly* 17:1 (Fall 1978): 5–14.

A perceptive discussion of three Ozark writers, Vance Randolph, Otto Rayburn, and Charles Morrow Wilson, and their place in the broader picture of regional literature generally. Clements teaches English at Arkansas State University and is the former editor of *Mid-South Folklore*, now known as *Mid-America Folklore*.

1545. Cochran, Robert. "Folklorist Vance Randolph, Ozark Mountain Man and Teller of Stories." *Arkansas Times* 6:4 (January 1980): 42–51.

This touches the high points of Randolph's life. Of special note are the accounts of his brief career as a Hollywood scriptwriter, his early troubles with chambers of commerce, and, until recently, the lack of recognition of his work by the academic community. One full page is devoted to a portrait, complete with cigar and fedora, taken in the late thirties while Vance was living in Galena, Missouri.

Arkansas Times is a monthly publication of the Arkansas Writer's Project, Inc. The author, who is in the English Department at the University of Arkansas–Fayetteville, is working on a biography of Randolph.

1546. ———. "People of His Own Kind: Vance Randolph's Kansas Years." *The Little Balkans Review* 1:2 (Winter 1980–1981): 1–18.

This is a candid look into the early years of Randolph's life: his birth in Pittsburg, Kansas, in 1892; his childhood, with memories of Buffalo Bill Cody and Carry Nation; the somewhat rebellious school years (he did not finish high school but graduated from Pittsburg State Normal); and his early adulthood, which included teaching biology, a flirtation with socialism, and service in the army during World War I. The article ends shortly before his move to Pineville, Missouri, in 1919. The author makes liberal use of Randolph's personal reminiscences, acquired by many hours of taped interviews during the last years of Randolph's life. This article is a condensation of the early chapters of Cochran's forthcoming biography of Randolph. *The Little Balkans Review* is published quarterly in Pittsburg, Kansas.

1547. Conroy, Jack. "Musings of the Sage of Moberly." *Foolkiller* 3:2 (Winter 1977): 1, 9.

This is a lively account of Vance Randolph's fifty years of folklore collecting in the Ozarks, with special attention to traditional erotica. Conroy quotes the story of nude waitresses in Kansas City in the 1930s (from *We Always Lie to Strangers*, Columbia University Press, 1951) and the recent *Pissing in the Snow* (entry 515). Conroy is a native of Moberly, Missouri, and a long-time collector of bawdy folksongs and folktales. He is remembered as the author of *The Disinherited* (see volume 1 of this bibliography, p. 358), one of the best of the Missouri novels, which deals with the mining camps around Moberly.

1548. *Conversations with Congressman Dewey Short: Senior Officers Debriefing Program.* Carlisle Barracks, Penn.: United States Military History Institute, 1975. 72p.

Congressman Short was from Galena in Stone County, Missouri. He represented the Seventh District of southwest Missouri for twenty-four years (1928–1930, 1932–1954). These interviews were conducted on three different occasions in early 1975 when Congressman Short was seventy-seven years old. They are primarily concerned with his long political career, but in the first few pages he tells of his political beginnings with reminiscences about court days and early campaigning in the Missouri Ozarks. (Vance Randolph lived with the Short family in Galena in the early 1940s.)

1549. Croley, Victor A. "The Hermit of Hemmed-In Hollow." *The Ozarks Mountaineer* 22:3 (April 1974): 24–25.

The story of William Patrick O'Neill and his sojourn in Newton County, Arkansas. I believe Croley's account is true in the main. Some of the details differ from Rose O'Neill's story as she told it to me at Bonniebrook, but it's a good article anyhow.

1550. Croy, Homer. *Country Cured.* New York: Harper and Brothers, 1943. 282p.

A straight autobiography. The first part of the book—about the farm near Maryville, Missouri—is good reading. The latter part deals with Croy's writing and his life in St. Louis, New York, and Hollywood, and is of small interest. Croy is a skilled writer.

1551. Crump, Bonnie Lela. *Carry A. Nation.* Eureka Springs, Ark.: Times-Echo Press, 1959. 52p.

This pamphlet is just another rehash of the standard accounts, except for some anecdotes about Carry's last years at Hatchet Hall in Eureka Springs, Arkansas. Crump has several letters from Carry's grandchildren, and two or three photographs that I had not seen before.

1552. Dalton, Captain Kit. *Under the Black Flag*. Memphis: Lockard Publishing Company, 1914. 252p.

The first part of this book, pp. 1–115, covers the author's experiences during the Civil War. He says, as the title infers, that he was a Confederate guerrilla under the command of the infamous Quantrill. The second half, pp. 116–252, are concerned with the postwar years. Dalton claims to have been an outlaw with the Jesse James gang. What follows are stories of bank and train robberies, gunfights, and brawls, all related with the air of a bard extolling the virtues of an American Robin Hood.

See Harold Preece's comments about Dalton on pp. 211–12 and 290 in his *The Dalton Gang* (see entry 1620).

1553. Deane, Ernie. "A Man Inspired by the Hills, and Hill People, of the Ozarks." In *Proceedings of the Conference on Ozark In-Migration*, pp. 1–2. Green Forest, Ark.: Larimer Publications Commercial, 1976.

Mostly about Vance Randolph's many years of study of the Ozark dialect and folklore, reprinted from the *Arkansas Gazette* with a large picture of Randolph by George Fisher of Little Rock, famous for his cartoons of Governor Faubus.

1554. ———. *Ozarks Country*. Branson, Mo.: The Ozarks Mountaineer, 1975. 191p.

"Vance Randolph Knows Folklore," p. 107, appeared on 10 February 1971, when Vance was approaching his eightieth year. In speaking of the changes he had seen in the Ozarks, his dislike of some of those changes was summed up by his statement, "I hate a damn clock that doesn't tick." "Mary Randolph, Folklore Teacher," on p. 108, tells of folklore classes she taught at the University of Arkansas–Fayetteville for more than twenty years. She and Vance were married in 1962. "The Editor of the Mountaineer," p. 118, is about Clay Anderson and his accomplishments as editor of *The Ozarks Mountaineer*, a slick-paper magazine devoted to reporting the past, present, and future of the Ozark region.

1555. ———. "Vance Randolph: Legacy from a Lifelong Love of the Ozarks." *The Ozarks Mountaineer* 29:2–3 (April 1981): 28–29.

In this brief overview of Vance's life and accomplishments, the author pays tribute to a commitment of over sixty years of documenting a vanishing way of life, ". . . a man absolutely dedicated to his life's mission of bringing together in an orderly way uncounted thousands of bits of information about the Ozarks and their people." Deane, a close friend of Randolph's, covers the significant facts and recounts important qualities of his character, one of which was his determination to continue this work until he was neither physically nor mentally capable of doing so.

1556. Dorson, Richard M. "A Visit with Vance Randolph." *Journal of American Folklore* 67:265 (July-September 1954): 260.

In 1953 Dorson spoke at the meeting of the Arkansas Folklore Society in Fayetteville. He recounts here his first meeting with Randolph. At that time Dorson was teaching at Michigan State University. He later became head of the folklore department at Indiana University and was instrumental in getting the press of the Indiana University Research Center for the Language Sciences to publish the first volume of this bibliography.

1557. Edwards, John N. *Noted Guerrillas, or the Warfare of the Border*. St. Louis: Bryan, Brand, & Company, 1877. 488p.

Much material on Quantrill, the James and Younger boys, and many lesser-known outlaws who operated in Missouri and Arkansas in Civil War days and the decade that followed.

1558. ———. *Shelby and His Men, or the War in the West*. Kansas City, Mo.: Hudson-Kimberly Publishing Co., 1897. 461p.

Joe Shelby was a Missouri bushwhacker who became a major general in the Confederate army and led his wild cavalry in many bloody raids and battles in Missouri and Arkansas. This book describes his exploits in great detail and presents a vivid picture of the period. Major Edwards was a romantic writer, and a fire-eating sesesh. I'm afraid there is a good deal of fiction in this story, but it is good reading, anyhow. The book was first issued by the author in 1867 and "re-published by his wife Jennie Edwards" thirty years later.

1559. Elfer, Maurice. *Opie Read*. Detroit: Boyten Miller Press, 1940. 339p.

The Opie Read that Elfer writes about is very different from the man who wrote the novels. According to this book, Read was vain and silly and sentimental and religious. The man I knew from reading his novels was perhaps sentimental at times, but I never thought of him as silly, and he was certainly not religious. As for vanity, probably he did have a measure of it—who doesn't? The author of Read's novels was a good storyteller, but Elfer's friend was not. Read the tale "An Escape in the Night" (pp. 266–77) and you'll see what I mean. Still, I met Opie Read only once, while Elfer was intimately acquainted with him for many years.

1560. Ellis, John Breckenridge. *Adventures in Living*. Cedar Rapids, Iowa: Torch Press, 1933. 310p.

Autobiography of an Ozark novelist. Chapter 11 (pp. 195–259) is "Down in Arkansas." He spent most of his life in the Ozarks, and wrote several regional novels. But he shows little firsthand knowledge of the Ozark people. His stories might have been written anywhere in the rural South.

1561. Ernst, John. *Jesse James*. Englewood Cliffs, N.J.: Prentice-Hall, 1976. 76p.

A very condensed version of James's life and exploits. See chapter 14 (pp. 70–72) for some discussion of the legends.

1562. Faubus, John Samuel. "John Samuel Faubus. Correspondence and Miscellaneous Records, 1913 . . . 1934, 1942–1966." Special Collections, University of Arkansas Library, Fayetteville.

John Samuel (Little Sam) Faubus of Madison County, Arkansas, was a man very much like John Quincy Wolf, Sr., of Independence County. Little Sam also wrote regional news and editorials for local newspapers (the *St. Paul Mountaineer*, and later the *Madison County Record*), just as John Quincy had. But John Quincy's writings were compiled by his son, John Quincy Wolf, Jr., into the book *Life in the Leatherwoods* (entry 584). Many of us wish that Little Sam's papers might also be published. Past Arkansas governor Orval Faubus is no scholar as was John Quincy Wolf, Jr., but he writes good straightforward prose, and he could do a wonderful job of editing his father's papers.

1563. Faubus, Orval Eugene. *In This Faraway Land*. Conway, Ark.: River Road Press, 1971. 736p.

This is a World War II diary, all about the author's military adventures. Faubus had a good war record. Of greater interest to the folklorist is the section (some forty pages) titled "Background of the Writer," a fascinating account of his early life in Madison County, Arkansas. For six terms (1954–1966) Faubus was governor of Arkansas—one of the best governors Arkansas ever had. Now retired, he lives quietly in Huntsville. Orval Faubus is quite a fellow, by anybody's standard.

1564. Fletcher, John Gould. *Life Is My Song*. New York: Farrar & Rinehart, 1937. 406p.

A very frank autobiography. See pp. 382–83 for Fletcher's reaction to the Ozark backwoods. In later years he was converted to a passionate regionalism and founded the Arkansas Folklore Society.

1565. Freyder, Doris K. "City Learning Takes to the Country." *The Ozarks Mountaineer* 26:3 (April 1978): 18.

A brief article about Ernie Deane, well-known newspaper columnist, former professor of journalism at the University of Arkansas, and author of books and feature stories about the Ozarks. Includes a good photograph of Deane.

1566. Funk, Ernest M. *Ozark Farm Boy to University Professor Emeritus: An Auto-biography*. Columbia, Mo.: College of Agriculture, University of Missouri, 1975. 80p.

This booklet is just the autobiography of a moderately successful college professor, and is listed here only because a few pages (pp. 8–14) deal with life on a farm in Iron County, Missouri.

1567. Garrison, J. H. *Memories and Experiences, a Brief Story of a Long Life, An Autobiography*. St. Louis: Christian Board of Publications, 1926. 269p.

Beginning with the author's childhood near Ozark, Missouri, this book carries him through four years in the Union Army. He served the whole Civil War in Missouri and Arkansas. After the war he entered Abington College, a Campbellite school in Illinois, graduating in 1868. He describes himself on the title page as "Editor, Minister, Author." He was, I take it, a man of some prominence in the Christian (Campbellite) Church. He gives a vivid and well-written account of his boyhood in the south-central Missouri Ozarks.

1568. Gibbons, Robert H., and Robert P. Neumann. *Wild Bill: The Legend and the Truth of the Wild West's First Shootout in Springfield, Missouri, July 21, 1865*. Springfield, Mo.: Published by the authors, 1975. 32p.

This paperback reprints George Ward Nichol's well-known account in *Harper's New Monthly Magazine*, February 1867, in a very fine print. The remainder of the pamphlet (pp. 15–32) is a hodgepodge of "new matter"—local tales, testimony of old settlers, court records, old drawings and photographs—which the authors think are more reliable than Nichol's article.

1569. Godsey, Helen, and Townsend Godsey. "Millions Share Her Ozark Adventures." *The Ozarks Mountaineer* 26:1 (February 1978): 22–23.

About Edith McCall of Hollister, Missouri. She's a popular author of a juvenile series, the adventures of a young Ozarker called Butternut Bill.

1570. ———. "Queen of the Hillbillies." *The Ozarks Mountaineer* 25:10 (November 1977): 14–15, 26.

Good story about May Kennedy McCord of Springfield, Missouri. McCord will be long remembered for her "Hillbilly Heartbeats" radio talks, and her weekly newspaper columns. She grew up at Galena, in the wilds of Stone County, Missouri, and knew more about the Ozarks than most of the people who write on the subject. She died in 1979 at age ninety-nine.

1571. Godsey, Townsend. "'Bull Goose' of the Ozarks." *Missouri Life* 1:6 (January-February 1974): 46–52.

A flattering piece about me and my books on Ozark folklore, with several good photographs.

1572. ———. "The King of the Floaters." *Missouri Life* 5:1 (March-June 1977): 67–74.

For twenty-five years, beginning in the 1930s and ending with his retirement in 1958, Jim Owen's Float Service sent more than ten thousand fishermen down Ozark streams. He made Ozark float fishing almost a national pastime and allegedly made himself a fortune in the process. He operated out of Branson, Missouri, and hosted nationally known businessmen, politicians, and movie stars. His enterprise was publicized by the *Saturday Evening Post, Life, Look,* and countless other periodicals that made Ozark rivers famous. Godsey floated with Jim many times and gives a good description of one of these float trips (pp. 70–71), which were hardly what one would call "roughing it." Jim was a promoter first class! He owned a local movie theater and in 1941 convinced Paramount Pictures to hold the premier showing of *Shepherd of the Hills* in Branson (though not one foot of it was shot in the Ozarks). He was a well-known dog breeder, once serving as president of the National Fox and Fox Hound Protective Association (folks still tell some good stories about Jim and his champion foxhound, Ozark Wing Bone). He raised fighting cocks, engaged in real estate, wrote columns for area newspapers, and was a politician, serving as mayor of Branson for twelve years. He had planned to write a book titled *The King of the River* but decided the financial benefits wouldn't be worth the undertaking. He did later put together a collection of anecdotes that was published as a paperback, *Hillbilly Humor* (see entry 502). This article is as good as I've seen about Jim and has lots of fine photographs. But now Jim's gone (he died in 1972), and so is the mighty White River, obliterated by Corps of Engineers lakes. For those of us fortunate enough to have known them both, the Ozarks will never be quite the same.

1573. ———. "Pioneer Life Preserved." *Springfield News and Leader*, 21 March 1976.

About Lennis Broadfoot, artist and author of *Pioneers of the Ozarks* (see volume 1 of this bibliography, p. 43). Broadfoot was born and reared in the Current River country of the Missouri Ozarks and knew intimately the subjects he sketched and wrote about.

1574. ———. "Struggles and Reward." *The Ozarks Mountaineer* 23:1 (February 1975): 17.

Story of D. H. Pickett, a preacher who came to the White River country in 1871 with sixteen dollars in his pocket.

1575. Hagen, Lyman B. *Douglas Jones.* Jonesboro, Ark.: Craighead County and Jonesboro Public Library, 1982. 14p.

An informative biographical sketch about this accomplished author. Jones was raised at West Fork just south of Fayetteville, Arkansas, and after a career in the military and as a university professor returned home and began writing historical novels. His first four were about the Indian uprisings, but in 1979 he began a trilogy that followed the lives and adventures of a family in northwest Arkansas. He has proven himself one of the most adept narrators of the Ozark past. This publication is part of a series on Arkansas authors and was funded by the Arkansas Endowment for the Humanities.

1576. Hail, S. A. "A Short Story of My Long Life." *The Independence County Chronicle* 20:4 (July 1979): 4–37.

Reminiscences, written in 1912, of the author's life in and around Batesville, Arkansas. During the Civil War he fought with a regiment of Arkansas Confederate volunteers. What he tells about the Reconstruction period in north Arkansas after the war is worth reading—all about carpetbaggers, freed blacks, and the Ku Klux Klan.

1577. Hale, Donald R. *They Called Him Bloody Bill: The Missouri Badman Who Taught Jesse James Outlawry*. Clinton, Mo.: The Printery, 1975. 118p.

This is an historical account, well documented, of Bill Anderson, a Missouri guerrilla leader during the Civil War, one of Quantrill's lieutenants. Chapter 11, "Outlaws" (pp. 100–111), tells of the lesser-known members of his band, aside from Jesse James, who lived outside the law in the postwar days. Also see Chapter 13, "The Legend" (pp. 116–18). Bloody Bill was killed in October 1864, but his name came to public attention again in the 1920s when he was "discovered" still living in Texas.

1578. ———. *We Rode with Quantrill*. No place or publisher cited, 1975. 197p.

The first part (pp. 8–75) is a well-documented account of Quantrill's life and his exploits as leader of the Confederate guerrilla bands that terrorized Missouri and Kansas before and during the Civil War, especially the Lawrence, Kansas, raid (pp. 49–59), and the Baxter Springs, Kansas, massacre (pp. 59–64). The rest is a series of short biographies of thirty-three principal members of his band. But of special interest is the chapter titled "Reburial of Quantrill's Remains" (pp. 68–75). Through a series of bizarre events, his bones are now alleged to be scattered across the country in the possession of historical societies and private collectors. For many years his skull was reportedly used in the initiation rites of a small college fraternity in the Midwest. See photographs on pp. 70–71.

1579. Holbrook, Stewart H. *Wild Bill Hickok Tames the West*. New York: Random House, 1952. 179p.

This is the Hickok story for juveniles, ages nine to fourteen, the library says. But it is interesting to me that the accounts of Hickok's exploits, notably that of his duel with Dave Tutt, don't sound much different from those in most popular adult publications.

1580. Holden, I. E. *Hillbilly Preacher.* Peace Valley, Mo.: Published by the author, 1970. 92p.

Reverend Holden was born in Oregon County, Missouri, in 1896. In his youth he loved dance halls, picture shows, the bottle, and cards. Then he entered the church, first getting an "Exhorter's License" and then a "Full License" to preach in the First Baptist Holiness Church. This little book, first printed in 1959, is his autobiography, all about his ministry throughout the Midwest, his sermons, revivals, and faith healing. But there is little of value for the folklorist in this book.

1581. Horine, Maude M. *Memories of Rose O'Neill, Creator of the Kewpie Doll.* Branson, Mo.: Published by the author, 1950. 33p.

This author was an old friend and neighbor of the elder O'Neill's, but she first met Rose in the early 1930s. In this book she makes Rose romantic and sentimental, even a bit silly sometimes. Rose did not seem so to me, but I didn't come to Bonniebrook until about ten years later. This book chronicles the chief events of the O'Neill career accurately enough, and is doubtless based upon interviews with Rose's mother, "Meemie," rather than with Rose O'Neill herself.

1582. ———. *Memories of Rose O'Neill: Creator of the Kewpie Doll.* Branson, Mo.: N.p., 1979. 38p.

This reprint of the 1950 edition says on the cover, "Revised Edition—New Material Added," but these additions are only two poems and two photographs, all of which have appeared previously in other publications.

1583. Huffman, Peggy. "A Page from the Past." *Rural Arkansas* 34:5 (March 1980): 4–6.

A biographical sketch of Tate C. "Piney" Page, who was raised on Moccasin Creek in the Leonard Valley of Pope County, Arkansas. After high school he attended Tulane University and then took a Ph.D. from Kansas University. He became a noted educator and at the time of his retirement was dean of the College of Education at Western Kentucky University. He then returned to Pope County. His story is not so different from that of other Ozarkers who left the hills to follow successful careers, but Page authored an excellent book on the early lifestyle and folkways of his part of the Ozarks, *The Voices of Moccasin Creek* (entry 503).

1584. Hunt, Martha Alice. "Autobiography of Grandmother Hunt." Typescript, Springfield, Mo., 1956. 24p.

The paperbound copy I saw begins with an item from a Springfield newspaper dated 12 February 1959 about Mrs. Hunt's death at age ninety-eight. Her "autobiography" begins in September 1954, and the last page she wrote is dated May 1956. She evidently wrote in longhand, but her children typed it later and had copies made and bound to give relatives and friends. She tells the facts of her life clearly enough. She was born in a log house near Springfield before the Civil War, and was left motherless at four. When she was seven her father and stepmother took her to Tennessee in a wagon—a twenty-day trip. Her father served in the Confederate army. She married Taylor Hunt in 1886, and they returned to Missouri and bought a farm near Dadeville, where they raised six children. After thirty years on the farm, they moved into Springfield, where she lived the rest of her life.

1585. "In Memoriam: Otto Ernest Rayburn." In *Ozark Guide Yearbook*, pp. 12–17. Reeds Spring, Mo.: Gerald Pipes, 1961.

Some good early photos of Rayburn and reprints of a few of his better writings. Also some memorial letters from friends, including one from Vance Randolph that is worth reading.

1586. Keesee, Irene. "The Occupants of 106." *The Ozarks Mountaineer* 27:6–7 (July-August 1979): 14–15.

Brief account of a visit with Vance and Mary Randolph in their living quarters in the Sunrise Manor Rest Home in Fayetteville, Arkansas. The author is a freelance writer who lives on a farm near Elkins, Arkansas, where she raises laying hens.

1587. Kirkpatrick, John Ervin. *Timothy Flint: Pioneer, Missionary, Author, Editor, 1780–1840*. Cleveland: Arthur H. Clark Company, 1911. 331p.

The life and work of a Presbyterian missionary from New England, who came west and spent most of his life on the frontier. For a brief period he worked in Missouri and Arkansas (1816–1822). While at Jackson, in southern Missouri, where he preached for two years, he encountered the new religious character of these frontier people. See his account of the "holy laugh" (p. 136). He also makes some interesting observations on the various nationalities living there. The Germans, he said, were the most prosperous, then the Anglo-Americans, next the Scotch, then the direct emigrants from England, whom he placed only slightly better off than the French, whom he considered the poorest of the lot (p. 138). This is a careful and plain-spoken biography, with footnotes and bibliography.

1588. Knight, Edward. *Wild Bill Hickok: A Contemporary Portrait of a Civil War Hero, Champion Pistoleer, Deadliest Gunfighter of the Old West*. Franklin, N.H.: Hillside Press, 1959. 61p.

Of special interest is the chapter titled "Origins of a Legend" (pp. 9–21), discussing fact and fiction of the Hickok myth. The rest is pretty much a rehash of well-known incidents.

1589. Lance, Donald M. "Max Hunter Remembers Vance and Mary." *Missouri Folklore Society Journal* 4 (1982): 1–29.

Max Hunter became acquainted with Vance Randolph and Mary Parler at the 1954 Ozark Folk Festival held in Eureka Springs, Arkansas. This meeting began a friendship that was to encourage and guide Hunter to develop his Ozarks ballad collection into the most extensive in recent times. Reading this interview carefully is a must for those interested in a glimpse of Randolph from other than the usual scholarly viewpoints published in academic writings. It is full of truisms about his character not customarily seen in print.

1590. Launius, Philip. "Fouke Monster Up His Alley." *Arkansas Gazette*, 2 November 1978.

Good account of Bill Clements, who teaches folklore at Arkansas State University, Jonesboro. Launius praises *Mid-South Folklore*, the scholarly journal Clements founded in 1973.

1591. Lee, Robert. "Roscoe Winfield Stewart 1887–1969." *The Ozarker* 6:7 (August 1969): 6.

A half-page obituary. Lee was closely associated with Stewart for several years, but Lee didn't know much about him, and neither did anyone else. He talked freely and pleasantly enough, but said very little about himself. Stewart founded and edited a monthly magazine, but he was never a skilled writer, and the village intelligentsia poked a little gentle fun at his literary efforts. A teacher of English at the University of Missouri once remarked that Stewart could not tell a noun from an adjective, nor tar from wild honey. Maybe his grammar was a little shaky, but his readers got the message all right. He graduated from Drury College, got through the Harvard Law School, and practiced law successfully for several years. I was only slightly acquainted with Stewart, in his latter years. I thought he was a fine fellow and a dedicated student of the Ozark culture.

1592. Long, Kathy. "Little House on Rocky Ridge." *Bittersweet* 7:2 (Winter 1979): 4–17.

Good account of Laura Ingalls Wilder of Mansfield, Missouri, with many photographs. See p. 10 for a picture of Rose Wilder Lane that I had never seen.

1593. Love, Robertus. *The Rise and Fall of Jesse James*. New York: G. P. Putnam's Sons, 1926. 446p.

Many old-timers in Carroll County, Arkansas, say that a member of the James gang lived there under another name. I thought it was just a migratory legend. But Love says (p. 442) that Jim Cummins *did* spend two years near Eureka Springs, where he was known as Jim Johnson. This same Jim Johnson crossed over into Barry County, Missouri, where he bought a farm—and became a constable!

1594. Luneau, Teresa Irwin. "A Critical Biography of Charlie May Simon." Typescript, University of Arkansas, Fayetteville, 1978. 51p.

There is a bound copy in the Special Collections of the University of Arkansas Library at Fayetteville. The list of Simon's published works is valuable, of course, and so is the critical annotation. But the best material is in chapter 1, a very personal and intimate account of Simon's private life, with excerpts from her letters unavailable elsewhere. Luneau was a graduate student at the University of Arkansas; this is a good piece of work.

1595. Luster, Michael. "Vance Randolph: A Chronology." *Missouri Folklore Society Journal* 4 (1982): 37–41.

A chronology of significant events in Randolph's life and career. Luster also recounts his first meeting with the folklorist, which occurred while Luster was a graduate student at the University of Arkansas.

1596. Lyon, Marguerite. "Lady of the Hills." Unpublished manuscript, Forsyth, Mo., 1948. 234p.

Marguerite "Marge" Lyon lived in Chicago, but in the late 1930s she and her husband moved to the Arkansas Ozarks. She was a keen observer and a good writer and authored four books about the Ozarks, all published in the early 1940s (for listings of those, see volume 1 of this bibliography). In 1943 she began a weekly column of Ozark stories for the *Chicago Tribune* titled "Fresh from the Hills," which ran for many years. In 1953 she joined the staff of the School of the Ozarks and lived in Hollister, Missouri, until her death in 1965. Mary Elizabeth Mahnkey, the "Lady of the Hills" referred to in the title of this manuscript, lived most of her life in Taney County, Missouri. For many years she had been a correspondent for the county newspaper and wrote a column about local happenings, in which she included her poems. It was all good, so good in fact that in 1935 she was selected as the best rural correspondent in the nation by Crowell Publications and received a trip to New York and Washington, D.C., where she was fêted by literary greats and politicians alike. In April 1948, Lyon and Mahnkey began work on Mahnkey's autobiography. For a number of weeks Mahnkey reminisced about her life and Lyon took it all down. Within a short space of time a sizable and nearly complete manuscript was composed. But a rift developed between the two, whether over how the book was to be written, the publishing arrangements, or possibly a clash of personalities, no one knows for sure. But whatever the cause, that was as far as the autobiography got. Shortly after this incident, Mahnkey became ill, and died four months later. Nothing was heard of the manuscript. After Lyon's death in 1965, it was assumed by those few who knew of its existence that the manuscript had either been destroyed or lost. Then, in 1981, it was discovered that Mahnkey's son, living in Forsyth, Missouri, had been given a carbon of the original typescript by Lyon. Now there is renewed interest in the project, and work has begun to enlarge and ready it for publication. Mahnkey is best remembered for her verse, which is as good as any ever written about life in the Ozarks.

1597. McCann, Gordon. "'Come See Us When You Can!': Some Memories of Vance Randolph." *Mid-America Folklore* 9:2 (Fall 1981): 29–33.

A friend reminisces about Randolph's last years in Fayetteville, Arkansas.

1598. ———. "What Do You Know About Horseheads and Crow Poison?" *Missouri Folklore Society Journal* 4 (1982): 31–34.

A brief character sketch of Vance Randolph concerning the day-to-day problems he faced in the nursing home in Fayetteville, Arkansas, where he spent his last years. McCann first met him in March 1975. A common interest in the written word about the Ozarks led to a cooperative effort to develop a supplement to *Ozark Folklore: A Bibliography*. As with Max Hunter, McCann was just an interested collector of Ozarks folklore with neither academic credits nor formal training in this field.

1599. McCanse, Ralph Alan. *Titans and Kewpies*. New York: Vantage Press, 1968. 220p.

The life and art of Rose O'Neill. Large segments (pp. 57–96, 177–89) deal with the backwoods of Taney County, Missouri. McCanse is a native of Monett, Missouri, who is now a professor of English at the University of Wisconsin. O'Neill lived for many years near Day, in Taney County, Missouri.

1600. McCord, May Kennedy. "May Kennedy McCord Papers." Unpublished papers, School of the Ozarks, Lyons Memorial Library, Point Lookout, Mo.

May was a longtime friend of Randolph and a major contributor to his work. She was also one of the most vocal speakers and prolific writers about Ozark life and ways. For more than thirty years her newspaper columns, magazine articles, radio shows, and public appearances were immensely popular throughout the Ozarks. When May died in 1979 the library received her personal scrapbooks containing material accumulated over a period of fifty years, as well as cassette tapes of many of her "Hillbilly Heartbeats" radio programs.

1601. McCorkle, John. *Three Years with Quantrill.* Armstrong, Mo.: Herald Print, 1914. 157p.

Written by O. S. Barton "from the dictation of McCorkle, who served with Quantrill." Details of raids in Arkansas, at Fort Smith, Cane Hill, Van Buren, and the Crowley's Ridge country. See Allsopp's *Folklore of Romantic Arkansas*, 1931, 1:309–12.

1602. McCulloch-Williams, Martha. "John Murrell and His Clan." *Harper's New Monthly Magazine* 94:560 (January 1897): 302–8.

A brief, well-written summary of Murrell's career. Very little documentation.

1603. McCullough, Florence Woodlock. *Living Authors of the Ozarks and Their Literature.* Joplin, Mo.: Published by the author, 1945. 288p.

She lists more than two hundred names and provides photographs of thirty, not one professional writer among them and none important enough to be included in *Who's Who in America*. There were three or four good newspaper writers in Arkansas in 1945, but McCullough doesn't know any of them, not even our Pulitzer Prize poet. Many of her "authors" have not published anything more than a few miserable rhymes in some country newspaper. It was interesting to me, however, and contains much information about these obscure scribblers not available elsewhere.

1604. McNeil, William K. "Mary Alicia Owen: Collector of Afro-American and Indian Lore in Missouri." *Missouri Folklore Society Journal* 2 (1980): 1–14.

During her lifetime (1850–1935) Mary Alicia Owen compiled and published an extensive collection of Negro folk narratives. These tales were published in dialect, much in the manner of Joel Chandler Harris's "Uncle Remus" stories. The extent of her collection was a remarkable feat as it was confined to the immediate vicinity of St. Joseph, Missouri. Her mentor was Charles Godfrey Leland, a noted American folklorist who spent much of his time in Europe. McNeil contends that had Leland been more closely identified with the United States she would have received as much acclaim as did Harris.

1605. McRaven, Charles. "Home to His Heritage." *The Ozarks Mountaineer* 23:1 (February 1975): 22, 36.

About Dr. Tate C. "Piney" Page, who returned to his home town of Dover, Arkansas, after an absence of thirty-seven years. Page is a past president of the Arkansas Folklore Society.

1606. Marshall, Mrs. A. J. *Autobiography of Mrs. A. J. Marshall, Age 84 Years.* Pine Bluff, Ark.: Adams-Wilson Printing Company, 1907. 232p.

The author was an Englishwoman who came west from New York as a missionary-teacher and taught in Miss Sophia Sawyer's Female Seminary in the 1840s and 1850s in Fayetteville, Arkansas. Pages 29–112 describe her life in "Arkansaw" (she spells it thus always) as the wife of a wandering preacher. There are scattered references to pioneer customs.

1607. Massey, Ellen. "Vance Randolph." *Bittersweet* 8:3 (Spring 1981): 38–41.

The author, who is the teacher and guiding force of the *Bittersweet* class and publication, took some of her students to Fayetteville, Arkansas, for a visit with Vance in 1974. She recounts their conversation, her impressions of that visit, and his contributions to our knowledge of Ozark folk culture. Vance thought very highly of Massey and her Bittersweet project. He often paid her one of his highest compliments, "She knows her stuff!" On p. 38 is George Fisher's portrait of Vance that first appeared in the *Arkansas Gazette*.

1608. May, Leland C. "The Story of Harold Bell Wright." *The Ozarks Mountaineer* 29:1 (February 1981): 28–29.

A brief biography of Wright that concludes with a list of all his books and their publishers. He published nineteen in all, the second being his famous *The Shepherd of the Hills*, which has sold well over a million copies.

1609. Miller, E. Joan Wilson. "Vance Randolph, Folklorist." *Mid-South Folklore* 3:3 (Winter 1975): 63–69.

A very flattering brief biography, listing all my books about folklore. The only errors of fact concern my personal life, and are of no importance. Miller is an English geographer who came to the United States and turned folklorist. I believe she took her second Ph.D. at Indiana. Dorson sent her to see me in the 1950s. She has published several good papers about the Ozarks. This article includes a fine photograph of me sitting on a bench with the big shots—Stith Thompson, Archer Taylor, Dick Dorson, George Korson, and others.

1610. Morgan, Tom P. "The Long Boy from the Limekilns." *Country Gentleman* 84:51 (20 December 1919): 10–11, 51.

A lengthy article, with good photographs, about John E. Brown, who founded the John E. Brown College at Siloam Springs, Arkansas. It was called a "Collegiate Institute" at first, but it's a university now. Much about Brown's youth at Rogers, Arkansas, where he worked in a rock quarry and was converted to Christianity by the Salvation Army.

1611. Morrill, O. R. *The Story of Uncle Ike and The Shepherd of the Hills Characters*. Springfield, Mo.: Cain Printing Co., 1948. 44p.

Another account of Levi Morrill, postmaster at Notch, Missouri, the "Uncle Ike" of Harold Bell Wright's novel *Shepherd of the Hills*. The author was the son of "Uncle Ike." His book begins with an introduction by Gerald H. Pipes, who used to run the dancehall at Reeds Spring, Missouri.

1612. Newton, Margaret. *Shad*. Springfield, Mo.: Pin Oak Publishing Company, 1982. 294p.

This is the biography of an actor named Lloyd Heller. After his early days of acting with the Smoki Indian Dancers in Arizona and then as a clown with the Ringling Brothers Circus, Heller came to the lakes country of the southern Missouri Ozarks. For the past twenty years he has played the part of "Shad," the blacksmith and mayor of a tourist attraction called Silver Dollar City, located close to Branson, Missouri. Before playing this role, he was the "Old Shepherd" in a production of Harold Bell Wright's *Shepherd of the Hills* staged by another tourist attraction, the Shepherd of the Hills Farm. He and his wife also have the Wilderness Theater, where they put on Toby shows using, as do many of the theme parks in the Ozarks region, "Hilarious . . . baggypants Ozarkian clown characters of every description." (Thomas Jackson lives!)

1613. O'Neill, Rose. Rose O'Neill Memorabilia and Papers. Shepherd of the Hills Farm, Branson, Missouri.

The Shepherd of the Hills Farm is a tourist attraction outside Branson that includes Old Matt's cabin and stages a version of the Harold Bell Wright drama in an outdoor amphitheater. Its owner, the late Mary Trimble, gathered over a period of years a collection of O'Neill material including illustrations and sketches, photographs, newspaper clippings, and the like concerning Kewpies, HoHo's, sculptures, monster drawings, and other forms of O'Neill's art. These are contained in some fifteen notebooks. Among this material are two dozen or more letters Rose wrote to Vance Randolph in the late thirties and early forties. There are also twenty-four typed pages of six unrelated chapters of what are apparently parts of the unpublished O'Neill autobiography that Randolph spent most of a year helping her with. Much of this material is duplicated in the School of the Ozark's collection.

1614. ———. "Rose O'Neill Papers." School of the Ozarks, Lyons Memorial Library, Point Lookout, Mo.

This is a collection of more than two hundred items, mostly correspondence, and the majority of that between Rose and Vance Randolph. One section of fifty-eight pages is typed material of Rose's autobiography with notes and corrections in Randolph's handwriting.

1615. ———. "Story of Rose O'Neill: An Autobiography." Unpublished manuscript, School of the Ozarks, Lyons Memorial Library, Point Lookout, Mo. 266p.

In the thirties Rose contracted with a major publisher to publish her autobiography. When she submitted it to them it was rejected and returned. Rose asked Randolph to help her, and in 1940 he accepted and for a time lived with Rose and her sister Callista at Bonniebrook, their home in the wilds of Taney County, Missouri. He worked with Rose for almost a year, and when he left he assumed Rose was resubmitting the revised manuscript to the publishers. But there evidently were a number of Rose's memories in this revision that Callista and other members of the O'Neill clan felt shouldn't be there, and, according to Randolph, they proceeded to "blue pencil" it to the point of evisceration before it left for the publisher. Again it was rejected. After Rose's death in 1944 Callista tried her hand at rewriting the work—which was again rejected. Since that time possibly two other writers have reworked the manuscript, so by the time it was laid to rest it's doubtful it bore any resemblance to Rose's original. As to which "edition" the School of the Ozarks possesses, it would be anyone's guess.

1616. Owen, Lyle. *Memories of an Ozarks Mother: The 100 Years of Stella Owen*. Branson, Mo.: The Ozarks Mountaineer Press, 1978. 96p.

Stella Tibbits Owen was born in 1877 in southeast Nebraska. She grew up there, married, and moved to Oklahoma where she and her husband homesteaded and began their family. In 1921 they moved to Taney County in southwest Missouri. After her ninetieth birthday she began writing her memoirs. By 1972 she had completed 870 handwritten pages, approximately 160,000 words. She was encouraged in this undertaking by her son, a retired college professor, who compiled this little book. As she entered her second century she proofread and made corrections to his writings and lived to see the volume in print. Stella passed away in 1980 at age 103. There is little folklore per se in this story, which is narrated by her son with a liberal use of quotes from her manuscript; it mostly concerns events of interest primarily to her family and descendants. There must be a wealth of material that the son did not draw upon, but Dr. Owen is a trained scholar and will undoubtedly see that this voluminous work is preserved and made available to future generations.

1617. Pendleton, G. W. *50 Years of Roses & Thorns: 1930–1980*. Mountain Home, Ark.: Trumpet Publications, [c. 1981]. 159p.

Autobiography of a Church of God minister. There are some folklore references in the reminiscences of his boyhood in Maries County in the north-central Missouri Ozarks. The rest is an account of his career as a minister and as a publisher of religious matter.

1618. Pilant, Richard. *George Washington Carver . . . the Poor People's Scientist*. Point Lookout, Mo.: School of the Ozarks Press, 1971. 35p.

Carver gave respectability to the lowly "goober," but this author stresses his importance to the civil rights movement and his symbolism to the poor of the world. Pilant was a political science Ph.D. and writes that way. But he lived close to Diamond, Missouri, and knew Carver. He initiated and promoted the establishment of a Carver National Birthplace Monument.

1619. Potter, Marian. "Laura of the Little House." *Missouri Life* 5:1 (March-June 1977): 12–18.

Good account of the late Laura Ingalls Wilder, author of many popular juvenile books, who lived in Mansfield, Missouri. A detailed story of her life, with many good photographs.

1620. Preece, Harold. *The Dalton Gang: End of an Outlaw Era.* New York: Hastings House, 1963. 320p.

This is the best book on the Daltons that I have seen, much better than Emmett Dalton's *When the Daltons Rode* (see volume 1 of this bibliography, p. 465), which was ghosted by Jack Jungmeyer. The only other reliable book is the pamphlet by David S. Elliot, *Last Raid of the Daltons* (1892), which is still in print, published by the Dalton Museum in Coffeyville, Kansas. Preece is remembered as the author (with Celia Kraft) of *Dew on Jordan* (see volume 1 of this bibliography, p. 507).

1621. Preston, Bill. "I Wonder What's Become of Sally . . . ." *Missouri Life* 5:1 (March-June 1977): 30–31.

Brief account of Sally Rand of Hickory County, Missouri, with some splendid photographs.

1622. Quaife, M. M., ed. *Absalom Grimes, Confederate Mail Runner.* New Haven, Conn.: Yale University Press, 1926. 216p.

Grimes was a river pilot and friend of Mark Twain. As boys, he and Twain enlisted in the Confederate militia near Hannibal, Missouri. Later he made his living by smuggling letters, money, medicines, and the like to Confederates in Southern camps and Federal prisons. He was often arrested by the Yankees as a spy and was twice sentenced to death. This book was put together by Grimes and his daughter Charlotte in 1910, based upon a wartime diary. After Grimes's death in 1912, the manuscript was edited and polished by Quaife for the Burton Historical Collections.

1623. Ray, Sally Cooksey. "Enoch Obed Wolf: His Life and Family." *Izard County Historian* 11:4 (October 1980): 18–25.

Wolf, who lived in Ash Flat, Arkansas, and, in later life, Myron, Arkansas, completed his autobiography just before his death in 1910. He fought in the Mexican War and took part in the Battle of Buena Vista, where he heard "the owl squawk." In 1850 he followed the California gold rush; in 1861 he raised a company of men who enlisted in the Confederate army. He was captured and confined to a prison in St. Louis, where an order for his execution was issued. This was rescinded by President Lincoln due to an appeal on his behalf because he was a Mason. There are interesting accounts of life in the Arkansas Ozarks at this time and on the battlefield.

This article is made up of excerpts from a more complete version that has appeared previously in two Arkansas newspapers, once in the *Sharp County Record* in June 1911, and again in the *Salem Headlight* in 1968.

1624. Richolson, Betty. "Suggins Expert Also a Prominent Artist." *Arkansas*, 17 July 1977.

Full-page article, with one good photograph, about Josephine Graham of Little Rock, president of the Suggin Folklife Society. Richolson is a native of Newport, Arkansas. *Arkansas* was a monthly publication by the Department of Journalism at the University of Arkansas–Fayetteville. It was delivered as a Sunday supplement to the *Springdale News*.

1625. Robertson, Vesta-Nadine. "Midwife to Greatness." *The Ozarks Mountaineer* 23:11 (December 1975): 20–21.

Born into slavery, Mariah Watkins came to Neosho, Missouri, in the 1870s. She became the town's midwife, and among her deliveries was one Thomas Hart Benton. George Washington Carver lived with her while he attended the only school for blacks in southwest Missouri. She died in 1925.

1626. Rogers, Cameron. *Gallant Ladies*. New York: Harcourt, Brace & Co., 1928. 363p.

Chapter 4 (pp. 117–44) is a study of Belle Starr, the most colorful female outlaw the Ozarks ever knew. Rogers says (p. vii) that this sketch was first published in the *Pictorial Review*. A good story, but there is no documentation, and many of the familiar anecdotes about Belle cannot be substantiated. Cf. James D. Horan's *Desperate Women* (New York, 1952), pp. 201–26.

1627. Rosa, Joseph G. *They Called Him Wild Bill: The Life and Adventures of James Butler Hickok*. Norman: University of Oklahoma Press, 1974. 377p.

See pp. 72–85 for more details of the legendary Hickok-Tutt duel that took place in Springfield, Missouri, in 1865. This is the most thorough treatment of this event I have read.

1628. Sanderson, Jane. "If Billy Joe Tatum's Pots and Pans Rattle, It May Be Just Snakes Alive." *People Weekly* 11:19 (14 May 1979): 91–92, 95.

This begins with a fine photograph of Billy Joe, her husband Halley, and a four-foot rattlesnake (which she later confided to me was out of the freezer). The rattler was subsequently on the menu of a "wild dinner" given for Arkansas governor Bill Clinton at the Tatum's mountaintop home near Melbourne. Besides biographical information about Billy Joe, the article gives complete recipes for dandelion bud omelet and apple-spearmint salad, both of which I intend to try.

1629. Saults, Dan. "The Man Who Knew Frank James." *The Ozarks Mountaineer* 27:4–5 (May-June 1979): 55–57.

A very fine brief article about the Missouri outlaw. Note Saults's endorsement (p. 57) of William Settle's *Jesse James Was His Name* (see next entry).

1630. Settle, William A., Jr. *Jesse James Was His Name or, Fact and Fiction Concerning the Careers of the Notorious James Brothers of Missouri*. Columbia: University of Missouri Press, 1966. 263p.

There are scattered Ozark references throughout the book. On p. 118 Settle says: "The gold watch worn by Jesse when he was killed was returned to its owner, John A. Burbank of Richmond, Indiana, who had lost it in the stage robbery at Hot Springs, Arkansas, in January, 1874." See pp. 171–73 for the author's example of a typical James legend. Although Frank James was an equal leader of the band, explanations are given why Jesse has become the central figure in our folklore. Fine scholarly notes and bibliography.

1631. Shirley, Glenn. *Belle Starr and Her Times: The Literature, the Facts, and the Legends*. Norman: University of Oklahoma Press, 1982. 324p.

An attempt to separate fact from fiction found in mostly written accounts of the career of Belle Starr, "From Richard Fox to 20th Century-Fox," as he titles his first chapter. See his comments (p. 23) about Vance Randolph and two of these accounts: *Belle Starr, the Bandit Queen* by William Yancey Shackleford (see volume 1 of this bibliography, p. 206), and *Wildcats in Petticoats* by Anton S. Booker (Girard, Kans.: Haldeman-Julius, 1945). He concludes his book with an extensive bibliography.

1632. ———. *Henry Starr, Last of the Real Badmen*. New York: David McKay Co., 1965. 208p.

The best book on this outlaw. Much detail about life among the Cherokee of eastern Oklahoma.

1633. Shumate, Fern. "Rose O'Neill—Neither Saint Nor Sinner." *The Ozarks Mountaineer* 30:2–3 (April 1982): 48–49, 51.

Some candid reminiscences by one who knew Rose personally. Quite a departure from the usual panegyrics that emerge from such present-day celebrations to her memory as the Kewpiesta held each year in Branson, Missouri. Shumate, using the pseudonym Nancy Nance, has written extensively about the Ozarks.

1634. Slater, Harold. "The One, the Only, Sally Rand." *Missouri Life* 5:1 (March-
      June 1977): 24–29.

The story of the famous fan-dancer. She lived her last years (died 1979) in California, but she was born at Elkton, in Hickory County, Missouri. Her name was
Helen Gould Beck, and she attended Christian College at Columbia. Slater thinks
she is probably the most celebrated Missourian of our time, except maybe Jesse
James and Harry S. Truman. Those of us who remember Sally in her prime always
realized that she was no ordinary stripper.

1635. Snelling, Lois. *Coin Harvey, Prophet of Monte Ne.* Point Lookout, Mo.:
      School of the Ozarks Press, 1973. 66p.

Lois Snelling is a native Arkansan and a long-time resident of Rogers, Arkansas. The local people tell me she writes "good books for children" but I have not
seen any of her juveniles. This Coin Harvey book is a good job—earthy enough, but
without the dirty wisecracks so many local people have dragged out in writing about
the pyramid-builder of Monte Ne. A pleasant, enjoyable book, well bound and
printed, it is one of the best jobs the School of the Ozarks Press has ever turned out.
Snelling did not know Colonel Harvey personally, but she knew many of his intimate associates and set down their opinions fairly and without too much prejudice.

1636. Steele, Phillip. *The Last Cherokee Warriors.* Gretna, La.: Pelican Publishing
      Co., 1974. 111p.

Careful, detailed account of Zeke Proctor and Ned Christie, two celebrated
Oklahoma desperadoes. Both were Cherokee, and both were active in the Keetoowa
fraternity, bitterly opposed to the United States government. Phillip Steele is a resident of Springdale, Arkansas (formerly known as Shiloh), and has written several
articles about pioneer history.

1637. ———. "Ozark's Last Horseback Outlaw." *The Ozarks Mountaineer* 29:6–7
      (August 1981): 20–21.

Henry Starr began his career by robbing the People's Bank of Bentonville,
Arkansas, in 1893 and ended it (and his life) in 1921 with an attempt to rob the
People's Bank of Harrison, Arkansas, thirty miles distant. Between these two
events, his exploits supplied legends for generations yet unborn. He was the nephew
of the equally famous Henry and Belle Starr. For a more complete story, see Glenn
Shirley's *Henry Starr, Last of the Real Badmen* (entry 1632).

1638. ———. "The Saga of White River Red." *The Ozarks Mountaineer* 23:2
      (March 1975): 16–17, 29.

White River Red was a strange character, well known throughout the White
River country. Her name was Forrestina Campbell. She had been a beauty, with

flaming red hair, who spent her early life with the circus and carnival people. When she came to the Ozark country, she was just a tough, foul-mouthed old woman dressed in men's clothing, but she always wore diamond earrings. An inveterate gambler, she always paid her debts—her credit was always good. She was charitable and generous. Though she was not particularly religious, the poor and friendless regarded her as a kind of saint. She died in a geriatric clinic in Fayetteville, Arkansas, in 1973, at age eighty-two. There are some very fine people around West Fork and Springdale who speak of her today with a kind of superstitious reverence. I have always wished that I had known her better.

1639. ———. *White River Red*. Springdale, Ark.: Published by the author, 1979. [7p.]

This is the same article that appeared in the March 1975 issue of *The Ozarks Mountaineer* (see preceding entry). It is here presented in booklet form and contains some passages that were expurgated from the *Mountaineer* version. The cover is a fine photograph of Forrestina Campbell. I knew her, and she was all Steele says she was.

1640. Thompson, Henry C. *Sam Hildebrand Rides Again*. Bonne Terre, Mo.: Steinbeck Publishing Co., 1950. 113p.

Story of a Civil War outlaw who operated mostly in southeast Missouri. A serious biography, but not much documentation. There is now a second edition, "with a few changes and additions" (Bonne Terre Printing Company, 1967).

1641. Triplett, Frank. *The Life, Times and Treacherous Death of Jesse James*. Chicago: Swallow Press, 1970. 344p.

This is a reprint, of course; the first edition appeared in New York in 1882, just a few months after Jesse's death. Nothing is known about Triplett except that he once lived in St. Louis, claimed to be a mining engineer, and was sometimes called "Colonel" Triplett. See pp. 67–68 for a short and matter-of-fact account of the robbery of the Hot Springs stage in 1874—very different from the elaborate yarns told by Sam Leath and other Arkansas raconteurs.

1642. Turrentine, G. R. "The Arkansas Traveler." *The Ozarks Mountaineer* 4:1 (September 1955): 7.

Mainly about Edward Washburn and his two paintings.

1643. Vaughn, Columbus, Sarah Snow, and Lester Snow. *This Was Frank James*. Philadelphia: Dorrance and Company, 1969. 180p.

Joe Vaughn lived at Wayton, in Newton County, Arkansas, where he served as county surveyor for thirty-eight years. Shortly before his death in 1925 he wrote a book claiming that he was really Frank James, the celebrated Missouri trainrobber. He entrusted the manuscript to his daughter, Sarah, directing that it be published after his death. I met several members of the Vaughn family at Fayetteville in 1950 (cf. *Ozark Folklore Society Bulletin* 1:1 [July 1950]: 10), and one of Joe's sons showed me a tattered copy of the paperback that was published from Joe Vaughn's manuscript, *The Only True Story of the Life of Frank James, Written by Himself* (Pine Bluff, Ark.: Norton Printing Co., 1926, 134p.).

Columbus Vaughn is old Joe's grandson, Sarah Vaughn Snow is Joe's daughter, and Lester Snow is Sarah's son. They have collected a vast amount of evidence that Joe Vaughn really was Frank James. The first eighty-eight pages of their book is a vivid and detailed account of Joe Vaughn's family in Newton County, Arkansas, with much valuable information about backwoods customs and the like. The rest (pp. 89–180) is a reprint of Joe's book of 1926.

1644. Walston, Marie. *These Were My Hills*. Valley Forge, Penn.: Judson Press, 1972. 128p.

The childish story of a Baptist preacher, a widower, who brings his teenage daughter to the Ozark backwoods during the Depression and tries to build a little church and school. This book contains a few references to superstitions and children's songs and rhymes, but consists mostly of church politics, quarrels with liquor dealers who try to bribe the poor but honest preacher, and so on. Virtue always triumphs in the end.

1645. Watkins, Paul, Jr. "Thomas Hart Benton Remembered." *Missouri Life* 3:1–2 (March-June 1975): 46–57.

A good story of the painter, with fine reproductions of some of his best pictures, including one of his several self-portraits.

1646. Watson, R. R. *Boyhood Days on an Ozark Farm*. New Market, Iowa: College Hill Press, 1978. 166p.

Growing up in Polk County, Missouri, in the early 1900s. Watson is a graduate of Drury College in Springfield.

1647. Wiley, Dorothy B. "Book Man of Mt. Sherman." *The Ozarks Mountaineer* 19:4 (May 1971): 21–24.

Ted Richmond homesteaded land on Mt. Sherman in the wildest part of Newton County, Arkansas. In 1931 he began a lending library for his impoverished neighbors. As word of the Wilderness Library spread, donations of books from all parts of the country were sent to the "Book Man." Some even came from Franklin D. Roosevelt's personal library, sent by Eleanor after his death. Richmond continued this endeavor for nearly thirty years, when he suddenly left without notice. He died in 1975 at age ninety-two. This article includes a fine photograph of Richmond by Townsend Godsey.

1648. Williams, G. L. "Charles F. M. Noland—One Aspect of His Career." *Independence County Chronicle* 10:3 (April 1969): 52–58.

The author contends that no really thorough work has been printed about Noland and his influence upon the frontier literature of the nineteenth century. He says that the one extensive collection of letters, *Pete Whetstone of Devil's Fork: Letters to the Spirit of the Times* by Ted Worley and Eugene Nolte (1957), is far from complete. I'm not so sure he's correct, but this is a well-documented article and presents yet another conclusion to the Whetstone letters. It is worth reading.

The author was a graduate student in the English Department at the University of Louisville and is now a member of the English faculty at the University of North Alabama in Florence. He published an edition of Noland's work under the title *Cavorting On the Devil's Fork: The Pete Whetstone Letters of C. F. M. Noland* (entry 582).

1649. Wilson, Charles Morrow. "Modern Frontiersman." *Scribner's Magazine* 99:2 (February 1936): 106–10.

A good account of Ted Richmond, who homesteaded land in Newton County, Arkansas, and founded a lending library. Ted is a bit idealized perhaps, but it is a good article. See Godsey's *These Were the Last* (entry 1377) for more about "Twilight Ted."

1650. Wilstach, Frank J. *Wild Bill Hickok*. New York: Garden City Publishing Company, 1926. 304p.

Wilstach tells of the famous duel between Hickok and Dave Tutt that took place on the public square in Springfield, Missouri (pp. 117–36). He also recounts the legend of the Wild Bill–Calamity Jane love affair on pp. 253–65.

1651. Winn, Robert G. *Belle, the Bandit Queen—Pearl, River Front Madame: Two Starrs*. Fayetteville, Ark.: Washington County Historical Society, 1979. 62p.

Slick-paper pamphlet about Belle and her daughter Pearl. The author thinks that Belle was murdered by her son Eddie Reed. Eddie was the father of Pearl's daughter Flossie, according to Winn's informants. See p. 38 for a photograph of the bronze statue of Belle by Jo Moro, in the Woolaros Museum in Bartlesville, Oklahoma. This book contains two pictures of Pearl and one of Flossie that I have not seen elsewhere.

1652. Yeo, Wilma, and Helen K. Cook. *Maverick with a Paint Brush*. Garden City, N.Y.: Doubleday and Co., 1977. 125p.

Another book about Thomas Hart Benton, with photographs of some of his best paintings. I like especially "Fish Camp on Buffalo River." Benton made many floats along the Buffalo, and this painting was one of his favorites.

1653. Zochert, Donald. *Laura, the Life of Laura Ingalls Wilder*. Chicago: Henry Regnery Co., 1976. 260p.

This is a very good book, but it deals mostly with the prairies of North Dakota, Nebraska, and Kansas; only the last few pages are concerned with the Ozarks, where Wilder wrote most of her books.

1654. Zomar, Karl. "Berryville, Arkansas." *Ozarks Journal*, 5 April 1935.

Good newspaper story about Burton Sanders and his gun collection. *Ozarks Journal* was published in Springfield, Missouri, by John D. Harris in 1935 and 1936, according to Springfield directories, and was later issued by radio station KWTO, with Floyd Sullivan as editor and Leslie L. Kennon as business manager. I have seen only two copies.

INDEX OF AUTHORS